D0984727

RECONSTRUCTING THE HOUSEHOLD

STUDIES IN LEGAL HISTORY

Published by the

University of North Carolina Press

in association with the

American Society for Legal History

Thomas A. Green & Hendrik Hartog

editors

PETER W. BARDAGLIO

Reconstructing the Household

FAMILIES, SEX, AND THE LAW IN

THE NINETEENTH-CENTURY SOUTH

The University of North Carolina Press

Chapel Hill & London

The paper in this book meets the guidelines for permanence and
durability of the Committee on Production Guidelines for Book Longevity of the
Council on Library Resources.

Library of Congress Cataloging-in-Publications Data

Bardaglio, Peter Winthrop.

Reconstructing the household: families, sex, and the law in the nineteenth-century South /

Peter W. Bardaglio.

p.   cm.—(Studies in legal history)

Revision of the author's thesis (Ph.D.)—Stanford University, 1987.

Includes bibliographical references and index.

ISBN 0-8078-2222-1 (cloth: alk. paper)

1. Domestic relations—Southern States—History.   2. Family—Southern States—History.

3. Southern States—Social conditions.   4. Reconstruction.   I. Title.   II. Series.

KF505.B37   1995

306.85′0975′09034—dc20   95-11798

CIP

99 98 97 96 95   5   4   3   2   1

Portions of Chapters 2 and 6 originally appeared in somewhat different form in
" 'An Outrage upon Nature': Incest and the Law in the Nineteenth-Century South," in
In Joy and in Sorrow: Women, Family, and Marriage in the Victorian South, edited by
Carol Bleser, pp. 32–51 (New York: Oxford University Press, 1991).
Reprinted by permission of Oxford University Press.

Portions of Chapter 2 also appeared in "Rape and the Law in the Old South: 'Calculated
to Excite Indignation in Every Heart,'" *Journal of Southern History* 60 (November 1994):
749–72.

Portions of Chapters 3 and 5 originally appeared in somewhat different form in "Challenging
Parental Custody Rights: The Legal Reconstruction of Parenthood in the Nineteenth-Century
American South," *Continuity and Change* 4 (August 1989): 259–92. Reprinted by permission
of Cambridge University Press.

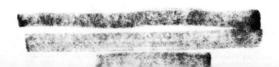

FOR WREXIE

Maybe nothing ever happens once and is finished.

Maybe happen is never once but like ripples maybe on water after the pebble sinks, the ripples moving on, spreading, the pool attached by a narrow umbilical water-cord to the next pool which the first pool feeds, has fed, did feed, let this second pool contain a different temperature of water, a different molecularity of having seen, felt, remembered, reflect in a different tone the infinite unchanging sky, it doesn't matter: that pebble's watery echo whose fall it did not even see moves across its surface too at the original ripple-space, to the old ineradicable rhythm.

WILLIAM FAULKNER, *Absalom, Absalom!*

CONTENTS

The catalyst for this study was a very simple observation. Thumbing through the pages of antebellum statutory codes from some of the southern states, I was surprised to find that chapters on the law of what was called "domestic relations" often included not only the headings "husband and wife," "parent and child," and "guardian and ward," but also "master and slave."[1] As I puzzled over the meaning of this arrangement, it struck me that southern lawmakers had organized the statutes in this fashion because they did not consider these sets of social relations as isolated categories but as intrinsically connected. If this was so, then these connections deserved a closer look. What was the impact of slavery, I wondered, on the rules and regulations governing relations between husbands and wives as well as between parents and children? What changes did the end of slavery bring about in the law of domestic relations? How did the legacy of slavery continue to shape legal attitudes toward women, children, and families after its demise?

As I delved into these questions, it became increasingly clear that in order to understand fully the legal dynamics of southern households, I needed to examine the regulation of sexuality as well as domestic relations.[2] Since the sexual access of slaveholders to their wives and bondswomen provided the undergirding of patriarchy as a system that shaped both race and gender relations, understanding how the law interacted with sexuality was critical. I discovered in the process of this investigation that, important as the household was as a private institution in the Victorian South, it was even more important as a political institution in the broadest sense: it not only constituted the chief vehicle for the exercise of power in southern society but also served as the foundation of southern public beliefs and values. A distinctive variation of republicanism developed in the household of the Old South, one based more on hierarchy and dependence than on egalitarianism and consent. It was this version of republicanism, forged in the crucible of households on plantations and farms throughout the slave South, that planters and yeomen sought to defend in 1860 when they called for secession from the Union.

The laws regulating domestic and sexual relations furnish an entry point, then, for raising fundamental questions about the ideological and social character of the nineteenth-century South and its relationship to the rest of the nation, a way to track the ripples of change and continuity across the pools of the region's past. A study of these laws can help illuminate debates over the nature of the antebellum South (was it "bourgeois" or something else?), over the nature of the law (was it "relatively autonomous" or a reflection of larger power structures?), over the nature of the postbellum South (was it marked more by continuity or discontinuity?), and over the degree of convergence among American regions in the Gilded Age (did a national vision of governance take hold or did regional variations persist?). I do not pretend to have fully answered these questions about the temper of southern society and social thought during the nineteenth century in this study, but I do believe that I have posed a new way of considering them.

Apart from the topics of slavery and race, the legal history of the South has only recently attracted systematic and sustained attention.[3] There is now a growing body of work on women and the law in the South, but the legal regulation of southern families and sexual behavior remains largely overlooked, and the issue of regional variation has not been adequately addressed.[4] This work seeks to reconstruct southern legal developments during the nineteenth century in order to examine the crucial differences between North and South, and at the same time establish that they were, after all, regions in a common country rather than entirely separate civilizations. "Southern lawyers and statesmen," Maxwell Bloomfield observes, "have always shared the core values of the Anglo-American legal tradition and have never tried to create an alternative system, even in antebellum times."[5] Although the North and South shared a common core of values, before the Civil War the two regions diverged significantly in their understanding of the household order, a development mirrored in the state statutes and court opinions of these two regions. As the North moved toward an increasingly contractual view of domestic relations, one that challenged the traditional ideal of the patriarchal family, the white South saw itself as the defender of the organic model of the household.

In his groundbreaking investigation of family law in Victorian America, Michael Grossberg argues that "the end of the eighteenth century and the early nineteenth century was the time when jurists, legislators, litigants, and commentators most fundamentally redirected the governance of the American home." According to Grossberg, legal changes set in motion during this period led to "a republican approach to domestic relations" that created a new distribution of power among family members, and between the household and the state. Focusing on central tendencies rather than on regional diversity, he contends that the republican ideal of the family, in which members of the household were "bound together by a new egalitarianism and by affection," became the controlling paradigm in American law, society, and culture. As Grossberg puts it, "A middle-class creation, the republican family dominated household ideology and practice in an increasingly bourgeois nation."[6]

The problematic character of this assertion becomes clear as soon as one considers the slaveholding household in the antebellum South. If we take seriously the claims of slaveholders that slaves as well as wives, children, and other kin belonged to their families (and, of course, the slaves were biologically part of the family when they were offspring of the master or his sons), then it becomes very difficult to see how a middle-class, egalitarian form of republicanism provides the key to explaining the evolution of southern domestic relations law before emancipation.[7] In fact, the distinctive nature of the southern domestic order (that is, the presence of slaveholding households) helps account for the coming of the Civil War. "In this one particular slavery doomed itself," Rebecca Latimer Felton, a Georgia planter-class woman, wrote after the war. "When white men put their own offspring in the kitchen and the cornfield and allowed them to be sold into bondage as slaves and degraded them as another man's slave, the retribution of wrath was hanging over this country and the South paid penance in four years of bloody war."[8] One does not have to subscribe to Felton's notions about guilt and sin to see that the southern understanding of the household differed in significant ways from that of the North, making it impossible to generalize accurately about antebellum developments in American domestic relations law without taking into account the question of regionalism and, more specifically, the varied meaning of republicanism across place and time.[9]

This is not to say that the family dynamics of the slaveholding South had nothing at all in common with those of the North. Although white southern society departed from the bourgeois experience of the Northeast and western Europe in many aspects of its domestic life, it shared with the broader Victorian culture a growing emphasis on affectionate love between husband and wife, as well as between parent and child. At the same time, however, white southerners clung to traditional notions of patriarchal authority that stressed the importance of harmony, dependency, and hierarchy.[10] "The law regards the father as the head of the family, obliges him to provide for its wants, and commits the children to his charge, in preference to the claims of the mother or any other person," the Alabama Supreme Court intoned in 1858. Emphasizing the legitimacy of the father's rule, a South Carolina judge maintained that "a divided empire in the government of a family . . . is not consistent with the welfare of the wife and children, and has not the sanction of law." Southern whites, in short, found themselves caught between contradictory impulses.[11] *De Bow's Review* captured this sense of being poised between two worlds in 1856, describing the southern home as "not simply a theatre for the development of the affections appropriate to friendship and the domestic relations, but a school of discipline in the general proprieties of life. In the household was displayed the deference due to age, to office, to social position, to personal merit of any kind, to the claims of the gentler sex." [12]

The sense of intensifying contradictions within the household, contradictions that rippled outward into the society at large, drove white southerners to look for some resolution of these tensions. As developments such as individualism and contractualism made inroads into domestic relations law before the Civil War, most southern lawmakers and judges, as well as social theorists and writers, upheld the organic ideal of the household. Indeed, they felt compelled to defend this ideal, because it served as the governing metaphor not only for husbands and wives, parents and children, but also masters and slaves. By 1860 southern elites viewed secession as the most effective way to defend the traditional domestic order in which bondage acted as the linchpin.

What might be called the "household theory of secession" does not presuppose that domestic relations law remained static in the South before the Civil War. The Civil War did not mark a sharp dividing line between continuity and change in this sense. In fact, important alterations in slavery, married women's property rights, divorce, and child-custody law did take place, especially in the 1850s, largely as a result of ideas such as individualism and contractualism beginning to penetrate southern culture.

While slaves gained rights in southern courts, divorce rates grew, child-custody contests became more child-centered, and married women became increasingly assertive about their property rights, northern abolitionists launched a vehement attack against the slaveholding household, a campaign that culminated with the publication in 1853 of Harriet Beecher Stowe's novel, *Uncle Tom's Cabin*. Conservative intellectuals and politicians perceived the threat posed to the social order by this deadly combination of changes in domestic relations law and assaults on slavery, and they became convinced that only secession could keep the fabric of their households and society from unraveling. Disunion, in other words, was an

attempt to slow down the pace of change and manage the changes that had
already taken place, rather than an effort to prevent change from occurring at all. To the horror of those who led the South out of the Union, the
outbreak of war in 1861 accelerated the pace of change, unleashing a flood
of unanticipated consequences, not the least of which was emancipation.

Despite the transformation of southern legal culture by 1900, undercur-
rents of continuity generated by deep-seated attitudes toward race, blood,
and gender made themselves felt. Dramatic change had taken place, most
assuredly, but the change had not led to any sense of clear resolution.
Contradiction and paradox persisted, the push and pull of southern history continued. The transformation went only so far and developed some
peculiar forms, forms that stubbornly resonated with prewar attitudes
and beliefs.[13]

Beyond the issue of regionalism, the nineteenth-century South provides
a dramatic case study of how a society undergoing profound social change
develops new channels of legal control over family norms and behavior.
During the first half of the century, the South experienced massive geo-
graphic expansion with the rise of the cotton kingdom and the opening
up of the black belt, and then in the 1850s underwent a wave of economic
prosperity that brought about the first stirrings of industrialization and
urbanization. The Civil War, of course, put a halt to the cotton boom, but
wartime pressures hastened industrialization and urbanization. After 1865
the region not only had to cope with the physical destruction of the Civil
War and the psychological trauma of military defeat but also experienced
the wrenching shift from a slave to free society and the corresponding
upheaval in race and class relations.

These changes, especially after 1865, severely disrupted the traditional
structure of power and authority in the households and larger society of
the South. The dominant classes viewed the war and its consequences as
a watershed in the legal transformation of the southern household. When
a Georgia judge in 1866 referred to the period before the Civil War as
"the days beyond the flood" in a case involving the public apprenticeship of a black youth, he invoked this biblical metaphor to underscore
his point that there was no going back to the time in which slavery provided the cornerstone for social relations and that, in particular, former
slaveowners could not expect to maintain custody over the offspring of
parents who had been their slaves.[14] This was only the most obvious manner in which the end of bondage had an impact on household governance.
Southern white elites were compelled in many other ways to fashion new
public policies and laws that reshaped the regulation of relations between
blacks and whites, husbands and wives, and parents and children. The

primary result of these legal innovations was an unprecedented intrusion of the state into what heretofore had been considered the private lives of southerners, a development I term "state paternalism."[15]

This study, then, explores in detail the ways in which war and emancipation, among other social changes, transformed the legal understanding of the southern household and its relationship to the state, and suggests how these developments shed light not only on family dynamics but also on political developments such as the origins of progressivism in the late-nineteenth-century South. In this sense, it is an effort to build on Eric Foner's observation that "Reconstruction was not merely a specific time period, but the beginning of an extended historical process: the adjustment of American society to the end of slavery."[16]

The key assumption underlying this approach to the southern past is that law deals with social relations and that legal changes should not be considered apart from society. Law is not simply an institutionalized system of jurisprudence; it is a process that both reflects and shapes the arrangement of power relations in society. Legal change, in this context, is the product of conflict between dominant elites and other groups that seek to share power with these elites or replace them entirely. Hence, legal history must be understood as part of social, economic, and political history, rather than as a self-contained force driven by its own rules and logic.[17]

Although the law does not evolve solely by its own inner momentum, it does possess a partial autonomy, a valuable insight that the critical legal studies movement has underscored. Law makes itself felt as a distinctive ideology in part by fostering values such as due process and equal protection that are defined and implemented through legal procedures, and by generating vested interests in these values and procedures.[18] Southern law did not simply reflect the narrow economic interests of the planters and merchants, in other words, but mediated social relations in such a way as to place certain constraints on the actions of those in power while legitimizing the position of these governing elements and contributing to their dominance. In this way, southern law displayed a degree of independence beyond its purely instrumental function sufficient to persuade groups besides those in power that the law was just.[19] Thus, when judges paid close attention to the procedural rights of slaves charged with rape, murder, or some other serious crime, they demonstrated a commitment to legal formalism that went beyond the mere protection of property rights, although such economic considerations played a role as well.

Given this theoretical framework, four major questions will guide the discussion: (1) What changes took place during the nineteenth century in southern laws governing domestic and sexual relations? (2) Where did the pressures for these legal changes come from? (3) What was the impact on the relationship between the household and the state? (4) What does all of this tell us about the character of southern society in the nineteenth century?

These questions will be answered primarily through a close analysis of the content of the statutes and appellate court opinions from the southern states concerning incest, miscegenation, rape, child custody, and adoption. The study also draws extensively on other legal sources, such as legal treatises, state and regional law journals, state bar association reports, and published and unpublished material from the collections of southern lawyers and judges. In addition, I have examined literary periodicals, fiction, diaries, memoirs, and travel accounts in an attempt to reconstruct southern legal culture and the dynamics of the household. This range of sources has allowed me to probe into the nature of the southern legal system, to examine how the system intersected with the household and the rest of society, and to reconstruct the values and attitudes that bound the system together.[20]

For the purposes of this study, the South is defined as the eleven states that formed the Confederacy. Although a somewhat arbitrary definition, it focuses attention on those states where slavery thrived and where ruling elites and their white followers were most self-conscious about their southernness, to the point that they ultimately left the Union. Occasionally, this study incorporates material from the border states, but it does not examine them in any detail.

Because this is a study in social as well as legal history, the strengths and limitations of state statutes and appellate court opinions for understanding the social character of the South should be noted at least briefly. Statutes in themselves do not furnish evidence of actual social conditions; they tell us, for example, what husbands and fathers could do, not what they really did. On the other hand, statutes allow us to ascertain how society thought its members ought to behave, and more specifically, they allow us to determine the social values and attitudes of the elite that made and shaped the law. In the words of William Wiecek, "Statutory law is thus a valuable window on the hopes and fears of a society, of its image of itself and of the ways it hoped to shape the time to come."[21]

Like statutes, judicial decisions at the appellate level reveal the aspirations and anxieties of society, as well as significant aspects of the social outlook of those who wield power in society. Judicial decisions, moreover, frequently interpret and flesh out the reasoning behind the statutes, thus clarifying the intentions of lawmakers. But the decisions can be difficult to cast in ideological terms because of the formal constraints under which a judge operates and, as a result, a decision may obscure rather than reveal the social attitude of a particular judge. Fortunately, the remarkable willingness of southern jurists in many of the cases under study to go beyond the settlement of the precise legal point at issue, and to hand down broad statements about their understanding of domestic relations and the place of the state in these relations, largely offsets this difficulty.[22]

Appellate court opinions not only expose the ideological structure of society, they are also more useful than statutes in telling us about how people behaved, since this is what brought them into court. Judicial decisions, in addition, provide us with insights into how individuals were treated in the southern legal system, at least to the extent that the judicial decisions themselves amounted to treatment in particular cases. Of course, only a small minority of cases involving incest, miscegenation, rape, child custody, and adoption reached state supreme courts in the nineteenth century, so appellate opinions are not necessarily representative of the experience of those who entered southern courtrooms. Still, these decisions are especially valuable because the supreme courts established guidelines for the lower courts adjudicating cases in these areas of the law.[23]

To sum up, appellate opinions and state statutes are well suited to an examination of what southern elites believed the distribution of power, rights, and obligations ought to be among members of the household, and what role the law ought to play in governing sexual and domestic relations. This book, then, will concentrate on the attitudinal and ideological dimensions of the law in an attempt to excavate the underlying assumptions, values, and norms of the men who held power in the nineteenth-century South.

ACKNOWLEDGMENTS

My father is a certified public accountant. I mention this because he would be appalled if I submitted to him the balance sheet of credits and debits acquired while writing this book. The latter far outweigh the former, and he would have me filing for bankruptcy so fast my head would spin.

Despite this precarious state of affairs, it is a pleasure to acknowledge the generous assistance I have received from many people and institutions. Financial aid from a National Endowment for the Humanities Summer Stipend, a Littleton-Griswold Research Grant from the American Historical Association, and various faculty awards from Goucher College—including a Mary Wilhelmine Williams Fellowship in the Social Sciences and an Elizabeth Nitchie Fellowship Fund Research Grant—supported the research and writing. The School of English and American Studies at the University of Exeter in England, where I spent a memorable year as a visiting professor in the American and Commonwealth Arts program, also provided assistance in the final stages of preparing the manuscript.

This study would not have been possible without the fine holdings at the Library of Congress, the Southern Historical Collection at the University of North Carolina at Chapel Hill, the Thurgood Marshall Library at the University of Maryland Law School, and the Julia Rogers Library at Goucher College. The staff at all of these institutions were unstinting in their efforts to answer my questions and facilitate my research, but I particularly want to thank Larry Boyer; his good-natured interest and involvement in this project during his tenure at the Library of Congress went way beyond the call of duty. The contributions of Ben Karp as my research assistant came at a critical point, and I hope that his work for me as an undergraduate at Goucher inspired him in part to pursue graduate study at Yale University.

This book has evolved more slowly and painfully than I care to admit out of a doctoral dissertation at Stanford University, where it was supervised by Carl Degler. His meticulous reading of the dissertation set a standard that I strive to achieve in working with my students. I also owe a debt of gratitude to Edward Ayers and Michael Grossberg, who read the manuscript for the University of North Carolina Press. Their astute appraisals provoked me to embark on a new round of research and to re-conceptualize the organization of my argument. Although I did not always follow their advice, this is a far more subtle and sophisticated book as a result of their searching critiques.

Other friends and colleagues who kindly read all or portions of the manuscript at various stages and offered much-needed suggestions include Jean Baker, Maxwell Bloomfield, Victoria Bynum, Catherine Clinton, Laura Edwards, and Julie Jeffrey. Catherine also offered crucial assistance in collecting the late-nineteenth-century appellate decisions dealing with rape that are analyzed in chapter 6, making sure in this and other important ways that I maintained forward momentum. As the book took shape, I presented papers at the Berkshire Conference on the History of Women at Vassar College, the Fort Hill Conference on Southern Culture at Clemson University, the Summer Research Seminar on Race, Class, and Gender in Southern History at the University of California–San Diego, the Southern Conference on Women's History at the University of North Carolina at Chapel Hill, and the annual meetings of the Southern Historical Association in Fort Worth, Texas, and Louisville, Kentucky. The criticisms and comments of people who participated in these sessions have also significantly improved the final product.

My editors at the University of North Carolina Press, Thomas Green and Lewis Bateman, had the good sense to allow me to stew in my own juices until I was ready to place this manuscript in their capable hands. Their cogent assessments of my work, unstinting professionalism, and loyal friendship provided a steady source of encouragement and support for me during the writing of this book. I also appreciate the skilled guidance and contributions of many others at the Press, including Pamela Upton and Karin Kaufman.

My family deserves special recognition for their patience while I spent endless hours investigating the trials and tribulations of families in another time and place. I have been lucky in having a mother who introduced me early on to the joys of reading and a father who knew no price could be put on acquiring an outstanding education. Most of all, I want to acknowledge my good fortune in finding a partner, Wrexie, who has had the grace and intelligence to keep me involved in life outside this project: her work in Native American policy, the bookstore that we founded together, and most important, our children, Sarah, Jesse, and Anne.

Besides keeping me firmly planted in the twentieth century, I am grateful to my wife for having listened as I worked through the ideas that developed into this book and for having read the manuscript as it emerged, keeping a watchful eye out for the all too-tempting sins of arrogance and obscurity. This book is dedicated to her, although it is clearly inadequate repayment for the sense of humor and proportion that she has offered all these years, resources that helped me to keep my wits about me as I moved toward the completion of this study.

PART ONE

THE DAYS BEYOND THE FLOOD

The LORD saw that the wickedness of man was great

in the earth, and that every imagination of the thoughts of

his heart was only evil continually.

Genesis 6:5

CHAPTER I

PATRIARCHY AND THE LAW

IN THE OLD SOUTH

On November 1, 1843, Governor James Henry Hammond of South Carolina received a fateful letter from his brother-in-law Wade Hampton II, one of the wealthiest and most powerful men in the state. In his letter, Hampton accused the governor of trying to seduce Hampton's nineteen-year-old daughter Catherine. It remains unclear whether Hampton knew the entire story at the time, but the incident with Catherine marked the climax of an extraordinary relationship between Hammond and his four teen-aged nieces, Catherine, Harriet, Ann, and Caroline.

AN AFFAIR BETWEEN MEN

The Hampton sisters frequently visited their uncle's home in Columbia while he was governor, and over a long period of time the relationship developed to the point where Hammond became sexually intimate with the young women during their encounters, which occurred at least once a week and often more frequently. In a remarkable passage from his diary, Hammond recounted the illicit meetings with his nieces, noting that the transgressions involved "all of them rushing on every occasion into my arms and covering me with kisses, lolling on my lap, pressing their bodies almost into mine, wreathing their limbs with mine, encountering warmly every portion of my frame, and permitting my hands to stray unchecked over every part of them and to rest without the slightest shrinking from it, in the most secret and sacred regions, and all this for a period of more than two years continuously." Hammond observed that his intimacies with the four girls "extended to every thing short of direct sexual intercourse," but he insisted that he "had never designed anything criminal."[1]

Wade Hampton finally discovered at least some of the particulars of Hammond's relationship with his daughters when Catherine reported to her father in the autumn of 1843 that the governor had become too familiar with her. Hampton immediately wrote Catherine's uncle, denouncing

Hammond for the attempted seduction and severing all ties with him. In 1844, following the end of his term as governor, Hammond left Columbia and returned to his plantation at Silver Bluff, leaving behind a swirl of rumor and speculation about the falling out between the two brothers-in-law. Although the sordid details of the affair had not become public knowledge, Hammond suspected that his political prospects for the near future had suffered serious damage due to Hampton's influential position in the state. Conclusive evidence of Hammond's political difficulties came in 1846 when Wade Hampton moved to block Hammond's candidacy for the U.S. Senate by threatening to expose the family scandal. Hammond stayed in the race but lost the Senate seat on the third ballot of the legislative vote.

For the next thirteen years, James Henry Hammond remained in exile at Silver Bluff. Not until 1857 did he hold political office again, when he won a seat in the Senate following Hampton's removal to Mississippi. As for the Hampton daughters, they lived out the rest of their lives under a cloud of innuendo and disgrace, and none of them ever married. As one state legislator summed up, "After all the fuss made no man who valued his standing could marry one of the Hampton girls."[2]

Because Hammond's sexual involvement with his four nieces was one of the most sensational scandals in the antebellum South, it is important not to make too much of so bizarre an affair. Still, the deviant nature of the incident and the way in which it was handled reveal much about the dynamics of gender in southern society.[3] Most obviously, the outcome of the affair exposed the traditional double standard of sexual conduct that held sway in the Victorian South, one which condemned female sin but downplayed the consequences of male lust. Thomas R. Dew in 1835 sought to explain the reasoning behind this double standard; as he put it, woman's "virtue is the true sensitive plant, which is blighted even by the breath of suspicion. . . . Man may, by reformation, regain a lost character, but woman rarely can."[4] Accordingly, Hammond's political career experienced a setback as a result of his sexual indiscretion, but he eventually returned to public office. Once the four Hampton sisters came under suspicion, however, they could never restore their good name. Unlike Hammond, they were permanently driven to the outer edges of proper society.

In the aftermath of the scandal the rival politicians demonstrated their adherence to the ideal of patriarchal authority. Hammond announced to his younger brother Marcellus that "Women were meant to breed—Men to do the work of the world."[5] As the father of the wronged girls, Wade Hampton perceived the incident as an assault on his good name, for he was responsible for preserving the sexual purity of white women under his care and any tarnishing of his daughters' virtue reflected upon him.[6] From Hammond's perspective, though, it appeared as if Hampton had threatened to publicize the disgrace of his children in order to block him from gaining a seat in the U.S. Senate. Hammond's sense of honor dictated that he remain silent about the affair, and he viewed the father as having betrayed the girls' reputation for his own selfish purposes.[7]

At any rate, Hammond and Hampton both understood the episode as a matter that primarily concerned the two of them. The four young women assumed only a secondary role in the rivalry between these men, and neither brother-in-law gave any indication that he viewed the Hampton daughters as autonomous individuals. The very terms of the struggle for power between these two planter-politicians reflected the subordinate position of women in southern society, as well as a severely circumscribed sexual identity for females.

THE MAKING OF SOUTHERN LEGAL CULTURE

Like Hammond and Hampton, many white men in the Old South preferred to settle private disputes and matters of morality and sexual misconduct outside the legal system, and they viewed the courts as a last resort.[8] A vigorous attachment to the concept of honor—the constellation of ideas and values in which one's sense of self-worth rested on the degree of respect commanded from others in the community—led white southerners to believe that such affairs did not belong before the bench and should be handled without turning to the third party of the state. Honor, in short, placed a premium on personal rather than impersonal justice.[9]

Members of the southern bar were as quick to subscribe to this ethos as anyone. Samuel H. Hempstead, a lawyer newly arrived in Little Rock, Arkansas, wrote his uncle in 1836, asking to purchase his pistols. "No menaces or threats shall ever deter me from discharging my duty of whatsoever nature it may be," explained Hempstead, "and as on the one hand I shall always use every honorable means to avert a quarrel, so on the other I am equally fixed in protecting my person from attack and my reputation from insult." Nineteenth-century southern fiction suggests that even judges were not immune to the demands of honor. Judge York Leicester Driscoll in Mark Twain's *Pudd'nhead Wilson* (1894), a caustic account of social mores in a Mississippi River town during the antebellum era, is a case in point. Informed that his nephew has taken an assailant to court rather than challenge him to a duel, the judge berates his kinsman for having violated the code of honor: "You cur! You scum! You vermin! Do you mean to tell me that blood of my race has suffered a blow and crawled to a court of law about it?"[10]

The predisposition to engage in extralegal action did not gain the support of all white southerners. Some recognized that taking the law into one's own hands could have harmful consequences in the long run. A lawyer who initially supported the resort to private retaliation as a way to regulate the behavior of individuals in the community explained his change of heart in 1839: "Tolerate this in one case, and you authorize it in a thousand; and that is anarchy at once."[11] For many southerners, the law represented a crucial source of stability in society, a reliable bulwark against anarchy and disorder. As a New Orleans minister proclaimed in 1847, "Amid all the busy scenes of life, the eagerness of competition, and the violence of conflicting passions, LAW lifts up her majestic front, calm, unmoved, and unaffected by the various changes which agitate us, like some lofty mountain towering far above the surrounding plain, unshaken by storms, and ever irradiated by heaven's own light."[12] More than a guarantor of social order, law legitimized the ideas of interdependence and stratification that formed the basis of slave society. As J. D. B. De Bow held, law "is the ligament which binds society together; and the whole machine must tumble into pieces if that ligament be disturbed. . . . Superiority and inferiority are contained in it; law is the language of a superior to an inferior."[13]

The southern reputation for lawlessness stemmed mainly from the conviction that only the pursuit of personal vengeance could properly restore one's injured honor, and that state intervention was of little use in such circumstances—hence the customs of brawling and disfigurement among backwoodsmen and dueling among planters, all of which disclosed the preoccupation of white men with the world of appearances. The duel, in particular, was a ritual that revealed the dependence of the individual male on community opinion and public image to confirm his status. Always occurring between social equals, the duel publicly expressed the membership of the parties in the ruling elite and displayed the values of this elite, as well as its solidarity, for all to see. In this social drama, instead of the written law, an elaborate code understood and shared by gentlemen mediated the resolution of the dispute.[14] The unwritten laws of honor, as Twain observes in *Pudd'nhead Wilson*, "were as clearly defined and as strict as any that could be found among the statutes of the land." For Judge Driscoll, a member of the Virginia gentry who moved west, "those laws were his chart; his course was marked out on it; if he swerved from it by so much as half a point of the compass, it meant shipwreck to his honor; that is to say, degradation from his rank as a gentleman." There was no question in the minds of white southerners like the judge about which set of laws would have to give way in the event of a conflict between them; in Twain's words, "Honor stood first."[15]

Although the culture of honor and deference to the written laws often clashed, this did not prevent the legal system from occupying an important place in southern society. Except for Louisiana, which adopted the civil law of France as the basis of its legal system, the South drew extensively on English common law as a source of inspiration. Settlers of the American colonies along the southern Atlantic seaboard who came from England carried with them the set of rights, procedures, and customs that made up the common law. Subscribing to a unitary view of the legal and political order during the seventeenth century, southern colonists established a layered system of courts that combined legislative and judicial functions. The main tribunals were the general court, consisting usually of the governor and his council, and the county court, composed of the justices of the peace. This system prevailed in Virginia until the American Revolution. In Maryland, however, the highest court divided into two after 1692: the Provincial Court, headed by a chief justice and members of the upper house of assembly, and the Court of Appeals, made up of the governor and council. In South Carolina an even more elaborate judicial system emerged at the provincial level, with the more serious criminal and civil suits going to one of three tribunals located in Charleston, either the Court of Common Pleas, General Sessions, or Chancery. A chief justice and four associate justices (usually laymen who went unpaid) constituted the former two courts, and the governor and council sat as the Chancery Court. The highest provincial courts exercised original jurisdiction over capital criminal cases (except for those involving slave defendants), heard appeals from the lower courts, and often handled chancery and admiralty proceedings. For much of the colonial period, appeals could be made from the general courts to the assemblies, but eventually the final appellate court became the Privy Council in England.[16]

The legal system of the colonial South was first and foremost a local system. County courts became the primary centers of power, wielding a broad jurisdiction that extended to nearly all aspects of daily life. Besides trying criminal offenders and settling disputes, the county courts assessed taxes, oversaw their collection, supervised road and bridge construction, and licensed taverns and inns. They also recorded deeds, granted poor relief, and supervised the proper administration of estates, the transfer of land titles, and the care of orphans.[17] Members of the landed gentry dominated the county courts, and court day became an important occasion for the ritual expression of their social position and authority. Court day brought together the scattered community, providing a welcome opportunity to debate politics, conduct business, and socialize. Wearing wigs and fine attire, the gentlemen judges administered oaths and handed down justice to their less prosperous neighbors and kin. These men were amateur justices whose administration of the law was rudimentary and unsophisticated. Their lives centered on the planting and marketing of tobacco and other staple crops, and they came to the bench with little or no legal training.[18]

The county court was one of the few institutions that could effectively maintain order and harmony in the colonial South, and it played a crucial role in defining and promoting the values of the community. Members of the grand jury, as well as justices of the peace, contributed to the accomplishment of this task. The justices were supposed to call together a grand jury made up of freeholders twice a year to present those accused of committing a wide array of minor offenses, such as bearing a bastard child, not attending the local parish church, and failing to keep up roads. Free persons and indentured servants indicted for felonies were tried in the general courts, whereas slaves were brought before special slave-trial courts consisting of two or three justices of the peace and several local freeholders. Crimes that threatened the social order—contempt, assault, homicide, and moral misconduct—generated the highest conviction rates, but convictions for crimes against property increased as economic growth accelerated. The grand jurymen, courts, and law enforcement officers, including the sheriff, his deputies, and the constables, all worked together to enforce the law and uphold gentry authority at the local level, establishing a legal system that reflected the social order in which they lived.[19]

As the rule of law became a more significant part of life in the southern colonies, the bar attained increasing influence. Like the magistrates, lawyers during the seventeenth century were often unschooled in the law. By the eighteenth century, however, law had emerged as a distinct profession, and the flowering of a complex agricultural and mercantile economy produced a need for specialists who had legal training. Not only did the southern bar grow in numbers and prestige, but also the level of legal education and practice underwent significant improvement. A few colonial lawyers trained at the Inns of Court in London, but most would-be lawyers read law in the office of a practicing attorney. Stratification of the bar developed as lawyers who resided and worked in the colonial capitals came to believe that they were superior to the county court attorneys. Virginia lawyers who practiced at the general court in Williamsburg, for example, made clear their disdain for what they saw as the lack of proper preparation of the justices and lawyers at the county level, and in the early eighteenth century the general court bar called for a more formal, learned, and technical approach to the law.[20]

The growing authority and sophistication of attorneys in the colonial South went hand in hand with an expanding role in politics, and by the outbreak of the revolutionary crisis, members of the bar had assumed a place in the forefront of the colonial elite. During the Revolution, lawyers helped to write the new state constitutions in the South that established more highly differentiated legal and political systems, reflecting the new emphasis on balanced government and separation of powers. Virginia in 1776 became the first of the new states to define the judiciary as a distinct third branch of government, and other states soon followed. Although separation of powers and balanced government created an enhanced position for the judiciary in the implementation of the rule of law, the doctrine of judicial review, by which the courts exercised the power to strike down on constitutional grounds legislative and executive acts, generated great controversy in the new Republic, and the highest appellate courts in the southern states employed their new prerogatives cautiously.[21]

Popular distrust of lawyers and the courts surfaced in the wake of the Revolution, although less so in the South than in the Northeast. Radical Jeffersonian Republicans, suspicious of concentrated power, were the most vociferous critics of the bench and bar. Portraying attorneys as "swindlers" and "parasites," they launched efforts to replace the complexities of the common law with a simple code of laws drafted by the legislature, and they engaged in other attempts to hinder the growth of an elite body of judges and lawyers. Even as critics attacked the legal profession, however, lawyers regularly won election to public office and increasingly replaced lay judges on the bench.[22] Thomas Jones, observing the great number of attorneys running for election to the general assembly of Virginia, complained in 1807 that "we shall 'ere long be as completely lawyer ridden as ever the people in Europe has been priest ridden."[23]

Gradually and somewhat haphazardly, amidst the tumultuous debate during the early nineteenth century over the proper place of lawyers and judges in a republican society, judicial systems evolved in the southern states. Variations existed from state to state in the form and content of the new legal arrangements, but by the middle of the century a fully developed structure of lower, circuit, and appeals courts had emerged in the South. The county courts continued to act not only as courts of law but also as administrative bodies directing local affairs. In this latter capacity, the courts exercised jurisdiction over county taxes, poor relief, local schools, and the construction and maintenance of roads, bridges, courthouses, and jails. The bulk of judicial business involved probating wills, overseeing the administration of estates, and appointing guardians for orphaned children.

With the expansion and overhaul of the legal system following the Revolution, an increasing number of states established trial courts organized in districts that eventually restricted the judicial role of the justice of the peace. The new superior courts possessed an original criminal and civil jurisdiction, and three or more judges staffed each court. Like the justices of the peace, these superior court judges were often planters rather than lawyers, and their formal legal education was minimal.[24]

Directly above the trial courts were the circuit courts, which sat in specific locations at different times of the year to review petitions of error or complaint from lower-court proceedings. The supreme court, which oversaw the work of these intermediate courts of appeal, originally consisted in many southern states of the circuit court judges or the chief justices of these courts sitting together. By the Civil War, however, each of the states had established the supreme court as a separate and distinct institution, usually composed of a chief justice and two to four associate justices.

In order to bolster the effectiveness of the appellate tribunals, states provided funds for court reporting, which involved the collection, arrangement, and publication of appellate court decisions and some trial-court proceedings. Many states also adopted measures early on to ensure the existence of an independent judiciary, generally appointing appellate judges for life tenure during "good behavior." The principle of judicial review survived in the appellate courts, although state jurists did not begin to employ this power widely until the mid-nineteenth century. All in all, these developments added up to a judicial system that was somewhat decentralized yet hierarchical.[25]

Within this evolving legal structure, the local courthouse endured as one of the most influential institutions in southern culture. An essayist in *De Bow's Review* extolled the virtues of the county court in 1856: "Here have the isolating tendencies of agricultural life been incessantly counteracted. Here have republican citizens been formed and trained to the difficult art and duty of self-government. Here has each citizen an opportunity of showing himself for what he really is and of taking that position in society to which he is justly entitled. . . . Here, in truth, has society insensibly organized itself, recognized its leaders, and assigned to each member his appropriate task in the general business of the community." The county court not only remained firmly rooted in the more settled areas of the South along the seaboard but also sprang up quickly in newly opened areas of the Old Southwest. Even W. J. Cash, who emphasized the frontier individualism of the Old South, has noted that "when the Southern backwoodsman moved out into the new cotton country west of the Appalachians, he immediately set up the machinery of the State, just as his fathers before him had done in the regions east of the mountains; everywhere he built his courthouse almost before he built anything else. And here in the South, as in all places in all times, the State, once established, inevitably asserted its inherent tendency to growth, to reach out and engross power."[26]

Cases jammed the criminal and civil dockets of the antebellum South, and spectators flocked to court whenever it was in session. John Pendleton Kennedy, in his novel *Swallow Barn* (1851), describes the carnival-like atmosphere that prevailed at the local level: "The sitting of this court is an occasion of great stir. The roads leading to the little county capital were enlivened by frequent troops of the neighboring inhabitants, that rode in squadrons, from all directions. Jurors, magistrates, witnesses, attorneys of the circuit, and all the throng of a country side interested in this pie-powder justice, were rapidly converging to the centre of business." In the same way that all roads led to Rome, so it seems that all the roads of this small southern town led to the courthouse, the seat and symbol of power.[27]

Of course, it was one thing to construct what Cash called "the machinery of the State" and it was another to run it in an effective fashion. The uproar that characterized the courthouse scene could be especially disconcerting to a young lawyer attending his first term. Pressing the flesh with the local folk was far removed from studying Coke and Blackstone. One attorney recalled his shock when arriving at the county court with his newly acquired license: "The political rivals had commenced haranguing the mob; the shrill cry of the Yankee pedler [*sic*] vendueing his goods, the hoarse laugh of the stout Virginia planter, the neighing of horses, the loud voice of the stump orator, and the menaces of county bullies, met for the purpose of testing their pugilistic talents, broke upon the tympanum in no agreeable confusion." In the more rural and isolated areas of the antebellum South, local courts dispensed justice in a crude and somewhat informal manner. Micajah Clark, having witnessed a magistrate's court in northeastern Georgia in 1857, wrote in his diary about the ignorance and self-importance of the judge and other people in attendance. According to Clark, the lawyers who addressed the jury on behalf of their clients "had a hard time to make the fool officers, witnesses, and people understand what was law."[28]

For many years historians have emphasized the inefficiency and laxness of the southern legal system.[29] Recent investigations, however, have cast new light on this traditional interpretation. It now appears that the ineffectiveness of southern courts may not have been a distinctive regional phenomenon. Growing evidence indicates that the inability of local southern courts to complete prosecution in a large percentage of criminal cases had striking parallels in other regions of the country, and that this problem was characteristic of rural communities in both the North and South. Just as important, patterns of prosecution in southern jurisdictions seem to resemble those found elsewhere. White, propertyless males made up a high proportion of those brought before the courts. Not only did theft and other property offenses show up regularly on court dockets, but the prosecution of moral disorder occupied much of the attention of local authorities as well. The major exception to this adherence to national patterns of prosecution was the large percentage of indictments for crimes against persons, a fact that highlights the violent nature of the region. Finally, although it is commonly believed that the penitentiary was a product of the urban North, prison systems developed in every antebellum slave state except the Carolinas and Florida. The elevated rhetoric of northern reformers did not accompany the spread of the penitentiary in the South and the appearance of this institution provoked an intense debate, but southerners built the same kind of prisons and at the same rate as most northern states.[30]

Although the legal system was not necessarily ineffective, localism imposed significant constraints on the extent of state interference in southern society. Local opinion and custom held a central place in southern public life and, consequently, the criminal justice system tended to put the power of the state at the disposal of the community. The different grades of society worked out their own arrangements with a minimum of external interference and, as Bertram Wyatt-Brown contends, the various elements of white society participated in the administration of criminal law according to the distribution of power in the community: "The rich, as judges and sometimes jury foremen; the middling ranks, as sheriffs, constables, magistrates, and younger attorneys; the yeomanry, as freeholding jurors and patrol leaders; and the poor, at times, as members of patrols, witnesses, informers, and active spectators at the trials."

The legal institutions themselves thus reflected the tendency to view justice in personal terms and to place as much weight on social custom as the rule of law. This does not mean that the law was purely the product of local sentiment, but the will of the community was a crucial factor in the legal process. Whatever the end result, justice was a neighborhood affair in the slave South.[31]

Given the local character of southern justice, the bench and bar occupied a sensitive position in antebellum society. Lawyers and judges were generally among the most educated members of the community and an important connection to the outside world, especially on the frontier. As attorneys, together with merchants and bankers, played an increasingly prominent role in promoting the economic and social changes sweeping over the South, they generated a complex reaction from the public at large. The ambivalence that most white southerners felt about the bar is reflected in the two contradictory images of lawyers that prevailed in antebellum popular culture: the gentlemen practitioners and the mercenary pettifoggers.[32] Philpot Wart, the hero of Kennedy's *Swallow Barn*, represents the best of the legal elite. An engaging storyteller with an intuitive feel for the law rather than a lot of technical training, Wart is held in high regard by his friends, colleagues, and neighbors. Not only is he a popular figure on the circuit, but he "has been elected to the Assembly for twenty years past without opposition; and, indeed, the voters will not permit him to decline."[33]

Wart is a man of honor with close ties to the planter class, but not all antebellum lawyers found such favor in the community. Major Trimmer, in Thomas B. Thorpe's *The Master's House* (1854), personifies a more predatory style of lawyering. Always on the lookout for new clients, Trimmer does not hesitate to defend Toadvine, an overseer accused of murdering a slave in a drunken rage. As a result of the attorney's legal maneuvering and oratorical talents, he is able to ensure that the overseer is declared innocent, infuriating General Bledsoe, the great planter, and his supporters, who want to see Toadvine punished for the reckless destruction of slave property. Indeed, convinced that "the law was a mere farce, gotten up for no other purpose than to enable lawyers to rob the community, and escape the consequences," Bledsoe and his friends try to take matters into their own hands after the trial, but Toadvine escapes down the Mississippi before they can locate him.[34]

A more humorous version of the pettifogger appears in Joseph G. Baldwin's *The Flush Times of Alabama and Mississippi* (1853). Among the memorable cast of characters introduced in this classic account of frontier law is Simon Suggs Jr., who wins his law license in an Alabama card game, moves to Arkansas, and there applies himself "to the duties of that learned profession." Suggs prepares diligently for his cases, developing a special knack for packing the courtroom with his friends for important trials in order to guarantee the impanelling of a sympathetic jury. As one courtroom victory follows another, Suggs soon cultivates a reputation for having mastered "all the arts and contrivances by which public justice is circumvented." Needless to say, his practice flourishes and he becomes a wealthy man.[35]

Despite fictional accounts that suggested otherwise, the legal field in the antebellum South was difficult to break into and often did not yield impressive economic rewards, especially in the first several years of practice. The outlook could be fairly intimidating for young men at the outset of their careers. David Schenck of North Carolina, contemplating the prospects for his success, exclaimed in his diary in 1854, "Oh! the legal profession is a thorny path. People suppose it to be a lazy occupation fit only for the idle and are apt to sneer at a young man who embraces it, whereas there is no science so difficult, so arduous, which requires so much application and then to obtain no credit where so much is merited."

Like increasing numbers of his colleagues, Schenck studied for a year at law school, in this case one established by Judge Richmond Pearson of the North Carolina Supreme Court. The program consisted of three lectures a week by Judge Pearson, attended by twenty-three students. One month after he began his formal legal training with the judge, Schenck related, "I am highly delighted with his mode of teaching and already experience greatly its benefits."[36] Whether his experience at Judge Pearson's school was as valuable as Schenck believed, a small but vocal group of southern legal writers launched a campaign supporting law schools as the most effective way to train potential attorneys.[37]

Despite the appearance of such schools in the South before the Civil War, the apprenticeship system continued to provide the primary means for acquiring a legal education. Assistance from relatives facilitated the careers of many young lawyers, who often studied in the offices of their older cousins and other male kin, and received guidance from them in the early years of their legal practice. The relatively unstructured character of law practice in the antebellum South and the lack of professional organizations made kinship networks particularly important.[38] Those without such support often found themselves facing grim circumstances. James Graham, an attorney trying to drum up business on the circuit in western North Carolina, complained in 1817 to a colleague, "There is not one of the profession who in this circuit makes anything more than a tolerable competency by his profession, hence several of the lawyers here, (chiefly those who have families to support,) have turned their attention, in part, towards some other pursuit." Things were so bad that Graham was considering the possibility of moving to Alabama or Mississippi, where he thought the situation might be more promising.

Many southern lawyers, faced with overcrowding at the bar in the seaboard states, in fact went west to seek opportunity in the new settlements on the frontier, but it appears that it was as difficult to establish a law practice there as anywhere else.[39] Enough examples of failure existed to provide material for a satiric poem about a county court lawyer down on his luck that appeared in the *Southern Literary Messenger* in 1846:

> Gaunt seems his hack,—mean his caparison,
> Lank the valise, which little hath therein;
> For he his wardrobe bears his back upon,—
> The same doth reptile hight the terrapin;—
> And whilst for fees, he patiently doth wait,
> Small is the stock within his pouch I ween,
> Which he from dearest friend y' borrowed late,
> With promise to repay, when prosperous his estate.

No doubt these verses sent shivers of recognition down the spine of more than one attorney caught in a similar plight.

Although young attorneys attempting to gain a foothold in the profession faced a series of daunting obstacles, the law had no trouble attracting aggressive, resolute men. Consequently, the bar expanded rapidly, becoming an important avenue of social mobility. Acutely aware of his poverty and "want of birth," John W. Brown, who went on to become an Arkansas lawyer and planter, ruminated in 1821 about his plans for the future while studying at John Rowan's law office in Louisville, Kentucky. "I feel ambitious to be known in the world, to procure property, to marry an amicable and respectable girl and at the same time of considerable rank," he bluntly announced in his diary. Brown was certain that the practice of law would help him achieve these goals. Almost a year later, recounting the challenges of setting up a practice in a small settlement on the Mississippi River, he noted, "There is a degree of ambition necessary to carry a man thro any profession with credit and this ambition ought to be strong enough to bear him up well in all the difficulties attending his pursuits." Samuel Hempstead struck a similar note in an 1836 letter to his uncle describing the legal scene in Little Rock: "I flatter myself, that by perseverance, and industry, I can *at least* make an honorable support—The bar here is somewhat crowded—but competition makes the good lawyer."[40]

Such determination, in fact, paid off for a sizable portion of the legal profession. During the decade before the Civil War the bar as a whole experienced a dramatic rise in wealth. Occupying a strategic position as a bridge between agricultural and business interests, lawyers took full advantage of southern economic prosperity in the 1850s, joining the ranks of the most powerful and financially well-off elites in their communities.[41] The growing number of attorneys at the top level of the economic and political order went hand in hand with an emerging professional self-consciousness about the vital role that lawyers played in antebellum society.[42] As B. F. Porter maintained in 1846, "When we consider how extensively the professional influence of the lawyer is exercised upon the affairs of mankind—that he has it often in his power to save the life, liberty or property of his fellow men, it will be evident that no time is too long, no labor too great to be devoted to his profession." New efforts to upgrade the bar also reflected the growing self-consciousness of lawyers. Calling on the legislature to tighten admission requirements for the profession, the *Carolina Law Journal* in 1830 contended that the problem of incompetent lawyers was "growing daily worse, and should be speedily corrected. Our bar is sinking instead of rising."[43]

Along with attempts to make entry into the bar more difficult, the antebellum legal profession sought to improve the lay image of the lawyer. In an attempt to counter the stereotype of the ill-mannered, money-grubbing pettifogger, the *Southern Literary Messenger* published in 1854 a portrait by Lucian Minor of "the model lawyer." According to Minor, a member of the Virginia bar, the ideal lawyer would always keep in mind the interests of his clients, avoid needless litigation, charge reasonable fees for his services, champion the public good, and never take advantage of his colleagues.[44] Of course, contained in the very effort to establish such a high standard was an acknowledgment that many, if not most, lawyers fell short of it. As Jeremiah Battle wrote his younger cousin William, who was about to become the first member of the family to practice law, "It is, unfortunately, a prevailing opinion that a Lawyer cannot, or need not be a man of veracity & truth." Suggesting that "a lawyer may be as virtuous, as humane, as charitable to the distressed, as free from the avaracious love of money, & as great an advocate for truth & honesty as other men," Jeremiah wondered, "Well, why are they not so?" Such questions about the legal profession persisted throughout the antebellum period.[45]

Although the bar produced at best an ambivalent response among white southerners, the judiciary nearly always commanded great esteem. Like Judge Driscoll of *Pudd'nhead Wilson*, who was "beloved by all the community," southern jurists at the local level tended to be seen as upholders of stability and tradition rather than as agents of change. In a larger environment of flux and fluidity, such an image of stolidity could be a source of great comfort to white southerners anxious about the future. Kennedy, in *Swallow Barn*, captures this symbolic function of the justices of the peace. Describing the county court coming to order for its monthly session, Kennedy observes that "the whole bench presented a fine picture of solid faces and figures, that might be said to be a healthy and sturdy specimen of this pillar of the sovereignty of the state." According to Kennedy, this judicial portrait "was well calculated to inspire a wholesome respect for that inferior and useful magistracy which has always been so much a favorite of the people of Virginia."[46]

Judges who served on the state tribunals also occupied positions of honor and influence. Although a relatively new institution, the appellate court on the eve of the Civil War was the final arbiter in most disputes involving civil and procedural rights, and thus exercised much more authority than after the adoption of the Fourteenth and Fifteenth Amendments, when federal courts possessed jurisdiction in these areas. Appellate jurists usually came from relatively affluent, well-established backgrounds, and they often had political careers before they reached the bench. The seven men who sat on the bench of the Georgia Supreme Court during the late antebellum period, for instance, were all prominent leaders of their state, including a former governor and three legislators. In addition, they were all slaveholders and substantial landowners. Six of the thirteen Alabama Supreme Court justices in the prewar decade were former state legislators; all held large properties, and several pursued interests in planting as well as law.[47]

The southern courts produced a number of remarkably accomplished appellate jurists before the Civil War. Thomas Ruffin, who served as chief justice of the North Carolina appellate court from 1833 to 1852, was arguably the most influential judge in the Old South. Ruffin graduated from Princeton and held offices as a state legislator and superior court judge before moving up to the state's highest court in 1829. A Jeffersonian Republican from the eastern part of the state, he wrote some of the most important and controversial appellate opinions in slave law before the Civil War, including the landmark decision of State v. Mann (1829).[48]

Judges in both local and appellate courts acted as official agents of the community, helping to establish boundaries between what was acceptable and what was unacceptable, a set of limits that confirmed social norms. This was particularly true in cases involving domestic relations disputes and sexual offenses. The courts operated as a form of "moral theater," seeking to reconcile the sometimes contradictory assumptions of Victorian culture with the competing claims of the legal parties. As judges sought to mediate these disputes, they did so from a distinctly masculine stance, creating what Michael Grossberg has called a "judicial patriarchy."[49]

Admirers described nineteenth-century members of the bench using language that reflected the patriarchal role of the judiciary. Commenting on the appointment of Richmond Pearson to the North Carolina Supreme Court in 1848, William D. Valentine observed that the judge "is very learned, of a mind remarkably legal, analytical, clear, and simple. He professes great confidence in his legal conclusions, and is firm. He investigates and understands for himself before he assents to an opinion." Likewise, another lawyer, Augustine Harris Hansell, remembered Judge Lott Warren of Georgia as "a man of high order and character, with a strong mind and strong body, and [who] well deserved the great popularity he long enjoyed, both as Congressman and Judge, for high order of ability and rigid integrity." By depicting judicial authority in such terms, Victorian legal culture helped to institutionalize masculine values such as impartiality, reason, and independence, as well as to designate the law as a male domain.[50]

In the largely rural South, where circuit riding persisted well into the nineteenth century, the conviviality of lawyers and judges traveling as a group from county seat to county seat reinforced the male orientation of the profession. The ideal of the bench and the bar joined together in fraternal solidarity lay at the heart of the antebellum legal culture, although the judiciary occupied the position of senior partner in this enterprise. "The beautiful fiction of Law, by which the members of the profession are considered as brethren, of whom the judge is but the elder, hardly deserves the name of fiction," Beverly Tucker, a law professor at William and Mary College, maintained in 1835. "There is no corps animated by a spirit so truly fraternal, nor is there any member of it to whose comfort this spirit is so essential, as the judge himself."[51]

Attorneys and jurists in the Old South had plenty of time to contemplate such lofty sentiments as they traveled the judicial circuits in all kinds of weather by coach or horseback over rough roads that were at times nearly impassable. Not surprisingly, the wear and tear of circuit riding was a frequent topic in the correspondence of those who took part in this time-honored ritual. Frederick Nash, a North Carolina judge, wrote his daughter Susan in 1819, "Another week has passed & left me wearied & disgusted—disgusted with the unceasing . . . quibbles of the law—& wearied in body & mind by the continued recurrence of the same dull monotonous round of labour." Despite the oft-stated desire to be home with family and friends, judges and lawyers did not experience unrelieved loneliness and boredom while on the road. Arguing, swapping tales, drinking, and living together strengthened the ties among members of the bench and bar, and afforded numerous opportunities for the younger attorneys to become closer acquaintances with their older, better connected colleagues.[52]

At least some of the appellate jurists escaped the rigors of circuit riding once the supreme courts became established as separate institutions.

Representative of the more cosmopolitan elements of southern society, these judges usually had a broader outlook than those who sat on the lower courts. Keenly aware that the rest of the Anglo-American world increasingly looked down upon the slave South as backward, the southern supreme court judiciary paid careful attention to the ideological role of appellate justice, using its position to make the case that the region possessed an unquestionable commitment to the rule of law. This does not mean that southern appellate jurists calculated each decision handed down in terms of its impact on neutralizing abolitionist propaganda. Instead, they largely embraced the moral framework of Anglo-American law and sought to demonstrate what they perceived as their rightful place within this framework.[53]

Despite the high regard they usually enjoyed, southern judges even at the appellate level belonged to the community and could not afford to overlook local feelings. This became especially true as southern states moved during the early nineteenth century towards the popular election of jurists. In 1812 Georgia initiated elections for inferior court judges and justices of the peace, and in 1832 Mississippi became the first state to elect its entire judiciary. Other states in the South followed suit in the 1850s, although on the eve of the Civil War the legislatures in Georgia, North Carolina, and South Carolina still appointed all judges for the higher state courts.[54]

As the drive to choose the judiciary by popular election made headway in the antebellum South, jurists paid increasing attention to the necessity of cultivating public approval. Alexander A. Allen of Georgia wrote to his brother in great detail about his effort to get elected to the circuit court in 1855. "It would gratify me exceedingly to hold the position of Judge of the Circuit," he remarked. "It is the point to which my ambition has looked since I came to the Bar." Several months after winning the hard-fought election, Allen expressed a profound sense of relief regarding the community's apparently favorable evaluation of his performance in office, telling his brother, "I am much gratified that the public seems to be satisfied with my mode of doing business & with my decisions."[55] The effort to democratize the selection of the judiciary left few members of the bench untouched. Where efforts to reform the judicial system ran aground, like South Carolina, the democratic impulse expressed itself in a flourishing tradition of judicial impeachments that were directed against unpopular as well as incompetent judges.[56]

White southerners respected the judiciary, then, but they expected those who sat on the bench to remain responsive to the larger community of which they were part. Chief Justice Thomas Ruffin, among others, deplored developments such as popular elections, which he believed undermined the independence of the courts. As he declared upon his resignation from the North Carolina Supreme Court in 1852, "All experience and all just reasoning concur in proving a dependent Judiciary to be, practically, the heaviest and the most enduring curse that can befall a deluded, depraved, and gain-saying people, and especially, a nation having a popular form of government." Nonetheless, even those who opposed legislation limiting the tenure of the judiciary granted that jurists must be held accountable to the public. As one such writer conceded in the *Southern Quarterly Review*, judges "were created certainly for the immediate interest of communities, and when they fail to subserve this purpose, they should not be allowed to occupy situations which might enable them to do irreparable mischief."[57]

Given the emphasis on the accountability of the judiciary, it is not surprising that respect for the bench did not always translate into deference. In George Tucker's *The Valley of the Shenandoah* (1824), one of the earliest plantation novels, an idealistic lawyer contends that "both magistrates and juries should be addressed by the title of citizens, for they were nothing more, and which, indeed . . . was the most dignified of all titles." Although this fictional attorney stakes out an egalitarian view that not all white southerners shared, jurists clearly had to maintain a well-honed appreciation of their mediating role in southern society, a role that required them to balance statutory and common law against local circumstances and needs.[58]

The dictates of honor, which gave so much weight to community opinion, contributed in large measure to the localistic nature of the southern legal system. But the distinctive meaning of republicanism in the slave South was just as influential. In New England economic and political elites viewed an active state as the essence of republicanism, while northern artisans and farmers embraced the notion of egalitarianism. Most white southerners, in contrast, retained an agrarian conception of republicanism that underscored the necessity of maintaining freedom from the control of others, and they believed that centralized power posed a serious threat to this freedom. Whenever power impinged on the lives of southern planters and farmers, they reacted predictably. As Cash put it, the South exhibited "an intense distrust of, and, indeed, downright aversion to, any actual exercise of authority beyond the barest minimum essential to the existence of the social organism."[59]

Southerners did not equate freedom with the complete absence of government; instead, they believed that the primary function of the state was to preserve individual autonomy, albeit for a select few: adult, white males. As the *Southern Literary Messenger* explained in 1851, "The end of government is simply to protect the individual in the enjoyment of his rights and in the proper pursuits of his calling; not a protection and patronage by direct acts of government power to promote his interests, but a simple protection from interruption or disturbance in his own efforts to enrich himself." [60] The suspicion of state power and distinct preference for decentralization led to a restriction of government activities and the imposition of severe restraints on public spending, except when a source of nontax revenue became available that allowed the state to increase spending without raising taxes. Reluctance to shoulder the costs of constructing and maintaining penitentiaries during the antebellum period thus drove southern states to experiment with several schemes to get these institutions to pay their own way, including putting inmates to work in prison factories and using them for contract labor.

The three main achievements of state governments in the antebellum period mirrored the economic and racial definition of liberty that formed the basis of the political outlook of white southerners: the protection of slave property, the distribution of Indian land, and the building of railroads. Public investment in railroad construction and other internal improvements not only fueled economic growth but also generated state revenues that helped pay for services such as elementary schooling and higher education. Overall, however, white southerners favored limited government and they emphasized local initiative on matters requiring state intervention such as poor relief and education. [61]

In the judicial arena, the southern variant of republicanism led courts during the early nineteenth century to employ the power of the state with noticeable circumspection. As the *Carolina Law Repository* insisted in 1814, the judge's "province is not to make the law, but to dispense it as made; nor ought he in any case to exercise a discretion, unless it is confided to him by the Legislature." [62] While their northern counterparts embraced a view of the law as an instrument of policy and forged legal doctrines with the self-conscious aim of stimulating social change, southern jurists generally took a much more cautious approach. As state courts elsewhere redefined property law to foster economic growth, for example, southern courts retained a traditional view of vested property rights well into the nineteenth century, protecting owners of state-granted franchises for mills and ferries against competition and interference. In short, members of the southern bench sought to maintain social and political stability, shying away from innovation and sanctioning forms of property rights that had the potential to impede economic development. [63]

This is not to say that there were no advocates in southern society for a more fluid view of the law. George Fitzhugh argued strenuously that "law is like language, it is constantly modifying and changing. Neither lexicographers, nor grammarians, critics, commentators, legislators, or judges, can arrest the ever-varying course of either." Fitzhugh emphasized the need for the law to adapt itself to changing times, and he underscored the central role of the courts in overseeing this process. He scornfully attacked those who contended that judges should "only discover and declare the common law." "The whole theory is as false and absurd as the stories told by priests about fragments of the Holy Cross," claimed Fitzhugh. "The judges make law and do not merely discover, expound and declare it."[64]

Few southern jurists, however, agreed with this approach, and they generally expressed hostility toward the idea of judges as lawmakers. This unwillingness to adopt a more dynamic understanding of law became especially apparent when the southern courts addressed issues related to criminal procedure. William Gaston, a leading member of the North Carolina Supreme Court from 1833 to 1844, insisted that in criminal cases judges had a responsibility "to hand down the deposit of the law as they had received it, without addition, diminution, or change; although it was a duty the faithful performance of which was exceedingly difficult— they must refrain from all tempting novelties, listen to no suggestion of expediency, give in to no plausible theories, and submit to be deemed old fashioned and bigoted formalists, at a time when all around were running on in the supposed career of liberal improvement." This highly conservative approach to the law, with its stress on a strict adherence to precedent-bound rules and procedures, characterized the judicial style of most antebellum southern jurists, even when it came to the criminal prosecution of slaves. Appellate judges, in particular, struggled to fashion a law of slavery that took into account the humanity of the slave, the property interests of masters, and a longstanding commitment to due process.[65] Certainly, judicial power grew during the early nineteenth century and, like members of the northern bench, southern judges at all levels of government became active agents of the state, but not on the scale achieved elsewhere in the United States.[66]

Honor and republicanism, important as they were in the antebellum South, did not exist as self-contained and autonomous value systems; instead, they combined to form the core of the white southerner's outlook. Honor rested on the maintenance of personal liberty, and the absence of liberty and honor conjured up the image of a degraded slave, an image that had tremendous resonance in the South. "For white southerners," William J. Cooper Jr. notes, "escaping the dreaded status of slave necessitated the maintenance of their liberty and honor no matter the cost." A preoccupation with the preservation of personal autonomy, the drive for honor shaped the southern tradition of republicanism, leading to an understanding of republicanism that involved not only equality among citizens—in this case defined as adult, white males—but also an assertion of power over others in the household and society.[67]

Honor and republicanism were not only connected with each other, they were grounded in master-slave relations. Slavery perpetuated a rural and localistic culture in which these value systems could take root and grow. White southerners saw bondage as the very opposite of republicanism, and their physical and psychological proximity to slavery strengthened their commitment to liberty and honor. Indeed, as Edmund Morgan has argued so incisively, slavery furnished the foundation of southern republicanism, for it eliminated the need for a white underclass and hence promoted a social structure in which no white man would ever become so dependent upon another that he would completely lose his independence and self-esteem.[68]

Slavery, republicanism, honor, and localism: these were the crucial forces that shaped the southern attitude toward state intervention. Together they combined to encourage the development of a weak state in the region, reducing the area of life that was controlled by law. But, as Charles Sydnor points out, to say that southerners placed significant limits on the reach of the law "is not equivalent to saying that law, within its restricted zone, was held in disrespect."[69]

DOMESTIC ORDER IN THE OLD SOUTH

The relationship between patriarchy and the law in southern society must be understood within this framework of attitudes toward the state.[70] The household, embedded in networks of blood, marriage, and kinship, provided the key source of order and stability in southern society. In the older areas of settlement along the seaboard an extensive network of kinship tied neighborhoods together and people looked to their relatives for assistance and security. In the Old Southwest and the upcountry, recent immigrants who had left behind family eagerly sought other kin with whom they could reconstruct support networks. Planter family life, in particular, generated vibrant emotional bonds among a variety of relatives, and recent research suggests that many planter households included relations from beyond the nuclear core. Closely woven circles of kin rippled out from both slaveholding and nonslaveholding households into the surrounding community, and together with the racial caste system that accompanied slavery, blunted the potential for class conflict among whites and gave southern society its unique sense of social cohesion.[71]

Daniel Hundley insisted in 1860 that in American communities outside the South "the family has long since ceased to be an institution at all."[72] This, plainly, was a gross exaggeration. The family was alive and well above the Mason-Dixon line, but not in its traditional form. As external influences such as the market and state penetrated families in the North and reshaped them, significant ideological differences emerged between northern and southern households. The triumph of capitalist social relations and the reorganization of work away from home in the urbanizing northeastern United States and western Europe led to the crystallization of separate spheres for men and women, and the enthusiastic acceptance of individualism. The bourgeois rhetoric of domesticity recast the home as a haven for nurturing, rather than a center of production, and empowered women to maintain the private sphere.[73]

In the overwhelmingly rural South, however, the household retained its role as the fundamental productive unit of society. Southern slaveholding ideology ascribed a more important position to the male head of the household than did bourgeois ideology, and the rigid separation of home and work that characterized middle-class life in the North did not exist. Because the household continued to be the focus of economic and domestic activities on southern plantations and farms, gender boundaries overlapped to a greater degree. Slave women toiled alongside the men in the fields, and on yeoman farms, white women helped with the agricultural work. When their husbands traveled, the wives of planters acted as deputies in their absence, supervising the plantation in addition to attending to the details of household management. Women were no less restricted to the domestic arena in the slave South than they were in the North, but the distinctive nature of the household meant that it did not become transformed into a woman's sphere and that patriarchal control over the home remained firm.[74]

English colonists had carried the patriarchal values of the Old World with them to the Chesapeake in the seventeenth century. According to the understanding of domestic relations that characterized the mentality of premodern England, a unity of family interests existed and the male head of the household best represented these interests. As the dominant authority, the patriarch was responsible for the women, children, and any other dependents under his roof. Each person had a special ranking within this organic hierarchy, and all subordinates owed obedience to the patriarch in return for his economic support and protection.[75]

When the settlers first arrived in the Chesapeake, white immigrants found it difficult to put these values into practice due to demographic conditions. The short life expectancy of adults during the seventeenth century made ties between the generations tenuous. The high ratio of men to women among the immigrants, furthermore, meant that men delayed marriage until they were nearly thirty years old, and they often married much younger women. Consequently, most marriages were short, and few men lived long enough to exercise much influence over their children. As demographic conditions improved at the end of the seventeenth century, many more families took on patriarchal characteristics and kinship networks became broader and denser.[76] Long before English settlers firmly established the biological patriarchal family in the Chesapeake, however, the patriarchal values and traditions that governed the relationships of family members in the Old World had begun to take root in the tobacco colonies. Thus female immigrants found their roles shaped by men in ways that would ensure the continuance of male dominance.[77]

William Byrd II, the eighteenth-century Virginia planter, best expressed the southern patriarchal ideal in an oft-cited passage: "I have a large Family of my own, and my Doors are open to Every Body. . . . Like one of the Patriarchs, I have my Flocks and my Herds, my Bond-men and Bond-women, and every Soart of trade amongst my own Servants, so that I live in a kind of Independence on every one but Providence." Of course, this remark ignored the reality that the very basis of Byrd's independence, his income, depended on the forced labor of others; this contradiction lay at the heart of the struggle for power between the master and slaves, and created tensions that shaped the whole of southern society.[78]

Central to the world view of Byrd and other slaveholders was a broad conception of family, one that went beyond the nuclear unit to encompass nonnuclear kin, slaves, servants, and all other inhabitants of the plantation, in the house and slave quarters alike. The incorporation of dependent laborers into the household and the identification of the "household" with "family" were not simply elements in a proslavery propaganda campaign designed to mask the exploitative character of bondage, for these beliefs underscored the southern commitment to organic hierarchy as the basis of social order. Often referring to the residents as "my people," the planter considered it his God-ordained task to govern them all, black and white, with a firm but benevolent hand.[79]

Southern social thought, however, did not envision the household as an absolute monarchy. Instead, the notion of stewardship insisted that reciprocal duties and responsibilities linked the members of the household, including the master and slave, and provided protection against abuse of power. This domesticated form of patriarchy gained increasing headway in the late eighteenth and early nineteenth centuries, particularly in the more settled areas of the South, and eventually flowered during the antebellum period into a full-blown ideology of paternalism.[80] In contrast to "the absolute power of a prince on his throne," Judge Thomas Ruffin asserted in a public address in 1855, "authority in domestic life, though not necessarily, is naturally considerate, mild, easy to be entreated, and tends to an elevation in sentiment in the superior which generates a humane tenderness for those in his power, and renders him regardful alike of the duty and the dignity of his position."[81]

Clearly, Byrd's depiction of his estate and Ruffin's portrait of paternalism were both more than a little idyllic. Pressures and disagreements plagued the slaveholding household, and conflict often erupted, not just between master and slave but also among white family members. Migration to the southern frontier, a decision often made by planter men without consulting their wives and children, led to even greater sexual inequality within the planter family, heightened stresses between men and women, and undermined the development of planter paternalism.[82] For those families that remained on the seaboard, the patriarchal impulse to impose domestic order found itself increasingly at odds with the growing influence of romantic love, intimacy, and affection in the family, a development that both reflected and bolstered the rise of individualism and led to a discernible tension in planter families between authority and autonomy.[83] In slaveholding and nonslaveholding families alike, the practice of taking in needy relatives, whether they were older parents, newlyweds, or orphaned children, also generated strains within the household.[84] Nevertheless, altered in significant ways over the years and frequently departing from reality to a considerable degree, the patriarchal ideal persisted well into the nineteenth century.

The modified version of patriarchy that ruled within the home also provided the great organizing principle for the exercise of state power in southern society. Liberty in the South, as elsewhere in America, was generally the exclusive prerogative of white men. For slaves, women, and children, subordination and stratification, rather than liberty and equality, shaped their social experience. Employing a rationale that combined elements of protection and coercion, southern governing elites argued that these subordinate groups could not survive the competitive and volatile world of the antebellum South on their own, and that granting them personal autonomy would lead to social chaos. Challenging those who would grant women political rights, for example, an essayist for the *Southern Quarterly Review* in 1842 outlined the reasons for his opposition: "The proper place for a woman is at home. One of her highest privileges, to be politically merged in the existence of her husband. Whenever a married woman has a *separate and individual reputation*, a position, a power independent of her husband, she nurtures misery for herself and injury to the community. There can be, at home, but one head,—one chief. If both attempt to govern, anarchy ensues."[85]

The state supported the family in the person of its male head, and state power flowed through the network of patriarchs who ruled over their households. George Fitzhugh, the proslavery apologist, explained the operation of this form of governance in 1854: "Two-thirds of mankind, the women and children, are everywhere the subject of family government. In all countries where slavery exists, the slaves also are the subjects of this kind of government. Now slaves, wives and children have no other government; they do not come directly in contact with the institutions and rulers of the State."[86] The subordinate members of the household, according to this ideal, were connected to the state only through the patriarch.

Despite differences in social class, the status of having dependents provided most adult, white males in each community with a common bond. Planters and yeomen alike based their claims to independence and autonomy on the capacity to exercise authority over dependents in the household. The ideology of male-dominated households allowed white southerners to uphold the ideal of egalitarian political relations among free men in a society rooted in the precepts of hierarchy and inequality. In this way, the private and public relations of power became inextricably linked.

The preservation of social order, not just domestic tranquility, rested on the smooth and effective functioning of the patriarchal network. In the organic model that served as the ideal of the Old South, people were supposed to know their own places as well as what part they played in the overall functioning of society. Two fundamental assumptions governed the relationships between male and female, and master and slave: (1) women and blacks were naturally suited for subordination, and (2) the male head of the household and master was naturally fitted to command this subordination. These underlying assumptions crystallized race and gender as transhistorical phenomena and obscured the extent to which they were social constructs.[87]

Legislators and judges in the Old South operated with these assumptions, and they placed a high value on upholding patriarchal authority. Consequently, the effect of their law making and decision making was often to provide heads of households—whether they were slaveholders or nonslaveholders, planters or yeomen—with the leeway necessary to patrol their own domestic domains. The law excluded women and slaves from the public sphere and remained largely absent from the private sphere, reinforcing the subordination of these two groups.[88]

The state intervened only when the male head of the household abused his rights or neglected his obligations in such an obvious and undeniable way that he posed a threat to the legitimacy of patriarchy as a social system. Such intervention, however, particularized his behavior by treating him as a deviant and making it clear that it was his individual behavior rather than the larger structure of power that was at fault. The goal, in other words, was the restoration of social order in the community rather than the extension of rights to subordinate groups. This careful balancing of patriarchal power and community constraints during the early nineteenth century had important implications for slaves and married women, and eventually opened the way for expanded intervention on the part of the state after the mid-nineteenth century.[89]

Most planters felt that the law should interfere in master-slave relations as little as possible, and that the self-interest of slaveholders provided those held in bondage with adequate protection. This view of the law reflected the attitudes of a powerful elite that was used to running things its own way on the plantation. Planters believed that the existence of slavery depended upon a variety of informal arrangements, the most significant of which was leaving control of slaves to the master's discretion. J. D. B. De Bow captured perfectly this attitude toward the role of law in slavery, insisting, "On our estates we dispense with the whole machinery of public police and public courts of justice. Thus we try, decide, and execute the sentences in thousands of cases, which in other countries would go into the courts."[90]

In fact, by law and custom the master exerted enormous power over his slaves, who were required to show proper obedience and respect to him. "The condition of the slave being a merely passive one," declared the Louisiana slave code of 1806, "his subordination to his master and to all who represent him is not susceptible of modification or restriction . . . he owes to his master, and to all his family, a respect without bounds, and an absolute obedience."[91] Those slaves who did not fully submit to the dictates of whites risked harsh retaliation, sometimes even death. Although slaveholders enjoyed wide latitude in the management of slaves, most employed the lash with at least some discretion. If nothing else, the fear of damaging valuable property acted as a restraint on imposing physical punishment too arbitrarily. But there is little question that the fear of such punishment was a powerful deterrent in the slave quarters.

During the early nineteenth century, after the closing of the international slave trade and the subsequent need to encourage the reproduction of the slave labor force, paternalism increasingly shaped social relations between masters and their human property. Reacting not only to the suppression of the slave trade but also to the increase in free blacks, the rising proportion of slaves born in America, and the growing influence of evangelical religion, southern slave owners sought during the postrevolutionary era to domesticate slavery, making it safe and profitable in a way that violated their private consciences as little as possible. Although planter paternalism carried with it certain obligations on the part of slaves that expanded white control, it also affirmed the rights of slaves and helped to sustain their self-respect, leading to more humane treatment.[92]

Legal historians have now examined in considerable detail how the dynamics of planter paternalism and antebellum law interacted. Most recent studies center on the tension in slave law between the slave as person and the slave as property, a tension that southern legal authorities found impossible to resolve.[93] Every slave state had a slave code, and the law undergirding slavery varied from state to state. These codes established the property rights of those who owned slaves, spelled out the duties owed by slaves to masters, provided safeguards for the white community against slave uprisings, and delineated the treatment that masters could exercise over their slaves. Despite their diversity, the codes shared some fundamental assumptions, such as generally defining slaves as personal rather than real property. As "chattels personal," slaves could be purchased, sold, leased, used as collateral, inherited, and even freed under certain circumstances.[94]

While the law stressed the character of the slave as property, it also recognized the humanity of the slave. Southern slave codes, at the very least, conceded that slaves had volition, will, and personality in exacting punishment from those who committed criminal acts. The courts had to acknowledge the free will of slaves or be prevented from holding them accountable for antisocial behavior.[95] But some southern appellate courts went even further. Judge Nathan Green of the Tennessee Supreme Court, for example, emphatically addressed the humanity of the slave in *Ford v. Ford* (1846), a case in which the family of a deceased slaveholder challenged his effort to free a slave by will. Finding in favor of the slave's freedom, Judge Green proclaimed that a slave was "not in the condition of a horse or an ox" but was "made in the image of the Creator," fully "equal to his owner but for the accidental position in which fortune has placed him."[96]

A profound contradiction thus lay at the heart of the law of slavery.

Defined as a chattel in the eyes of the law, the slave's personhood could not be denied. In the words of the Kentucky court in 1836, "Although the law of this state considers slaves as property, yet it recognizes their personal existence, and, to a qualified extent, their natural rights."[97] The slave codes sought to implement a system of social control that cut deeply against the grain of common-law and middle-class, republican values. Common-law doctrines emphasized a person's natural rights of life, liberty, and property; bourgeois republican ideology fostered a commitment to individualism and personal autonomy. The very basis of slave property contradicted these principles. Having inherited a legal and ideological tradition that it could not wholly embrace or wholly reject, the South found it impossible to clarify the ambiguities that permeated the law of slavery, resulting in a distinctive legal tradition and an understanding of republicanism that diverged significantly from that of the North.[98]

The fact that slaves were subordinate to the masters in the Old South did not mean that the master's power was absolute. The idea of slave law itself represented a significant constraint on the behavior of masters in a slave society, for in an ideal slave society all matters involving master-slave relations would be left to the discretion of the master. The state regulated the master's power in a number of ways, not the least of which was reserving for itself the right to say who was a slave. The law did not simply reflect the interests of slaveholders, then, but rather made major inroads into their rights to exercise uncontrolled dominion over slaves. Most important, the new laws prohibited the master from using excessive coercion to obtain compliance; dismemberment and other cruel and extreme punishments became illegal, and killing a slave with malice was murder. Additional restraints that had less favorable consequences for slaves included restricting the master's ability to manumit the human property in his possession. Southern grand juries played a particularly crucial role at the local level, checking upon the enforcement of laws regulating slavery and monitoring the treatment of slaves. Slave patrols, moreover, supervised the slave owner's management of blacks under his authority and could correct any laxity in discipline that seemed to threaten social order in the community.[99]

As the right of personal autonomy in slave management came into increasing conflict with the larger societal need to preserve the slave system, southerners found themselves turning more and more to the law to resolve this conflict. The power of the state to intervene in the master-slave relationship became legitimized, gaining a momentum of its own and becoming difficult to control. What was on the books may have differed from the day-to-day reality of slave life, but it indicated the changing sentiment of the law regarding what was desirable or necessary, providing at the very least an arena within which slaves tried to wrestle what power they could away from the masters. In the process, slaves made certain modest gains in achieving recognition as individuals with legal personalities.[100] After 1830, however, they encountered tightened constraints on their behavior and movement. Furthermore, slaves never made any headway at all in gaining legal protection for their families, only for themselves as individuals. Throughout the antebellum period slaves had no right to marry and no right to custody of their children. Although the law may have ascribed to other families a near-sacred status, it left the slave family outside the realm of legal protection.[101]

White women in the antebellum South did not experience anywhere near the same curbs on their freedom as did slaves, but their individual rights were still narrowly circumscribed relative to those of white men. In Louisiana and Texas, as under Spanish law, the personality of both spouses received legal recognition, and community property—the equal sharing of the gains of marriage—prevailed in these two states.[102] The rest of the South, however, subscribed to the common-law notion of marriage in which the wife's legal identity merged with that of the husband, a doctrine known as coverture.[103] As a result, the right of a wife to own and manage any property that she brought to the marriage was seriously limited. Personal property belonged to her husband absolutely, and her assets could be seized to meet his debts. Title to land remained in the wife's name, but the husband could manage or rent her land as he saw fit and keep any profits. Married women, in addition, could not control their wages, make independent contracts, initiate suits at law, execute separate wills, administer an estate, or conduct sales. For her part, the wife was entitled only to a minimal level of support and maintenance from her husband, and he was held accountable for any debts incurred before and during the marriage. Upon a husband's death, under common law, the widow had dower rights to one-third of his estate to ensure that she had some means of support.[104]

The legal system of the colonial and postrevolutionary South provided some married women with substantial loopholes to protect their economic position. Equity courts, which originated in England and were transplanted to the colonies, developed a more flexible system of justice than common-law courts. Sympathetic to the financial plight of wives, equity courts had long departed from the strictures of the common law by recognizing a wife's separate estate in her property. Under a trust or antenuptial agreement, a married woman's property could be managed for her benefit completely free of interference from her husband. Because equity jurisdiction was strongly established in the South, judges endorsed marriage settlements for women and vigorously supported a wife's separate estate in equity. But the courts granted such arrangements only on an individual basis, and they were expensive and required considerable legal knowledge, serious drawbacks for less affluent and less educated whites.[105]

Southern state legislatures during the antebellum period moved to enlarge the property rights of married women. The territorial legislatures in Arkansas and Florida enacted laws as early as 1835 that protected a wife's property from debts incurred by her husband prior to marriage, but these jurisdictions—having adopted common law—simply sought to ensure women's rights that had existed previously under former civil-law regimes.[106] More significant was the passage of legislation in Mississippi in 1839 that provided a model for other common-law jurisdictions in the United States seeking to protect married women's estates from their husbands' creditors. The product of the economic collapse set off by the Panic of 1837, the Mississippi law allowed wives for the first time to hold property in their own name, but it left the traditional marital estate and coverture rules largely intact.[107] Subsequent legislation in the 1840s and 1850s enlarged women's legal rights so that by the Civil War married women in Mississippi could retain profits earned from their property, sign contracts and deeds connected to their property, and manage their holdings independently without their husbands' consent. Other states in the South followed. Overall, these reforms were modest in intent and scope, and the provisions varied widely from state to state. Newer states in the South tended to be more open to reform; legislatures along the seaboard for the most part did not grant such rights to women until Reconstruction.

Pressure for these reforms stemmed in large part from the need to protect family property from the mismanagement of husbands and the claims of creditors in the boom-and-bust economy of the antebelllum period. The rising importance of women's domestic role in Victorian society also accounted for the expansion of married women's property rights, reflecting the belief that because of their increased responsibilities within the family, women deserved greater protection and support.[108] But by no means did this legislation intend to place women in an equal position with men; granting women special treatment under the law, the married women's property acts provided equity, not equality.[109]

As with the growth of married women's property rights, antebellum reforms in divorce law brought some positive changes in the lives of southern wives, but fell short of putting them on an equal legal footing with their husbands. Unlike New England colonies, the South before the Revolution followed the traditional English view that marriage was indissoluble. Thus absolute divorce was not available in the southern colonies, although one could obtain a divorce from bed and board, essentially a legal separation that did not allow either spouse to remarry. After Independence, southern states slowly accepted absolute divorce under certain circumstances, granting them by means of a private legislative act. Petitions for divorce, however, became a burdensome drain on the time and energy of state legislatures, and by the Civil War all but one state in the South had enacted general divorce statutes that authorized courts to end marriages on the grounds of adultery, cruelty, and desertion, among others. South Carolina was the sole exception, refusing until Reconstruction to make any provision for divorce.[110]

One of the most significant developments in antebellum divorce law was the evolution of the doctrine of mental cruelty. In English law during the early nineteenth century, cruelty endangering life or limb warranted a legal separation but not a divorce.[111] In many southern states, cruelty not only became a cause for divorce, but the legislatures enlarged the conception of cruelty to include mental abuse. Lawmakers in North Carolina, Arkansas, Tennessee, Louisiana, and Texas embraced the notion that "excesses" or "personal indignities" making cohabitation "intolerable" should be a cause for divorce. Justice Christopher Scott of the Arkansas Supreme Court provided perhaps the broadest understanding of cruelty, contending in an 1849 case that acts constituting a "personal indignity" included "rudeness, vulgarity, unmerited reproach, contumely, studied neglect, intentional incivility, injury, manifest disdain, abusive language, malignant ridicule and every other plain manifestation of settled hate, alienation and estrangement, both of word and action." Such indignities had to be "habitual, continuous and permanent," but they clearly went far beyond a narrow understanding of cruelty as physical violence.[112]

The number of divorce petitions increased during the prewar years, but rising state populations rather than a surge of assertive women seeking redress from the courts probably accounted for this development. Judges were not always enthusiastic about implementing the broad discretionary authority granted to them under the new laws. Justice Ruffin of North Carolina expressed serious misgivings about his state's new divorce statute of 1827: "I can not suppose . . . that the discretion conferred is a mere personal one, whether wild or sober, but must from the nature of things be confined to those cases for which provision was before made by law, or for those of a like nature."[113] The North Carolina Supreme Court not only refused to consider adultery as grounds for divorce but also turned down divorce petitions from women subjected to physical violence and abuse by husbands. "The law gives the husband power to use such a degree of force necesary to make the wife behave and know her place," declared Chief Justice Pearson as he denied a divorce to a woman who had been beaten and horsewhipped by her husband.[114]

Although the expansion of causes for divorce met resistance among appellate southern judges, the available evidence suggests that local judges and juries exhibited a far greater willingness to grant divorces. Few poor whites and free blacks had the resources or time to pursue a divorce, however, and many unhappy couples simply went their separate ways without a legal decree. Furthermore, the adversarial nature of the divorce process meant that the concept of fault or moral wrongdoing was central. In order to obtain a divorce one had to demonstrate that the party at fault had violated his or her domestic role in a fundamental way, while the person seeking the divorce had preserved his or her innocence. Thus the wife had to show that she had remained virtuous despite any behavior to the contrary on the part of her husband. Domesticity, propriety, and submissiveness all played an important part in determining whether a divorce would be granted to a woman. The qualities of compliance and docility that southern jurists admired in women seeking a divorce underscored the judicial commitment to the husband's place as patriarch. On balance, then, antebellum divorce reforms reinforced more than they undermined the traditional family hierarchy and division of labor, bolstering contemporary notions of wifely and husbandly behavior.[115]

Rather than ushering in a new age of egalitarianism, antebellum legal changes in southern society helped to shape and maintain the subordination of white women and slaves. The law contributed to the perpetuation of patriarchal dominance mainly through its reluctance to intervene in household matters, thereby buttressing the dependence of these two subordinate groups on the husband/master. Important changes, however, became apparent by the late antebellum period in the legal status of white women and slaves. The white, male head of household still exercised authority over the other coresidents, but an individualistic notion of domestic relations began to creep into the law. As slaves and white women won limited individual rights, the state assumed a growing responsibility for supervising relations among members of the southern household. In this way, a new paternalistic ideal of government regulating the treatment of dependents came into increasing conflict with the older model of domestic governance that relied on a network of patriarchs who held undisputed sway over the household.[116]

also master's paternalism

The conflict that intensified during the 1850s in the South between the traditional form of household patriarchy and a slowly evolving state paternalism grew out of the contradictory impulses shaping this historically unique society. As the world's most powerful slave society within a transatlantic civilization that was increasingly vehement in its condemnation of everything bondage stood for, the antebellum South was faced with the dilemma of creating and maintaining slave relations within a market framework. Market relations rested on the principle of each person's right to self-ownership, whereas slave relations assumed an absolute right in human property. Slaves had no right to withhold their labor power from the masters who owned them, and slaves had no right to the fruits of their toil. In a market system, however, workers exchanged their labor power for wages or some other form of compensation. Thus the fundamental premises underlying each of these social systems were mutually exclusive.[117] The conflict between the two systems escalated in the South during the 1850s as the cotton boom gained momentum, the value of slave property increased, and railroad construction brought areas of the South previously isolated in contact with the market economy. Although planters experienced unprecedented prosperity, they also had to grapple with the pressures of capitalist development as never before.[118]

Of critical importance here was the tendency of encroaching market relations to generate an undifferentiated individualism, in contrast to southern slave society, which gave rise to social arrangements based on personal dependence. Involvement in the international market economy and the interests of planters as a class in perpetuating the slave system made it impossible to repudiate wholly the individualism of a market-oriented world view. At the same time, though, slave owners remained strongly committed to a belief in the organic nature of their society. The growing tension during the late antebellum period between the patriarchal ideal of a household in which the discretionary authority of the husband/master went nearly unchecked and the emerging concept of a paternalistic state that granted dependents certain legal interests and rights mirrored the incompatibility of these two approaches to social control. Nonetheless, at the heart of both approaches lay a strict adherence to the concepts of stratification and subordination. What was involved was not the decline of patriarchy, in other words, but its transformation.

The conflict between traditional patriarchal authority and state intervention was not, by any means, confined to southern society. This tension strongly influenced the development of domestic relations throughout antebellum America.[119] The ideological struggle was more intense and drawn out in the South, however, because slavery encouraged patriarchal control over the household, thereby hindering (but not preventing entirely) the development of individualism. The South during the nineteenth century underwent many of the same profound legal changes that took place in other parts of the country. Southern lawmakers and judges shared a number of similar concerns and responded to many problems in the same manner as their counterparts elsewhere. But in more than a few areas of the law, especially regarding the regulation of race and sexual relations, southern courts carved out a distinctive path, or at the very least, adapted innovations to their own purposes. Crucial differences can be discerned, furthermore, in timing, pace, and sources of change, all of which stemmed from the uniqueness of the South's historical experience. Ultimately, the demise of slavery and the emergence of new social relations during the postwar years necessitated the development of alternative forms of social control, leading to the triumph of the paternalistic state over household patriarchy as the main source of authority and order in southern society. How this took place, and why, will be the central concerns of the chapters that follow.

— does not differentiate btw patriarchy → paternalism in terms of master's managerial style

CHAPTER 2

SEX CRIMES, SEXUALITY, AND THE COURTS

In December 1851 a grand jury in Houston County, Georgia, indicted Stephen, a slave who belonged to Nunn Miller, for the rape and attempted rape of Mary Daniel, a white girl who had been picking cotton in a field adjoining the one where the defendant was working. At the trial, John W. Johnson testified that, following Stephen's arrest, the constable left the prisoner temporarily in Johnson's custody. Johnson, a local white man, cautioned Stephen against discussing the crime because anything he divulged might be used against him.

THE ENGINE OF SUBJUGATION

Despite Johnson's warning, the slave began to talk. He had heard from one of his fellow bondsmen, according to Johnson, that "if a girl was not large enough, that to tie something around her waist, would make her big enough." Stephen confessed that, in order to test this proposition, he had lured the girl across the fence dividing the two fields by pretending he had a splinter in his finger. He asked Mary Daniel to bring him a pin so that he could remove the splinter, and when she approached him, he tied a handkerchief around her waist, throwing her to the ground in an effort to carry out the sexual assault. The prisoner told Johnson that the experiment failed and that "he did not succeed in accomplishing his ends, [because] she was too small." Based on this confession and corroborating evidence from the girl's mother, the jury found Stephen guilty of "an attempt to commit a rape," and he was sentenced to death.[1]

Counsel for the defendant petitioned the Georgia Supreme Court to reverse the conviction on a number of technical grounds, the most important of which challenged the validity of the confession. According to Stephen's attorney, the confession had been "extorted by duress and the excitement of hope and fear" and thus should not have been admitted into evidence. Justice Joseph Henry Lumpkin, who dominated the Georgia Supreme Court during the late antebellum period and had a profound impact on the development of slave law in Georgia, issued the appellate decision in February 1852, refusing to overturn the verdict. "The crime, from the very nature of it," declared Lumpkin, "is calculated to excite indignation in every heart; and when perpetrated by a slave on a free white female of immature mind and body, that indignation becomes greater, and is more difficult to repress."

Despite the heated rhetoric, the Georgia judge took pains to demonstrate that the court had reached its decision as dispassionately as possible. "The very helplessness of the accused," he observed, "like infancy and womanhood, appeals to our sympathy. And a controversy between the State of Georgia and *a slave* is so unequal, as of itself to divest the mind of all warmth and prejudice, and enable it to exercise its judgment in the most temperate manner." After careful consideration of the record, the court found that the confession was voluntary and that there was "nothing which would require these confessions to be excluded; no threats or promises, or improper contrivances of any kind, were used to influence the prisoner to make them." Lumpkin insisted that the condemned slave was "unworthy to have a place longer among the living."[2]

Stephen v. State underscores the extent to which the interplay of race, gender, and sexuality kept the Old South simmering, and how the law tried to keep the lid on this volatile mixture. To understand the dynamics of sexuality, and how they fueled the racial, gender, and economic systems of the Old South, is to grasp the essence of power relations in this society.[3] The sexual subjugation of women and blacks provided the chief engine for the advancement of patriarchal authority, a process illuminated by a close examination of state statutes and appellate court opinions regarding incest, miscegenation, and rape. Such an analysis reveals, furthermore, the extent to which the growth of the state during its early stages in southern society depended upon the patriarchal household, and how white southerners perceived the proper functioning of the household as crucial to the maintenance of social order.[4] Besides the resiliency of the patriarchal ideal, the public regulation of what was defined as sexual misconduct discloses the intimate links between domestic governance and the commitment to white supremacy, what Jacquelyn Dowd Hall calls "the web of connections among racism, attitudes toward women, and sexual ideologies."[5]

The majority of incidents involving incest, miscegenation, and rape probably did not come to the attention of local and state authorities in the South. Court records therefore do not reliably indicate the extent of these sexual offenses in southern society. In addition, because only a fraction of the cases concerning prosecutions of these crimes reached the state supreme courts, appellate opinions do not necessarily indicate how the southern legal system in its entirety treated sexual misconduct. But the state supreme courts provided guidance to lower courts adjudicating these cases and thus had a discernable impact on overall judicial behavior.

The point here is not to condemn the South for its sexual sins but to determine how it handled the issues of sexual misconduct and what the means of control reveal about southern culture and society.[6] Indeed, the whole of sexuality, not just attitudes toward sexual misconduct, offers us a valuable window on the South because sexual feelings and activities do not exist in isolation from culture but are embedded in it. Sexuality, in other words, is not simply a set of biological facts; in the Old South it embodied the relations of race, class, and gender, and was itself one of the motors that drove the unequal distribution of power in this society.[7]

THE TROUBLE WITH INCEST

The psychodynamics of Victorian family life on both sides of the Atlantic had a distinctly incestuous character. The emphasis placed on the cultivation of affection and sentiment in Victorian culture, together with the great concern about the need to control sexuality and promote purity, produced an intense and intricate emotional climate within the household that led, in many cases, to latent incestuous feelings. To say the least, the explosive nature of incest made its regulation a highly sensitive matter among Victorians.[8]

Appellate opinions handed down in the courtrooms of the Old South lay bare the anxiety and ambivalence that this form of sexual behavior generated. On the one hand, judges recognized that incest threatened the integrity of the family. The Alabama Supreme Court proclaimed in 1847 that the crime involved an "offense against decency and good morals." Most important, incest confused the roles and duties of individuals and eroded the stability of the family, thereby weakening its effectiveness as an institution of social control. To commit incest, consequently, was to violate one's responsibilities both to the family and society at large. As the Mississippi high court insisted in 1852, failure to punish those who committed such crimes "would undermine the foundations of social order and good government."[9]

Of all the forms of incest, father-daughter sexual relations drew the most heated reaction from antebellum southern jurists. The Texas Supreme Court asserted that committing incest with one's daughter "was so shocking to the moral sense of every civilized being" because it reduced "man from his boastful superiority of a moral, rational being, to a level with the brutal creation." [10] For the patriarch to indulge his carnal appetite in this fashion posed an immediate danger to the legitimacy of his rule and called into question his ability to exercise the self-control necessary to carry out his responsibilities to the members of his household.

Although the southern judiciary acknowledged that abuse of male power sometimes resulted in the practice of incest, such abuse did not weaken its support for the patriarchal concept of the household. A South Carolina judge articulated in 1858 the rationale behind the commitment to patriarchy, a position widely held by his colleagues: "The obligation imposed on the husband to provide for their wants and protection, makes it necessary that he should exercise a power of control over all members of his household." The law, for this reason, "looking to the peace and happiness of families and to the best interests of society, places the husband and father at the head of the household." [11]

The tension between the condemnation of incest and the commitment to patriarchy shaped judicial findings in cases that came before the state supreme courts in the Victorian South, leading to the expression of outrage against incest and to the conviction of those men who clearly misused their patriarchal prerogatives in committing the crime. But judges, even when they imposed criminal punishment, tended to emphasize the infrequent occurrence of incestuous sexual assault, isolating men who undeniably exploited dependent females in their family and treating these males as deviants, rather than locating the source of incest behavior in the hierarchical nature of the household itself. In doing so, southern jurists helped to preserve the patriarchal ideal and minimize state intrusion in the private sphere. [12]

In the area of incest regulation, state legislatures rather than the courts dominated the process of formulating policy, enacting legislation that restricted kin marriages and criminalized incest. Southern appellate judges left no doubt during the antebellum period that they preferred to let legislators take the lead in governing incestuous behavior. The firm adherence of the courts to the common law, which traditionally did not recognize incest as a crime and left its regulation to church authorities, made it almost certain that jurists would not impose incest prohibitions without legislative initiative. Even with the enactment of anti-incest statutes, many jurists appeared wary about controlling incest through legal intervention, a caution that reflected in part the high value placed on family autonomy by the southern judiciary as well as a general suspicion of state power.

Of course, incest was not just a troubling issue in the nineteenth-century South. Most human societies have prohibited sexual relations between closely related persons, and the banning of certain marriages has been nearly universal.[13] Although societies generally have frowned upon marriage and sexual relations between parent and child or brother and sister, the range of incest restrictions beyond the nuclear family has varied widely. Furthermore, not all societies have made incest, however defined, a criminal offense. Hence the central issues for any analysis of the sanctions against incest are the extent of the prohibitions and the punishment exacted from those who violate them.[14]

The legal sanctions against incest in the Old South had their roots in English canonical rules, which imposed numerous marital constraints based on both consanguinity (relationship by blood) and affinity (relationship by marriage). Originally, canon law had imposed extensive prohibitions on marriages between persons connected by consanguinity or affinity, although dispensations could be procured in individual cases. Ecclesiastical courts could annul incestuous marriages, excommunicate offending individuals, and declare any offspring illegitimate, thus preventing them from inheriting property. Statutes passed during the reign of Henry VIII decreased the number of banned consanguineous relationships. Under these statutes, only unions that violated the sanctions in Leviticus against marrying nearer than first cousins were voidable by ecclesiastical courts. The Church of England drew up a table of degrees in 1563 that incorporated the narrower range of prohibitions, and the table provided the basis for most succeeding Anglo-American legislation on the topic.[15]

Colonial statutes in the Anglican South stipulated that every parish must display the table of forbidden degrees. Whereas New England Puritans strongly opposed first-cousin marriages, white southerners followed English tradition in accepting such unions. Marriages in eighteenth-century Virginia were prohibited "within the levitical degrees," and the children of such marriages were deemed illegitimate. The Virginia General Court had the authority to separate offenders and to impose fines at its discretion. In South Carolina, a 1704 statute prevented unions "not allowed by the Church of England" and "forbidden by the table of marriage." Those who married contrary to this act could be fined fifty pounds or imprisoned for twelve months, but civil authorities in the colony did not have the power to annul such marriages.[16]

With the founding of the new Republic, southern legal authorities maintained their relaxed attitude toward cousin marriages. Only Georgia prohibited first-cousin unions before the Civil War, and it lifted this ban in 1866.[17] Antebellum southern statutes outlawed matrimony between members of ascending and descending lines of a family, and between uncles and nieces or aunts and nephews.[18] Several states included illegitimate children and their relations, as well as half-blood kindred, in their marital restrictions.[19]

Although state legislatures in the Old South agreed for the most part that kin marriages between first cousins and those more distantly related by blood needed little regulation, they found it more difficult to achieve a consensus on unions involving those related by affinity. Indeed, a significant disparity in attitudes toward such matches existed in the antebellum state laws. Arkansas, Florida, North Carolina, and Louisiana imposed no legal impediments whatsoever to matrimony on account of affinity.[20] The majority of southern states, however, did not allow one to contract matrimony with a daughter-in-law or son-in-law, or with a stepparent, stepsibling, or stepgrandchild. Virginia law went even further, sticking with the English prohibition against unions with a broad range of affines, including an uncle's widow, a nephew's widow, a deceased wife's sister, and a brother's widow.[21]

Marriage, according to the traditional view, was less a personal matter involving the private emotions between two individuals than an event that brought together two families and promoted the ties between them.[22] Limitations on marriages of affinity proceeded from the conviction that the relations created by matrimony did not cease following the dissolution of the union by death or divorce. Rules prohibiting affinal marriages underscored the permanent status given in-laws who were brought into what sociologists call "the intimate kin group." Bans on unions between affines sought to protect the integrity of the family formed by the matrimonial contract and to minimize the threat to the family's unity. Thus, in Victorian England, marriages with a deceased wife's sister and a brother's widow were frowned upon, for both of these individuals had been incorporated by marriage into the man's intimate kin group to the extent that they were expected to be treated as consanguineal sisters.[23]

Despite these traditional views, a reduction in the number of legal restrictions on affinal marriages took place during the antebellum era in both the North and South.[24] The loosening of prohibitions against such unions mirrored a growing belief that marriage joined two individuals, not two families. Once the original matrimonial contract ended, according to this line of reasoning, the surviving spouse was free to wed just about anyone, regardless of the marriage's impact on family unity and stability.[25] As an Arkansas judge declared in 1852, "The relationship by affinity ceases with the dissolution of the marriage which produced it. Therefore though a man is by affinity brother to his wife's sister, yet upon the death of his wife, he may lawfully marry her sister."[26]

The paring down of bans on affinal marriages in the antebellum South suggests that the region was moving with the main currents of American social change as far as the selection of marriage partners was concerned. This evidence of southern legal change supports the view that, during the postrevolutionary period, personal preferences and romantic love—as opposed to family needs and prospects—played an increasingly significant role throughout the country in the choice of a mate. The gradual reduction of legal controls on persons related by affinity was part of the larger trend toward individualism and sentiment taking place in the early nineteenth century, a trend that allowed a person greater freedom to contract matrimony with whomever he or she wished.[27]

But too much emphasis should not be placed on the slackening of constraints regarding marriages of affinity, for the fact of the matter is that on the eve of the Civil War most southern states still prohibited many such matches.[28] These limitations on affinal marriage combined with a generally tolerant attitude toward first-cousin unions to form a type of kinship that Bernard Farber has termed the "Biblical system." This system, predominant in much of the older South and New England, was based on the admonitions in Leviticus and English tradition.

In contrast, a "Western American system" arose outside of these two regions, prohibiting first-cousin marriages but permitting matrimony between any affines. Farber asserts that the kinship system of New England and the older South helped sustain a stable, family-oriented social hierarchy by incorporating in-laws into the intimate kin group on a permanent basis and consolidating economic resources within the family. The Western American system, on the other hand, encouraged the development of a more open society in the nineteenth century by facilitating marriages with a wide selection of affines and outsiders, thus leading to a greater diffusion of family wealth.[29]

Undoubtedly, the practice of cousin marriage in the South (except in the slave community, where, apparently, a proscription against unions between cousins prevailed), allowed whites to concentrate property within the family and keep the family name alive. Whether these were the main considerations prompting the arrangement of such matches, however, is unclear. Surely, another important factor behind this southern marital custom was the social geography of plantation society. Kin made up a large part of the pool of potential spouses due to the vigorous family ties in long-established communities or the social isolation of more sparsely settled areas. Therefore it was not unexpected when cousins who had long known each other decided upon marriage.[30] Economic and social forces worked together, in short, to foster marital unions between blood kin.

This kind of intermarriage in the South helped to promote strong bonds among relatives beyond the nuclear core, in contrast to much of the rest of the country, where kin ties appeared to be weakening during the first half of the nineteenth century due to the increasingly fluid nature of society.[31] Although some planters disapproved of cousin marriage, the practice remained relatively common during the antebellum period; there is even some evidence that matches between cousins in one generation produced more such unions in succeeding generations. In any event, these intricate marriage patterns generated extensive kinship networks that provided crucial connections in both economic and political arenas, as well as a sense of social stability.[32]

The antebellum evolution of legal rules concerning forbidden degrees of marriage in the South, then, revealed a continued preoccupation with marriage as a way to build alliances between two families, to intensify kin-group solidarity, and to concentrate family property holdings. Although personal preferences and sentimental love played a growing part in marital decisions, the laws regulating such decisions reflected the fact that matrimony was still a family and public concern. The primary aim of these laws before the Civil War was to promote with a minimum of state intervention marriages that would sustain a highly stratified and close-knit society. Southern policy makers accomplished this in most states by allowing first-cousin marriages and continuing to prohibit unions between certain affines. But in some states fewer legal restraints were placed on those related by affinity, reflecting a greater emphasis on the rights of individuals. The developing law of prohibited degrees, in short, exhibited a fundamental tension between viewing marriage as a voluntary, contractual act and as an organic institution that provided the foundation of social order.

The development of legal rules regarding forbidden degrees of marriage provided the framework for the criminalization of incest in the South and the rest of the country. Incest statutes in antebellum America defined the crime generally as marriage or sexual intercourse between two parties related to each other within the prohibited degrees. In England, as mentioned earlier, incest was not a crime at common law; ecclesiastical courts traditionally had handled the matter, imposing excommunication or public penance on offenders. Parliament did not make incest a criminal offense until the passage of the Punishment of Incest Act in 1908. Consequently, the criminalization of incest occurred in the United States long before it did in England, due perhaps to the separation of church and state in this country.[33]

By the mid-nineteenth century, most southern states had laws on the books making incest either a felony or high misdemeanor.[34] The main objective of the anti-incest legislation was to prohibit matrimony and in-breeding between near kin, not to protect women or children from sexual abuse. This legislation thus punished only intercourse and did not encompass other forms of sexual conduct. The penalties for those convicted of this crime varied widely during the antebellum period, ranging from a maximum prison sentence of twelve months and a fine not exceeding one thousand dollars in Florida to life imprisonment in Louisiana. Several southern states also passed laws pronouncing incestuous marriages absolutely void from the outset or requiring the courts to declare such unions void upon conviction of the accused parties.[35] These statutes reversed the common-law tradition that made marriages within the forbidden degrees merely voidable rather than void, and hence subject to challenge only in an ecclesiastical court.[36]

In most southern states, the man only was punished for incestuous sexual relations.[37] Southern jurists did not consider incest a joint offense, so mutual consent of the parties was not required for an incest conviction. In instances in which force was used, the man might be guilty of incest and the woman innocent, and in such cases either rape or incest might be properly charged.[38]

Because incest was a statutory rather than common-law crime, state supreme courts in the antebellum South rarely strayed from a narrow interpretation of the incest legislation,[39] and where no statutes existed, the courts refused to take on the role of ecclesiastical courts and impose prohibitions. The appellate court in South Carolina demonstrated such prudence when it considered the question of marriages within the forbidden degrees. The court shied away from assuming any authority to annul incestuous marriages without first gaining explicit legislative support for such an enlargement of judicial power. *State v. Barefoot*, an 1845 bigamy case, revealed this reluctance. Scion Barefoot had married his mother's sister in 1838, and he married again seven years later, this time to a Miss Elizabeth Odum. Indicted for bigamy, Barefoot came up with an imaginative if flawed defense: he argued that his first marriage to his aunt was void because of the consanguinity of the parties, and as a result, he had not committed bigamy when he married the second time. Barefoot's counsel held that if the nephew was "guilty of any thing, it is the crime of incest." But the lower court believed otherwise, and it convicted Barefoot of bigamy.

In the appeal, Barefoot's attorney tried to arouse the justices' presumed disgust with incest and thus persuade them that his client's first marriage had no validity. As he put it, "It is impossible that any enlightened system of jurisprudence can regard as valid contracts which do violence to the decencies of society, and which, if permitted by law, must so often degrade and debase the people of any country where they are allowed."[40] Judge J. S. Richardson immediately grasped the thrust of Barefoot's defense: the nephew offered "to defend himself by insisting that the first marriage was intrinsically immoral and sinful, and therefore a nullity, in order to arrest the criminal consequences and legal punishment of bigamy." But Richardson pointed out that no legislation existed in South Carolina granting courts the power to annul marriages within the forbidden degrees. Consequently, Richardson contended, he and his fellow judges could not intervene in Barefoot's union with his aunt, because at common law only church authorities could invalidate incestuous marriages. Although the South Carolina jurist recognized that "there may be deep feelings enlisted in this case," he believed that the negative consequences — of nullifying marriages and bastardizing children made it imperative for him to adhere to the common law on this matter. Richardson observed, however, that "it may well be deplored that a legislative Act has not been passed to reform the common law in this respect . . . and such incestuous marriages declared to be utterly null and void, if contracted after the statute."[41]

Despite Judge Richardson's thinly disguised summons for action, the state legislature had still not pronounced incestuous marriages voidable thirteen years later, when the South Carolina high court once again had to rule on the validity of such unions, this time in an estate dispute involving a marriage between an uncle and his niece. As before, the court refused to appropriate any ecclesiastical powers to annul incestuous unions until it had the statutory authority to do so. Once again the appellate judges called on the state legislature to take corrective measures and authorize the court to nullify marriages "within the Levitical degrees." Without such statutory backing, the court refused to act. "It is far better to leave to the Legislature the appropriate duty of defining and prohibiting such evils," the jurists decided, "rather than arm the Court of Chancery with ecclesiastical powers on a subject of great delicacy and pervading interest."[42]

These cases and others underscored the desire of most antebellum southern judges to leave the power to develop marriage rules in the hands of the state legislators. This is not to say, however, that the courts shrank from passing moral judgment on incestuous marriages; clearly, they disapproved. Furthermore, when state legislatures invested the courts with the power to annul unions within the forbidden degrees and to punish the parties involved, appellate jurists approved the use of this judicial power, however restrained their exercise of this authority might have been.[43]

The circumspect manner in which southern judges wielded their authority to exact criminal punishment was apparent not only in cases of incestuous marriage but also in those involving sexual relations within the forbidden degrees. In *Ewell v. State* (1834), the Tennessee Supreme Court granted a new trial to Dabney Ewell, who had been convicted of carrying out a felonious sexual assault on his brother's daughter, not because there was a lack of evidence establishing incestuous intercourse between the parties but because no evidence was introduced during the trial proving where the offense was committed. Without proof of venue, the Tennessee judges felt compelled to reverse the judgment of the circuit court, displaying their high regard for the defendant's procedural rights. Judge Peck, in his written opinion, underscored the unwavering adherence of the high court to the technicalities of the common law: "I will not relax old and inflexible rules in the administration of the criminal law; there is no reason for it. Whenever we depart from the great landmarks which have been the guides for ages, we enter on a sea of uncertainty and hazard every thing."[44]

Although such utterances represented the mainstream opinion among southern members of the bench, Judge Eugenius A. Nisbet of the Georgia Supreme Court refused to adhere to proceduralism and instead issued a remarkable call for judicial discretion regarding the legal process in incest cases. Nisbet in 1852 rejected out of hand the argument that an indictment accusing George Cook of committing incestuous adultery with his daughter ought to be quashed on technical grounds, and he vigorously supported the lower court's decision to let the indictment stand:

> I have but little fear of judicial power in Georgia so aggrandizing itself, as to endanger any of the powers of other departments of the government; or to endanger the life and liberty of the citizen; or to deprive the Jury of their appropriate functions. The danger rather to be dreaded is making the Judges men of straw, and thus stripping the Courts of popular reverence and annihilating the popular estimate of the power and sanctity of the law. I am not, therefore, disposed to watch with great vigilance every act, phrase or sentiment, that may fall from the Court, with the hope of detecting an indiscretion, or fabricating an error. Surely some discretion ought to be allowed to able, pains-taking, conscientious men, as to the *mere etiquette* of judicial procedure.[45]

This energetic endorsement of judicial discretion was a striking exception in the antebellum South, however, cutting sharply against the grain of a pronounced predisposition on the part of judges to cleave to the prescribed forms of criminal procedure and to construe strictly the language of the statutes in making appellate decisions, even if it sometimes led to the release of incest offenders.[46]

The impact of incestuous assault on women and children was only a secondary consideration, if that, in antebellum decisions. This form of sexual misconduct appeared to disturb southern judges primarily because it undermined the family as an effective institution of social control. Exposing the coercion that underlay patriarchal authority, incest threatened the legitimacy of this authority. It was important, then, not only to condemn such behavior but also to stress that any incidence of incestuous sexual activity was an isolated occurrence rather than an abuse inherent in the imbalance of power in southern households. Commenting on a father accused of engaging in sexual relations with his daughter, for example, Judge Goldthwaite of the Alabama Supreme Court proclaimed in 1847 that the crime "is so revolting to natural propriety and decency, that it would seem almost incredible." The Texas Supreme Court maintained in 1849 that "our pride and respect for our species" required it to accept only the "most indisputable proof" that a father "had disturbed the harmony of the family" by copulating with his daughter. In the case before the Texas appellate judges, they found that there was not "the slightest legal proof, that our country has been degraded by the commission of so loathsome, so heartsickening an offence, in our midst," and they awarded a new trial to the father.[47] This mixture of rhetorical condemnation and reluctance to prosecute patriarchs disclosed the conflicted emotions of southern jurists who heard incest cases before the Civil War.

INTERRACIAL SEX AND MARRIAGE

Although judges in the antebellum South exhibited a noticeable ambivalence about punishing incest, they demonstrated few reservations about the enforcement of measures penalizing interracial sex and marriage. The importance of slavery and the commitment to white supremacy fostered a widespread antipathy toward race mixture in southern society. Attacking those who had the temerity to suggest intermarriage as a solution to the problem of racial prejudice, W. W. Wright insisted in 1860 that, on the contrary, "it is this prejudice of color, or rather *aversion to hybridity* (as we may more properly term it), on the part of the whites, that will preserve the black and white races from destroying one another and prevent all those evils which we have shown to be everywhere entailed upon the mulatto breed."[48]

Whites feared that sexual relations between blacks and whites, if not controlled, could undermine the sharpness of the two-caste racial system that characterized American slavery. The relegation of mulattoes to the lower caste of blacks also aimed at preserving this sharpness. Mulattoes blurred the clear boundaries between the races essential to slavery in the South, and thus posed a threat to the maintenance of a biracial society.[49] Mark Twain, in his novel *Pudd'nhead Wilson* (1894), etched in acid the efforts of antebellum whites to prevent intermixture from sabotaging the color line: "To all intents and purposes Roxy was as white as anybody, but the one sixteenth of her which was black outvoted the other fifteen parts and made her a Negro. She was a slave, and salable as such. Her child was thirty-one parts white, and he, too, was a slave, and by a fiction of law and custom a Negro." By lumping mulattoes and blacks into the same category, whites in effect denied the existence of race mixture.[50]

The restrictive policy toward intermixture that emerged in the slave South, however, was not all-encompassing. Antimiscegenation laws sought not so much to eliminate interracial sexual contacts as to channel them. Those in power employed these laws, as well as laws against fornication, mainly to keep white women and black men apart. The legal process was relatively tolerant of white males who had sexual relations with black females, as long as the liaison was kept casual and discreet. This sort of illicit intercourse—between men of the higher status racial group and women of the lower—reinforced rather than challenged the existing system of group stratification in the Old South.

Those southerners in power vehemently opposed any sexual relations that implied either sexual or racial equality, such as white female relations with black men or legal interracial marriages.[51] The deepest fear of southern white men was that one of their daughters might marry a black man. Wright, in his polemic against amalgamation, cut to the heart of the matter: "Do away with the social and political distinctions now existing, and you immediately turn all the blacks and mulattoes into citizens, co-governors, and acquaintances: and acquaintances . . . are the raw material from which are *manufactured friends, husbands, and wives.* The man whom you associate with is next invited to your house, and the man whom you invited to your house is the possible husband of your daughter, whether he be black or white."[52] The twofold goal of antimiscegenation laws, then, was to keep black men and women in their place and protect the purity of white womanhood, a goal that reflected the degree to which the structure of power in the South rested on both gender and color classifications.[53] Some regional variations existed in southern attitudes toward miscegenation, but generally speaking, only white men could cross racial lines in the South without incurring severe social and legal penalties, and then only in certain circumstances.[54]

Although the early evidence of attitudes toward interracial sexual unions is ambiguous, southern authorities took a decisive stand against racial amalgamation following the legislative enactment of slavery in the late seventeenth century.[55] The rise of legal barriers to interracial sex and marriage in the southern colonies proved to be a notable exception to the general hesitancy about monitoring the private lives of individual whites. Indeed, antimiscegenation laws offered the strongest example of state intrusion in southern domestic life before the Civil War.

The fact that white southerners—who usually opposed mobilizing the machinery of the state when matters of local morality were concerned—passed such legislation and reenacted it on a regular basis gives some indication of the depth of feeling against racial intermixture. The early passage of antimiscegenation laws underscores the central role of race relations in prompting the expansion of public governance over the southern household. Lawmakers sought to preserve white dominance and to stigmatize white women who had sexual relations with black men. The legacy of these early patterns left their imprint on nineteenth-century efforts to control miscegenation, and for this reason, the colonial statutes require a closer look.

English settlers who came to America brought with them notions about African sexuality that influenced colonial policies concerning miscegenation. It was widely held, for instance, that black women were extraordinarily passionate and had virtually no self-restraint; they were "hot constitution'd Ladies" who possessed a "temper hot and lascivious," one Englishman reported. Black males also were associated with a "beastly" sexuality, and European travelers to Africa commented often on the "extraordinary greatness" of the men's "members" as confirmation of their exceptional virility.[56] These perceptions regarding the supposedly uncivilized nature of African sexuality helped to legitimize the legal control of interracial sexual encounters in America.

Just as important in shaping attitudes toward racial intermixture were the very different demographic conditions that existed in the various New World colonies. In the Caribbean and Latin America, where blacks overwhelmingly outnumbered whites and the white sex ratio was heavily weighted in favor of males, sexual relations between black women and white men became socially acceptable and widely practiced. The abundance of black women in the Caribbean and Latin America, together with the relatively small number of white women, overcame whatever reservations white settlers may have had about interracial sexual contact.

A similar gender imbalance among whites could be found in North America during the earliest decades of settlement, but whites outnumbered blacks in all the colonies except South Carolina. Before the number of blacks in America began to increase significantly, white settlement patterns shifted toward families, and hence white men had more opportunity for satisfying their sexual desires with women of their own race. As a result, miscegenation never achieved the broad public acceptance in America that was characteristic of colonies in the Caribbean and Latin America.[57]

English settlers in North America especially frowned upon racial intermarriages, and such unions were relatively rare. Interracial sexual contacts outside of marriage, however, occurred frequently, a fact made sufficiently clear by the presence of large numbers of mulattoes. This illicit intercourse usually took place between white men and black women, but ample documentation exists of sexual relations during the colonial period between white women and black men. Perhaps a majority of interracial marriages in New England involved these two groups, and even in the plantation colonies, miscegenation between black males and white females was by no means unknown.

Interracial sexual relations were extensive in colonial America, then, but few whites thought intermixture was a good thing. Public feeling about miscegenation was potent enough to make its way into the statute books of many colonies.[58] The development of these antimiscegenation statutes was an American legal innovation, for no such ban existed at common law or by statute in England at this time. The laws against miscegenation generally took two forms, those banning fornication between blacks and whites and those prohibiting marriage between these two groups.[59]

The Maryland and Virginia assemblies led the way in legislating against miscegenation, beginning in the 1660s. Maryland at first punished only interracial marriage, and Virginia only interracial fornication, but by the end of the seventeenth century the two colonies penalized both acts.[60] From the beginning antimiscegenation legislation in Maryland manifested an intense concern with controlling the sexual behavior of white women. In 1664, for example, the legislature enacted a law that denounced "diverse freeborne Englishwomen [who were] forgetful of their free Condition and to the disgrace of our Nation doe intermarry with Negro slaves." To discourage "such shamefull Matches," the statute stipulated that any white woman who married a black slave was to serve her husband's master until the slave died. The offspring of these interracial marriages were to "be slaves as their fathers were," in accordance with the English custom that children inherited the status of their fathers. White women already married to black men were not punished under the statute, but their children were indentured to the father's master until they reached the age of thirty.[61]

Although the aim of the 1664 statute was racial separation, it actually created incentives for masters to encourage matrimony between white female servants and black slaves because the law required the enslavement of any children born of such interracial unions and it locked the white mothers into terms of service that ended only when their black husbands died. In an attempt to eliminate these incentives, the Maryland assembly in 1681 altered the penalties for mixed marriages, shifting the burden of punishment from the female servants and their offspring to the masters who allowed matches with black slaves to take place. The legislators disclosed their continued anxiety about the sexual proclivities of white women, however, insisting that interracial marriages were "*always* to the Satisfaction of their Lascivious & Lustfull desires."[62]

Still not satisfied with the effectiveness of legal deterrents against interracial marriage, Maryland lawmakers again revised the punishments for this crime in 1692, calling for the enslavement of free black men who contracted marital ties with white women, among other changes. This legislation not only established new penalties for interracial marriage but also established a distinctive set of punishments for fornication between whites and blacks in the colony for the first time. The law provided that a white woman who had a bastard child was to serve for seven years, and if the black was free, he also had to serve for seven years. The mulatto issue of the illicit union were to be indentured until they were thirty-one years old. Although the statute stated that white men who "begett with Child any negro woman" were subject to the same penalties as white women, this provision was tacked on almost as an afterthought.[63] To put it mildly, restrictions on the right of blacks and mulattoes to testify in court against whites made it difficult to carry out successful prosecutions of white males who engaged in interracial sex.

Maryland's antimiscegenation law, in short, was directed primarily at white women, black men, and their mulatto offspring.[64] Recognizing that only the reproduction of "pure white" children by white women could maintain the fiction of a biracial society, the legal system was particularly determined to keep white women from interracial sexual unions. This preoccupation, combined with the custom of lumping mulattoes and blacks into the same category, provides a crucial insight into the social and legal construction of reproduction. Under the social rules that operated in the South, a white woman could give birth to a black child; thus the need for strict legal regulation of her sexual behavior. But, under the same rules, a black woman could not give birth to a white child. Such a construction of reproduction clearly served the interests of white men in the South, allowing them to roam sexually among women of any color without threatening the color line itself.

A similar thrust characterized antimiscegenation legislation in Virginia. The colony's assembly decided in 1662 that interracial fornication demanded special penalties, and it imposed a fine for this crime which was twice that stipulated for illicit intercourse between persons of the same race. Legislators moved at the same time to clarify the status of mulatto offspring of interracial unions. Declaring that the child of a black woman by a white man would be "bound or free only according to the condition of the mother," the assembly broke with English common law—which stated that the status of a child followed that of the father—in favor of the Roman custom that a child inherited the status of the mother. Maryland in 1712 also adopted this practice, abandoning its earlier adherence to the status-of-the-father rule for offspring of mixed parents. Southern lawmakers in these two colonies, as a result, ensured that the transgressions of white men would lead to an increase in the population of the slave labor force, providing a powerful economic incentive to engage in interracial sex even as criminal sanctions were imposed for such behavior. At the very least, this new legislation delivered a mixed message to white males regarding intercourse with black females.[65]

That the Virginia assembly was primarily concerned with regulating the sexual behavior of white women became apparent when it set out in 1691 to ban interracial marriage. Although the 1691 act prohibited mixed marriages involving white males as well as females, making any free white person who contracted such a union liable to permanent banishment from the colony, its stated purpose was to prevent "that abominable mixture and spurious issue which hereafter may encrease in this dominion, as well as by negroes, mulattoes, and Indians intermarrying with *English, or other white women*, as by their unlawfull accompanying with one another." The new legislation dropped the earlier sanctions against white males who indulged in interracial fornication, focusing its attention on the illicit relations of white women with black or mulatto men. Both white men and women were subject to punishment if they sought to legitimize their relationship with a black person by marriage. But the statute did not impose any penalties on a white man for having sexual relations with a black woman, and it was not a crime for a black woman to have a bastard child by a white man. Engaging in interracial sexual relations outside of marriage only became a crime when a white woman had a black man's child.[66]

The other three plantation colonies also adopted some form of statutory prohibition against miscegenation, although South Carolina did not explicitly ban marriages between whites and blacks.[67] In contrast, only two northern colonies passed antimiscegenation legislation, Massachusetts in 1705 and Pennsylvania in 1725–26.[68] The lack of statutory bans against race mixture in other northern colonies did not necessarily indicate support for such practice, but rather a reliance on social custom and prejudice to maintain racial purity. The near uniformity of opinion among legislatures of the plantation colonies, however, suggests the more pronounced nature of southern opposition to miscegenation, opposition that exhibited a growing belief among southern whites in their racial superiority.

Statutory proclamations in the colonial South declaring that interracial sexual contacts were "shamefull" and would result in an "abominable mixture and spurious issue" reinforced as well as reflected white beliefs that blacks possessed a degraded nature. By passing legislation that fostered racial contempt among whites, southern lawmakers sought to promote white solidarity and discourage lower-class whites from uniting with blacks to mount a serious challenge to the power of slaveholders. Antimiscegenation laws, in the words of historian George Fredrickson, revealed that "racial caste was an acknowledged principle of social organization," and these laws "certified that all whites were members of an exclusive and privileged community by virtue of their racial origin, thus establishing a foundation for solidarity in defense of slavery."[69]

Besides helping to implement a racial caste system, the colonial bans on miscegenation aimed at strengthening the sexual control of white men over women of their own race. The patriarchal assumptions of those men who held power in southern society found expression in statutes prohibiting intermixture to the extent that these laws had the effect of retaining white women for the use of white men. Moreover, by winking at intercourse between male slaveholders and female slaves, antimiscegenation legislation provided masters with an important economic advantage. Most of the South by the early eighteenth century had followed Virginia, which adopted the legal doctrine that black and mulatto offspring inherited the mother's status, so any children born of sexual encounters between white men and female slaves were potential additions to the plantation labor force. This form of interracial sex also allowed slaveholders to further their social control of the slave community through sexual subjugation.

"White men extended their dominion over their Negroes to the bed," observes Winthrop Jordan, "where the sex act itself served as ritualistic re-enactment of the daily pattern of social dominance."[70]

The fact that mulatto children derived their status from their mother also helps to explain why southern lawmakers struggled to prevent sexual relations between white women and black men. Although mulatto children of black female slaves were subject to enslavement, mulatto offspring of white females could not be placed in slavery. These free mulattoes threatened the racial caste system ideologically, if not practically, because their presence could lead to the blurring of the distinction between slave and black, on the one hand, and free and white, on the other. As a Virginia court asserted in 1770, by requiring the severe punishment of white women who had mulatto children, antimiscegenation statutes sought to deter white women "from that confusion of species, which the legislature seems to have considered an evil."[71]

Although sexual contacts between white women and black men involved serious legal risks, evidence of such encounters continued to surface in southern courts before the American Revolution.[72] The persistence of these unions posed a significant challenge to the social hierarchy of the colonial South. The elaborate set of legal regulations that had evolved by the mid-eighteenth century to deal with race mixture, however, served to keep this challenge within manageable proportions.

Following the Revolution, public control of intermixture in southern society became even more stringent. The growth of the free black population in the new nation and increasingly vehement attacks on slavery by northern abolitionists, beginning in the 1830s, convinced most white southerners of the need to bolster the color barrier and prevent an undermining of racial distinctions.[73] A few proslavery apologists did speak out in favor of interracial sex between white men and slave women, the most popular argument being that the practice sheltered white women from the degrading task of serving their husbands' lust. But in public the majority of slave owners, however divided they may have been in their own minds, disapproved of illicit intercourse with slave women.

As in the colonial period, the sexual unions of white women with black men generated the most inflamed condemnations.[74] The extreme response elicited by the specter of white females pairing off with black males can be seen in the outburst of Henry Hughes of Mississippi, who in 1860 equated miscegenation with the violation of the incest ban: "Hybridism is heinous. Impurity of races is against the law of nature. Mulattoes are monsters. The same law which forbids consanguineous amalgamation forbids ethical amalgamation. Both are incestuous. Amalgamation is incest." Legal prohibitions against interracial marriage, Hughes argued, maintained the social subordination of blacks and the racial purity of southern society, while restraining the rise of a population of mulatto "monsters."[75]

Despite the strictness of the proscription against interracial sex, the color barrier in the antebellum South did not prevent miscegenation. The available evidence suggests that the numbers of white females who violated this social dictate were far from negligible.[76] Most miscegenation, however, occurred between white men and black women, much of it resulting from slaveholders and their sons, as well as overseers, taking sexual advantage of female slaves. The most highly ritualized form of miscegenation involving white men were the famous "quadroon balls" of New Orleans, where wealthy whites courted prospective mulatto mistresses and entered into formal liaisons with these women.[77]

Although some liaisons between white men and black women became enduring relationships based on mutual affection, female slaves confronted a limited choice in sexual matters involving their masters. The tremendous disparity between the social and legal position of white men and that of black women ensured that psychological, if not physical, coercion was a significant component of such encounters.[78] In *Incidents in the Life of a Slave Girl* (1861), Harriet Jacobs recounted the stratagem employed by her fictional self, Linda Brent, to deal with the intense sexual harassment of her master. In an effort to make her master jealous and compel him to sell her, Linda Brent begins a relationship with another white gentleman in the neighborhood that eventually leads to Brent's becoming pregnant. "It seems less degrading to give one's self," wrote Jacobs, "than to submit to compulsion." In such a situation, the line between seduction and forced intercourse was fuzzy, to say the least.[79]

Northern abolitionists concerned with the abuses of southern slaveholders charged that these men seduced or forced most of the younger, sexually attractive bondswomen under their rule. Although such charges were probably exaggerated, the sexual abuse of female slaves was widespread, generating considerable tension and conflict in southern households. Above all, black women who were sexually exploited and black men who could not protect their women experienced the most pain and distress.[80] White women often resented mulatto offspring as reminders of their husbands' sexual infidelity, and miscegenation caused them much anguish, too. Mary Boykin Chesnut's outspoken attack on interracial liaisons is the best known: "What do you say to this? A magnate who runs a hideous black harem and its consequences under the same roof with his lovely white wife and his beautiful and accomplished daughters? He holds his head as high and poses as the model of all human virtues to these poor women whom God and the laws have given him."[81] The sexual exploitation of slaves, then, disrupted the family life of both races, giving all women good reason to condemn this practice. As Harriet Martineau remarked, observing the extent of sexual relations between white men and female slaves during her visit to the southern states, "Let any one look at the positive licentiousness of the south, and declare if, in such a state of society, there can be any security for domestic purity and peace."[82]

Even white men in the antebellum South could not entirely escape the repercussions generated by their pursuit of interracial sex.[83] Of course, there were more than a few males who slept with black women without feelings of affection or guilt. But the situation was not always so simple, and some white men found it difficult to manage their interracial affairs without becoming emotionally involved. Perhaps one of the most remarkable instances of a long-term, interracial relationship has been documented recently by Adele Logan Alexander: Nathan Sayre, a superior court judge in antebellum Georgia and a prominent member of his community, established a household with a free woman of color, Susan Hunt, that produced three children and lasted for a quarter of a century. Although not legally married, the couple lived in an impressive mansion with private apartments for Susan Hunt and her offspring. Hunt managed the household during Sayre's frequent absences and supervised a sizable staff of servants.[84] In cases like this, sexuality that crossed social boundaries had the potential to undermine as well as reinforce the hierarchy of southern society.[85]

Those white men not afflicted by a sense of attachment to black women with whom they had sex might still feel responsible for any children. The development of increasingly strict manumission laws during the antebellum period hindered the capacity of masters to free their slave mistresses and children, but many made efforts to provide for their mulatto offspring.[86] Such efforts, sincere as they might have been, did not significantly diminish the contradiction that sexual exploitation of slave women posed to the paternalistic vision of those planters who argued that duty and responsibility, not abuse and avarice, linked master and slave. Not all slaveholders adhered to the organic ideal of planter paternalism, but those who did had to deal with the charge that, at bottom, their rule rested on coercion, not consent. In an effort to excuse miscegenation, southern whites frequently cited the "natural lewdness of the negro" as the main cause of interracial sex. This attempt to place the responsibility for race mixing onto the shoulders of blacks, however, could not disguise the extent to which white men imposed their sexual desires on slave women.[87]

Given the widespread indulgence of white men in illicit intercourse with female slaves, white women became the primary vehicle for the protection of racial purity. Placed on a pedestal, they found themselves honored for their moral virtue yet hemmed in by the severe constraints on their social and sexual behavior. They were the key point of vulnerability in the edifice erected to maintain the color line; they had to be protected from the danger of interracial intercourse at all costs.[88]

Whereas white women were installed on a pedestal, mulattoes were commonly relegated to the status of blacks. Indeed, some white southerners argued that mulattoes were inferior to blacks of purely African heritage. In the words of W. W. Wright, mulattoes were "the most utterly abandoned and profligate of any civilized people on earth."[89] In contrast, other whites demonstrated a pronounced promulatto bias, asserting that the offspring of intermixture were more intelligent and responsible than blacks. However much antebellum whites might disagree about the superiority of mulattoes to blacks of purely African heritage, there was a solid consensus that too many mixed-bloods were slipping into the ranks of the white race. By using the law to classify the mulatto as a black, southern whites were able to reinforce the boundary between the races and prevent the breakdown of racial demarcations.

During the colonial period, there had been little preoccupation with the question of strictly defining who was a mulatto and therefore subject to the laws governing the conduct of slaves and free blacks. Only Virginia and North Carolina passed legislation establishing guidelines for racial identification. Both colonies decided that anyone with black blood within the last three generations should be lumped together with "negroes," although sometimes North Carolina stretched the definition to include four generations. Other colonies simply grouped mulattoes loosely with blacks without writing the custom into law. In all the colonies, legal definitions aside, anyone who displayed the physical characteristics of African ancestry was deemed black.[90]

An increased concern with strengthening the color barrier in the post-revolutionary era led most southern states to pass legislation setting the limits of blackness and whiteness. As Twain pointed out in *Pudd'nhead Wilson*, social custom decreed that any amount of African blood made one black; however much the law may have approved of this social custom, it found the notion impossible to apply literally. Some measurable standard was necessary in the courtroom in order to make racial background susceptible to proof. Consequently, by the early nineteenth century, various southern states applied one-fourth or one-eighth rules about African blood to determine one's legal color. This legislation, by establishing precise definitions of what constituted blackness, meant that some individuals with African blood slipped through the legal net, however fine the mesh. Virginia lawmakers proclaimed in 1785 that an individual with one African ancestor in the previous two generations was a mulatto and hence subject to laws regulating free blacks. This definition was subsequently adopted by Arkansas, Florida, and Mississippi. Alabama, Georgia, Tennessee, and Texas passed more restrictive legislation that pushed the line back three generations.[91]

One would be hard pressed to find a better example of the extent to which race is an ideological construct rather than a physical fact than these various legislative efforts to define the racial boundary in the slave South.[92] The attempt to establish a fractional definition of blackness for mulattoes accompanied the spread of statutory bans on intermarriage, making it easier for authorities to enforce these bans. The use of state power to regulate mixed unions stood in stark juxtaposition to other areas of antebellum marriage law in the North and South, which usually encouraged a hands-off approach to matrimony. The most significant illustration of this overall commitment to free choice in marital matters was the broad acceptance of common-law marriage, in which unions were consummated without procedural formalities or state involvement of any kind.[93]

The perceived need to clamp down on intermarriage in order to preserve racial distinctions, however, prodded the overwhelming majority of states in the antebellum South to enact rigorous public controls. This new legislation made marriages between blacks and whites null and void rather than merely voidable. In addition, some of these states established special penalties for interracial couples who cohabited outside of wedlock. Conviction for miscegenation could draw punishments of anywhere between a hundred dollar fine in North Carolina to a jail sentence of two to five years in Texas.[94] Five states, moreover, imposed stiff fines on clerks who issued licenses for mixed marriages and on officials who performed ceremonies for such unions.[95]

The proliferation of southern laws forbidding intermarriage, together with those setting the limits of blackness and whiteness, testified to the deeply rooted commitment in the Old South to a racial caste system.[96] Yet not all southern states mounted such elaborate legal efforts to buttress the color barrier. The South Carolina legislature refused to impose a single standard for distinguishing the races. Afraid that a rigid definition of who was what might lead to an overly crude application of the color line, lawmakers left the problem of determining racial identification up to the courts. In this way, judges and juries could weigh on a case-by-case basis factors such as social reputation as well as color and blood line.[97] "Color was sometimes a deceptive test," a South Carolina judge commented in his instructions to a jury in 1842. "It ought to be compared with all the circumstances of the case," he insisted, "and if the jury were satisfied that the color, blood, and reception in society would justify in rating the [plaintiffs] as free white men, they had a right to do so."[98] John Belton O'Neall, one of the state's most prominent jurists, provided somewhat more detailed guidelines in an 1848 treatise, *The Negro Law of South Carolina*, advising that "whenever the African taint is so far removed, that upon inspection a party may be fairly pronounced to be white, and such has been his or her previous reception into society and enjoyment of the privileges usually enjoyed by white people, the Jury may rate and regard the party as white. . . . When the [Negro] blood is reduced to, or below ⅛, the Jury ought always to find the party *white*. When the blood is ¼ or more African, the Jury must find the party a mulatto."[99] Even these guidelines, however, underscored the flexibility and ambiguity of the state's law.

surprisy— South Carolina not only refused to establish strict definitions about who was white and who was black but also did not implement any legal sanctions against intermarriage. In addition, Mississippi and Alabama —lacked effective statutory measures to prevent interracial marital unions.[100] The less systematic nature of legal efforts in these three states to reinforce the boundary between the races reflected the somewhat different conditions that characterized portions of the Lower South. Race relations in this area, including Louisiana, evolved in a pattern borrowed from the West Indies, one that tended to treat free mulattoes as a social group with special privileges and status. The influence of the West Indies, together with the high proportion of black slaves to the number of whites, predisposed many whites to perceive the mulattoes who made up the bulk of the free black population in the Lower South as an intermediate element between the races. This more sophisticated system of race relations, with its keener awareness of the complexities of color, encouraged the development of a more porous racial boundary than elsewhere in the South, at least until the intensifying racism of the late antebellum era pushed free mulattoes downward toward the lower caste.[101]

The development of a distinctive attitude toward mulattoes, most evident in South Carolina and Louisiana, does not mean that intermarriage was common in the Lower South. An examination of the manuscript schedule of the 1860 federal census for South Carolina (outside the city of Charleston) revealed only sixty-one coresiding interracial couples in the state. Forty-four of these families were headed by black or mulatto men with white wives, and seventeen families were headed by a white man with a black or mulatto wife. If anything, the tremendous social chasm between most whites and blacks made intermarriage so inconceivable that it did not have to be legislated against.[102] Support for this point of view can be found in the *Charleston Mercury*, which insisted in 1823 that "there is not a white person in the community who would hazard a defence of it [intermarriage between blacks and whites]. The feeling on this subject is universal. A white person so acting would be considered as degraded in society without a dissenting voice." Legislation to ban intermarriage was not necessary because "such a marriage would be a fraudulent contract" due to the unequal status of the parties and would "amount to an indictable offence against public decorum and public morals."[103] The *Columbia Telegraph* in 1848 recognized the legal status of intermarriage but editorialized that "the policy of the State is decidedly against it. Whatever tends to break down the barriers between the two classes of colors must weaken the institution."[104]

Although there may have been little need for legal prohibitions against interracial marriage in South Carolina, the absence of any statutory ban left state judges in a quandary when faced with determining the validity of matrimony between blacks and whites. In 1842, for example, the South Carolina court considered a property dispute involving the legality of a union between an emancipated slave woman and a white man. The mulatto children of this marriage sought title to a tract of land that had been given to their deceased mother under the terms of her former owner's will. The lawyer for the children asserted that the mother's marriage was valid and therefore the offspring had inheritance rights to the property in question that must be recognized. Acknowledging the great hostility toward interracial unions, the attorney remarked that "such marriages are *revolting*, and justly regarded as *offensive to public decency*," but he held that they were "not contrary to *existing laws*." Because no ban on intermarriage existed at common law, he contended, only "*express statutory provisions*" could "make such marriages unlawful," and these provisions were absent from the law books of South Carolina.[105]

The question of whether the black woman's marriage was valid created much consternation among the members of the South Carolina court. Admitting that the case involved "points that are not free from difficulty, and on which there might be some diversity of opinion," the majority of jurists opted to sidestep the question. Instead, they decided against the mulatto offspring on a technicality regarding the will left by the slaveholder who had emancipated their mother and given her the land. Two of the judges, however, issued dissenting opinions in which they claimed that the inheritance rights of the children could not be denied. Without legislative initiative, they agreed, marriage "was good and legal between a white person and a free negro."

Antebellum jurists in other southern states also maintained that the absence of common-law authority made it impossible to impose the restriction on intermarriage without a statutory ban.[106] Of course, most southern legislatures supplied the necessary statutes, and when such legislation existed, it won the whole-hearted endorsement of the southern judiciary. Antebellum courts, in particular, firmly backed those laws making interracial unions null and void. The racial prohibition was "one eminently affecting the public order," announced the Louisiana Supreme Court in 1860. "Hence the *nullity* declared by the [statute] is absolute, and cannot be cured by ratification. The law is of that rigorous nature that it will not permit a marriage to exist between persons of two different races for a moment."[107]

Legislation making marriage between blacks and whites void was the most significant antebellum development in antimiscegenation law. Judicial endorsement of this legislation had several important consequences. First, it meant that when an interracial couple attempted to contract matrimony, the result was precisely the same as if no license had been obtained or ceremony performed and the parties had simply indulged in illicit sexual relations. As the North Carolina appellate court observed in 1852, the parties were thus subjected "to the risk of being indicted for fornication and adultery, as long as they continued to cohabit." In many cases, this is exactly what happened.[108]

Furthermore, because a marriage violating the racial prohibition was void and of no legal effect, someone who was not a party to the marriage could attack it collaterally (as in an estate proceeding).[109] The possibility also existed that a couple who contracted matrimony in a jurisdiction where the union was not prohibited might find its validity challenged when they entered a state that banned intermarriage. In 1855, for instance, the Louisiana Supreme Court denied the legality of an interracial marriage when the parties went to France to contract matrimony and then returned to Louisiana. The jurists denounced the union, calling it an "unnatural alliance," and they proclaimed that "the Courts of Louisiana cannot give effect to these acts, without sanctioning an evasion of laws, and setting at naught the deliberate policy of the State."[110] All in all, such judicial rulings made it nearly impossible for interracial couples who married to achieve any peace of mind in the antebellum South.

Southern law before the Civil War not only opposed interracial marriage but also continued to mirror deep-seated fears concerning illicit sexual intercourse between the races. Public antagonism toward sexual relations between white women and black men had a noticeable impact on judicial policy, as two North Carolina cases demonstrated in 1832. In both appeals, Chief Justice Thomas Ruffin faced white men who sought divorces from their wives because these white women had given birth to mulatto children shortly after their marriages. The men, who admitted taking part in premarital sexual relations with their future spouses, charged nuptial fraud, each asserting that the woman he had married was not a fit marital partner because she had given herself to a black man.

In the first ruling, Ruffin refused to grant Marville Scroggins a divorce. The chief justice decided that he had no choice but to uphold the common-law principle that "persons who marry, agree to take each other *as they are*." Reminding Scroggins that he knew his wife was not chaste at the time of their marriage, Ruffin admonished him: "He who marries a wanton [woman], knowing her true character, submits himself to the lowest degradation, and imposes on himself."

The North Carolina judge was well aware of the powerful prejudices operating in this case, and he acknowledged that the sexual involvement of Scroggins's wife with a black man had made it extremely difficult for him to deny the divorce. In Ruffin's words, "The stigma in our state of society is so indelible, the degradation so absolute, and the abhorrence of the community against the offender, and contempt for the husband so marked and unextinguishable, that the court has not been able, without a struggle, to follow those rules which their dispassionate judgment sanctions."[111] Indeed, public revulsion against race mixture involving white women was so intense that in the second case it proved impossible to overcome.

Ruffin, in *Barden v. Barden*, made it clear that his personal inclination was to issue the same verdict as in the Scroggins case. But the majority of the North Carolina court felt otherwise. Ruffin was compelled to modify his previous stand on the common-law rule of nuptial fraud, and he granted the divorce that Jesse Barden sought. Apparently, the public opposition generated by Ruffin's first opinion was enough to surmount the court's commitment to common-law tradition. As Ruffin frankly concluded, his decision to award the divorce was "a concession to the deep rooted and virtuous prejudices of the community" regarding miscegenation. The dramatic reversal of the North Carolina court in *Barden v. Barden* underscored the power of the community in the southern society to mobilize state sanctions against racial intermixture, especially when it involved white women crossing the barrier of color, and served as a sobering counterpoint to the unrelenting adherence of the southern judiciary to the common law in incest cases.[112]

RAPE IN THE SLAVE SOUTH

Like antimiscegenation statutes, southern rape laws sought to prevent sexual relations between white women and black men, and consequently, race ran through these laws in the same way that veins streak a marble tablet. Nonetheless, slaves accused of raping white women received relatively fair trials, at least in contrast to the widespread outrages committed after emancipation against African American men charged with similar crimes.[113] Although slaves obtained a degree of due process, their trials took place within a statutory framework that usually imposed far harsher punishment on blacks convicted of rape than on whites. Antebellum appellate opinions reveal how the legal treatment of rape reinforced class as well as racial stratification, for poor white women bringing sexual assault charges to the courtroom frequently encountered negative stereotypes that underscored their inferior social position.[114]

White southerners, both inside and outside the legal system, widely shared the belief that black males were obsessed with the desire to rape white women. Such fears may very well have been a projection of white men's sexual passion for black women, a passion that society and the individual found largely unacceptable and hence not easily acknowledged.[115]

The anxieties of southern white males about black sexual aggression found their most morbid expression in the passage of legislation during the colonial era that sanctioned castration of African American men convicted of raping or attempting to rape white females.[116] The rise of humanitarian sentiment in the late eighteenth century placed significant constraints on this form of slave punishment. The 1755 slave code of Georgia made it illegal for masters to maim or emasculate their slaves, and in 1758 North Carolina specifically excluded rape from those crimes punishable by castration. Still, as late as 1819, the Virginia legislature declared this penalty permissible for any slave convicted of an "attempt to ravish a white woman."[117]

Rather than prescribing castration, southern states in the antebellum period called for the execution of black men convicted of rape or attempted rape of a white female.[118] The appellate judiciary wheeled out its strongest denunciations for cases involving assaults by slaves on white women and girls. For example, expressing his dismay over the attempted rape of young Mary Daniel in *Stephen v. State*, Judge Lumpkin bemoaned the consequences to "the unhappy victim, her family and friends, and to society at large." He protested that "the defendant's unhallowed lust, has thrown a dark cloud, which will hang over them forever." [119]

Members of the southern bar concurred with the judicial assessment that blacks' sexual assaults on white women deserved unequivocal condemnation. William D. Valentine, a North Carolina lawyer, wrote in his diary in 1838 about an African American male accused of such an attack. "If ever one's sympathy, mortification and vindictive feelings were excited to the highest and hurt most delicately," said Valentine, who observed the trial, "mine were when I saw this unfortunate woman returning from the prison where the monster was examined by the magistrates and counsel." The crime, in his judgment, was a "diabolic outrage"; and the accused black man "a vile devil." [120]

The rape of white females by black men provoked such profound rage among southern white men because they viewed female sexuality as property that they owned, like slaves, and protection of this property was a key to preserving their position in society.[121] Woman's proper place was in the home, one southern writer exclaimed in 1836, where "her diadem is the social affections; her sceptre love; her robe chastity, pure as the driven snow, enveloping her form, so that the imagination can find nought to blush at, even in the impropriety of an attitude." [122] In a culture that emphasized the purity of white female sexuality, rape was less the violation of a woman's autonomous will than the theft of her honor. Indeed, rape brought dishonor upon not only the woman but also her entire household, and the male head of the household most of all. As far as a southern man was concerned, anyone who sexually assaulted his wife, mother, or daughter assaulted him as well. Rape or attempted rape of a white woman by a bondsman demanded especially fierce retribution because it challenged slavery and the racial order of southern society.[123]

Southern statutes following the American Revolution stipulated execution for white men convicted of rape, and a few states retained capital punishment in the late antebellum era for whites who committed this felony.[124] Especially in cases involving the sexual assault of female children, southern courts did not hesitate to inflict the death penalty on white men. Justice Abraham Nott, sitting on the South Carolina appellate court, refused in 1813 to overturn the conviction of Francis Le Blanc, who was condemned by a jury to die for raping a seven-year-old girl. In Nott's words, despite his doubts that complete penetration and emission had taken place, "I am not disposed to look with eagle's eyes, to see if I cannot, by some legal subtlety, rescue him from the punishment he so justly deserves." [125] By the mid-nineteenth century, however, most states in the

South imposed lesser penalties on white offenders, usually not more than twenty-one years in prison, although the punishment in some states was as little as two years and in others as much as life.[126]

The southern racial hierarchy is revealed by laws that prescribed prison terms for white men found guilty of assault with intent to rape and capital punishment for black men convicted of the same offense.[127] In 1850 attorneys for an Arkansas slave challenged the constitutionality of this disparity in penalties for attempted rape. Basing their argument on a provision in the state constitution that "a slave convicted of a capital offence, shall suffer the *same degree* of punishment as would be inflicted on a free white person, *and not other*," the appellant's lawyers contended in *Charles v. State* that the legislature could not call for the execution of a slave when a white man convicted of the same crime was punished only by imprisonment. The Arkansas Supreme Court reversed the conviction on other grounds, but it upheld the legality of the statute in question, interpreting the constitutional provision to mean that a black convicted of a capital crime must be executed in the same manner as a white. In the court's words, "The provision was doubtless inserted in the constitution from a feeling of humanity towards the unfortunate African race, and in order to secure them against that barbarous treatment and excessive cruelty which was practiced upon them in the earlier period of our colonial history."[128]

Although southern law during the antebellum era protected white females from sexual assault, except in cases of married women whose husbands attacked them, female slaves usually had no legal recourse against rape or attempted rape.[129] The bondswoman's status as property meant that the law treated the rape of one man's slave by another white man as a trespass against the slave woman's master rather than a crime against the woman herself. Thomas R. R. Cobb, whose influential treatise on slave law sought to provide a comprehensive justification for the peculiar institution, explained that only the master could seek compensation in the courts because "the violation of the person of a female slave, carries with it no other punishment than the damages which the master may recover for the trespass upon his property."[130] When a master raped one of his female slaves, the law did not hold him accountable for the attack.[131] But such systematic sexual assault was double-edged, for the physical coercion of slave women cracked open the veneer of paternalistic concern that planters applied to the surface of bondage. As Elizabeth Fox-Genovese notes, "The masters' unchecked power over their slave women brought into the center of the household that public violence against which white women were protected."[132]

The rationalization for the sexual exploitation of slaves sprang from the conventional wisdom of southern whites that black women were naturally promiscuous and sought to copulate with white men. Therefore, masters and overseers often approached female slaves expecting sexual favors. When such favors were not forthcoming and these men encountered opposition to their requests, many resorted to outright force to achieve their purpose.[133] Sometimes the threat of violence was enough to resolve the matter. As one slave explained to Fanny Kemble, the English actress who married a well-to-do Georgia planter, "We do anything to get our poor flesh some rest from de whip; when he made me follow him into de bush, what use me tell him no? he have strength to make me." Although slave women resisted sexual abuse, employing physical means as well as less overt forms of defiance, the outcome was rarely in doubt. "No matter whether the slave girl be as black as ebony or as fair as her mistress," observed Harriet Jacobs. "In either case, there is no shadow of law to protect her from insult, from violence, or even from death; all these are inflicted by fiends who bear the shape of men."[134]

The relative silence of the law on the subject of female slaves who had been raped spoke volumes about the structure of power in southern society, dramatizing the double burden of race and gender that these women endured.[135] Opponents of slavery pointed to the legal vulnerability of slave women to sexual assaults as one of bondage's greatest crimes. Sarah Grimké, the southern abolitionist and women's rights advocate, confessed that the predicament of female slaves gave her "feelings of the deepest shame and sorrow." "In our slave States," she wrote in the famous tract Letters on the Equality of the Sexes (1838), "if amid all her degradation and ignorance, a woman desires to preserve her virtue unsullied, she is either bribed or whipped into compliance, or if she dares resist her seducer, her life by the laws of some of the slave States may be, and has actually been sacrificed to the fury of disappointed passion."[136]

The lack of legal protection for African American women in bondage surfaced as an issue in George v. State, an 1859 opinion that overturned the conviction of a Mississippi slave sentenced to death for the rape of a female slave under ten years of age. The lawyer for the accused candidly noted the impact of slavery on the law of domestic relations for blacks: "The crime of rape does not exist in this State between African slaves. Our laws recognize no marital rights as between slaves; their sexual intercourse is left to be regulated by their owners. The regulations of law, as to the white race, on the subject of sexual intercourse, do not and cannot, for obvious reasons, apply to slaves; their intercourse is promiscuous, and the violation of a female slave by a male slave would be a mere assault and battery." The original indictment could not be sustained under common law or the state statutes, agreed Justice William Harris of the Mississippi high court, because "it charges no offence known to either system." As he pointed out, "the common law is not applicable to the *status* of the slave," and hence only statutes could protect slaves or hold them responsible for criminal behavior. But, Harris noted, "there is no act which embraces either the attempted or actual commission of a rape by a slave on a female slave." Under the circumstances, the appellate jurist believed that he had little choice but to reverse the decision of the lower court and discharge the prisoner.[137]

This case reveals the difficulty inherent in the efforts of southern jurists to construct a separate body of slave law apart from the general law. "Masters and slaves cannot be governed by the same common system of laws: so different are their positions, rights, and duties," declared Judge Harris. But this attempt to set off slave law as a distinct category ran afoul of political and ethical considerations: namely, the need to make bondage more palatable to the public in nonslaveholding states and the presence of genuine humanitarianism in southern society, the two of which combined to alleviate some of slavery's most distasteful features.

The brutality exposed by the unambiguous finding of the Mississippi Supreme Court in *George v. State* may have provided the impetus for the passage the following year of legislation making it a crime punishable by death or whipping for a black man to rape or attempt to rape a black girl younger than twelve years old. The requirement that the victim be extremely young in order to have a black perpetrator punished underscored the vulnerability of African American women in the slave South; only a black female under the *legal* age of consent was considered rapeable. Even the law seemed to regard all black women as "Jezebels" who were so sex-driven that they were incapable of withholding consent. In addition, of course, the law punished only black assailants and said nothing about white men who sexually assaulted black girls.[138]

On the eve of the Civil War a number of southern jurists, legal scholars, and theologians began to express concern about the legal susceptibility of slave women to sexual assault, and they suggested that the rape of a slave woman should be considered a crime. T. R. R. Cobb, for example, believed that the "occurrence of such an offence is almost unheard of," but that making provision for "an adequate punishment" would preserve "the honor of the statute-book" if the crime ever did take place.[139] The 1861 Georgia code, which Cobb helped to prepare, asserted that rape was "the carnal knowledge of a female, *whether slave or free*, forcibly and against her will." Despite this more inclusive definition, the new code did not punish all those convicted of rape equally. The penalty for a white male found guilty of raping a white female was imprisonment at labor in the penitentiary for two to twenty years, whereas a black man convicted of such a crime was subject to the death sentence. Raping a slave or "free person of color" was penalized by "fine and imprisonment at the discretion of the court."[140] Thus the laws by which Mississippi and Georgia extended to black females limited protection against sexual assault perpetuated the dual character of southern society.

Surviving court records at the local level indicate that rape and attempted rape of white women by black men did not occur frequently in the slave South. But white fear of black sexual assault guaranteed that legal authorities would vigorously prosecute African American males accused of this crime. In Virginia between 1785 and 1865, fifty-eight slaves were executed for raping white women, and the lynching of slaves suspected of sexually assaulting white females was not unknown in the state during the antebellum years.[141]

Black defendants who escaped the lynch mob and reached the courtroom found themselves in a precarious position. As Kermit L. Hall cautions, one must be careful not to overemphasize the equitable treatment of slaves in the criminal trial courts of the antebellum South. "The criminal procedure accorded whites let alone slaves was primitive," he observes, "especially in rural areas."[142] Southern states attempted to protect the rights of slaves in criminal trials by ensuring that slaves had counsel in cases involving the prosecution of capital crimes such as rape. In some states, if the master refused to provide counsel, the court appointed an attorney to defend the slave and billed the master for the fee. In other states the government took on the responsibility and the costs of providing counsel for slaves whose owners refused to furnish an appropriate defense.[143]

Nonetheless, the procedures to ensure the fairness of the trials of slaves were extremely flawed. Most important, slaves could not contradict the statement of a white witness or prosecutor, although they could testify against other bondsmen and bondswomen. Slaves could not have a jury of their peers, and, consequently, the protection of trial by jury—central to the common law—provided noticeably less security for slaves than for white males. Southern states such as Alabama and North Carolina required that juries be composed of slave owners, and in Virginia, South Carolina, and Louisiana, special tribunals sat in judgment on all slaves accused of capital crimes without any jury whatsoever. In such a situation, obviously, the slaves' right of appeal was critical.[144]

A three-year struggle in the Tennessee Supreme Court centering on a slave charged with attempting to rape a sixteen-year-old white girl highlights the pitfalls that blacks faced in a legal system in which they were dependent upon the protections afforded by white juries and the right of appeal. Major, the slave, had known the girl for quite some time and had even "slept in the same room with her and her mother." Following his conviction in 1854, Major appealed, and the Tennessee high court ordered a new trial because the girl's identification of Major as her assailant was insufficient.[145] In 1857, when the case arrived in the state supreme court for the second time, there had been three different convictions, two of which had been overturned, one due to jury misconduct. A review of the evidence reveals a tangle of conflicting testimony that made it impossible to determine what had happened. Given the glaring flaws in the prosecution's evidence, the appellate judiciary felt obliged to set aside the jury's guilty verdict on the grounds of insufficient evidence rather than on some procedural issue, as was usually the case. In its opinion, the Tennessee court stressed the importance of the right to a trial by jury: "This case strongly admonishes us of the necessity of a watchful vigilance and an unyielding firmness on the part of judicial officers to see that the invaluable right of a fair trial by an 'impartial jury' should not be disregarded."[146]

Of course, if a black found guilty of rape believed that he had not received a fair trial, he had the right to appeal in most southern states. In cases involving slave convictions, the master often initiated the appeals process, trying to save his valuable property.[147] When convicted black men reached the appellate level, the state supreme courts in the Old South not only consistently paid close attention to the appellants' procedural rights and safeguards but also granted a new trial to a majority of the appellants. In fact, of the thirty-seven appeals by African American men prosecuted for rape or attempted rape of a white female that appear in the published records of state courts in the antebellum South, twenty-two were successful; in only fifteen of these cases did the courts uphold the conviction.[148]

In appellate decisions involving an enslaved defendant, the appearance of a high regard for the slave's rights cast bondage and the legal system in a favorable light, which was well understood by members of the southern bench. For instance, considering the appeal of a slave convicted for the rape of a white woman, the Florida Supreme Court announced in 1860 that "the majesty of the law has been insulted by the commission of a most heinous and revolting crime that strikes at the very foundation of society." Nonetheless, Chief Justice Charles H. DuPont contended that "it is the crowning glory of our 'peculiar institutions,' that whenever life is involved, the slave stands upon as safe ground as the master. The same tribunals of justice are open to each—the same forms of proceedings—

the same safeguards that are extended to the one are fully and freely awarded to the other." [149] Behind such judicial pronouncements lay the understanding that the law had to display a degree of evenhandedness sufficient to persuade groups other than the governing elites that it was just. The commitment to due process helped not only to legitimize the authority of those in power in the eyes of other southerners but also to counter the northern abolitionists' attacks on slavery. Jurists who sat on the southern high courts were keenly aware that appellate justice played a crucial ideological role in shaping the outer face of the South, the face the region presented to the rest of the world. [150] Such a sharp awareness of public sensibilities does not, of course, indicate that these judges were insincere or that their efforts were simply calculated to produce a favorable image of southern slavery and the southern legal system.

The commitment of the southern appellate courts to ensuring that African Americans accused of rape received a proper hearing appear most vividly in the courts' dismissal of indictments for rape or attempted rape if they were not framed in the language of the relevant statute. When a black man was convicted on a charge in *State v. Martin* (1832) that he "feloniously did attempt to ravish" a white female, the North Carolina Supreme Court affirmed the decision of the lower court to arrest judgment because the indictment was not properly drawn. According to Judge Thomas Ruffin, to be sufficient the indictment had to state that the assault was made "with an intent to commit a rape." Especially in cases dealing with allegations of a capital crime, Ruffin insisted, the precise terms of the statute must be used in the charging complaint "not only to denote the disposition of the accused, but also to describe and identify the crime, as that for which the particular punishment is prescribed." "If one departure is allowed," he concluded, "it cannot be told how far astray it may lead us." [151]

Antebellum appellate courts also dismissed indictments for rape if the race of the female was not explicitly stated, and they overturned convictions if adequate evidence of her race was not presented or if the trial judge failed to instruct the jury on the need for such evidence. These actions were taken because in order for a crime to have been committed the victim had to be white—the sexual violation of a black woman was usually not a crime. As Judge Nathan Green of Tennessee pointed out in 1841, what gave "the offence its enormity" was that the victim was white. "Such an act committed upon a *black woman*, would not be punished with death," Green remarked, throwing out an indictment that did not disclose whether the female was "black or white, bond or free." [152]

Not only could insufficient evidence of the woman's race lead to favorable treatment of the accused, but also inconclusive proof of the defendant's race could result in a new trial. For example, in 1850 the Alabama Supreme Court reversed the conviction of a man charged with raping a white woman based on evidence that he was the offspring of a white mother and mulatto father, and therefore did not fall within the statutory definition of a mulatto. In the words of the court, "If the statute against mulattoes is by construction to include quadroons, then where are we to stop? If we take the first step by construction, are we not bound to pursue the line of descendants, so long as there is a drop of blood remaining?"[153]

Slaves and free blacks charged with the rape or attempted rape of a white woman, then, could take advantage of small mistakes in indictments or other technicalities to gain new trials or escape conviction altogether.[154] Similar outcomes testifying to the commitment of southern appellate courts to procedural fairness for subordinate blacks occurred in prosecutions for assault and battery, murder, arson, and robbery. An adherence to legal formalism—the notion that the law was an autonomous body of rules that had to be applied equitably—thus significantly influenced the judicial treatment of criminal cases involving African Americans.[155] More than formalism was at work here, however. Extending procedural rights to slaves in the courtroom protected property rights as well as human lives. The death or injury of a slave represented a significant loss to the owner, for slaves were valuable both as property and as workers. Even when states compensated masters for the execution of their slaves, the compensation often fell short of the full market value of the slave. The financial interest of the master class in mitigating the harshness of the slave codes and the interest of the legal community in maintaining the integrity of the law therefore coincided to create a legal system that conceded the humanity of blacks in criminal trials.[156]

Besides legal formalism and economic self-interest, factors unique to rape cases also contributed to overturning the convictions of slaves and free blacks. The traditional view that rape brought dishonor to the woman and her family made it almost inevitable that not only the race but also the class and reputation of the female victim would be taken into consideration in prosecutions for sexual assault, whether the accused man was white or black. If a woman was poor, without social position, and did not behave in a prescribed manner, then, in the eyes of the community, she lacked honor and worth, and, in the judgment of legal authorities, the likelihood that she had been raped decreased.[157]

Southern lawmakers generally defined rape as "the unlawful carnal knowledge of a woman forcibly and against her will."[158] Lack of consent on the woman's part was obviously a critical component in the legal definition of rape, and just as obvious to the white men who dominated the judicial system of the Victorian South was the notion that a chaste woman was more apt to withhold her approval than a woman without virtue. "Now, who is more likely to consent to the approaches of a man," the Georgia Supreme Court asked in 1847, as it overturned the conviction of a white man for attempting to rape a white woman, "the unsullied virgin and the revered, loved and virtuous mother of a family, or the lewd and loose prostitute, whose arms are opened to the embraces of every coarse brute, who has enough money to pay for the privilege?"[159]

To put it bluntly, a white woman who had previously engaged in an illicit sexual relationship was often presumed to have agreed to any subsequent activity. The woman's chastity could be impugned in rape cases, the Arkansas Supreme Court held in *Pleasant v. State* (1855), in order to raise "the presumption that she yielded her assent, and was not forced in point of fact; and this presumption would doubtless be stronger or weaker, according to the degree of prostitution or degradation established by the impeaching evidence."[160]

This aspect of rape law reveals southern white men's deep distrust of female sexuality. Although the Victorian ideology of feminine "passionlessness" made significant headway among the northern middle classes, the understanding of female sexuality remained ambivalent in the antebellum South, and slaveholding culture still perceived women as subject to sexual desire. White females needed to be insulated from possible threats to their virtue, and they themselves had a responsibility to be constantly vigilant.[161] The sexual nature of woman, proslavery apologist Thomas R. Dew decreed, "renders circumspection and virtue more absolutely indispensable to her than to man. Guilt and infidelity are much more certainly detected in her case than in his, and are attended with much more lamentable consequences. Her whole moral character is formed in some measure in view of this state of things: chastity and virtue become her points of honor; modesty becomes her most pleasing and necessary attribute."[162]

Not only were unchaste women more likely to consent to sexual intercourse on any given occasion, but they were also more prone to lie about their sexual behavior. Having succumbed to their passions, their testimony was inherently suspect. As the Georgia high court put it, "No evil habitude of humanity so depraves the nature, so deadens the moral sense, and obliterates the distinctions between right and wrong, as common, licentious indulgence. Particularly is this true of women, the citadel of whose character is virtue; when that is lost, all is gone; her love of justice, sense of character, and regard for truth."[163] Such a statement exhibits how definitively the image of woman as a "lying temptress" shaped rape law. The image is not confined to the South by any means and, in fact, it continues to shape the law today.[164]

In addition to the prior sexual history of the victim, another issue that exposed the distrust of women's testimony in rape cases was the emphasis placed on the length of time between the alleged act and the woman's complaint. As the Virginia Court of Appeals explained in 1853, "In prosecutions for rape the fact that the person injured made complaint recently after the commission of the offence, is admissible, and the absence of such complaint would be suspicious. The proof of such offences depends in great measure upon the testimony of a single witness, and therefore every test should be applied to her integrity for the safety of the accused." When a sixteen-year-old girl waited seven months before disclosing that her stepfather had sexually assaulted her, Chief Justice William Lewis Sharkey of the Mississippi Supreme Court expressed great skepticism that the sexual acts had taken place against her will, suggesting that the lapse of time was a "circumstance powerfully calculated to induce suspicions that she had been a willing victim to the perfidy of a seducer, rather than a resisting subject of a brutal outrage." [165]

Distrust of women's testimony influenced southern judges even when they considered cases involving intercourse between black men and white women. Appellate jurists in these cases expressed their understanding of the connection between a woman's prior sexual history and the credibility of her accusations in ways that underscored the class dimension of sexual violence in the antebellum South. Judges had little doubt that a "respectable" woman would never submit willingly to a sexual relationship with a black man. As the Arkansas appellate court insisted in 1855, only white women who "had sunk to the lowest degree of prostitution" would yield "to the embraces of a negro, without force." [166]

Southern jurists maintained that rape statutes protected white females "regardless of their character or position in society," but clearly class was an important factor in the calculus employed by the courts to determine a woman's reputation. Whether the male defendant was black or white, judges had little doubt that poor women were much more susceptible to indulging their sexual impulses and hence less deserving of protection under the rape statutes.[167] In cases involving women who lacked social standing or whose conduct did not conform to societal expectations, convictions of black males were sometimes reversed or a lesser penalty than death ordered. For example, of sixty Virginia blacks sentenced to death between 1789 and 1833 for rape or attempted rape, the judge or members of the jury recommended mercy for twenty-seven based upon the belief that the women had either encouraged or consented to the copulation.

Petitions to the Virginia governors exposed the preoccupation with the social position and prior sexual behavior of the female. In one of these cases, a petitioner in 1807 requested transportation rather than execution for the condemned slave, noting that the woman was "under a very infamous character" and had "lived as a concubine for some time past" with a black man.[168] Combining a sentence of death with a recommendation for mercy demonstrates that the impulse to control white women's sexual behavior could collide with the need to maintain the subordination of blacks, sometimes generating an ambivalent attitude toward a black man accused of raping a white woman, especially if she was poor.[169]

In some cases the issue of a woman's reputation became so entangled with the question of what constituted force that it was nearly impossible to distinguish between the two. For instance, in the 1807 request for mercy just mentioned, the petitioner not only assailed the woman's character but also wrote to the governor of Virginia that she "appears large and strong enough to have made considerable resistance if she had been disposed, yet there was by her own confession no mark of violence upon any part of her."[170] The Florida Supreme Court in *Cato v. State* (1860) demonstrated the extent to which the previous sexual relations of a white woman could cast doubt on the plausibility of her allegation that she had been coerced. Pointing to "abundant proof" that the woman and the female housemate who testified on her behalf were "common prostitutes of the lowest grade," the court argued that the accusation of rape should be considered in light of the woman's active sexual history. "Want of consent" did not necessarily imply "force or violence." In its words, "A woman may revolt at the very idea of yielding herself to the embraces of a man. Her moral sense may be shocked at the bare thought, and she be totally unwilling to commit the act, but impelled by the stress of circumstances growing out of her own necessities, she may be induced to take the fatal step in the total absence of any force or violence." Arguing that the distinction between force and persuasion was "peculiarly applicable to the circumstances of this case," the appellate jurists chided the trial judge for not making this clear to the jury, and they ordered a new trial for the black prisoner. "Taking into consideration the degraded character of the witness, and that she was *contradicted* in several important particulars by the other witness on the part of the State," the court contended, "we think that it was a case which eminently demanded that the question of *force* and *violence* should have been kept directly before the minds of the jury."[171]

Antebellum judges in other southern states shared the view of the Florida judiciary that the woman had to exhibit overt resistance to the violent behavior of an alleged attacker in order to substantiate a charge of rape. The stringent standards imposed in prosecutions of black men for attempted rape, like the issue of the woman's character, suggest how attitudes toward female sexuality could temper or sometimes outweigh the need to exert racial domination. Consider, for example, the Virginia case of *Commonwealth v. Fields* (1832), a decision that led to the release of a free black indicted for attempting to rape a white woman. According to the special verdict of a Virginia jury, the defendant "made the attempt to have such carnal knowledge of her when she was asleep, but used no force except such as was incident to getting to bed with her, and stripping up her night garment in which she was sleeping, and which caused her to awake." Based on the conclusion of the jury that the black man did not employ force, the court pronounced him innocent.[172] To say the least, such a limited view of coercion attests to the callous disregard for the autonomy of women that was shared by the members of the jury, who were, of course, all men.

Judge George W. Stone of the Alabama Supreme Court illustrated the degree to which a determinedly male perspective molded the construction of rape law. In 1857 he held that a slave who had been accused of trying to have sex with a woman while she was asleep by pretending to be her husband could not be convicted of attempted rape. Judge Stone was reluctant to render this decision, but, given the legal understanding of force that prevailed in Alabama, he saw no alternative. He expressed his misgivings by means of a striking parallel between virtuous womanhood and private property: "Under our penal laws, one who obtains the goods of another under false and fraudulent pretenses, is held guilty in the same degree as if he had feloniously stolen them," he commented. "He who contaminates female purity under like pretenses, goes unwhipped of justice."[173] Several states, in response to similar judicial findings, enacted laws that punished a man for rape when he employed fraudulent measures to engage in sexual intercourse with a woman, either by pretending to be her husband or by administering some substance to her that prevented or weakened her resistance.[174]

The Alabama Supreme Court in 1860 summed up the thinking of southern jurists on the question of force. The court insisted that an "indecent advance, or importunity, however revolting," was not sufficient to constitute an assault with intent to commit rape. If the defendant, however, "actually intended and attempted carnally to *know* the prosecutrix, by violence and against her consent, and prosecuted his purpose so far as to put her in terror, and render flight necessary to escape from his wicked attempt, then he was guilty of an attempt to commit a rape, within the meaning of the statute."[175] Before the Civil War the vast majority of southern states did not formulate a precise statutory definition of the use of force in rape, but the Texas legislature declared in 1856 that in cases of rape the degree of force "must have been such as might reasonably be supposed sufficient to overcome resistance, taking into consideration the relative strength of the parties, and other circumstances of the case." In addition, according to this law, where a threat existed that might "reasonably create a just fear of death, or great bodily harm," the offender could be convicted for rape.[176]

The application of these standards to both black and white men who were accused of sexual assault demonstrates that southern judges were eager to ensure the appearance of evenhanded justice. Although slaves and free blacks put on trial for rape or attempted rape received substantial procedural protections, the effort to grant some degree of due process to blacks was offset by the racially determined disparity in punishments for men convicted of rape or attempted rape. This dual statutory framework exposed the contradictions generated by a slave society caught in the larger web of a liberal, capitalist system committed to the rhetoric, if not reality, of egalitarianism.[177]

Furthermore, African American men suspected of sexually assaulting white women were often punished by a lynch mob, and hence were denied even the semblance of a trial. The Louisiana planter Bennett H. Barrow recalled an incident in which two runaway slaves killed an elderly man, raped and whipped his daughter, and went on to commit a series of other violent crimes. The fugitives were tracked down and burned alive, but Barrow believed that "burning was even too good for them."[178] Such incidents undermine southern claims of procedural equality for blacks charged with serious crimes. As Edward L. Ayers observes, "The law, it seems, protected slaves when they were on the highly visible stage of the courtroom, but did little to protect slaves from their masters when both were out of the spotlight."[179]

Not only does the judicial handling of rape prosecutions in the Old South reveal the tension between the need to exert racial control and the effort to provide due process, it also exposes the limitations of male thinking about the crime of rape, especially in regard to the issues of coercion and consent. As feminist legal scholar Catharine A. MacKinnon points out, the requirement that to prove the woman's lack of consent one must demonstrate both the use of force by the man and resistance by the woman overlooks the woman's perspective that "force is present because consent is absent."[180] The ways that appellate jurists assessed the reputation of poor white women in rape cases make it clear, moreover, that class as well as racial divisions shaped legal attitudes toward sexual violence. The prevailing assumptions that only "respectable" white women could be raped and that black men had a predilection to rape such women combined during the antebellum period to create a cultural and legal consensus that remained unchallenged for more than a century.

Appellate court opinions and state statutes dealing with incest, miscegenation, and rape illuminate the complex interaction of race, gender, and sexuality that lay at the core of southern social relations. Most important, these laws and decisions disclose the degree to which ideological support for the exercise of patriarchal authority remained deeply entrenched during the antebellum period. Southern judges endorsed the notion that the state should be subject to significant constraints when it came to the regulation of private morality. The legal prohibitions against interracial sex and marriage, rooted in the dictates of slavery, were among the most significant exceptions to the antistatist character of the Old South. Even this form of state intrusion did little to limit the sexual access of white men to female slaves. The primary aim of antimiscegenation legislation, as well as the rape laws, was to prohibit sexual contact between white women and black men. The limited legal protection that white women received against incestuous assault and rape rested less on a recognition of their rights as individuals than on their status as dependents. Southern women, white and black, thus encountered a tenacious commitment to patriarchal attitudes in cases involving the prosecution of sex crimes, a commitment that continues to cast its long shadow over the criminal justice system.[181]

KEEPING THE CHILD

One of the key changes that took place in the Victorian household was the growing influence of legalistic conceptions of consent and contract in domestic relations. Early nineteenth-century commentators on family government increasingly argued that parents should avoid resorting to coercion and should seek to secure the voluntary obedience of their children through moral and psychological influence. The rising importance of contractualism in domestic relations, which also manifested itself in the new emphasis on the consensual nature of marriage, stemmed from a world view that embraced an individualistic rather than organic model of society, one that recognized separate identities within the home.[1]

The family culture of the slave South generally did not provide fertile soil in which to nurture an egalitarian understanding of domestic relations. But the laws regulating the relations between economically self-sufficient white parents and their children suggest that ideas about consent and contract made noticeable headway before the Civil War, highlighting an important area of convergence between the North and South. Powerful sentiments about the importance of proper child rearing and the role of motherhood undercut the common-law emphasis on paternal custody rights in both regions, leading to a more child-centered approach to resolving custody disputes between parents.

The alterations in southern child custody and adoption laws that first appeared during the 1840s and 1850s provide a graphic illustration of the push and pull forces at work in nineteenth-century southern society. New notions about the welfare of the child began to reshape the traditional understanding of domestic governance. These changes preserved the dominant position of the husband/father, but granted women and children individual legal personalities and increased rights, a move that paved the way for the introduction of a contractual model of domestic relations based on voluntary cohesion rather than a fixed order. A very different story unfolded during the antebellum period for poor white and free black families, however, one that disclosed the coercive side of state intervention and that clearly reflected a continued commitment to hierarchy and subordination in southern society.

THE PATRIARCHAL TRADITION

Child custody involves the right of a parent or person acting as a parent to keep a child and control his or her upbringing.[2] The majority of custody cases in the antebellum South grew out of disputes between two parents after separation or divorce. As in divorce law, the reformulation of policies regulating parental custody battles led to an improved legal position for white women within families.

Expanded rights to children, however, provided southern women with few gains in status outside the household because these new rights were based on a vision of mothers as innately suited for the task of nurturance within the home. The development of enlarged maternal prerogatives thus reinforced the restriction of white women in the South to the domestic arena. Changes in custody law, however, did lead to a shift in the distribution of power between families and the state. Increasingly preoccupied with the welfare of the child and standards of parental fitness in the resolution of legal conflicts between mothers and fathers, the courts opened up new channels of state intervention in southern households.

Traditionally, English common law granted the father a nearly unlimited right to the custody of his minor children.[3] The law paid little attention until the early eighteenth century to the welfare of children or the rights of mothers. The father's right to custody of his offspring rested on the control that he exercised over the family property. English custody law, in fact, considered children as little more than pieces of property in which fathers had a vested interest, rather than as individuals whose welfare and interests were legitimate issues.[4] The mother had no legal right over her children; in William Blackstone's words, she was "entitled to no power, but only to reverence and respect." Even after his death, the husband could exercise authority over the children, for he had the power to award custody by will.[5]

Gradually, the idea began to emerge in English law that custody involved not only rights but also responsibilities for the welfare of the child.[6] The father's power over his children, according to Blackstone, derived from his duty to provide support, and to protect and educate them. In addition, English chancery courts began to assume jurisdiction over the welfare and property of children. Employing the doctrine of parens patriae, which held that the state should protect all those unable to care for themselves, the courts intervened for the first time on behalf of the children of living parents, and exercised a right to make a custody decision based on the child's welfare.[7] During the late eighteenth and early nineteenth centuries, this judicial doctrine was incorporated into a broader move among the English ruling classes toward a self-conscious ideology of paternalism. Government intervened not so much to maximize happiness, or to defend private right or public honor, but to protect the weak and helpless.[8]

Despite a deepening concern for the welfare of the child, the ideal of the family in English law remained strongly patriarchal and hierarchical. As a Tennessee court observed, under English common law women and children were held "as the property of the husband and the father, having no will of their own, no rights in contradiction to his power and authority, and only considered *through him* as a portion of the community in which they lived." The father, in other words, was the unchallenged head of the family, and through him the state dealt with the other subordinate, dependent members.[9]

In the colonial South, as well as the rest of British North America, the law made few changes in the paternal orientation of English custody rules, and the father's custody right remained superior to maternal claims. Because divorce was impossible, and separation from bed and board infrequent in the southern colonies, child-custody disputes rarely made their way into the courts. As in England, southern fathers could delegate guardianship by will. Few husbands assigned custody of their children to anyone other than their wives, but sometimes the husband appointed his wife guardian on the condition that she remain a widow, and provided that if she remarried, another person would have custody of the children.[10]

Although American colonial law did little to alter the common-law notion of custody rights, postrevolutionary courts developed an expanded authority to employ judicial discretion in deciding child-custody contests. Consequently, American jurists began to modify the father's paramount right to custody in contests involving the mother. These custody fights between parents now commonly occurred as a result of divorce, because by 1800 divorce statutes existed in the North and had begun to spread to the southern states. American jurists in custody battles began to take into account the welfare of the child and maternal rights. In exercising judicial discretion, state courts during the early nineteenth century not only increasingly examined the needs of the child but also developed notions of parental fitness, evaluating the ability of mothers and fathers in custody disputes to supply children with the special nurture that the courts believed necessary for infants to develop fully.[11]

These early decisions in American courts drew some of their legal authority to consider the child's welfare in employing discretion from *Rex v. Delaval*, an English case of 1763. Lord Mansfield's opinion in this case provided the legal foundation in the United States for the use of a habeas corpus writ to try custody contests.[12] Mansfield insisted that upon issuing a writ of habeas corpus, the court was bound to release the child from an improper restraint, but was not required to deliver the child to any particular party. What was important was that the British jurist did not address the issue of whether judicial discretion included the authority to determine custody as well as to protect the child from illegal restraint.[13]

A few American courts, however, went beyond *Rex v. Delaval* to argue that judicial discretion embraced the broader authority to sustain or award custody. In doing so, they transformed the negative power of the parens patriae doctrine to withhold custody from unfit fathers into a more positive use of discretion. American judges, furthermore, began to link this expanding discretionary power with a developing concept of the child's best interests. The father's traditional common-law right to custody of his children began to give way to the right of the courts (and behind them the state) to determine the best interests of the child. Judicial discretion, when linked to this new concern for the child's welfare, enabled postrevolutionary jurists in many states to rewrite the common law of custody.[14]

Enlarged judicial power and concern for the welfare of the child developed to a great extent out of changing attitudes toward gender roles, childhood, and the family. By the 1830s the "cult of domesticity" had emerged in American culture. Behind this cluster of ideas and values lay a view of women as morally superior yet in need of male protection in a competitive, commercial world. Despite similarities between the rhetoric of domesticity in the North and South, writers below the Mason-Dixon line placed a special emphasis on the ideal of the lady as the highest position to which women could aspire.[15] Thomas R. Dew outlined this ideal for his southern audience in 1835: The man "is the shield of woman, destined by nature to guard and protect her. Her inferior strength and sedentary habits confine her within the domestic circle; she is kept aloof from the bustle and storm of active life; she is not familiarized to the out of doors dangers and hardships of a cold and scuffling world: timidity and modesty are her attributes."[16] Whereas men took responsibility for activities outside the home, women remained within the family, where her duties included rearing the children, supporting the husband, and maintaining the household. As C. R. Carroll rhapsodized in the *Southern Literary Journal*, "Her pride should be, to convert home into paradise, to fix her affections there, and to have an eye to this in every thing she says and does. For this is her proper place, wherein she shines most and is every where else a stranger. If she have no content here—if home be not a temple, at whose altar she can offer the incense of love, what other spot will she find sacred?"[17]

The emphasis on the domestic role of women was closely associated with a new conception of children as individuals who were distinct from adults and thus required special attention.[18] Childhood, rather than a time to demand absolute submission to authority, was increasingly perceived as a period of growth and development in preparation for the independence and self control of adulthood. "It should never be forgotten that the child's mind is his own mind, and not the property of his parents; and the parent should learn to respect it as such, and to watch over it with the deepest solicitude," advised one southern writer on female education in 1835.[19] A greater appreciation for the family's role in shaping the character development of the future citizens of the Republic meant that the mother became entrusted in theory and practice with the proper rearing of children, and her role in providing the appropriate training for her sons was seen as especially important.

The ideal of the republican mother, with its stress on the responsibility of women to imbue their youngsters with precepts of patriotism and morality, came to dominate the lives of white women in the antebellum period. The *Southern Literary Messenger* in 1840 vigorously endorsed this view: "With a nation of virtuous and enlightened females to lay the foundation of masculine character, to doubt the durability of the Republic would be to doubt the influence of virtue and intelligence."[20] In response to the new notions about childhood and child rearing, a wide range of reformers, primarily in the urban Northeast, established numerous institutions to meet the unique needs of children. The age-graded common school, high school, children's aid society, orphan asylum, and reformatory school all aimed at insulating children from adult society, prolonging the period of dependency, and administering an education appropriate to a child's distinctive requirements.[21]

The increased willingness of American judges to grant custody rights to mothers and to recognize the welfare of the child as a legitimate legal concern reflected this new interest in children and the growing stress on the importance of maternal care. But American child-custody laws were still very much in transition. Although courts by the 1830s had made notable advances in the use of judicial discretion to resolve custody disputes, some jurists clung to older notions of the father's paramount right to custody.[22]

This vacillation between older and newer views of custody was particularly apparent in antebellum southern courtrooms. The seeds of domesticity, with its stress on the importance of motherhood, took root in the South, but the culture in which they were planted was still very much committed to the male-dominated household. One result, as Elizabeth Fox-Genovese points out, was that "southerners, unlike northerners, did not view either families or households as primarily female preserves, but as terrain that contained woman's sphere." Important though it was, there could be no doubt that the female sphere was subordinate to that of the man. Domesticity may have brought about some measure of equality within the family and the emergence of autonomous women's networks in the Northeast, but in the rural South women continued to defer to their spouses in most matters regarding family concerns, and they remained rooted in neighborhood kinship networks that discouraged the formation of an independent women's culture.[23]

With the persistence of this deferential model of marital relations in the South, the presumption that fathers had a superior right to custody widely prevailed, even as the judiciary began to grant custody of children to mothers. Moreover, although southern justices increasingly employed their discretionary authority to award custody, the exercise of this authority remained controversial well into the 1850s. The outlines of a more child-centered theory of guardianship became discernible in the South by 1860, yet many courts during these years denied the father custody only upon a strong showing of his misconduct or unfitness.

An 1812 case in Louisiana involving a custody dispute between parents underscored the reluctance of southern judges to interfere with the father's authority. The husband in this contest had been out of the state for about eight years, but he had made arrangements for the support of his wife and children, who went to live with the wife's brother. On the husband's return, the wife refused to live with him or send their two sons and daughter to him. She insisted in court upon her right to retain the children, especially the eleven-year-old girl, "to whom, in her judgment, the cares and attentions of a mother were more necessary than those of a father."

The court expressed no sympathy for the mother's position; instead, it ordered her to deliver the children to the father. The judges declared that the father was "the master of the family," and that his authority was "founded in nature, and the care which it is presumed he will have of their education." "While his conduct is proper," contended members of the Louisiana bench, "the Court cannot interfere with his authority, and will cause it to be respected." Even if the mother had some claim to the custody of her children, her voluntary absence from "the paternal house" without justifiable reason automatically denied her any such claim.[24]

The Louisiana court in this decision paid scant attention to the age and gender of the child, and it revealed little concern for parental ability to provide special care and nurture. The primary preoccupation of the judiciary was to bolster the father's position as head of the household. In doing so, it expressed the belief that the other members of the family each had his or her place in the family hierarchy, and that the court should do nothing to disrupt this carefully ordered arrangement.

The aversion of southern justices in the early nineteenth century to disturbing paternal authority went hand in hand with an uncertainty over whether they had the power to award custody in legal disputes over children. Many judges argued that the courts upon a writ of habeas corpus had only the authority to protect a child from illegal restraint. In *Ex parte Ralston* (1821), for example, a Georgia superior court asserted that it did not have the discretionary authority to remove a child from the custody of the legal guardian designated by the father. Justice William Charlton observed that the child in question was only seven years old, and hence too young to "make a free and unbiased selection" between the legal guardian and the grandmother with whom the girl lived. The court, instead, ordered the grandmother to return the child to her legal guardian.[25] Georgia justices insisted on a narrow conception of judicial discretion that excluded the power to sustain or grant custody upon a writ of habeas corpus. The Richmond Superior Court maintained in 1831 that it was required in custody contests "to set the infants free from all improper restraints; but *it is not* bound to deliver them to *any body* nor to *give them any privilege.*"[26]

During the first third of the nineteenth century, Georgia courts confined the exercise of judicial discretion largely to custody cases involving orphans and illegitimate children. As in the colonial period, fathers in postrevolutionary Georgia had the right to grant custody of their children by will. The father might, and frequently did, name the mother as their guardian. For married women, this was the only way during these years in which they could ever gain complete control over legitimate children, but doing so depended on the express wishes of the father. Although the courts possessed the statutory authority to appoint the mother if the father died without providing for the guardianship of offspring from the marriage, upon remarriage the mother's right to guardianship ended, and the court could exercise its discretion to reappoint her or to name someone else as guardian. When the father was still alive, judges had the power to appoint a guardian only for an illegitimate child or when property descended to a child and the natural guardian refused to give bond and security for the performance of the trust.[27]

Members of the South Carolina bench also adopted this strict interpretation of judicial authority. In the 1834 case of *In re Kottman*, a father sought to regain custody of his son. Kottman had severely beaten the fifteen-year-old boy and later placed the child with a Mrs. Mary Thompson, who without charge furnished boarding and lodging for the youth. When Kottman demanded the return of his son, Thompson refused to turn over the boy to him. The father then sued for custody in a lower court, but the judge noted Kottman's previous treatment of his son and declined to transfer custody. In response, Kottman appealed the decision.

Like the Georgia bench, the South Carolina Supreme Court held in this case that it did not possess the discretionary authority to award custody. In the words of Justice William Harper, "Perhaps it might be more correctly said that the office of the court is to discharge the infant from illegal restraint, and the discretion is to protect the infant in returning." The court refused to return the child to the father because it found that Thompson was not holding the boy against his wishes; to this extent the court stepped in to protect the son from his abusive father. Justice Harper, however, was certain that the father still retained legal custody of the youth, asserting that "the father has the legal right to take him where he can find him," as long as he did not trespass in his attempt to regain custody.[28]

The breakthrough came in 1836 when a Georgia court embraced a broader view of judicial discretion in the case of *In re Mitchell*, and announced that it possessed the power to award custody as well as to free a child from improper restraint. Dr. John J. Mitchell filed a habeas corpus petition in Chatham Superior Court to recover custody of his three-month-old infant, who had remained with the maternal grandparents since the mother's death during childbirth. The court exercised its discretion to give the father custody in this case because it found that he had neither abandoned the child nor released his right to custody by contract. "This court," Justice Robert Charlton maintained, "has the power to determine the right of custody of an infant of tender years." But Charlton also believed that fathers had a "legal, natural right" to the possession of their children, and that this right should remain undisturbed except in cases of extreme abuse or unfitness.[29] In short, although the Georgia court expanded judicial authority to include the right to award custody, it insisted that this discretionary authority should only be used to take custody away from a father when he exhibited a pronounced lack of fitness.

Before the Civil War, southern courts usually hesitated to give the mother custody in a legal battle between parents unless there was strong evidence of both the father's incompetence and her suitability.[30] The Alabama Supreme Court made it clear in two cases during the late antebellum period that without such evidence, the father's rights would prevail. In *Ex parte Boaz* (1858), the mother sought a writ of habeas corpus to gain custody of her two-year-old infant after the father abandoned her and took the child with him. He had left his wife not for any failing on her part as a mother, but because she had brought a legal suit against him to recover certain property that she claimed as a separate estate. A lower court denied the mother's attempt to gain possession of the child, and she appealed.

Her lawyers argued before the high court that "the good of the infant" required that the judges give the mother "custody of her infant child for nurture." The attorneys maintained, furthermore, that the wife's separate estate made it possible for her to support the child on her own. The court, however, did not find these arguments persuasive. "The law regards the father as the head of the family, obliges him to provide for its wants, and commits the children to his charge," it proclaimed, "in preference to the claims of the mother or any other person." The father, according to the Alabama jurists, could forfeit his right to custody "by misconduct" or lose it "by misfortune." But when the father had custody of the child, and no improper restraint of the minor could be established, it was "beyond dispute" that the court must allow him to retain custody.[31]

The Alabama Supreme Court confirmed this finding a year later in another dispute between parents. The wife's charges that her husband was habitually intoxicated, physically and verbally abusive, and sexually unfaithful failed to convince the judges that she should be awarded control of the offspring. Justice Walker conceded that the husband drank "freely and in some cases to inebriation," but asserted that his drinking did not "materially interfere with his business habits or . . . make his association dangerous to his wife or children." Even though the children were only two and four years old, Walker felt that they were old enough to be separated from their mother because she no longer nursed them. "The strong favor with which the law regards the father's prior right to the custody of his children" *and* the mother's "want of peculiar fitness for the custody and care of the children," he contended, made it impossible for the court to intrude upon the husband's control of the children.[32]

Antebellum southern judges did not regard the extramarital sexual activities of men as serious enough to deny them custody of their offspring, but the courts took a much stricter stance toward mothers who committed adultery. The Louisiana Supreme Court, for example, refused in an 1843 decision to give the wife custody of the only child because she had slept with someone other than her husband. Justice Henry Bullard admitted that the mother's conduct prior to her extramarital involvement had been "ladylike and above reproach." Bullard also found that the husband had abused her before she became involved, and had killed her lover "in cold blood and in a manner both cruel and unmanly." Nevertheless, members of the Louisiana bench overturned the divorce that a lower court had awarded the wife, and granted custody of the child to her husband.[33]

The Georgia Supreme Court, in *Lindsey v. Lindsey* (1854), also revealed its firm opposition to giving custody to a mother who had engaged in sexual relations outside of marriage. When the wife in this case left her husband and took the daughter to live with another man, the husband sued out a writ of habeas corpus to regain possession of the child. Although the wife claimed that she had moved out because of the husband's cruel treatment and failure to support her, the appellate court refused to award her custody. The daughter, according to the Georgia judiciary, would be better off with the father, so it ordered the return of the child to him.[34]

Although the decision of the Georgia court disclosed a concern for the child's welfare, this concern stemmed more from a traditional, patriarchal attitude toward female sexual behavior than from a newer form of child-centeredness that weighed the abilities of the mother and father to provide nurture for their offspring. From a purely ethical point of view, the justices noted, "there may be no difference in the sins of the man and woman, who violate the laws of chastity"; still, "in the opinion of society it is otherwise." When a man committed adultery, he did not necessarily lose the respect of those who knew him. His children would not be excluded from association with "decent people" and "may be educated to become good and useful members of society." With "the frail female," however, the outcome was commonly quite different. Following the violation of the marriage contract, the wife inevitably found herself reduced to "utter and irremediable ruin, where her associations are with the vulgar, the vile, and the depraved." "If the children be with her," the court stated, "their characters must be, more or less, influenced and formed by the circumstances which surround them." Members of the Georgia bench believed that more of a stigma fell on women who committed adultery than on men who did so, and this was reason enough to grant the father custody of the children, even in situations where both parents pursued extramarital affairs.[35]

In legal battles between parents, then, men's custody rights received significant protection from the antebellum southern judiciary. State courts in Alabama, Georgia, Louisiana, South Carolina, and Texas held that fathers possessed a superior claim to custody in the absence of a strong showing of unsuitability.[36] Although southern jurists began to grant mothers some custody rights before 1860, they generally gave paternal prerogatives greater weight unless the father was distinctly unfit.

Paternal rights to custody gained strong support from the antebellum courts because they viewed the father-child bond as a critical link in the southern family. Through the paternal tie the child received his or her social position and inheritance. Southern justices placed great stock in the fact that the economic resources of the father were usually much greater than those of the mother; they saw this as the basis of the father's primary right to custody. As the Alabama Supreme Court put it, "Upon the separation of husband and wife, the father is entitled to the custody and control of the minor children, because he is bound for their maintenance — and support." [37]

The antebellum judiciary thus assumed that the economic interests of the child required the preservation of patriarchal authority. This was especially true in planter families. The South before the Civil War was an overwhelmingly rural and agricultural society; land and slaves formed the basis of planter wealth. Within the household, the planter's power rested on his estate, and this patrimony encouraged among his offspring the patriarchal characteristics of subordination and dependence rather than the bourgeois traits of autonomy and individualism fostered among children of the northern middle classes.[38] But the reciprocal nature of the relationship between the obligation to provide support and the right to control, in theory, disciplined and moderated the patriarch's domination of his children.

In this context, like the criminal law of incest, the primary role of child-custody law during the antebellum period was both to uphold and restrain the authority of the father; to see to it that his dominance was presumptive, but not absolute. Few southern jurists were willing to follow the logic of patriarchy to its end: an assertion of the despotic nature of the father's authority. The majority of judges maintained, instead, that the state should step in when the father clearly misused his power or overlooked his responsibilities. To this extent, antebellum developments in southern custody law led to important constraints on patriarchal actions, but without overturning the judicial commitment to the superiority of paternal custody rights.

Although courts in the Old South tended to safeguard the custody rights of fathers in legal contests with mothers, the state justices were not unbendingly patriarchal. In fact, between 1800 and 1865 the appellate judiciary granted custody to mothers in almost as many cases as it did to fathers: the former received control of the children in about 38 percent of the contests, and the latter in about 42 percent. The judges split custody of the children—giving some to the father and others to the mother—in 17 percent of the disputes.[39] Although southern jurists frequently granted custody to mothers before the Civil War, they usually did so only when a father proved to be particularly unfit as a parent or violated his obligation to support and protect his wife and children and thus had forfeited his right to control of the children.

Most judges before the Civil War granted custody to women with noticeable caution in part because doing so created a conflict with the traditional common-law commitment to paternal authority. This reluctance was particularly evident in the first southern decision that awarded control of the children to a mother, *Prather v. Prather* (1809). Jennet Prather petitioned the chancery court in South Carolina for a separation from her husband on the grounds of gross abuse, and she asked for custody of her daughter and two sons.[40] William Prather, according to his wife, had "used her extremely ill, and turned her out of doors"; he then began living with another woman "in open adultery." Chancellor Henry Desaussure, with little hesitation, awarded the wife a separation and alimony, for there was no doubt that her husband had treated her badly. But the question of custody gave the chancellor pause; he obviously felt uneasy about challenging the common-law prerogatives of the father to his children. As he put it, the father "is the natural guardian invested by God and the law of the country, with reasonable power over them. Unless therefore his paternal power has been monstrously and cruelly abused, this court would be very cautious of interfering in the exercise if it." Desaussure finally decided to give the father custody of the two sons, and to award the mother possession of the daughter. Even this compromise left the chancellor uncomfortable, and he observed that the court was "treading new and dangerous grounds."[41] Although the mother won a partial victory, she gained custody of the girl only because the father had undeniably violated his familial obligations.

This cautious judicial balancing of circumstances and traditional rights could also be seen in two other early South Carolina decisions that divided custody of the children between the parents. In *Williams v. Williams* (1811), the chancery court placed the three daughters under the guardianship of the wife when she proved that the husband had kept his mistress in the house with the family. Despite the father's "abandoned and flagitious conduct," the judges allowed the sons to remain with him. Four years later, Chancellor Desaussure again granted possession of some of the children to the mother; in this case the South Carolina jurist gave her custody of the youngest children, and left the oldest son with the father. According to Desaussure, the husband "has been habitually in a state of intoxication, and when in that state, has generally abused and ill used his wife, and sometimes beat her, and put her life in jeopardy; in two instances most barbarously." Desaussure admitted that he was "reluctant to intermeddle with the rights of the husband and father," but he felt compelled "to do something for the security of this unhappy family." [42]

Although southern judges in the early nineteenth century displayed a distinct aversion to disturbing the father's authority over legitimate children, most members of the judiciary assumed a very different attitude when children born out of wedlock were involved. English common law considered the bastard as the child and heir of no one, and consequently, his or her status regarding custody claims was ill-defined and uncertain. The English courts granted mothers moral and natural law rights to the guardianship of the illegitimate child, but they provided no clear guidelines as to how legally enforceable these claims were. [43]

American courts after Independence gradually staked out the position that mothers had a common-law right to the custody of a bastard. Behind the emergence of this new policy lay a twofold rationale. On the one hand, illegitimate children belonged to no legally recognized household, leaving the mother as the "natural guardian." The rapidly developing cult of domesticity, on the other hand, put increasing pressure on legal authorities to place children with their mothers whenever possible. [44] Judge Catron of the Tennessee Supreme Court declared in the 1825 case of *Lawson v. Scott* that by common law "the mother of a child born out of wedlock has the undoubted right to the possession thereof." The justice rested this opinion in part on his faith in "the disposition of the female to protect and support her offspring." Arguing that unmarried women with bastards should be treated as if they were men who had fathered children in wedlock, he overturned the lower court's decision granting the father custody of the child in dispute. [45]

Although most southern states upheld the maternal right to illegitimate children, some states balked at allowing any inroads into the custody rights of fathers. An 1811 act in Mississippi, for example, stated that the court should give the reputed father "preference to any other person" in appointing a guardian for an illegitimate child. The Texas high court contended in 1855 that once a bastard attained the age of seven years, "the father has an equal claim with the mother to the guardianship."[46] Such thinking demonstrated the continued hold of the traditional paternal orientation on southern lawmakers and members of the bench, even in cases involving children born out of wedlock.

Nevertheless, during the 1840s and 1850s, women in the South began to make notable gains in custody rights to both legitimate and illegitimate offspring. Appellate courts in these years found themselves faced with a steadily increasing number of divorce and separation cases in which women sought to gain control of their children. Many southern jurists began to assume that, if the mother received the divorce or separation, she deserved custody of the children as the injured party. This assumption was a logical extension of the same paternalism that led the judiciary to grant southern women expanded divorce rights in the nineteenth century. Confronted with a husband and father who failed to fulfill his patriarchal responsibilities, the court stepped in to ensure that the wife was not left unprotected nor that her children were taken away from her. Hence Justice Thomas W. Glover of South Carolina held in 1858 that an "inability or neglect to provide for the child's wants," a "brutal exercise of authority," and an "open practice of those vices which corrupt the infant mind" would all constitute grounds for taking custody away from the father.[47]

An 1860 appellate case in Mississippi illustrated the way in which this developing judicial paternalism helped to enlarge the custody rights of women. In this case John Cocke petitioned for a writ of habeas corpus to recover custody of his daughter from her mother, Louisa Hannum. The mother had divorced Cocke in 1856 on the grounds of adultery and subsequently remarried. At the time of the divorce no legal provision had been made for their daughter, and she remained with the mother. Justice Alexander Handy of the Mississippi Supreme Court awarded permanent custody to Hannum. Noting that Cocke had been divorced not once, but twice, for adultery and was "addicted to intemperance," Justice Handy commented that "there can be no doubt that the father is positively unfit" for his parental duties. The Mississippi judge believed that the father should not be permitted to retain his "paramount legal right" to custody when "his own violation of duty had produced the dissolution of the marriage tie." Handy's sense of responsibility for the subordinate family members was evident in his conclusion: "It would be most unjust both to the child and to the mother that it shall be committed to the keeping of an unworthy father."[48] Implicit in such an approach to the determination of custody was the supposition that awarding custody to the parent not at fault for the divorce or separation best served the welfare of the child.

This general concern on the part of southern jurists with furthering the welfare of the child in custody contests had first appeared in the 1836 case of *In re Mitchell.* Awarding custody to the father, the Georgia superior court maintained that the child's "interests and health would be best promoted" by such a decision.[49] Six years later, another Georgia court became the first southern bench to employ the best interests of the child approach to undercut, rather than buttress, the father's custody prerogatives.[50] Anna King sought to gain possession of her two-year-old daughter after she and her husband separated. King claimed in her plea for custody before the superior court that "the tender years of the said infant" meant that the child required "the constant care of its mother." The father responded, however, that the mother was "not a fit and proper person to care for the child," and that his sister would take care of the girl if he received custody. Justice John Shly found that the husband was "a good moral man, and no objection can be raised against him as a father." According to the judge, however, the court's "great and paramount duty is, to look to the interest and safety of the child—as well as its morals, its education, and even its pecuniary interests: And the legal rights of the father to the custody of his child will not be enforced, if those rights, in any manner, conflict with these interests, or the *welfare of the child*." The court felt that in this case the mother was more qualified to have custody because of the child's age and gender.[51]

Shly's decision represented an abrupt departure from earlier cases in which southern jurists expressed doubts about their discretionary authority, or paid little attention to the age and gender of the child in the resolution of custody contests. It demonstrated, in particular, increased judicial backing during the 1840s of the view that the court's discretionary power included not only the right to release a child from improper restraint but also to grant custody. The decision also revealed a new willingness on the part of southern courts to recognize maternal custody rights and the welfare of the child as legitimate legal issues.

Underlying this new willingness was the sentimentalization of childhood and the ideology of domesticity, phenomena that were closely linked. As Carl N. Degler notes, "Exalting the child went hand in hand with exalting the domestic role of woman; each reinforced the other while together they raised domesticity within the family to a new and higher level of respectability."[52] The link between these developments could be readily detected in the South as well as the North. Men's responsibilities might take them out into the world, observed a contributor to the *Southern Literary Messenger*. "But to women," he quickly added, "it peculiarly belongs, to preside, with grace and advantage, over the domestic and social relations—to give the mind its first impulse in the path of wisdom and virtue—to impart to the infant soul its earliest lessons of piety, as well as of worldly prudence—to give to society its principal attractions, and to life its greatest consolations and most animating hopes." [53]

Despite the support for domestic ideology among antebellum southern jurists, the use of judicial discretion to award custody to a mother remained a matter of substantial debate. The Mississippi court vigorously discussed this issue in the 1842 case of *Foster v. Alston*, which involved a custody battle over two girls (aged nine and ten) between their mother and legal guardian. The father's will had appointed James Alston, the girls' uncle, as their guardian. The mother, however, managed to gain possession of her daughters upon remarriage, and she refused to return them to Alston, who sued out a writ of habeas corpus to recover custody. The lower court then ordered the mother to turn the children over to Alston, and she appealed.

The mother's counsel in the appeal insisted that the court had the power to make final disposition of the children, and that "this discretion is to be exercised *for the benefit of the children*." Alston's lawyer, on the other hand, argued that only when there was strong evidence of unsuitability on the part of the father or legal guardian could the court employ its discretion to determine custody. Otherwise, "if no cause exists showing want of capacity in the guardian or father, the court must always deliver the children to them." Justice Edward Turner, in his decision, agreed with the appellant that the court could give custody to whomever it perceived would promote the welfare of the children. As he put it, "We are bound to consider the interests of the child, as paramount to all other considerations." With the concurrence of Justice James Trotter, Turner reversed the decision of the lower court and awarded custody to the mother. [54]

Chief Justice William L. Sharkey, however, issued a sharply worded dissent. He contended, as did Alston's attorney, that the only situation in which "the court could exercise a discretion for the benefit of the child" was "where the father or guardian is obviously the improper person to have custody of the child." Objecting to the court's award of custody to the mother, Chief Justice Sharkey expressed his commitment to the common-law tradition of the patriarchal family: "We are informed by the first elementary books we read that the authority of the father is superior to that of the mother. It is the doctrine of all civilized nations. It is according to the revealed law and the law of nature, and it prevails even with the wandering savage, who has received none of the lights of civilization. The father is considered the head and governor of the family. He controls even the mother, and must of necessity control the children." Sharkey asserted that a "system of training must be adopted which is often repugnant to the wishes of the child." "Which is best calculated to do these things," asked the Mississippi judge, "the doting, partial mother, with whom every fault is a virtue, every wish a command, or the less partial father, who looks to the future welfare, rather than the gratification of childish folly?"[55] Here, summed up neatly, was the patriarchal criticism of the new emphasis on maternal child rearing.

Similar arguments over the use of judicial discretion appeared elsewhere in the antebellum South. In each instance, however, the jurists decided in favor of the broader interpretation that they possessed the right to determine custody. Noting this trend with approval, South Carolina justice Joseph N. Whitner suggested in 1853 that "the day of danger, I trust, has passed."[56] Gradually, beginning with Georgia in 1836 and Mississippi in 1842, southern courts endorsed the view that judicial discretion should be exercised to further the best interests of the child. Tennessee in 1843, Virginia in 1852, South Carolina in 1853, and Alabama and Texas in 1858 all declared that the welfare of the child should be the "highest consideration" in the determination of custody.[57]

The gradual reassessment of maternal and paternal custody rights began to enter the statute books of the South. Antebellum laws in Louisiana and Tennessee extended to women the right to petition for the custody of their children in the event of abandonment by the husband.[58] Most important, Georgia, Mississippi, Tennessee, Texas, and Virginia amended statutes governing divorce and legal separation to provide for the exercise of judicial discretion in custody matters. These new laws allowed the courts to grant custody to either the father or mother, and they instructed the judiciary to base its decision on the welfare of the child.[59] A Georgia act of 1845, for example, proclaimed that "the Common Law rule vesting said custody always in the father, shall be abolished." The act authorized the court in a custody controversy "to award the custody of said minor or minors either in the father or mother, as may appear most beneficial to the interest of the said children."[60] The Alabama and Virginia statutes also gave the court additional power, pending the outcome of a divorce suit, to provide for the custody of the children as "their safety and well being may require."[61]

During the antebellum era, then, southern courts gained the power to overrule traditional paternal prerogatives in custody battles between parents. A growing preoccupation with the welfare of the child began to engender dissatisfaction with the common-law emphasis on the absolute paternal right to control of his offspring, and the older commitment had to compete with new concerns relating to child nurture and parental fitness. The *Southern Quarterly Review*, in an 1842 essay on gender roles, marriage, and divorce, laid out the competing views of child custody. On the one hand, "the pride of power indicates to the father that his offspring are under his rule and dominion. It is sort of a domestic monarchy. He has the burden of the support of the children till they are competent to take care of themselves; he must educate them;—he is, in a greater degree than the mother, responsible to society for their correct moral discipline." But the journal urged its readers to listen carefully to the mother's side of the debate: "The mother has an equal right to the person of the infant, for she brings it into the world. It is, as it were, an emanation from her own spirit, and this, too, secures her tenderness. She supplies the infant's first want, and her tenderest care and warmest solicitude are forever alive, to watch its growth, and promote its improvement." In the end, however, the *Southern Quarterly Review* supported the application of the best interests of the child standard. "The true position is, that the rights of neither party should be regarded, for nature declares them equal," it asserted. "The advantage, prosperity, and happiness of the children, should be alone consulted; and wherever it appears that one or the other parent will be the better custodian of the children, to that parent they should be given." [62]

Although more and more southern judges and lawmakers agreed with this child-centered approach, they sought to reshape rather than destroy the patriarchal basis of antebellum southern society. In the struggle to resolve individual custody disputes, judges recognized the importance of taking into account the interests of the child. At the same time, members of the bench operated with well-entrenched assumptions about the importance of paternal authority. Trying to balance these conflicting interests, the courts shored up southern patriarchy by acknowledging abuses of paternal power and trying to correct them. This process led to a questioning of the common-law emphasis on the father's rights, to a new concern with the child's welfare, and to the recognition that the wife had a legal personality distinct from that of her husband.

These new developments in child-custody policy disclosed an increasingly individualistic conception of domestic relations, but they did not lead to the dismantling of the patriarchal foundation of the southern household. As long as the family remained under one roof, the father still ruled unchallenged in the eyes of the law. As a South Carolina jurist put it in 1858, a "divided empire in the government of a family . . . is not consistent with the welfare of the wife and children, and has not the sanction of law."[63]

BLOOD TIES, APPRENTICESHIP, AND THE POOR

Custody battles between fathers and mothers did not compel the southern legal system to question its commitment to blood ties as the bedrock of the parent-child relationship. Instead, these sorts of custody contests required jurists to choose between two biological parents. Although such decisions made up the majority of custody cases that reached the appellate level in the nineteenth-century South, disputes that pitted parents against challenges from outside the home for the control of children constituted a significant proportion as well. Such legal struggles frequently occurred when a parent voluntarily transferred custody to a third party, and then tried to recover possession of the child.

The firm belief of the antebellum southern judiciary in the importance of the biological bond between parent and child led it almost always to side with the parent in contests with nonparents. Even the introduction of the best interests of the child standard in the South during the 1840s and 1850s did not immediately undermine the ability of mothers and fathers to gain custody of their young. Judges before the Civil War assumed that a child would be best cared for by the parent unless that parent proved utterly unfit.

Under the regime of English common law, the ties of blood and parental authority had appeared unassailable. Parents enjoyed nearly indisputable rights to the custody of their children in contests with nonparents. So highly valued was the integrity of the biological family that English law would only sanction the voluntary transfer of custody rights in the case of the appointment of a testamentary guardian or the contract of indenture. The development of the parens patriae doctrine in the eighteenth century did lead to a softening of this view as custodial power shifted slowly from a property right to a trust, and the courts extended their protection to children. English chancery courts, in particular, which had assumed jurisdiction over the welfare and property of infants in the previous century, manifested a greater willingness to intervene on the child's behalf in disputes involving third parties.[64]

In the colonial South, the law largely retained the traditional English stress on the custody rights of biological parents, especially fathers. As in England, the informal transfer of custody was discouraged, and the courts carefully regulated the transfer of custody rights that occurred with the formal appointments of guardians and indentures of apprenticeship.[65] The major exception in the South to the legal protection of parental custody prerogatives involved black parents in bondage, who received no legal sanction whatsoever for their rights to the custody and control of their children. This lack of protection persisted until emancipation, for under slavery masters could separate slave parents and their children at will.[66] For the parents of white and free black children, the main invasion of custody rights during the colonial era took place when the courts exercised their power to bind out poor and illegitimate children. Fathers and mothers in these instances had little say in the placement of their young, and magistrates sometimes apprenticed children over the objections of their parents.[67]

The expansion of the court's authority to employ judicial discretion in deciding child-custody contests not only led to a reassessment of paternal and maternal rights but also slowly reshaped the distribution of power between biological parents and those who came to stand in loco parentis. As American courts during the early nineteenth century entered increasingly into disputes between parents and third parties, new questions regarding the settlement of these controversies emerged. Most important, the struggle between a parent and nonparent for the custody of a child raised the issue of whether the parental claim to custody should always prevail. How might the evolving best interests of the child standard apply to contests involving parties outside the nuclear family? Should the courts assume that a biological parent would most adequately fulfill his or her child's needs unless proved unfit to have custody? How should the jurists treat agreements that involved a voluntary transfer of parental authority? Were these agreements void and hence revocable, or should the courts recognize and enforce them? Were there any instances in which the courts should step in and terminate parental custody rights because of neglectful or abusive treatment of children?[68]

In the process of resolving these issues, early-nineteenth-century American judges established new rights for surrogate parents, in many cases leading to the termination of the biological parents' custody rights.[69] A close examination of developments at the regional level, however, reveals that southern justices before the Civil War were notably more reluctant than their northern counterparts to grant new prerogatives to surrogate parents. Northern courts in the early Republic showed a growing willingness in disputes between parents and nonparents to evaluate parental fitness, and to make the claims of parents more dependent on their capacity as child rearers than on any absolute legal right grounded in blood ties. Consequently, conflict soon surfaced between the rights of biological parents and the child-welfare doctrine, and northern jurists often exercised their discretionary authority to strip parents of their children.

One of the most dramatic examples in the North of this use of judicial authority to challenge parental custody rights occurred in a case that reached the New York Supreme Court in 1816. Following the death of his wife, John Waldron attempted to regain custody of his daughter, who had been living with her maternal grandparents since birth. In denying the father possession of his daughter, Chief Justice Smith Thompson pronounced that "little doubt can be entertained that it will be more for the benefit of the child to remain with her grandparents than to be put under the care and custody of her father."[70] Numerous other cases confirmed the deepening belief of northern judges before the Civil War that they had the authority to overturn the custody claims of biological parents.[71] Members of the northern bench also exhibited an unprecedented sensitivity to the new family ties created when parents informally transferred the custody of a child. Although the rights of biological parents to custody remained superior in the North, jurists there demonstrated a widespread willingness to balance these prerogatives against the benefits of the new family ties.[72]

In contrast, courts in the Old South retained their traditional commitment to the custody rights of "natural parents" and to the maintenance of biological families. Before 1865, in fact, the southern appellate judiciary refused almost as a whole to support nonparental claims to the custody of a child in contests with parents. The justices granted custody to a third person only three times during this period, and two of these cases involved apprenticeship disputes over illegitimate African American children.[73] In backing the custody claims of biological parents, southern high courts employed the evolving best interests of the child standard in nearly every appellate case involving custody battles with nonparents. The weight of responsibility fell on the nonparent to demonstrate that the parent could not properly care for his or her child. In such cases, southern judges consistently maintained that the ties of blood between parent and child were the best guarantee of correct child rearing.

The antebellum commitment to the preservation of biological families was especially evident in those cases that pitted fathers against third parties for the possession of a child. In 1843, for example, Thomas Kershaw appealed to the Louisiana Supreme Court after a probate judge had denied him custody of his daughter on the grounds of "notorious bad conduct." Following his wife's death, Kershaw had become administrator of her estate, and he boarded his child with another family. Kershaw apparently had a serious drinking problem, and witnesses also claimed that he had engaged in sexual relations with a female slave belonging to his daughter. Despite this testimony, Justice Rice Garland insisted on the father's right to custody. Garland asserted that the "case must be a very strong one, that will justify the removal of a parent from the tutorship of a child, for notorious bad conduct." In this instance, he contended, Kershaw's behavior was "not so notoriously bad and immoral, or his heart so callous, as to be insensible to those parental affections, which induce a father to watch over the morals and welfare of his child." Thus the high court restored control of the girl to her father.[74]

Like the Louisiana high court, appellate jurists in Georgia made it clear that fathers could not be easily displaced in disputes with third persons. The Georgia Supreme Court expressed the prevailing judicial sentiment toward paternal custody claims in 1836: "The law of nature, the feelings which God has implanted both in the man and the brute, alike demand, that he who is the author of its being—who is bound to its maintenance and protection, and answerable to God for the manner in which it is reared, should have its custody, and the law of man which is founded upon reason, is not hostile to the assertion of this claim." The court recognized that it had the responsibility to place the child with the person "by whom its interests and health would be best promoted," but it had little doubt that this person should be the father, unless he was of "bad morals, of unsound mind, or of pecuniary inability to maintain his child."[75] In short, during the early nineteenth century, most southern jurists believed that the father had both a natural and legal right to custody of his child, and this right should remain undisturbed except in cases of pronounced unfitness.[76]

While judicial emphasis on fatherly care over that of a third person reinforced traditional paternal custody rights, the enlargement of married women's rights and the expanding faith in maternal child care in the new Republic provided mothers with a strong legal position in controversies with nonparents. Mothers, however, could only assert their custody rights after divorce, separation, or the death of the father. In the event of a father's death, the common law required the appointment of a new guardian, for it considered children without fathers to be orphans. Even when the mother was named guardian of the children after her husband's death, her rights were restricted in a number of ways. Most important, as noted earlier, common-law tradition called for the termination of a widow's guardianship rights upon remarriage. The underlying assumption of this rule was that the new husband would so dominate a woman who remarried that she might not fulfill her duties to her children.[77]

During the mid-nineteenth century, however, judges in the North and

South increasingly supported the guardianship rights of widows who married again. This shift went hand in hand with a deepening judicial conviction that the custody rights of women should be augmented because of their supposedly innate capacity for childrearing.[78] The Virginia Court of Appeals made this connection explicit in an 1852 opinion that supported the rights of a recently remarried woman in a legal contest with her former father-in-law. The court declared that, even though the mother had married again, "the facts and circumstances disclose nothing which should induce the court, in the exercise of its discretion, to deprive her of the custody." Indeed, the court observed, the child had a "natural right to the care and nurture of her mother," and "the interest of the child will probably be promoted by the custody being restored to her."[79]

In endorsing maternal custody claims in third-party disputes, jurists began to draw on the tender years doctrine. As the Alabama Supreme Court explained in 1860, children of "tender years . . . stand in need of that ever watchful care which none but a mother is likely to bestow, and for which it is next to impossible to find a substitute." Pursuing this same line of reasoning, Justice Edward Turner of Mississippi decreed in 1842 that the court would not "tear these tender female children, aged nine and ten years, from the care and custody of a fond, devoted, and capable *mother*, and place them under the care of a *bachelor uncle*," although the uncle had been appointed guardian by the father's will.[80]

Given their vigorous backing of biological family ties, antebellum southern courts not surprisingly frowned upon informal parental transfers of custody, and in large part refused to recognize and enforce any contract to relinquish custody. The judiciary agreed that a father could consent to his child living in another household; he could, however, withdraw this consent at will and retrieve his offspring. As Texas chief justice John Hemphill pointed out in 1855, the father "has very ample authority in the control, management, rearing and education of his children" and, as a result, he could place them for years under the superintendence of others. "But this is very different," noted Hemphill, "from an absolute transfer of his right of guardianship, and all control over the person and estate of the minor." In the words of the chief justice, such an absolute transfer of custody was "obnoxious to and void under the law."[81] Mothers, too, could not permanently relinquish custody of their young. As Justice James H. Bell of the Texas court stated in *Cook v. Bybee* (1859), "The guardianship which the law devolves upon the mother, in respect to the person and estate of her minor child is a right, which she may assert"; however, it was also "a trust which the law does not permit her to assign or transfer to another."[82]

The hesitancy on the part of southern jurists before 1860 to sanction informal parental transfers of custody contrasted noticeably with the prevailing attitudes of northern judges during this period, revealing the deeper commitment of antebellum southern law to a notion of parenthood based on blood ties. An opinion that the New York State Supreme Court issued in 1856 underscored the difference in outlooks. In this decision, the court pronounced that the parents had lost custody of their nine-year-old son to the boy's aunt and uncle. Although ordinarily a deed or will was necessary to transfer custody, Justice Roosevelt in this instance upheld a verbal agreement between the parents and relatives made eleven weeks after the disputed child was born. Despite the lack of a written contract, the New York judge claimed that the uncle and aunt were "entitled to a parent's rights" as far as custody of the boy was concerned. "Do not nine years of undisturbed possession on the one part, and of uninterrupted acquiescence on the other, constitute as good evidence of the understanding of the parties as any written instrument?" asked Roosevelt.[83]

Parents in the Old South, like parents elsewhere in antebellum America, did have one important means to transfer custody rights and obligations to another person: they could formally bind their child as an apprentice. Indentures involved the exchange of vocational education and child maintenance for a number of years of personal service. Such contracts created a legal relationship in which apprentices were considered dependent children and masters stood in loco parentis. But, unlike biological parent-child relationships, signed agreements rather than blood ties formed the basis of apprenticeships.[84]

Although the apprenticeship system in the colonial South involved all social strata, the practice of voluntarily binding children was most common among the lower classes. Parents too poor to educate all of their children in school often apprenticed them to learn a trade. Southern parents frequently placed their offspring in families to whom they had kinship ties; in such an apprenticeship, where the master was a relative, parents expected him to provide the child with a disciplined upbringing. Whether related to the child or not, masters assumed the role of surrogate parent.[85]

The family-oriented character of voluntary apprenticeship persisted in the South following the American Revolution, at least for white children. State statutes contained stipulations requiring masters to act like parents, and these laws spelled out the duties of masters, including the provision of adequate food, clothing, and lodging. The laws also called on masters to equip their apprentices with an education in such fundamentals as reading and writing, as well as religious instruction. To guard against abuse, statutes demanded that indentures be written rather than oral agreements between the master and parent. If a master did not fulfill his obligations, the county courts had the power to remove the child, and bind him or her to someone else.[86]

Southern appellate courts, at the same time, placed certain restrictions on the ability of parents to apprentice their children. Justice Dabney Carr of the Virginia Supreme Court, for example, held in the 1833 case of *Pierce v. Massenburg* that a father could not bind his son without the signed consent of the boy, although Carr admitted that no such statutory provision existed. Implicit in this decision was the belief that the rights of children restrained the paternal prerogative to indenture minors. Actions like this revealed the widening influence of the best interests of the child doctrine, an influence that undercut the older conception of parental rights as proprietary.[87]

The impact of the child-welfare doctrine also manifested itself in the way that antebellum southern courts confronted the complex question of the master's right to assign his apprentice to another person. Eighteenth-century statutes had sanctioned the practice, as long as the parent or guardian approved the transfer.[88] But judges in the first half of the nineteenth century increasingly refused to countenance such transfers. In the words of a Tennessee jurist, they began to view the indenture as "a personal trust and confidence reposed in and peculiar to" the original master; therefore it could not be transferred to others.[89] The Louisiana Supreme Court pointed out the perilous consequences for indentured children that flowed from the older practice: if an indenture could be assigned to another master without the consent of the apprentice, the court warned in 1833, then the apprentice would "have no higher protection against a transfer to a bad master, than a slave."[90]

Southern appellate jurists before 1860 thus demonstrated an growing sensitivity to the welfare of the child in formal transfers of parental custody through indentures. The Arkansas Supreme Court, in an 1860 apprenticeship case, put it this way: "The State has an interest in its children; that they may not be removed from the care and influence of parental affection, except upon conditions that shall ensure their suitable education, and shall commit them to persons proper to take the places of parents." Although the court believed that voluntary apprenticeship in "some useful art, trade or employment" could benefit the child, it took a new paternalistic interest in regulating the process.[91]

Certain groups of children could be taken away from their homes involuntarily. Colonial poor laws that gave local authorities the power to care for poor, orphaned, and neglected children continued in the South after the American Revolution. Antebellum county courts possessed a broad jurisdiction, in particular, to bind out poor orphans, and legislation in several states extended this authority to include all indigent children.[92] Statutes in some states also granted judges and other local officials the power to apprentice illegitimate children and the offspring of prisoners. All in all, this legislation gave county authorities a significant degree of discretion to interfere in the family life of less fortunate members of the community.[93]

Apprenticeship during the antebellum era took on an increasingly co-ercive character, especially for free blacks and mulattos. Several southern states specifically abolished any educational stipulation for free black ap-prentices, underscoring the extent to which the apprenticeship system had become an instrument of racial control rather than vocational training for this group. A majority of state legislatures in the Old South, further-more, passed laws that placed the children of free blacks under the control of white masters for security reasons, regardless of their parents' finan-cial position.[94] Illegitimate mulatto and black children found themselves especially susceptible to involuntary apprenticeship. Of the youngsters in-dentured by local courts in three North Carolina counties between 1850 and 1860, for example, 61 percent were black and mulatto children. Even when a free black woman clearly had the ability to support her offspring, she ran the danger of losing custody through the apprenticeship system. As the North Carolina Supreme Court proclaimed in 1855, the county courts had the "power to bind out *all* free base-born children of color, without reference to the occupation or condition of the mother." The primary aim of these laws, Judge Thomas Ruffin of the North Carolina high court re-marked four years later, was to subject free black and mulatto children "to the supervision of a strict police, so as to restrain their propensity to be idle and mischievous." [95]

Black parents challenged the power of the courts to take their offspring from them and attempted to maintain some degree of authority over their indentured children. These parents, often mothers, appeared in court to protest poor treatment, illegal indentures, and other abuses. In an effort to resist the apprenticeship of black children to whites, free blacks who were not parents of the children at issue had the youngsters bound to themselves. Despite such attempts, the southern courts largely succeeded in imposing the apprenticeship system on those who occupied the lowest rungs of southern society. Gradually, as James Ely Jr. notes, apprentice-ship for blacks during the years before the Civil War "was transformed into just another system of forced labor." [96]

Although antebellum southern courts demonstrated little reluctance to apprentice the offspring of indigent and free black parents, they showed an aversion to removing children from parental authority in white, eco-nomically self-sufficient families, even in cases where there appeared to be physical abuse. A commitment to the privacy of the family in these instances outweighed whatever concern there was for the children. When antebellum lower courts did attempt to terminate parental custody rights on the basis of neglect or abuse, they met vigorous resistance from appel-late jurists, who preferred to give parents a wide latitude in the treatment of their children. A Tennessee court, for example, overturned a lower-court ruling that ordered the removal of a girl from parents who had been convicted of beating and whipping her. Maintaining that whether the parents used excessive punishment was a question of fact for the jury to decide rather than a question of law, Justice William Turley declared, "The right of parents to chastise their refractory and disobedient children is so necessary to the government of families, to the good order of society, that no moralist or lawgiver has ever thought of interfering with its exis-tence, or of calling upon them to account for the manner of its exercise, upon light or frivolous pretences." In an 1838 case, the North Carolina Supreme Court demonstrated an even greater reluctance to interfere in the exercise of family discipline, deciding that child cruelty consisted of only those acts that "endangered life, limbs, health, or caused disfigurement or permanent injury."[97] Such a hands-off approach on the part of the courts is not surprising, given the crucial role that corporal punishment played in slave society. From this perspective, the reluctance to intervene in house-holds in which child abuse took place was one important way in which slavery shaped family life.

The judiciary contended, in general, that for white children from non-indigent families blood ties were the best assurance that their needs would be met, and the courts used the child-welfare doctrine to preserve these ties. An underlying assumption of this approach, however, was that the child's needs should indeed be taken into account in resolving disputes over the transfer of custody. This new assumption reflected a crucial change in the notion of parenthood from a property right to a personal trust. The custody claims of parents, antebellum jurists began to stress, should rest on their appropriateness as child rearers rather than on any inherent legal prerogative. As Justice Robert Charlton of Georgia insisted, "All legal rights, even those of personal security and liberty may be for-feited by improper conduct, and so this legal right of the father to the possession of his child, must be subservient to the best interests or safety of the child, and to the duty of the State to protect its citizens of whatever age."[98] These alterations in southern legal attitudes toward parenthood slowly led beyond a simple judicial faith in the superiority of biological bonds to the development of external standards of parental evaluation similar to those evolving in the North. Once southern jurists set out on this path, it was only a matter of time before they would apply such standards to remove children from their parents.

Before 1860, however, the persistence of a social system in which patriarchal authority and kinship provided the key sources of order and stability hindered the growth of state intervention in parent-child relationships and led southern courts to protect the rights of biological parents, as long as they were not slaves. Antebellum whites demonstrated an especially intense preoccupation with bloodline. As Bertram Wyatt-Brown has commented, white southerners believed that blood "was not an abstract concept but a determination that could so type a child that a sense of unworthiness could well develop. Like horses, human beings were supposed to exhibit traits of lineage." In large part, of course, this emphasis on family lineage stemmed from the racial character of slavery in the South, which generated an obsession among whites with preserving the purity of the family's blood. Another key aspect of the antebellum value system was the notion of honor, with its understanding of individual identity as rooted in one's standing in the ordered ranks of the community, an understanding that placed great weight on the role of traditions within the family and the connections between the generations.[99] Little wonder, then, that southern jurists during these years refused to stray far from a biological conception of the parent-child bond, and that they shied away from direct state interference with this bond.

THE EVOLUTION OF ADOPTION LAW

The appearance of the first general adoption statutes in the United States during the late antebellum era signaled the advent of a new domestic order: one in which legal relations between parents and children were increasingly viewed as contractual in nature and subject to state mediation. The endorsement of adoption marked the greater willingness of lawmakers and judges to recognize the legitimacy of "contractual families"; that is, families in which the tie between child and child rearer stemmed from a legal agreement rather than from birth.

Adoption provided a vehicle for the termination of blood bonds created by birth and the substitution of a new legal relation between a child and surrogate parent. Other methods of transferring child custody maintained a legal connection between the biological parent and child. But adoption resulted in the complete and permanent severance of this connection. In other words, adoption shifted the affiliation of a child and constructed a new parent-child bond.[100]

Adoption existed among the ancient Greeks and Romans, who relied on it to prevent the extinction of a family line. Adoption in ancient history also provided a means to preserve rites of family religious worship and to build alliances among clans or tribes. Civil-law adoption had its origins in the Roman practice, which served to meet the needs of the adopting patriarch more than the child.[101] It was the legal recognition of the child as an individual with distinctive needs that set nineteenth-century adoption procedures in the United States apart from these other forms of adoption.

Although adoption had long been practiced in civil-law countries, it never made significant headway in English common law. The English unwillingness to authorize adoption grew mainly out of the common law's preoccupation with the property rights of blood relatives, which made it difficult to accept the notion that nonrelatives had inheritance rights to a family succession. Furthermore, the existence of child placement alternatives such as guardianship, apprenticeship, and almshouses largely solved the problem of what to do with dependent children.[102]

The lack of a common-law tradition in England regarding adoption meant that there was little precedent for adoption procedures in colonial America. As in England, guardianship, "putting out," and almshouses played a major part in the colonial child-placement process. But there is also evidence that informal arrangements tantamount to adoption existed in the American colonies, North and South. Colonial wills sometimes gave children placed under these arrangements full family status and inheritance rights in the new family, and probate courts often accepted the distribution of property specified by these wills.[103]

Moreover, while Louisiana and Texas were under Spanish law, adoption practice existed in both states. Spanish and French jurisprudence were largely modeled on Roman civil law, and adoption was a well-established institution in those countries. Despite this civil-law heritage, legislators in Texas and Louisiana restricted adoption as soon as they had the opportunity to write their own codes. In fact, Louisiana's first code of 1808 specifically abolished the practice.[104] Such actions in states that had a civil-law background underscored the hostility toward adoption in early-nineteenth-century America.

Notwithstanding such obstacles to adoption, a legislative device existed in the new Republic that enabled individual adults to adopt children. As in divorce, private acts authorizing a particular adoption could be employed, and such acts were approved by many state legislatures. Most of this private legislation, which was expensive and time-consuming, simply involved name changes, but some of it actually gave the child complete legal rights in the new family.[105] Thus, although the civil code of 1808 abolished adoption in Louisiana, it was still possible to adopt a child thereafter in the state if a special legislative act authorizing that particular adoption was secured.[106]

Private adoption acts in the antebellum South received their most significant judicial backing in the Louisiana case of *Vidal v. Commagère* (1858). Pierre Jean Baptiste Vidal and his wife, Félicité Blanche Power, had obtained the passage of a bill in 1837 that enabled them to adopt a seven-year-old orphan named Adele, provided that they executed the adoption act before a notary public within six months after the passage of the bill. The couple had been rearing the child for six years, so the notarized adoption simply ratified their relations. It declared that the Vidals considered Adele a full legal member of the family: "She shall enjoy the same rights, advantages and prerogatives, as if she had been the issue of the marriage of the parties to the act and their legitimate child."

When Adele's adoptive mother died intestate some years later, several of the mother's nieces and nephews brought a suit to determine who was entitled to her property. The nieces and nephews argued that they should inherit as collateral heirs, and that Adele as an adopted child had no right to claim anything from the estate. Chief Justice E. T. Merrick dismissed the argument advanced by the mother's relatives. He insisted that the private act should be construed broadly, taking into account the civil law of adoption and the common use of the word. A narrow interpretation, contended Merrick, made little sense because "it cannot be presumed that a formal execution of the sovereign power was made for a trivial purpose." To accept the argument of the nieces and nephews would give the act only "slight significance," and this the chief justice refused to do. Instead, he concluded that the Vidals had intended to give Adele "the rights of a legitimate child." The court therefore awarded possession of the mother's entire estate to her adopted daughter.[107]

This appellate opinion widely influenced the interpretation of private adoption acts not only in states that had a civil-law heritage, but also in common-law jurisdictions.[108] Other legal challenges to private adoption acts in the Old South, however, underscored the precariousness of adoption under these special procedures.[109] Furthermore, sometimes a southern court endorsed a private adoption act but restricted the rights of the adoptive parents. This was especially true when the rights of adopters came into conflict with those of biological parents. An 1861 decision by the Louisiana Supreme Court revealed the reluctance of some southern jurists, even in adoption cases, to allow surrogate parents to displace completely the child's birth parents. The court held that a widow permitted by a private act to adopt a girl could not appoint a testamentary tutor (the term in Louisiana law for guardian) while the biological father was still alive. Although the father had given his consent to the adoption of his daughter, Justice A. Duffel maintained that the right of appointing a tutor by will for the girl still belonged to the father. In Duffel's words, "It can not be said that the act of the Legislature authorising the adoption in this case, took away, or diminished, in expressed terms or by implication, any of the paternal prerogatives conferred by the Civil Code." Indeed, the court concluded that the widow's death reinstated the father in all his rights. It thus rejected the application of the tutor named by the widow's will, and turned over control of the girl to her biological father.[110]

It can be seen, then, that the southern judiciary accepted the legitimacy of private adoption, but the rights assumed under this special procedure remained insecure. Many judges in the Old South plainly found it difficult to break away from their commitment to the primacy of blood ties. The strength of this commitment often expressed itself in a judicial emphasis on proceduralism or a narrow interpretation of the adoptive parents' rights in disputes involving private adoption acts.

General adoption acts first appeared in the United States during the 1840s and 1850s. Students of adoption law have commonly divided these statutes into two broad categories, based on the extent to which the acts granted judges the power to monitor the adoption process. The first group of statutes made no explicit provision for judicial supervision of the adoption arrangement or for the consideration of the child's welfare. These acts, instead, simply provided a way to make private adoption agreements part of the public record without involving the legislature in each and every adoption. The primary impetus for this type of legislation, which resembled the traditional civil law of adoption, stemmed from the desire to relieve the legislatures of routine action on private bills.

Southern statutes that fell into the first category were those passed in Mississippi (1846), Texas (1850), Tennessee (1851–52), Alabama (1852), and Louisiana (1865).[111] The Alabama act, for example, stipulated that any person who wanted to adopt a child merely had to submit a written declaration to the county probate court, including the name, sex, and age of the child, as well as the name that the adopter wished the child to carry thereafter. The probate judge had no authority to inquire about the child's welfare; the adopter had only to acknowledge his declaration before the judge, who then filed and recorded the written arrangement. The effect of the adoption, in the words of the statute, was "to make such child capable of inheriting such estate of the declarant, and of changing its name to the one stated in the declaration." The Mississippi adoption procedure, outlined in the act of 1846, was even more loosely constructed.[112]

Texas legislators in 1850 established a somewhat more elaborate adoption procedure that placed certain restrictions on the rights of the parties involved. If the adopter had any children "begotten in lawful wedlock," for instance, under the statute the adopted child could not inherit more than one-fourth of the adoptive parent's estate.[113] Aside from the imposition of these sorts of constraints, however, the antebellum adoption statutes were relatively crude and simple, largely because they were designed to streamline a cumbersome procedure and ease the burden of state legislators. In no case was the welfare of the child a central concern of this legislation.

In contrast, a more child-centered approach to adoption emerged in Massachusetts in 1851. The first truly comprehensive adoption statute in the United States, this act provided for judicial supervision over adoptions. It declared that the courts must be satisfied that the new parents had "sufficient ability to bring up the child, and furnish suitable nurture and education, having reference to the degree and condition of its parents, and that it is fit and proper that such adoption should take effect." The Massachusetts law also required the written consent of the child's birth parents, the agreement of the child if he or she was fourteen years of age or older, and a joint petition by the adoptive mother and father. The statute made it clear that adoption involved the complete legal severance of the relationship between the child and biological parents; the adopted child became "to all intents and and purposes" the legal child of the petitioners.[114]

The Massachusetts adoption act of 1851 became the model for many of the other state adoption laws passed during the last half of the nineteenth century. Although several other northern states passed child-centered adoption acts before the Civil War,[115] in the South only Georgia and Mississippi followed the path carved out by Massachusetts. The Georgia statute, passed during the legislative session of 1855–56, charged the courts with making certain that adoption was "to the interest of the child." It also provided for the written consent of the biological father, or of the mother if the father was dead or had abandoned his family. Another Georgia act, passed in 1859, pronounced that upon judicial approval of the adoption the relation between the new parent and adopted child was, "as to their legal rights and liabilities, the same as if the relation of parent and child existed between them," with the important exception that the adoptive father could not inherit from the child.[116]

The Mississippi legislature in 1857 also followed the Massachusetts model, in this instance replacing its adoption act of 1846 with a more child-oriented law. The new statute instructed the courts to assure themselves that "the interest and welfare of such infant will be promoted by such adoption." In addition, it required the consent of the biological parents, and of the child if he or she was over fourteen years of age.[117] These new adoption statutes represented the culmination of several developments in custody and guardianship law. The emphasis on the welfare of the child, the exercise of judicial discretion, the voluntary transfer of parental rights, and the agreement of older children were all included in the new laws. Hence the development of child-centered custody rules provided the framework for the creation of contractual families through legal adoption.

The passage of comprehensive adoption laws in the South lagged behind the rest of the United States before the Civil War in part because of the persistent commitment to the importance of blood ties and because slavery fostered a rural environment in which traditional child-placement techniques such as apprenticeship continued to function fairly well. In the North, however, the decline of apprenticeship, the outcry against the abuses of almshouses, and the expanding rights of surrogate parents generated support for the development of a formal system of child transfer. The greater propensity of northern judges to back the legal recognition of children as individuals was also a significant factor in the wider acceptance of child-oriented adoption laws in the region before the Civil War. It led to the construction of custody standards that stressed the importance of proper nurture rather than blood bonds, and to the recognition that biological ties did not always guarantee children stable, supportive homes.[118]

Despite resistance to judicially supervised adoption in the South, it began to emerge on the eve of war as a new domestic alternative. The first southern test of the general adoption statutes came in the 1858 case of *Rives v. Sneed*, in which the Georgia Supreme Court upheld an adoption against the claims of a guardian. Under the act of 1855–56, Dudley Sneed had adopted John Needham Massey, who was about seven years old, but Robert Rives, challenging the validity of the adoption, claimed that he had been appointed guardian of the boy in 1855. Rives contended that Sneed had obtained the adoption "without the knowledge, consent or approbation" of the boy's guardian, and thus the court should declare it void. Justice Charles J. McDonald, in his decision, pointed out that because the child's parents were dead there was no need to notify anyone of the adoption. McDonald maintained that the court order granting the adoption established a relationship between the adoptive parent and boy that was "the same as if he had been the natural legitimate child of the said Dudley Sneed." Accordingly, the court found that Sneed had a right to the custody of his adopted son, even if Rives was the child's legal guardian.[119]

Although the judges in this case took an important first step toward embracing a contractual conception of parent-child relations in the law, their support for adoption was qualified by the fact that the boy's parents were dead. Slavery and the dependent, patriarchal relations that it fostered among family members hindered the development in the South of a more sweeping judicial endorsement of adoption and the individualistic model of the household that lay behind this innovative domestic arrangement. The collapse of slavery and the expansion of market relations following the Civil War, however, removed an important barrier to change, producing tremendous consequences for the household and the legal system that increasingly intervened in it.

PART TWO

AFTER THE FLOOD

On that day all the fountains of the great deep

burst forth, and the windows of the heavens

were opened.

Genesis 7:11

THE TRANSFORMATION OF
SOUTHERN LEGAL CULTURE,
1860–1880

On September 3, 1864, Private Spotswood Rice, laid up with chronic rheumatism in a St. Louis hospital but itching to get back into action, wrote his children. A former slave from Missouri who had been in the Union army only a few months, Rice had discovered that his daughter's mistress prevented Mary from visiting him; even more infuriating, Mary's owner accused the father of trying to "steal" the child. Rice's anger boiled over in the letter to his offspring as he sought to assure them that he would gain control of "his own flesh and blood." The Union soldier announced to the girls that he would participate in a military operation moving through the area in several weeks and that, if the mistress didn't "give you up this Government will and I feel confident that I will get you." "You tell her from me," Rice commanded his daughters, "that She is the frist Christian that I ever hard say that aman could Steal his own child especially out of human bondage."

The former slave dispatched another letter directly to "Miss Kaitty" that same day. "Now I want you to understand that mary is my Child and she is a God given rite of my own and you may hold on to hear as long as you can," he apprised the owner of his daughter, "but I want you to remember this one thing that the longor you keep my Child from me the longor you will have to burn in hell and the qwicer youll get their." Making clear his understanding of parental rights under the new order brought about by emancipation, Rice added emphatically, "My children is my own and I expect to get them and when I get ready to come after mary I will have bout a pwrer and autherity to bring hear away and to exacute vengencens on them that holds my Child." [1]

THE "DOMESTIC INSTITUTION" IMPERILED

It is easy to imagine the astonishment of Kitty Diggs as she cast her eyes down the page of Spotswood Rice's letter. But just as important to consider are the remarkable developments that put Rice in a position to send it. We will never know how many other African American soldiers wrote letters to their masters, mistresses, and children after escaping slavery and joining the Union army. Even if most of the intended recipients of these letters never received them, the act of composing this correspondence was what counted most. It demonstrated in a remarkably concrete fashion the extent of the revolution that took place in the southern household during the Civil War, a revolution that began as soon as the first slaves started leaving the farms and plantations of the South and headed for Union lines.[2]

Southern masters grasped this crucial point as they watched slaves escaping during the war. Reverend Charles Colcock Jones, reporting on the large numbers of African Americans who began to flee the plantations along the Georgia coast in July 1862, asked, "Could their overt rebellion in the way of casting off the authority of their masters be made by construction insurrection?" There was little doubt as to the answer, in the judgment of Jones: "They declare themselves enemies and at war with owners by going over to the enemy who is seeking both our lives and property. They are traitors of the worst kind, and spies also, who may pilot the enemy into your bedchamber." Responding to his father's letter a few days later, Charles C. Jones Jr. concurred. "No mercy should be shown where the party has once obsconded and afterwards returns to induce others to accompany him in his act of desertion to the enemy," he exclaimed. "If allowed to desert, our entire social system will be upset if the supremacy of the law of servitude and the ownership of such property be not vigorously asserted in cases where recaptures occur."[3]

Despite the determination of southern slaveholders to stem the flood of runaway slaves, African Americans seized destiny in their own hands, and out of it shaped an understanding of what it meant to be free. For many blacks, more than anything else, freedom meant the right to create and nurture their families without the everpresent threat of white interference and control. Freedom also made possible the reunion of families that had been torn apart by slavery, although the search for loved ones was not always successful. African American youngsters, in particular, viewed the coming of freedom in terms of its impact on their family life. As Charlie Barbour, a former slave who was fourteen years old when the Civil War ended, recalled, "I wuz glad ter git free, cas I knows den dat I won't wake up some mornin' ter fin' dat my mammy or some ob de rest of my family am done sold."[4]

The breakup and reconstitution of the southern household was one of the key developments of the Civil War and Reconstruction. When we look at perhaps the two most momentous events in the political life of our nation from this perspective, it becomes clear that the ideological debates, military battles, and economic upheavals that mark this period flowed in large part from the contradictions and tensions that by 1860 churned the waters of the southern household. With the election of a Republican president that year, a domestic crisis in the broadest sense of the term had developed, one that compelled masters, husbands, and fathers to press for secession in order to rescue what they saw as the very essence of their reason for being: the traditional patriarchal order that not only gave them authority over all dependents—women, children, and slaves—but also made possible their own freedom and autonomy in society at large.

During the late antebellum period, changes in laws regarding slavery, divorce, married women's property rights, child custody, and adoption revealed the contradictions beginning to surface in the southern domestic order. Bending to the dictates of a market-oriented world view, southern legal change before the Civil War led to measurable improvements in the position of white women and children, and even slaves, within households. State intervention in domestic affairs, however, remained narrowly circumscribed despite these changes.

The major exception to the antistatist posture of elites in the slave South was in the realm of interracial marriage and sex, where authorities showed little hesitancy in erecting the legal prohibitions necessary both to buttress the racial divisions upon which slavery rested and to control the sexual behavior of white women. The major aim of this intervention was to support the authority of patriarchy as a system rather than to back the power of individual patriarchs. In other areas of the law regulating sexual relations, antebellum legislators and judges departed from the old ways with great reluctance, and they continued to uphold the right of planters and yeomen to patrol the domestic sphere, including slavery, with as little interference as possible from outside authorities.

The persistence of the household as the social unit of production in the Old South was the fundamental factor that sustained the traditional system of domestic governance. In the antebellum North, urbanization, capitalism, and economic development did much to undermine the patriarchal ideal, but until the 1850s the South contained such forces only in weak forms. Although individualism and market relations penetrated the southern household before the Civil War, coming into conflict with the organic model, the ideological commitment to the traditional model still prevailed. As one southern writer declared in 1855, northern reformers "divide the household into separate interests; the domestic hearth is no longer a common property to the family." In contrast, "a very different idea of government prevails" in "the slaveholding States." The hierarchical character of "the relations of parent and child, of husband and wife, of master and slave, and the right to property . . . all go to make up the great corner-stone of the social edifice—the family." This organic arrangement of "institutions and rights" stemmed from "the laws of nature, from God alone," and existed "independent of, and prior to, all government." The overriding duty of government, the writer concluded, was "to preserve these institutions in all their incidents, and all their derivative rights."[5]

A better example of the close connections between domestic governance and political order in the minds of white southerners would be difficult to find. In this essay, entitled "The South and the Union," the author contended that the conservative character of the South had been a major factor in the preservation of the Union. As long as the South remained in the Union, he asserted, southern influence would restrain the hands of northern reformers and agitators whose actions threatened the very foundation of the republic.[6] A few years later, however, increasing numbers of white southerners, planters and yeomen alike, began to wonder whether staying in the Union placed the patriarchal household at too much risk by continuing to expose it to northern influence. Indeed, planters and yeomen joined together to support secession in large part out of a perceived sense that only by making a strike for independence could they protect household patriarchy from the corrosive forces that threatened it.

These forces, it should be stressed, were not simply the product of a fevered southern imagination. Especially during the 1850s a sense of uncertainty about the future gathered momentum in the black belt areas of the South as wealth in land and slaves became increasingly concentrated, slave prices rose beyond the reach of many aspiring planters, and railroad construction integrated ever greater areas of the cotton South into a market economy over which individuals exercised little control.[7] All of these economic forces combined to foster a profound sense of anxiety among planters and yeomen about their ability to preserve a system of domestic governance becoming more and more whipsawed by the contradictions of maintaining a slaveholding society within an international capitalist market.

More was at stake than the defense of slavery, in short, when white southerners seceded from the Union. Slavery did not stand on its own; it had become, as LeeAnn Whites notes, "an organic part of the southern household" and "organic to the slaveowners' very conception of themselves as men and as women, as mothers and as fathers."[8] The rise of individualism and contractual social relations in the North, which southern traditionalists saw symbolized in such reforms as the expansion of married women's property rights and the liberalization of divorce, as well as abolitionism, endangered the entire "domestic institution" as southerners understood it: not simply racial bondage, but a network of households grounded in dependency and inequality.

Indeed, abolitionism struck such a fearful chord in the South because of its insistence on the oppressive nature of patriarchal power in the slaveholding household. Harriet Beecher Stowe, as much as any northern abolitionist, fixed on this line of attack in her antislavery writings, especially the 1852 novel *Uncle Tom's Cabin*. Her biting critique of slavery's deeply personal consequences for the family, both black and white, grew out of a developing ideology of domesticity that viewed the mother as the moral guardian of the home, the very same perspective that led southern judges in this period to begin endorsing the tender years doctrine in child-custody cases. Stowe deployed this ideology in her novel to focus on what she saw as slavery's greatest evil: the separation of mother and child. Thus, when asked why she escaped to freedom across the treacherous ice floes of the Ohio River, Eliza explains that her child "was my comfort and pride, day and night; and, ma'am, they were going to take him away from me,—to *sell* him,—sell him down south, ma'am, to go all alone,—a baby that had never been away from his mother in his life!"[9]

Stowe, in her "Appeal to the Women of the Free States," issued two years after the publication of *Uncle Tom's Cabin*, dealt even more explicitly with the domestic dimension of slavery. "I do not think there is a mother among us all," she observed, "who clasps her child to her breast, who could ever be made to feel it right that the child should be a slave; not a mother among us all who would not rather lay that child in its grave." Stowe asserted that the threat of slavery to the relationship between the mother and child was inherent in the institution, and the danger could not be eliminated by even the most paternalistic master. In her words, "It is not the abuse of slavery, but the legal nature of it."[10]

Here Stowe had driven to the heart of the matter: slavery, as both a system of social and legal relations, violated the sacred principles of the domestic order emerging in the North, an order that emphasized the individualism and autonomy of family members. It was in the name of nurturing such values, in fact, that northern culture paid homage to motherhood during these years. That a significant proportion of educated whites in the South shared a similar sense of almost religious fervor about the superior morality and innate capacity of women for rearing children was apparent in the very criticisms leveled at Stowe. In writing *Uncle Tom's Cabin*, the *Southern Literary Messenger* charged, Stowe had stepped into the public arena of males and had passed irretrievably "beyond the hallowed precincts—the enchanted circle—which encompass her with a halo of divinity." [11]

This attack on Stowe was telling because the ideology of domesticity that it employed had the potential to undercut the legitimacy of southern patriarchy; Stowe herself had used this constellation of values and beliefs to assail slavery. The separate-spheres doctrine, furthermore, had been wielded in southern courtrooms to challenge the custody rights of fathers and to grant limited recognition to mothers as legal personalities. To those southern whites who reflected on it, this observation must have been troubling, indeed. The only conclusion one could draw was that northern beliefs and values had begun to burrow within the southern sensibility to the point that the tensions between a patriarchal and individualistic understanding of domestic governance were beginning to shape the public discourse of the South.

Besides the abolitionist attack on slavery, southern conservatives viewed divorce reform as a major threat to the concept of the "undivided empire" that undergirded the traditional household order in the South. According to the *Southern Quarterly Review* in 1854, the administration of the new laws permitting divorce "has been attended with great laxity, and a severe blow has been given, in consequence, to the public morals." "The indissolubility of the marriage tie, the permanence of the family bond, the domestic order that the sentiment of its indissoluble character created, are fast leaving us," the journal chided its readers.[12] Linking the liberalization of divorce with the expansion of married women's property rights, southern traditionalists saw these developments as an indication that northern influence must be curbed. "The danger to the South *in the Union* from the force of Northern example in these and other particulars, is imminent and cannot be exaggerated," warned *De Bow's Review* in 1857. "Already, the South, with the honorable exception of South Carolina, have adopted to a fearful extent, Northern ideas on the subjects of divorce and the independency of married women, through separate estates and exclusive revenues." In an earlier time, *De Bow's Review* cautioned, similar enactments had undermined Roman virtue, leading to the loss of civil liberty, the onset of civil war and anarchy, and eventually the fall of a great republic.[13]

The historical parallel was obvious. Unless the traditional domestic dominion could be sustained, the holy trinity of southern manhood—what Stephanie McCurry has referred to as "manliness, masterhood, and republican citizenship"—was imperiled. A full-blown theory of constitutionalism had developed in the antebellum South to protect this distinctive conception of liberty. According to this theory, most powerfully espoused by John Calhoun, the states had acted as sovereigns in adopting the federal Constitution; in doing so, they had retained control over all their own "domestic institutions," and delegated only certain specific powers to the federal government. Now, with the election of Abraham Lincoln and the Republican Party to the White House, it appeared as if the federal government would no longer refrain from interfering with the internal affairs of southerners, including the structure and governance of their households. Faced with mounting political tensions within the South, as well as an organic patriarchy under assault by the market forces of individualism and the partisan forces of antislavery Republicanism, southern conservatives insisted finally that secession was the only alternative.[14]

THE RESORT TO PUBLIC AUTHORITY

Ironically, the southern effort to defend the patriarchal household, as well as the slave system that formed its underpinning, set in motion historical forces that hastened the demise of the old domestic and political order. As Thomas Settle, associate justice of the North Carolina Supreme Court, observed in 1868, "All of the movements of the secessionists & nullifiers have not only failed but have really accomplished exactly the reverse of what they intended."[15] In the political realm, the Confederacy may have begun as an experiment in states' rights, but the exigencies of wartime compelled the South to build a highly centralized state. In raising an army, controlling its citizens, and managing its economy, the Confederate government carried out an unprecedented expansion of state intervention, disrupting southern households and generating widespread discontent among those still committed to a decentralized vision of republicanism and suspicious of state authority. The conscription of white men for the military, the impressment of slaves for labor on fortifications, the establishment of a tax-in-kind, and the outright confiscation of food and supplies, to say nothing of the drastic restrictions imposed on citizens' rights—all of these actions by the Davis administration violated revered southern principles of liberty and local government.[16] Although the Confederate Congress never enacted a bill to establish a Supreme Court, and ultimate judicial authority remained in the state courts, the judiciary backed most of the Davis administration efforts to centralize its political power. As a result, Confederate authority expanded into all aspects of southern life, surpassing comparable measures carried out by the Union.[17]

Even at the state and local levels, government enlarged its powers significantly during the war. Poverty and food shortages provided the main impetus for the resort to interventionism. The Georgia state government regulated crop production during the war to assure a sufficient food supply, and the state legislature passed several extraordinary welfare measures in response to civilian needs. In North Carolina, the economic suffering of citizens by 1862 reached such proportions that county officials implemented elaborate new mechanisms to meet their basic dietary needs. The crisis overwhelmed traditional public and private aid efforts, leading to a sharp break with past notions about government involvement in the economy. In Virginia, the shortage of food in towns and cities became so serious by 1864 that Governor William Smith asked the state legislature to appropriate funds to buy and transport food to the needy communities. When the legislature refused, Smith dipped into his contingency funds, took out a personal loan, and managed to come up with $110,000 to hire a fleet of blockade runners and begin trading for supplies. Blockade running soon became too dangerous, but the resourceful governor confiscated a railroad train in the name of the state to facilitate his purchase of food supplies inland. His operation became so successful that he was able, in his words, "to make occasional loans to the Confederate Government."[18]

As food became increasingly scarce, riots erupted throughout the urban South, disclosing conflicts and resentments that had remained below the surface before the firing on Fort Sumter. Women, who experienced the hunger of their children and families most directly, led many of these food riots, the best-known of which was the uprising in the Confederate capital of Richmond on April 2, 1863. Similar protests occurred in small towns such as Salisbury, North Carolina, where a highly disciplined group of between forty and fifty soldiers' wives demanded that local merchants lower the prices for flour, as well as other essential commodities such as molasses and salt. When merchants failed to cooperate, the women seized the food supplies and divided them up among themselves.[19]

The southern countryside did not escape the ravages of poverty anymore than the towns and cities, and property crimes became rampant as the war went on. The Superior Court in rural Whitfield, Georgia, which had prosecuted few cases of theft before the war, handled more than a hundred indictments for this crime between 1861 and 1865. The dramatic increase in crimes against property was not simply confined to male offenders. Although between 1850 and 1860 grand juries in three North Carolina counties handed down only eight indictments against women for larceny, they issued eighty-eight such indictments between 1861 and 1871. As the conflict between North and South ground on after 1863, women in the upcountry demonstrated a pronounced level of disorderliness, not only rioting at grain mills but also encouraging men to desert the army and return to their families.[20]

Like many of his fellow planters, Thomas Watson in 1863 worried "that the lower classes . . . are engaged in robing [sic] and stealing every thing that comes in their way, and that people of property suffer more from these wretches than from the Yankees." Especially in the isolated mountains, where class tensions became intertwined with Unionism, guerrilla forces challenged Confederate rule. During the last months of the war, social disorder and violence spread as outlaw bands consisting of conscripts and deserters from the Confederate army terrorized the rural South. According to Nimrod Porter in 1864, the approach adopted by the local bandits in his Tennessee community involved "attacking [a] house in the dead of the night gitting the doore open & punishing the inmates by partially hanging & choking them until they tell where there moneys & valuables are."[21]

In territory controlled by the Federal army, many county courts closed as magistrates and clerks abandoned their duties, sometimes fleeing with their records. When General Benjamin F. Butler and his Union troops occupied New Orleans in May 1862, they discovered that the court system and much of city government had collapsed in the panic that preceded the city's fall. Butler immediately established a system of military courts to handle criminal and civil cases until civilian government could be at least partially restored. By late 1863, with General Nathan P. Banks now in charge of New Orleans, both the regular civil and criminal courts had been reopened. In highly contested areas of the South, local government returned when Confederate control resumed and then shut down again upon the recapture of the area by Union forces. Even where Federal authorities stepped in and tried to restore the operation of county courts, they encountered almost insurmountable difficulties. Uncollected tax revenues, missing records, damaged courthouses, and lawyers and litigants going off to fight in the army all hindered the smooth running of local government during the war.[22]

In the immediate aftermath of military defeat and emancipation, legal and institutional disarray prevailed throughout the South. The restoration of order was the key not only to economic revitalization, but also social and political progress. Union officers established martial law on a temporary basis at the end of the war, overseeing the administration of justice and monitoring the transition to civilian rule. County governments and courts struggled to get back on their feet so they could resume the overwhelming job of governing communities devastated economically and physically by the war.

During this period, the most serious threats to social order stemmed

—from the disbanding of the Confederate army, which released a wave of hungry veterans who usually faced a long march to get back to their families and farms. Not surprisingly, these men frequently resorted to thievery as they straggled homeward. With the upsurge in property crimes and violence, as well as disturbing signs of restlessness on the rise among poor whites, besieged southern property owners felt that they had little choice but to turn to the occupying forces for assistance, a reality that generated mixed emotions among the recently vanquished whites.[23] As John W. Brown, an Arkansas attorney and planter, noted in his diary on June 9, 1865, "We have at length a Federal Garrison. This secures us from Jayhawking, but makes us feel more keenly our degradation as a conquered people."[24]

The most challenging task facing the South after the war involved working out a new set of arrangements between the races to replace slavery. Emancipation led to an overhaul of the southern racial system and to a search for new controls over blacks. The state increasingly took over responsibility for the maintenance of social order. With the disintegration of slavery, planters largely abandoned the paternalistic ethos to which most of them had adhered to one degree or another before 1865. "All feeling must be discarded," a former master in Virginia remarked shortly after Appomattox. "Our own interests, although it result in [the freed slaves'] total ruin and annihilation, must alone dictate the course for us to pursue." Hence freedmen may have escaped the capricious power of the master, but they also relinquished the protection of the paternalist.

At first white southerners insisted that only legally sanctioned efforts to enforce racial subordination could preserve order and compel blacks to remain productive members of the work force. Planters sought, in particular, to have former slaves sign written contracts that tied them to the land for a full year. Such contracts underscored the transformation in the social relations of the South. Mary Jones, a mistress on a Georgia plantation who took great pride in her treatment of slaves before the war, recounted that "I had considered [the slaves] friends and treated them as such," but now "they were only laborers under contract, and only the law would rule between us, and I would require every one of them to come up to the mark in their duty on the plantation."[25]

Freedmen's Bureau agents generally approved this system of labor contracts, which the Union army and the bureau had developed during the war, because their main concern was to stabilize agricultural production and get former slaves back to work in the fields. Although former slaves were free to choose their employers, they were not free to refuse to labor.[26] As John William De Forest, a Union officer with the Freedmen's Bureau in South Carolina, wrote in his wartime novel *Miss Ravenel's Conversion from Secession to Loyalty* (1867), "We must civilize and Christianize [the freed slaves]. And we must begin this by teaching them the great elementary duty of man in life—that of working for his own subsistence." Bureau officials thus developed a system of compulsory contract in order to implement free labor in the postwar South, disclosing in the process the coercive side of the marketplace.[27]

By the fall of 1865 southern legislatures began to enact detailed codes regulating labor in their states. The Black Codes made violation of the labor contracts a serious criminal offense and they called for the arrest of those who refused to sign these contracts, punishing such individuals as vagrants. Although bureau officials were highly critical of the Black Codes, few took any sustained action to set the harsh and restrictive laws aside. Only a storm of protest among northern Republicans outraged by this racial legislation forced the repeal of the most flagrant provisions. Nevertheless, laws punishing vagrancy and breach of contract that made no explicit reference to race remained on the books.[28]

Southern courts responsible for enforcing these labor regulations and the criminal laws made little effort to maintain even an appearance of impartial justice, and local officials demonstrated a notable reluctance to prosecute whites accused of crimes against African Americans. Clearly, the judicial system during Presidential Reconstruction was much more interested in imposing disciplinary measures on blacks and pressuring them into the agricultural labor force than in upholding justice. "The idea of negroes getting justice before the magistrates of this county is perfectly absurd," a Freedmen's Bureau agent in Giles, Tennessee, charged in 1866. "They will hear the testimony of the blacks but will give it no weight unless it happens to suit their purposes."[29]

Governor Jonathan Worth of North Carolina worried that "the administration of justice to the prejudice of freedmen & those who claim to have been Union men during the late war" was so blatant that it might lead the Federal government to reimpose military rule in the state. In an 1866 letter to Superior Court Judge David Alexander Barnes, Worth urged him to make every effort to see that "justice is impartially administered in reference to negroes and all others." In particular, the governor suggested, the judge should make a special effort in his charges to grand juries to "dwell prominently on the importance of every justice of the peace and every citizen taking care that negroes recieve [*sic*] all the protection to which the law entitles them."[30]

The main aim of the police apparatus and courts in the postwar South, despite Worth's exhortations to the contrary, was to facilitate the state's assumption of control over blacks from their former masters. Sentencing African Americans to long prison terms, forcing them to work on chain gangs, and binding them out to employers who would pay their fines all represented different facets of the newly expanded role of the state in disciplining the African American labor force. The growth of the convict lease system, in particular, symbolized the new order of criminal justice in the postwar South, one which enforced white supremacy, provided employers with a cheap source of labor, and generated new public revenues.[31]

The controversy over the Black Codes led in large part to the undoing of Presidential Reconstruction and the onset of Radical Reconstruction in the southern states. During the period of Republican domination, the public life of the South underwent profound alteration and the state dramatically expanded its sphere of responsibility. James L. Alcorn, Republican governor of Mississippi, pointed out in his inaugural address that slavery had imposed sharp limitations on the range of public authority because it created a society of "patriarchal groupings," in which African Americans were subject to the governance of their masters rather than coming "under the cognizance of the government."

The state under Radical Reconstruction differentiated itself from the antebellum state not only in its scope but also in the interests it sought to serve. Especially in the areas of race and labor relations, the state took the initiative to break with the past and carve out a new path for the South, if only temporarily. The Radical constitutions were among the clearest expression of the new state of affairs, granting African Americans educational and voting rights previously denied them. Republican legislators, furthermore, enacted laws calling for equal access to transportation and public accommodations, repealed the remaining provisions of the Black Codes, reformed the harsh penal codes of Presidential Reconstruction, prohibited corporal punishment, and significantly decreased the number of capital offenses.[32]

Republicans also moved to take over the local and state courts, as well as other aspects of the machinery of justice. During the 1870s and early 1880s, for example, Republicans dominated the district court of Washington County, Texas. Furthermore, nearly one-fourth of the deputies in the sheriff's office were freedmen, and African Americans played a prominent role on the county's juries. Planters could no longer count on the state to serve unquestioningly as an instrument of labor and racial control. Although Radical Reconstruction was short lived and did not attain its goals, it underscored the extent to which the elimination of slavery demanded a new relationship between the state and society.[33]

The most far-reaching changes brought about by Republicans in the

South involved the granting of civil and political rights to blacks. Here Radical Reconstruction moved into virtually uncharted territory. Republicans evinced a deep faith in what Edward Ayers has termed "impersonal legalism," a faith that found its most vivid expression in the Freedmen's Bureau. The bureau acted as a temporary welfare agency, overseeing the transition from slavery to freedom, providing food, shelter, and clothing to the poor, and helping to establish schools for African Americans. Beyond offering this much-needed assistance, the bureau mediated relations between former masters and former slaves, bringing the power of the state to bear upon both parties in an effort to enforce northern notions regarding the rule of law. These notions, abstract and process-oriented, stood in stark contrast to the southern reliance on patriarchal authority and personal honor during the antebellum era.

In an effort to protect the legal rights of African Americans, the Freedmen's Bureau established courts in the South between 1865 and 1868 to deal with minor civil and criminal cases involving former slaves. The bureau interceded in disagreements between freed slaves and planters regarding labor contracts, but could provide only limited protection against crime and violence against African Americans. Appealing in desperation to General Davis Tillison, commander of the Freedmen's Bureau in Georgia, Abram Colby and three other freedmen pleaded, "We know from what we have seen that we have no chance of justice before the courts. We ask of you, sir, some right to defend ourselves and make those who contract with us stick to the contract. Our former masters are determined to oppress us." Even when the federal agency intervened in such labor disputes, African Americans had little success in achieving fair contractual arrangements. The bureaucratic legalism of the bureau made little headway against the commitment in the South to white supremacy, a fact made all too clear by the growing strength of the Ku Klux Klan in the late 1860s and 1870s. The rapid increase in the activities of this terrorist organization, including its infamous night rides, underscored the extent to which the social and political revolution imposed from the outside by emancipation and Radical Reconstruction lacked legitimacy in the eyes of most southern whites.[34]

Bitterness and hostility so infected politics in the South during these years that even members of the state supreme courts got swept up in the controversy. Richmond M. Pearson, chief justice of the North Carolina Supreme Court during the Civil War and Reconstruction, took the unusual step in 1868 of urging voters in his state to support Ulysses S. Grant, the Republican candidate, for president. More than a hundred Democratic members of the state's bar issued a protest against judicial interference in party politics, but a fellow Republican and colleague on the high court, Justice Settle, wrote to Pearson, expressing his approval of the endorsement in no uncertain terms. "I really believe that we are on the verge of another rebellion & it will require determination and boldness to crush it," Settle contended. "The election of Grant is a national necessity. The life of the government depends upon it." Settle made it clear to the chief justice that he had little patience with those who would employ "fraud & violence" to influence the outcome of the election. "It will not do to dilly dally and discuss questions of delicacy and propriety when we are dealing with desperadoes," the associate justice wrote Pearson. "We must be vigilant and if it is ascertained that fraud and violence are about to accomplish their purposes, we must do just enough and whatever is necessary to preserve the government, even if it should be extra constitutional." Such comments, coming from those sworn to uphold the constitution, were a mark of how politically polarized southerners were during Radical Reconstruction. In the fervent struggle over the South's future, white conservatives and Republicans alike engaged in measures that betrayed a lack of respect for constitutional values.[35]

The participation of African Americans in the political process of the South served as a lightning rod for much of the white hostility. Albion Tourgée, a carpetbagger who became a Republican judge in North Carolina, captured the anger that Radicals inspired among opponents to Reconstruction in his novel *A Fool's Errand* (1879): "After having forced a proud people to yield what they had for more than two centuries considered a right,—the right to hold the African race in bondage,—they proceeded to outrage a feeling as deep and fervent as the zeal of Islam or the exclusiveness of Hindoo caste, by giving to the ignorant, unskilled, and dependent race—a race who could not have lived a week without the support or charity of the dominant one—equality of political right!" Such convictions made it impossible for blacks to engage in even the most limited forms of political involvement in their communities without encountering intense hostility.[36]

The right of blacks to sit on juries served as a special source of grievance to southern whites at the local level. North Carolina attorney David Schenck noted in his diary the placement of two African American men on a Catawba Superior Court jury in August 1867. According to Schenck, this was the "First negro Jury" that he had encountered, and he pronounced the panel "the most inferior in intelligence I ever saw in N.C." "Thus has commenced negro political equality," the conservative Democrat declared. "God has permitted what seems to us a great evil." A. W. Dozier, who had left South Carolina for California, wrote to one of his kin who practiced law in South Carolina, putting the matter even more crudely: "How can you say '*Gentlemen* of the Jury' to a panel of loathsome, leather-headed negroes?"[37]

White antagonism to blacks serving on juries reached such a fevered pitch that Republican judges in the South sometimes had to ask for military protection so that the legal proceedings could go forward. Tourgée, after charging a grand jury made up of six blacks and twelve whites, wrote fellow Republican Thomas Settle in June 1869, noting that "things are in a bad situation." Indeed, Tourgée believed that it might be necessary for Governor William Holden to send help "at a minute's warning" in order to allow the jury to conduct its business free of interference. "Our friends here are the worst frightened you ever saw," Tourgée remarked.[38]

Republican policies regarding race relations and the labor system were not the only targets of wrath among conservative whites in the South. Greatly expanded programs in public schooling, including education for blacks, and aid for railroads, among other new initiatives, led to unprecedented increases in taxes, generating widespread antagonism among the white majority and undermining the political legitimacy of the Republican state governments. With the triumph of the Redeemers, the state once again took on the role of enforcing labor discipline and bolstering white supremacy, while at the same time adopting more parsimonious taxing and spending policies.[39] Nevertheless, a fundamental change had taken place in the legal culture of the South: public authority rather than the private household had become the key source of social order and stability.

DOMESTIC RECONSTRUCTION

During the Civil War and after, several profound changes in southern society disrupted the structure of household authority on the plantation and farm. First, the Civil War had a dramatic if temporary impact on the responsibilities and activities of white women. Not only did these women assist the war effort by carrying out such activities as sewing uniforms and making bandages, they managed farms, plantations, and businesses while husbands were away at war. Southern ladies, who had lived their lives within strictly patrolled gender spheres, now found themselves challenged to take on tasks for which they had little preparation. Slave management, in particular, proved to be an especially crucial responsibility for Confederate women on the homefront. While some women remained perplexed about how to handle the slave labor force effectively, others gradually assumed greater authority on the plantation and achieved a new sense of confidence that brought about significant shifts in the internal dynamics of their marriages.[40]

The legend of female sacrifice became a key part of Confederate wartime propaganda and eventually was incorporated into the mythology of the Lost Cause. George Fitzhugh wrote in August 1861 that the conduct of southern women showed "clearly enough that they fully understood and appreciated the consequences of war, and were prepared to meet them, without fear or trembling, and to give their money, sacrifice their luxuries and elegancies, and devote their labor to the support of our army."[41] As the war dragged on and suffering on the home front mounted, however, Confederate women of all classes increasingly expressed their discontent. "Is anything worth it? This fearful sacrifice—this awful penalty we pay for war?" wondered Mary Chesnut. The growing disenchantment, as well as such overt actions as the Richmond bread riot and other protests against food shortages, undermined the Confederate effort to repulse Union forces from the South. In engaging in such insurgent activity, women challenged the image of deference and frailty so central to the antebellum notion of womanhood.[42]

Besides the changing character of gender dynamics in the Confederacy, wartime casualties had a powerful impact on southern families. Sarah Morgan, writing just days after Appomattox, remembered with sadness the deaths of her two brothers during the war: "Since the boys died I have constantly thought of what pain it would bring to see their comrades return without them—to see families reunited, and know that ours never could be again, save in heaven." Traditional kin ties remained stable in the South, helping to mitigate some of the psychological trauma caused by the upheaval and loss, but the war left its mark on the composition of white families. A low birth rate, together with a high rate of infant and childhood mortality, left many white families without children born during the war years.[43] Moreover, the southern white male population experienced a devastating decline. Roughly 258,000 men were killed during the war out of a total white population of 5.5 million. In Edgefield, South Carolina, out of an enlistment of 2,137 white males, 613 died. Such losses led to a sharp increase in the number of widows with children and a noticeable reduction in the number of marriageable men.

Given these kinds of numbers, however, the long-term consequences for southern society were much less severe than might be expected. In Orange County, North Carolina, most of the soldiers who died were single, and those who were married had few children. Marriage rates skyrocketed in

the aftermath of the war, and by 1880 males too young to serve in the
army had also married, restoring the traditional sex ratio of young adults
in the county. By the end of the 1880s, the southern population had nearly
returned to prewar levels.[44]

The collapse of the slave system and the uprooting of the economic
order in the South as a result of the war proved to have much more lasting
effects. Slavery in the Old South had encouraged a deep concern with
the concepts of blood, race, and gender, notions that, in turn, fostered a
commitment to an organic social order. Under slavery, capitalist social
relations had been minimized, and the mass of the population had only
limited encounters with the national and world markets. With their defeat in the Civil War and the death of slavery, however, white southerners
advanced steadily toward a more market-oriented notion of social relations. Planters still dominated the countryside, but having undergone the
metamorphosis from masters to landlords, they now had to deal with
a nonslave labor market. Not only did emancipation remove slavery as
the dominant mode of production, it meant the end of bondage as the
organizing principle of southern society.[45]

As the southern countryside underwent this agricultural transformation, the spread of the factory system during the late nineteenth century,
and the accompanying increase in the employment of women and children,
brought about significant changes in family roles, as well as a separation
of home and work previously unknown to this agrarian society. The Civil
War had stepped up the process of industrialization in the South, but the
expansion of railroads after the war provided a more sustained stimulus
for the rise of mills and mines. The first wave of migrants to factories in the
Piedmont during the 1870s and early 1880s consisted largely of widows,
female-headed households, single women, and laborers. By the late 1880s
and 1890s, the credit squeeze in agriculture combined with a collapse of
prices to push an increasing number of families headed by men into the
factories. Traditional values persisted as entire families worked side by
side in the mill, but the sense of autonomy generated among women and
children by earning a wage and the family's dependence on these earnings
undercut the father's ability to act as master of the household.[46]

Confronted with these new challenges to patriarchal authority, southern elites developed new public policies in the late nineteenth century
that reshaped relations not only between former masters and slaves, but
also between husbands and wives, and parents and children. During Reconstruction, the law recognized the validity of slave unions, expanded
the grounds for divorce, and strengthened the property rights of mar-

ried women. The pressure of wartime, defeat, and the collapse of slavery compelled southern governing elites to abandon the household as the primary means of social control, and to turn to the state as the chief vehicle for maintaining social order. The increased resort to state intervention as a mode of social control was not, by any means, confined to the domestic arena. Labor relations and land-tenure arrangements, as well as hunting, fishing, and grazing rights, all became subject to intensified state supervision in the postwar years.[47]

African Americans experienced the most striking change in the relationship between the family and state after the defeat of the Confederacy. With emancipation, former slaves seized the opportunity to reaffirm and consolidate their family ties. The law under slavery had refused to recognize the autonomy of the black family, making it liable to separation at any time and treating it as part of the broader patriarchal household headed by the master. As the *Virginia Law Journal* pointed out in 1877, the slave "could not marry because he was legally incapable to consent, because the relation of husband and wife was inconsistent with that of master and slave, and because the slave had no status as a person before the law." Freedmen and freedwomen, however, now had the opportunity to establish their families on a firm and independent footing. Reunions of separated family members took place throughout the postwar South, and African American couples rushed to legalize their marriage bonds.[48] Most African Americans viewed the ability to solemnize their customary ties as a badge of freedom, a powerful symbol of their newfound status as citizens. In the words of one African American soldier, "The Marriage Covenant is the foundation of all our rights. In slavery we could not have *legalised* marriage: *now* we have it." Thousands of former slaves overwhelmed officials of the Freedmen's Bureau and other authorities with demands to validate both old and new unions. As a Union army chaplain attached to an African American regiment in Arkansas observed, "Weddings, just now, are very popular, and abundant among the Colored People."[49]

Teachers, missionaries, and Freedmen's Bureau agents encouraged African Americans to formalize their marriages, arguing that legal sanction would promote sexual and moral discipline among former slaves. The chaplain of a Louisiana black regiment asserted during the final months of the war that, because of the effort to legalize marriages between freedmen and freedwomen, "a deep and abiding foundation has been laid for a vast change in moral sentiment. . . . A revolution is rapidly going on among them in reference to the sacred nature and binding obligations of marriage." Many of the couples had more prosaic motivations for legalizing their unions, including the desire to legitimize their offspring and to qualify for soldiers' pensions.[50]

To meet the flood of requests, Union army officers, missionaries, local officials, and others carried out mass marriage ceremonies. Following the reorganization of the southern governments, state legislatures enacted validation statutes or constitutional provisions granting formal legitimacy of marriages initiated under bondage. These laws commonly pronounced slave unions legal if the couple continued to live together as husband and wife when they went into effect, although a few states stipulated that slave unions had to be registered. Such requirements, however, did little to stem the tide of marriages among African Americans. In seventeen North Carolina counties, for example, more than nine thousand couples registered their unions in 1866, and in Virginia that same year, four counties registered nearly three thousand marriages between former slaves.[51]

With the new laws, southern courts faced a wave of litigation regarding the status of slave marriages, including inheritance disputes, bigamy prosecutions, and divorces. As Leon Litwack notes, "The question facing numerous freedmen and freedwomen was not whether to formalize their slave marriage but which one should take precedence." Many spouses remarried following forced separation, and with the abolition of slavery and the legalization of slave marriage, they often faced a perplexing and sometimes even agonizing situation as they dealt with their multiple unions.[52]

The courts, seeking to resolve these legal difficulties, enthusiastically supported the acts making slave marriages legal and also drew on American common law to incorporate these unions into the law. The Alabama Supreme Court, in an 1881 dower suit, captured the feelings of the southern judiciary toward the new legislation. Upholding the marriage of a black couple under the Alabama act passed in 1865, the court asserted, "The ordinance commends itself to the moral sense, is eminently just, conservative of the social order promotive of morality, and preservative of the legitimacy and rights of innocent offspring of the preexisting union it ratifies. There is no room to doubt the power of the convention to enact it; and it belongs to the class of legislation which, when employed for such beneficial purposes, deserves the highest judicial consideration."

In general, when dealing with bigamy prosecutions or probate contests, judges held that marital cohabitation following emancipation and the enactment of the validation law made a slave union legally binding. Such cases fostered a strong sense of paternalism among members of the bench. As a Georgia jurist put it in an 1869 bigamy trial involving African Americans, "Under the peculiar circumstances surrounding them, a moralist will not judge them harshly, and it is perhaps a wise policy not to inflict upon them severe penalties for failing as in most instances they did, to comprehend the sacredness of the marital ties."[53]

Besides the legal recognition of slave marriages, the impact of the Civil War and Reconstruction could also be detected in the reform of divorce and married women's property rights. Southern legislatures after the war expanded the grounds for both absolute divorce and legal separation, as well as bolstered the property rights of married women, reflecting the new reliance on the state to mediate domestic relations.[54] Such reforms met with hostility from many conservatives, who saw them as indications of a corrupt society about to plunge into the abyss of anarchy and social disorder. Condemning the increasing availability of divorce, George F. Holmes insisted in 1867 that "if the closest links of family union are recklessly broken, it cannot be hoped that any other social tie will escape rupture." Divorce, according to Holmes, "almost invariably connects itself with, if it does not spring directly from, a festering tendency to social disintegration, and penetrates all parts of the society, vitiating all forms of thought and feeling."[55]

Despite such dire warnings, changes in divorce law after the Civil War tended to strengthen the power of men over women. In North Carolina, for example, the new Conservative legislature in the 1871–72 session built significant gender distinctions into its definition of adultery. While a wife could be divorced solely for the act of adultery, the husband's adultery had to accompany abandonment of his wife to be considered grounds for divorce. The North Carolina high court endorsed the double standard, contending that there was "a difference between adultery committed by a husband and adultery committed by a wife—the difference being in favor of the husband." A husband who overlooked a wife's adultery, Chief Justice Richmond Pearson explained, would be "disgraced," whereas a wife who did so would simply be "pitied."[56]

As with divorce reform, changes in the property rights of married women had little to do with meeting feminist demands for equality. Nine out of ten Radical conventions between 1867 and 1869 created new constitutions that guaranteed property rights to married women. Like the earlier married women's property rights acts, these Reconstruction measures stemmed in part from a paternalistic concern for the victimization of women. A delegate at the South Carolina constitutional convention in 1868 expressed this attitude perfectly: "I appeal to you who have lived here all your lives, and seen women suffer from the hands of fortune hunters; the plausible villains, who, after securing the property of their wives, have squandered it in gambling and drinking; a class of men who are still going about the country boasting that they intend to marry a plantation, and take the woman as an incumbrance."[57]

The constitutional provisions aimed not only at protecting women from fortune hunters, but also sought to provide relief from the extensive indebtedness of the postwar years. The provisions exempted whatever property the wife brought into the union from liability for her husband's debts, thus providing the family with a minimum of economic security in hard times. In this sense, the married women's property rights clauses were part of a larger debtor-relief package that included homestead exemptions, stay laws, and the abolition of imprisonment for debt. Especially in those states where the courts decided that the new married women's property clauses applied to women who were already married, and that these clauses applied to property acquired by the wife before the measure took effect, a substantial form of economic relief had been fashioned.[58]

Although the constitutional provisions did not define the property rights granted women with any precision, in some states they led to important new powers for women. In Georgia, where the common law had held sway prior to the Civil War, the state supreme court proclaimed that the husband's right to appropriate all the wife's property had been completely abrogated. According to the high court, the constitutional provision of 1868 transformed the husband and wife into "two distinct persons, with separate and distinct rights." Speaking before the Georgia Bar Association in 1891, Judge H. A. Matthews asserted that "in all essential respects a married women has the same rights to her property that the husband has as to his, or that the *femme sole* has as to hers." Matthews, however, overlooked that fact that the wife's wages remained the absolute property of the husband; in fact, Georgia women did not gain legal control over their earnings until 1943.[59]

The long-term significance of postwar reforms in divorce and married women's property rights lay in the extent to which they mirrored the breakup of the southern household into its individualistic components. Conservative southerners recognized the profound implications of these changes, and protested bitterly against them. Among the most vocal critics of the new notions about domestic relations was R. L. Dabney, who viewed these ideas as part of the "mighty tide of progress which has already swept away the Constitution, and slavery, and States' rights." Dabney insisted in 1871 that "the integers out of which the State is constituted are not individuals, but families represented in their parental heads."[60] The old domestic order celebrated by Dabney had passed, however, brought to an end by the social and legal transformation of the South during the Civil War and Reconstruction. Even the Redeemers, who over-threw Radical Reconstruction in the 1870s, could not bring the old order back. Instead, the state after Reconstruction focused its energies on re-shaping the old hierarchy of power into a new social order, one in which the patriarchal household was no longer the cornerstone.

THE EVOLUTION OF
CONTRACTUAL FAMILIES

Although individualism was by no means nonexistent in the southern household before the Civil War, slavery and the dependent, patriarchal relations that it encouraged on the plantation and farm had impeded the development of a full-blown contractual conception of parent-child relations in southern law. The expansion of market relations following war and emancipation, however, accelerated the transformation of southern family life and the legal system that increasingly regulated the household. Instead of an organic hierarchy, the contract became the central metaphor for structuring relations between members of the household, and the state assumed a growing responsibility for supervising these relations. Southern legislators and judges, in particular, reevaluated their attitudes toward the parent-child relationship. As a result of this searching reexamination, the law deemphasized the rights of biological parents and began to assess custodial qualifications on the basis of ability to fulfill certain duties.

The concept of contractual families first emerged in the South during the late antebellum period, but it did not gain dominance until after 1865. What was distinctive in the postwar era was the systematic attempt to link women and children directly with the state rather than through the male head of the family. Employing judicial discretion on an expanded scale, the state consolidated its power to determine the special needs of the child and the qualifications of parents to provide for these needs. By the late nineteenth century, courts throughout the South regularly employed their discretionary authority in custody, guardianship, and adoption disputes to advance what they considered to be the best interests of the child, as well as the interests of society at large.

THE RISE OF MATERNAL CUSTODY RIGHTS

Although appellate judges in the Old South awarded custody to fathers more often than mothers, this pattern underwent a significant transformation after the Civil War. The percentage of cases between 1866 and 1900 in which mothers received custody increased to 48 percent, whereas the proportion of fathers granted control dropped to 36 percent. In contrast, from 1800 to 1865 mothers won only 38 percent of the appellate contests between parents, compared to a rate of 42 percent for fathers.[1]

These figures, of course, indicated only the outcome of the cases, not the reasoning behind the judicial decisions. It was the reasoning that changed most dramatically after the war. Antebellum southern jurists had frequently granted custody to mothers, but more often than not they did so on the basis that the father had forfeited his dominant right to control of his offspring as a result of abusive or neglectful behavior. Thus, in E. D. E. N. Southworth's 1863 novel *Ishmael*, the father loses a custody battle because he has mistreated his wife, squandered her property, and ignored the children. Ishmael Worth, the young lawyer who defends the right of the mother to the children, asks the court not only to grant his client custody but also to secure her right to her property and earnings, and to require the father to provide child support. The father, outraged by this attempt to interfere with what he sees as his proprietary rights, exclaims, "The woman is my own wife! The children are my own children! And I have a lawful right to the possession of them."[2] By the end of the nineteenth century, contrary to such traditional paternal claims, most southern appellate courts no longer assumed that the father had a paramount right to his child. Instead, the courts generally concurred that the mother was best fitted to have responsibility for child rearing, and therefore in determining custody they gave her preference.

The most significant of the new judicial rules favoring maternal custody rights was the "tender years doctrine," which held that infants and young minors (especially those with health problems) ought to be placed in the care of the mother unless she proved unworthy of the responsibility.[3] This approach to determining the fate of younger children made a tentative appearance in several early-nineteenth-century cases, and became accepted policy after the mid-nineteenth century. "Nothing could replace a mother's assiduous nature and plastic government," Georgia justice Charles J. Jenkins pronounced, when a child was of "tender age."[4]

The tender years doctrine proceeded directly from the Victorian assumption that women were morally superior to men. As George Fitzhugh put it in 1861, "That woman is better than man, no true and brave and generous man will deny. She is of more delicate and refined fibre, more sensitive, more alive to impressions from without, more sympathetic, more benevolent; better, therefore, by nature." Southern ministers and moralists who celebrated the virtues of domestic life viewed women as almost incapable of sinning. On the other hand, evangelicals railed against the perceived tendency of men to indulge themselves in the world of temptation outside the home. In contrast to the self-restraint and humility of women, a Baptist preacher in Louisiana noted in his diary, "Man is verily an animal—sleeps like a hog—eats like an ox—and far too much forgets the source of all temporal and spiritual good." [5]

The belief in the moral superiority of women led to the conviction that mothers were more aptly suited for child rearing than men. Indeed, the Victorian South stigmatized mothers who did not pursue this responsibility as their primary interest, treating them as deviant. When Edna Pontellier, in Kate Chopin's novel *The Awakening* (1899), turns to painting as a way to explore her newfound sense of autonomy, she immediately suffers the consequences of trying to throw off the conventions of her society. Her husband, a New Orleans broker, angrily accuses her of neglecting the children and charges that she is letting "the family go to the devil." Bewildered by her behavior, he wonders "if his wife were not growing a little unbalanced mentally." [6]

Such attitudes toward women's autonomy represented the underside of the tender years doctrine. Nonetheless, mothers who took advantage of the doctrine in the courtroom made dramatic headway in the achievement of custody rights, and by the end of the century women had attained supremacy in legal struggles over the control of young children. Especially when the young children were female, southern judges were predisposed to place them with the mother. The Alabama Supreme Court revealed this predilection in 1876 when it refused to grant a divorce to the mother of a four-year-old girl but decided to give the separated wife custody of her daughter. "All must feel," the Alabama justices declared, "that no greater calamity can befall an infant daughter, than a deprivation of a mother's care, vigilance, precept, and example." [7]

Although women made some important advances as a result of the tender years doctrine, a mother might retain custody of her children for only a few years before the father regained possession. An earlier Alabama decision, for instance, ordered that the boy in dispute should remain with the mother "until he has reached an age when he can dispense with those tender offices which only a mother can bestow"; at that point, the court indicated, it might place the child with the father. The judges in this case declined to say at what age a youngster could be separated from the mother without undergoing serious psychological damage, but a year later members of the Alabama bench ruled in another case that the father could be awarded custody once his offspring had been weaned. In 1872, the Virginia Supreme Court removed a four-year-old girl from the possession of her mother and placed her in the father's custody. The court explained: "The tender nursing period has passed by, and the time for moral training and impressions has arrived." [8]

Southern jurists believed that whereas the mother was well suited for child nurture, the father was best fitted for imparting worldly knowledge to the children. Such an outlook occasionally led the judiciary to split custody of the children, giving the older minors to the father and the younger ones to the mother. In an 1898 contest involving two children, for example, Chief Justice Henry G. Bunn of Arkansas decided that the "elder of the boys, now nine years old, has probably arrived at that age when a father's peculiar character of oversight and control may begin to be more necessary than the mother's." On the other hand, the five year old was still "in need of a mother's care and control,—that care and control which a father is ill suited by nature to exercise." Revealing the increased role that the state played in monitoring the parent-child relationship, Chief Justice Bunn warned that the custody order was "temporary . . . and subject at all times to be revoked or modified, to the end that the care and control of the child may be under the strict supervision of the court." [9]

Splitting up the children, of course, ignored the possibility that it might be in the best interests of the child to maintain ties with his or her siblings. Southern courts paid little attention to this aspect of family dynamics in their custody determinations. Thus the recognition that the tender years doctrine gave to both the child's welfare and the mother's custody rights was seriously limited.

Besides taking into account the age of the youngster, southern judges in the late nineteenth century began to consult the wishes of the child when he or she was old enough to exercise a "reasonable discretion." The common law dictated that the age of discretion was generally about fourteen years old. The courts, however, frequently relaxed the rule to take into account the opinions of children who were younger but still capable of exercising a choice.[10] The expressed preferences of the youngster sometimes had a major influence on the outcome of the case. In an 1894 case, the North Carolina Supreme Court overthrew the order of a lower court that awarded custody of a nine-year-old boy to the mother. The jurists noted that the lower court had failed to inquire into the preferences of the child, "though this has weight always with a court in such cases according to the age and intelligence of the child." After determining that the boy did not want to live with his mother, the appellate justices granted custody to the father.[11]

The Florida Supreme Court in 1887 also adopted the infant discretion rule, on this particular occasion to uphold the decision of a circuit court that gave control of two teen-aged daughters to their father. Chief Justice Augustus E. Maxwell observed that the girls preferred to stay with the father, despite his "habitual indulgence of violent and ungovernable temper," and they voiced strong opposition to being placed in the mother's possession. Consequently, Maxwell deemed that it would be better to leave the children where they were, under paternal supervision.[12]

The infant discretion guideline could work in the mother's favor as well. B. W. Haymond, for example, instituted a suit in Texas against his wife for divorce and custody of their three children. According to Haymond, his wife had joined "a band of religious fanatics," made up mainly of women who "relate to each other the divine revelations communicated to them, which they interpret to suit their own views and then blindly follow in their business and domestic relations." The husband claimed that the membership of his wife, Ada Haymond, in the religious group had "poisoned the atmosphere of his once happy home, blighted his life, alienated his wife's affections, estranged his children, and made desolate all that was once happy and comfortable." A lower court awarded B. W. Haymond a divorce on the grounds of abandonment, and gave him custody of the children, but the wife appealed.

Justice John L. Henry of the Texas Supreme Court contended in his 1889 decision that the husband "wholly failed" to prove that Ada Haymond had abandoned him, and the appellate judge overturned the divorce. Henry pointed out that two of the children—both girls, one aged eight and the other twelve—had testified that they wanted to live with the mother rather than the father. In considering the fate of the daughters, the Texas jurist insisted that "we are not able now to see that those children should have been forced away from the mother." Hence he sent the case back to the lower court for a new trial, and in the meantime, gave the mother custody of the girls.[13]

Like the development of the tender years doctrine, the growing acceptance of the infant discretion rule in the late nineteenth century disclosed the evolution of an increasingly child-centered theory of guardianship among southern jurists. But the court did not always adhere to the child's wishes in settling custody struggles between parents. Particularly when the child did not want to return to the father, judges in the South tended to downplay the preference of the minor. The Texas Court of Civil Appeals, in fact, argued in *Jordan v. Jordan* (1893) that the natural right of a father to the custody of his offspring could not be changed at will by a child, even when he or she reached the age of discretion. In this case, despite the desire of a fourteen-year-old boy to remain with his mother, the Texas court restored control of him to the father, apparently perceiving the child's exercise of discretion in this instance as constituting too much of a threat to patriarchal power and family discipline.[14]

Besides the tender years and infant discretion precepts, postwar southern courts widely followed the practice—first introduced during the antebellum years—of awarding child custody to the parent not at fault for the divorce or separation. In Georgia and Louisiana, this judicial guideline even found its way into the late-nineteenth-century statute books, and judges in these states were instructed by law to place children under the control of the party that obtained the divorce or separation, unless he or she demonstrated a pronounced lack of fitness.[15] The use of parental fault in custody awards usually operated to the benefit of mothers, because they filed the overwhelming majority of divorce and separation suits. The paternalistic sensibilities of the judges in these cases generally led them to view the women as victims of irresponsible and abusive husbands. The jurists thus readily offered mothers the aid of the court in gaining custody of the children. As a member of the Alabama Supreme Court explained, "The law, equally with nature, clothes the husband with the highest and most ample authority to protect the wife. . . . But when the husband's love no longer exists, then the wife's protection becomes uncertain. When this uncertainty grows so great that the wife is evidently imperiled and made unhappy to such a degree as to effect her health, and interfere with the discharge of her duties as mother, then the courts will interpose for her protection."[16]

In their assessments of which parent should gain custody in divorce and separation cases, southern justices drew upon Victorian images of proper gender roles. Describing the women to whom they granted custody, the courts stressed characteristics such as domesticity, amiability, submissiveness, and purity of heart—all female traits much admired by men in the South. Extolling the virtues of the southern lady in 1894, Elton Eliot declared that she was "essentially refined, and even under the most aggravating of circumstances, the sweet perfume of refinement and politeness clings to her still. . . . There is something repulsive to her very nature in coarseness and vulgarity, and to be unladylike is something more than a fault in her eyes—it is a sin."[17]

In contrast, husbands denied custody in these cases were invariably "much given to obscene, rude and profane language, and inclined to drunkenness." A violent temper, lack of affection, and tyrannical exercise of authority were other common failings of men who were denied custody.[18] By taking these men to task in the courtroom, southern judges sought to lay down standards of proper behavior, challenging traditional male privileges and behaviors. This effort to redefine masculinity along more self-restrained, genteel lines during the late nineteenth century went hand in hand with the evangelical campaign to curb drinking, swearing, fighting, and carousing. Courts and churches joined together to temper male conduct and promote the values of self-control, domestic harmony, and sobriety.[19]

Underlying the judicial employment of the parental fault rule was the assumption that misconduct in one domestic relation presaged misconduct in another. President James Keith of the Virginia Supreme Court reasoned in *Owens v. Owens* (1898) that "as one who has done well or ill in the marriage relation will be likely to do the same in the parental all courts lean to the innocent parent when determining the custody of the child."[20] In this case, the mother was the innocent party and therefore received possession of the offspring. But the logic of parental fault meant that the doctrine could also be used against mothers who failed to conduct themselves properly in the eyes of the jurists.

As in the early nineteenth century, southern jurists after the Civil War displayed strong opposition to awarding custody to mothers who committed adultery. The Tennessee Supreme Court reversed the decision of a lower court that granted divorce and child custody to Laura Evans when the appellate judges found "abundant evidence" that she had been adulterous. "We are free to confess that we do not thoroughly apprehend the ground and reasoning upon which the learned chancellor reached his conclusions in the case," declared the state court, adding that the mother was unfit to have custody of her two sons, aged six and nine, because of her extramarital sexual activity.[21]

Desertion also proved to be a costly offense for southern mothers attempting to gain possession of their children. The Virginia Supreme Court in 1872 refused to grant Ascenith Ann Carr custody of her young daughter because she had broken "the sacred bond of marriage." In leaving her husband, the court observed, Carr had put herself in the socially and economically uncertain position of being a wife without a husband. Now "we are asked to compel the father and deserted husband to allow his innocent and unoffending daughter to share with the mother this undefined, ambiguous position, this burden of disgrace, during the critical period of moral training and education, when the mother has neither a home to which to take her (except at sufferance) nor means whereby to maintain her." This should not be done, asserted the Virginia judiciary, and it placed the girl in the custody of her father.[22]

Southern courts were not always unanimous in their feeling that wives who abandoned their husbands should automatically forfeit any custody rights. Six years later, faced with another case in which a wife left her husband, the Virginia high court found itself divided over who should receive control of the two-year-old son. Justice Waller R. Staples noted that both parties in the custody controversy, C. Fannie Latham and her husband Robert E. Latham, held prominent social positions; the wife was a "lady of many personal attractions, and of the highest culture and refinement," and the husband was a "man of excellent character, of amiable temper, and of unimpeached integrity." The couple separated in 1877 primarily because "they differed a good deal with respect to the management, control and training of the child." As a result of their differences, the wife decided not to have any more children, and "in that temper she had denied him access to her bed." Staples listened to the mother's request for custody with little sympathy. In his judgment, she was "to blame for the evils that have overtaken her, and she cannot ask, with any hope of success, for the aid of the courts so long as she persists in her present views and purposes." Under the circumstances, the Virginia judge felt that the father was entitled to control of the boy.[23]

Justice Francis T. Anderson, however, dissented from this opinion. "It is true that it is the husband's God-given prerogative to be the head of his family, and to be the ultimate authority in his domestic circle, and a good wife will respect his authority when exercised within proper bounds," Anderson contended, "but a woman when she marries does not *surrender* all her rights." The jurist pointed out that recent judicial decisions and legislation had granted the wife certain "rights and privileges within her sphere, which the husband cannot withhold from her except by an act of oppression." Child nurture was one of these rights and privileges that belonged to the wife's "peculiar province." A husband had no authority "to go into the nursery and take charge" of child rearing because he "has outdoor duties to perform" and "the mother is usually better qualified to train and instruct her children." The evidence in this case, Anderson concluded, "abundantly shows that the mother is eminently qualified, morally and mentally, to have the custody and training and education of her child, and no one can fill the place of a mother; and the child would be constantly under her care and supervision." Despite Anderson's vigorous argument for placing the young boy with his mother, an argument rooted firmly in the ideology of separate spheres, the majority of the Virginia appellate justices concurred with Staples, and the father received custody.[24]

Most southern jurists agreed with the majority opinion of the Virginia court that a wife who deserted her husband should not be granted custody. In an 1896 case, Chief Justice Milton H. Mabry of the Florida Supreme Court denied Lillian Belle Miller's efforts to recover custody of her two-year-old daughter because Miller was "without sufficient excuse in leaving her husband's home, and thereby breaking up the family ties." Mabry insisted that the Florida court should award the girl to her father, although she was of "tender years," because the mother's behavior was "of such a nature as to injuriously affect the life and character of the child."[25] Such a position stood in distinct contrast to that of northern courts, which even in cases of adultery would often separate the issue of a woman's parental fitness from her marital conduct when custody of a young child was involved. In any event, the use of adultery, desertion, and other charges to withhold custody from a mother showed how legal rules based on gender roles could be turned against women.[26]

Another area in which gender roles could operate against women in custody fights involved the continued connection after the Civil War between possession of the child and capacity to provide financial support. The assignment of support as a male responsibility had been the primary justification in the antebellum South for the judicial commitment to superior paternal rights. During the late nineteenth century, the southern judiciary still exhibited a strong respect for the close link between custody and support, but incorporated an examination of the parents' financial positions into a broader evaluation of the child's welfare. The greater economic resources of men sometimes put them at an advantage in custody battles, even when children of tender years were involved. The Virginia Supreme Court in 1894 refused to grant Anne Slater custody of her three young children because she was not financially independent. While Slater was, the court conceded, "a most affectionate and devoted mother," the father was "a sober and successful businessman" who had amply provided for the wants of his family. The father's monetary success, along with the mother's difficult economic straits, convinced the Virginia high court that he should have custody, despite the fact that he was "not shown to be an extremely affectionate person." In the court's judgment, the paternal capacity to provide financial support in this instance outweighed the benefits of maternal nurture.[27]

The postwar concern with parental ability to support children was especially apparent in custody contests between former slaves. Wartime separation sometimes led to the breakup of relationships, and mothers sought to gain support for the children of these unions. Likewise, African American men tried to acquire custody of children in cases where the mother had taken up with another man.[28] The Freedmen's Bureau handled most of these disputes in the period immediately following emancipation. The main preoccupation of the agency was to ensure that the state would not have to take on the responsibility of supporting the children, so it listened with heightened interest to the arguments of parents that they could provide economically for their offspring. Bureau officials took into account other grounds for custody, but they were most responsive to the claims of parents who had supported their children, or could demonstrate capacity to provide for them in the future.[29]

The judicial concern with the financial resources of both black and white parents involved in custody disputes during Reconstruction was due in large part to the desire to keep the lid on public spending during a period of economic austerity in the South. Although judicial consideration of financial resources often proved to be a disability for women attempting to gain custody, those mothers who showed that they could support their children were often in an advantageous position to retain them. In the 1879 case of *McShan v. McShan*, Mississippi chief justice Horatio F. Simrall noted that the father contesting custody had experienced a financial setback when he moved to Arkansas and attempted to set up a new medical practice there. The doctor abandoned his wife, leaving her with only a "very small supply of provisions" to support the two girls, aged three and five. The wife had little choice but to move into her father's home in Mississippi, where she and the two children were now living. In the words of Chief Justice Simrall, her father was "abundantly able and willing to support his daughter and her children." Although the doctor's circumstances "had greatly improved," the judge turned down his request for custody. The wife had found shelter and support for the children in her father's home, and the Mississippi jurist refused "to invade the happy home of the wife and children, and alter its conditions and relations, when we do not see that the condition of these little girls would be benefited thereby."[30]

The mother granted custody in this case depended upon her father's largess; those women who demonstrated that they could support the children on their own were in an even better position to keep them.[31] In any event, southern courts by the late nineteenth century regularly employed their statutory authority to make any order necessary for the maintenance and care of the children in a suit for divorce or legal separation, compelling fathers to provide child support when the mother received custody.[32] As the Arkansas Supreme Court remarked in 1883, "The dissolution of the marriage tie and decreeing the custody of the children, either permanently or temporarily to the mother, do not relieve the father of his obligation to support them." The high court contended that, if the children were too young to earn their own livelihood, "the father must continue to furnish them a maintenance out of his estate, regard being had to his means and condition in life."[33]

While southern jurists made it clear in the postwar period that granting the mother custody of the children did not relieve the father of his obligation to meet the economic needs of his offspring, they did not leave the interests of the fathers entirely unprotected in disputes over child support. The Texas Court of Civil Appeals, for example, held in 1896 that a court could not force a father to pay child support without taking into account his income and the necessities of the children. Emelia Pape had received a divorce and custody of the seven children, as well as the homestead and practically all of the community property. The district court had ordered the father to pay a monthly sum of eighteen dollars for ten years, and twelve dollars for seven more years, for the support of the children. Justice Fly of the appellate court affirmed the divorce and custody judgment, but maintained that the child-support order was "manifestly unjust and oppressive." Fly agreed that the father was "responsible for the necessaries of life for the children" after a divorce was granted. "We have seen no authority, however," declared the Texas judge, "that would permit a court to arbitrarily fix the amount that the father should pay for the maintenance of his children, without regard to his standing in society, and his resources and income." [34]

If southern appellate courts found that insufficient evidence existed on the financial condition of the father, they commonly sent the case back for a new trial to gather more information on the father's ability to support the children.[35] Sometimes, when the court determined that the mother possessed a large enough estate to provide for the children, it would not compel the father to contribute to the support of his offspring.[36] If neither the father nor the mother received custody upon divorce because the judge found them both unfit and placed the child in the possession of a third party, then both parents could be required to furnish funds for the maintenance and education of the children.[37] Moreover, when the court refused to grant a divorce and the mother gained custody, some jurists held that they did not have the authority to tell the father how much to provide for the support of his child. "The legal obligation and liability of the father for the necessary support and maintenance of his minor child remained," Texas chief justice James acknowledged, but the court was in no position to determine what precise amount of money constituted a fulfillment of this responsibility as long as the couple were still "man and wife." [38]

Although southern supreme courts developed new policies during the latter half of the nineteenth century that expanded the custody rights of women, the older reluctance to disturb patriarchal authority in the family continued to shape the judiciary's outlook. As the Arkansas high court pronounced in 1877, by "statute, as well as by the common law, the father (unless incompetent or unfit) is the natural guardian, and entitled to the custody, care and education of his minor children."[39] Therefore, in practice, southern courts after the Civil War still cited the common-law tradition when granting custody to the father, and increasingly cited the best interests of the child standard when awarding custody to the mother. This approach to settling custody disputes between parents grew out of an evolving state paternalism that expressed itself in the form of judicial discretion. For women, this was particularly significant because it meant that custodial equality did not achieve statutory form. Rather, the custody rights of women depended on a case-by-case evaluation carried out by male judges and jurors. In custody, as in other areas of family law, women gained greater legal standing, but their rights were largely dependent upon paternalistic judges and a rigid conception of gender roles.[40]

Furthermore, it should be stressed that southern women could claim rights to their offspring only after separation or divorce. While the family is intact, in the words of the 1861 Georgia code, "the husband is the head of the family, and the wife is subject to him; her legal civil existence is merged in the husband, except so far as the law recognizes her separately." As long as the parents lived together, the husband's right to custody and control of the children could not be challenged, for the law considered him the natural guardian.[41] Most southern states, in addition, continued to grant men the power to appoint guardians for their offspring by will, although some legislatures did limit paternal testamentary rights by insisting upon maternal consent to guardianship.[42]

In short, changes in southern child-custody law during the nineteenth century modified but did not eliminate patriarchal authority. The growing recognition of certain custody rights for southern women may have led to more power within families, but it did not bring about greater equality between women and men outside the home. Courts began to consider women as uniquely suited to raising children and, the courts agreed, this seemingly natural maternal instinct formed the foundation for women's custody claims. The cult of domesticity thus played an important role in undermining traditional conceptions of paternal custody rights. But granting married women custody rights to their children on the basis of their special capacity as mothers to provide nurture did not challenge gender roles in the larger society. Instead, it gave women the power to take legal action only within the narrow constraints of the domestic arena, confining the elevation of women's status to within the family and contributing to the consolidation of separate spheres for women and men. Changes in custody law, in this sense, undermined as much as they strengthened the notion of equality.[43]

At the same time that southern appellate judges broadened their efforts after 1865 to reevaluate the custody rights of mothers and fathers, a direct confrontation between the rights of biological parents and the child-welfare standard surfaced in custody disputes involving third parties. Judges before the Civil War had assumed that a child would be best cared for by the parent unless that parent proved utterly unfit. But in the postwar years the courts moved toward a different interpretation of the tie between child and child rearer that was more psychological and contractual, and less biological and organic. Most important, members of the southern bench began to take into account attachments that had been formed over time between surrogate parents and the child in dispute.

Several developments during the antebellum period foreshadowed this change in judicial thinking. The increasingly child-centered legal process could be turned against parents, because it rested on an assessment of the child's needs and the public good rather than the parent's interests. This potential manifested itself both in the court's willingness to appoint guardians for children who inherited property and whose fathers refused to give bond and security, and in its imposition of restraints on the capacity of parents to indenture their children.

Even more significant was an 1858 opinion by the Tennessee Supreme Court that employed a judicial conception of the child's best interests to deny custody to a biological parent, the first such appellate decision in the South. The Tennessee high court in *Gardenhire v. Hinds* refused to award control of an eight-year-old girl of "frail and unhealthy constitution" to Simeon Hinds, her father, after she had been raised by her grandmother. The court pointed out that Hinds had abandoned the child years ago, and that he now had no wife or home, and only limited financial resources to educate his daughter. The grandmother, on the other hand, was "eminently fit and able to raise her in a proper manner, and is willing to do so free of cost." In fact, the judges observed, "the child and grandmother are devotedly attached to each other," leaving little doubt that it was in "the interest and welfare of the child" that she remain with the grandmother.[44]

When a parent demonstrated a pronounced lack of fitness, a conflict between parental custody claims and the best interests of the child was inevitable. The decision in *Gardenhire v. Hinds* was based on the court's authority under the parens patriae doctrine to withhold custody from unsuitable fathers who had abandoned their children. In the postwar South, the influence of the child-welfare precept, together with an increasingly contractual notion of social relations, transformed this negative concep-

The Evolution of Contractual Families : 149

tion of judicial power into a more positive exercise of discretion. In custody fights between a parent and third party, southern courts demonstrated a dramatically greater willingness to take into account the special needs of the child, even if this meant removing children from their parents.

This greater sensitivity to the child's distinctive requirements, as well as the expanded awareness of the new emotional ties created when parents informally relinquished custody, led the judiciary to embrace a more psychological model of parenthood. This new understanding resulted in a dramatic shift toward the judicial approval of third-party custody rights after the Civil War. Between 1800 and 1865 southern judges awarded custody to nonparents in 17 percent of the cases that reached the state supreme courts. But from 1866 to 1900, third parties gained custody in 47 percent of the appellate decisions, a striking gain over the prewar period.[45]

The postwar breakthrough on the part of third-party applicants for custody was primarily a reflection of greater success by kinfolk. Not surprisingly, in a society that placed so much emphasis on the role of kin in providing child care, around 56 percent of the third parties seeking to gain custody in nineteenth-century southern appellate cases were related to the child. Grandparents, as well as aunts and uncles, made up the bulk of these relatives.[46] More often than not, they were in-laws of the parent whom they were challenging for possession of the child.

As with other third parties, these kin did not often emerge victorious in antebellum custody contests. But following the war, the relatives' rate of success at the appellate level grew impressively. Between 1866 and 1900 they won 52 percent of the battles in which they sought custody, as opposed to a pre-1865 rate of only 11 percent. The rate of success for unrelated third parties—both individuals and institutions—also improved during the postwar years, but it reached only 39 percent.[47] Although southern courts in the late nineteenth century moved away from a strict biological notion of custodianship, then, the blood connection between child and child rearer still played a crucial role in the outcome of custody struggles.

The Texas Supreme Court, in an 1894 opinion, articulated the dominant judicial attitude toward parental custody claims in the postwar years, an attitude that mirrored the central thrust of American legal thinking on this issue.[48] Justice Leroy Denman dismissed the idea that a parent had "any property interest" in his or her child. Instead, he sketched out a view of state paternalism in which parental authority was subordinate to governmental power:

> The State, as the protector and promoter of the peace and prosperity of organized society, is interested in the proper education and mainte-

nance of the child, to the end that it may become a useful instead of vicious citizen; and while as a general rule it recognizes the fact that the interest of the child and society is best promoted by leaving its education and maintenance, during minority, to the promptings of paternal affection, untrammeled by the surveillance of government, still it has the right in proper cases to deprive the parent of the custody of his child when demanded by the interests of the child and society.

In this forceful statement, the Texas judge made explicit the connection between the needs of the child and the public, and the primacy of these needs over the interests of the parent. Asserting that the two-year-old girl in dispute was "entitled to the benefit of that home and environment which will probably best produce the interest of the infant," Denman placed her in the possession of her foster parents, who had been mainly responsible for raising her.[49]

After the Civil War, as in custody disputes between mothers and fathers, southern justices gradually constructed a new set of legal rules to guide their assessment of parental qualifications and child welfare in third-party battles. The impact of these rules was to shift the burden of proof onto parents to show that the child would be better off with them than with the surrogate family. In contrast, of course, most antebellum judges had contended that it was up to the nonparent to demonstrate that the parent could not properly care for his or her child.

Although the application of these guidelines broke new legal ground, they disclosed the continued assumptions of the judiciary concerning proper gender roles and class responsibilities. The continuity in notions about gender roles could be perceived especially in the way that appellate jurists during the late nineteenth century expanded their implementation of the tender years doctrine. As we have seen, the courts used this doctrine before 1860 in contests between mothers and third persons to uphold maternal custody rights. After the war, members of the southern bench went on to apply the rule to surrogate mothers as well, employing sex-role stereotypes to undercut paternal custody rights. In such cases, the courts often considered even a woman without any blood connections at all to the child in question as more fit to have custody than the biological father.

The Arkansas Supreme Court drew on the tender years doctrine in this fashion in *Verser v. Ford* (1881). Verser had placed his daughter in the care of her maternal grandparents shortly after his wife had died giving birth to the child. The grandparents had raised her for three years when Verser remarried and sought to regain custody of his daughter. In his decision, Justice John Eakin strongly supported paternal rights and blood ties. Most of the time, the judge remarked, the father's "greater ability and knowledge of the world renders him the fittest protector." Yet the Arkansas justice also discerned that the court had an obligation to exercise its discretionary authority in the settlement of custody controversies. Although Eakin found both the father and grandparents in this case to be financially and morally suitable, he argued that the girl's young age and the maternal care provided by the grandmother made it necessary not to disturb the existing arrangement. The judge emphasized that the father was inexperienced in child rearing, and the grandmother had created a "safe asylum" for the child that would guard her "against pernicious influences."[50] The implication of this reasoning was clear: although the male role of provider strengthened the political and economic position of men in society at large, it did not assure them of superiority in the domestic sphere, at least when it came to rearing children.

Surrogate mothers thus gained important rights based on the tender years doctrine. But, as in contests between parents, a woman might retain custody for only a few years before the father regained control of the child. An Alabama court, for example, decided in 1883 that an infant boy should remain in the possession of his maternal grandmother because the child's delicate health made it "perilous to attempt his removal." The court indicated, however, that the father could renew his application for custody when his son's health improved.[51]

Biological mothers found themselves similarly vulnerable in custody fights with male legal guardians. In such a dispute, the Georgia Supreme Court held in 1869 that the mother should have possession of her two sons because of their young age, despite the fact that the father's will had appointed the paternal grandfather guardian of their persons and property. But the court declared that when the boys "arrive at an age which requires their transfer to the possession of their guardian for the purposes of their education, there can be no doubt of his right to have the control of them."[52]

Southern jurists carefully weighed not only gender roles, but also class responsibilities, a preoccupation that revealed itself in the way the courts took into account the social status and economic resources of biological and surrogate parents in the resolution of custody disputes. The judiciary presumed that a proper consideration of the child's welfare required a careful scrutiny of the financial resources of the legal contestants, as well as the social opportunities they could offer to the child in dispute. Members of the southern bench frequently cited the greater wealth and standing of the party to whom they awarded custody as support for their decision. In an 1873 battle over a teen-aged boy between his mother and grandfather, the Mississippi court maintained that the mother's "position, employment, and character, offer no guaranty of the proper care and training of her son." According to the court, she had "seven children, by different fathers" and had "no other ostensible business than that of cook, nor other means of supporting her children." The grandfather, on the other hand, was "a respectable farmer, in comfortable circumstances" who could offer the boy a "decent home, and some education." Hence the judge felt that it was in the best interests of the child to allow the grandfather to retain custody. In another case, which came before the North Carolina bench in 1876, the appellate jurists ruled against a stepfather, arguing in part that he was "a man of small estate, [who] has no land or fixed residence, and moved from place to place as a tenant or cropper." [53]

The concern of southern justices with class position also shaped the outcome of custody struggles between black litigants. In *Fullilove v. Banks* (1884), the Mississippi Supreme Court charged that a black mother attempting to recover possession of her illegitimate son had been a "common prostitute" until the boy's birth. Although the mother now earned a livelihood by taking in washing, and claimed "to have reformed morally," the court observed that she had left the child with his paternal grandparents, who belonged to "the most respectable and well-to-do class of their race." Largely because of the comfortable environment that the grandparents provided the boy, the members of the Mississippi bench affirmed a lower court decision to award custody to them. [54]

Appellate courts in other southern states used such expressions as "a man of substance," "moral, temperate and industrious," or "a frugal and saving man of good character" in describing men they looked upon favorably in custody controversies. [55] The judiciary characterized the women that it most admired in such terms as a "lady of good moral character and standing" and a "respectable married woman." Although these descriptions rested on obvious gender distinctions, they also revealed a strong respect for class standing. [56]

Besides the tender years doctrine and evaluation of socioeconomic status, the infant discretion rule was employed by southern justices in the late nineteenth century to enlarge the custody rights of surrogate parents. As in battles between parents, the expressed preference of the child regarding his or her placement sometimes had a major role in the court's settlement of custody contests between parents and third parties. For example, when a thirteen-year-old boy explained that he would rather remain with his uncle, the North Carolina Supreme Court reversed the decision of a lower court that awarded custody to his mother. Chiding the lower court for its failure to inquire into the boy's preferences, Chief

Justice Richmond Pearson contended that "being the party mainly concerned, he had a right to make a statement to the court as to his feelings and wishes upon the matter." Indeed, Pearson insisted, the lower court should have given such a statement "serious consideration" in resolving the dispute.[57]

The courts, however, did not always follow the child's preference in deciding custody cases. Southern jurists were particularly reluctant to adopt the wishes of the minor when he or she did not want to return to the father. Even if the child was old enough under common law to select his or her guardian, the judges maintained that they could order the delivery of the child to the father.[58] Nevertheless, courts in the postwar South embraced a more child-oriented decision-making process, one that occasionally conflicted with parental custody claims. For mothers and fathers, such rejections undoubtedly represented one of the most emotionally wrenching applications of the best interests of the child standard.

The final and most far-reaching custody policy that southern courts adopted after the Civil War involved a new sensitivity to the emotional ties formed after a child had been transferred to another family. Adherence to this rule led to a significant expansion of nonparental custody rights. The Georgia Supreme Court in an 1882 case, for instance, declined to return a child to the father after the boy's aunt and uncle had raised him for nearly nine years. The court asserted that it was right for the boy to remain "with her at whose breast he was nourished, a sucking child, and with him who supported the child and raised him to young boyhood, and to both who loved him as their own children."[59]

Other appellate courts in the postwar South also exhibited vigorous support for surrogate families under the "new ties" rule. The Virginia Supreme Court endorsed the more psychological view of parenthood implicit in this rule in *Merritt v. Swimley* (1886). The controversy involved the conflicting custody claims of an Ohio father and his deceased wife's family in Virginia. Hugh Merritt's wife had died in 1872 shortly after giving birth to their third child, a daughter. With Merritt's consent, the mother's sister brought the infant to Virginia, where she and her husband raised the girl. Thirteen years later, the father came to Virginia and announced that he wanted to take his daughter with him to Ohio. When the girl's maternal aunt and uncle opposed the move on account of the girl's ill health, Merritt sued out a writ of habeas corpus against them to recover custody.

Justice Benjamin Lacy took great pains in his appellate opinion to explain the rights of each party to the suit. Affirming the importance of parental prerogatives, he commented that "the legal rights of the parent or guardian are to be respected. They are founded in nature and wisdom, and are essential to the peace, order, virtue, and happiness of society." But Lacy also maintained that in all cases "the interest and welfare of the child is the great leading object to be obtained," and parental interests had to give way to his overriding goal. This was especially true when the parent allowed new family ties to develop; in such a situation, the rights of the biological and surrogate parents should be weighed equally.

The Virginia jurist believed that in the present case the welfare of the child would be best promoted by leaving her where she was. Although he found no evidence of the father's unsuitability to be a parent, Lacy stressed the significance of the warm, maternal care that the aunt had given the child. As the judge put it, "The father has permitted this child to grow up a stranger to him, almost unknown to him by sight, perhaps entirely so. In the new home the tenderest ties of affection have been wound around her." Hence Lacy ordered the child to stay with her new family.[60]

The heightened awareness of southern judges to the new emotional bonds created when a child lived on a long-term basis with another family led to a revised treatment of contracts involving the voluntary transfer of custody. Instead of refusing to validate such contracts, the judiciary began to recognize and enforce them. Justice Lacy was called on again in 1886 to resolve this issue. In 1882, when his wife became seriously ill, Daniel Black placed their three-year-old daughter with her maternal aunt and uncle, the Coffees. Black's child remained with the Coffees following his wife's death. Four years later, however, Black attempted to recover custody of the girl.

Justice Lacy conceded that generally the father was entitled to the possession of his child. Nevertheless, he declared that in cases "where the father has voluntarily relinquished the custody of an infant . . . the question is no longer to be viewed in the light of the father's legal rights, they having been abandoned by him, but in the light of a cautious regard for the happiness and welfare of the infant." In justifying the practice of voluntary transfer, the judge noted that a father had the power to emancipate his minor child, and that he could also forfeit the right to custody by improper conduct. "Why, then, may he not transfer this right of custody, which he may thus abandon or forfeit, especially when the interests of the child are not prejudiced by the assignment?" Lacy asked. The Virginia jurist, in other words, linked the voluntary transfer doctrine with the best interests of the child standard in awarding custody to the aunt and uncle. Another member of the Virginia bench summed up this approach in 1898: "Where a parent has transferred to another the custody of his infant child by fair agreement which has been acted upon by such other person to the manifest interest and welfare of the child, the parent will not be permitted to reclaim the custody of the child unless he can show that a change of the custody will materially promote his child's welfare."[61]

The Arkansas high court carved out a similar path to the recognition of voluntary transfer. The father in *Washaw v. Gimble* (1887) had asked a couple in his German Lutheran congregation to raise his son following the mother's death during childbirth. The father allowed his son to stay with the new family for more than four years before deciding that he wanted to regain custody. The couple refused to part with the boy, however, contending that they had taken him on the understanding that he would remain with them permanently.

After investigating the case, the Arkansas judiciary concluded that the boy would be best served by leaving him with the couple. Chief Justice Sterling Cockrill argued that the custody of a child was not the subject of a property transaction. In his words, "A father cannot by a mere gift of his child, release himself from the obligations to support it or deprive himself of the right to its custody." Yet he also held that the courts would not always aid the father in revoking his consent and retaking custody of his offspring. The guiding principle, urged Cockrill, should be the child's welfare. In this instance, the chief justice felt strongly that the father "ought not to be permitted suddenly to sunder the ties that he has allowed to grow up" between the surrogate family and child, and the boy "should not be suddenly removed to a new home, for his relatives are now comparative strangers to him."[62] Like the Virginia bench, then, the Arkansas court decided not to rest its order upon the transfer agreement alone, but rather to base it broadly on a conception of the child's best interests.

Most of the custody disputes over voluntary transfer agreements involved fathers' attempts to recover possession of their children from surrogate families. But even when both parents were alive and living together, and they attempted to revoke such a contract, postwar southern courts would frequently enforce the agreement. In an 1877 custody contest between the parents of a three-year-old girl and her maternal aunt, Justice James Jackson of Georgia asserted that the parents could not regain control of the child because they had consented to a transfer of custody. Jackson maintained that there was "no doubt" that parental power could be lost by a voluntary contract releasing the right to custody to a third person. According to the Georgia jurist, "The contract when made and executed . . . is clearly irrevocable by the parent, unless for good cause. . . . It would be wrong to hold that, after the child has been nursed, and loved, and cherished under the contract for five years, it could be revoked at pleasure by the parent."[63]

Underlying the support of southern justices for the concept of voluntary transfer was a growing sense that contractual and biological family bonds were not all that different. The central concern of the courts was no longer the maintenance of blood ties, but rather the promotion of stable family ties for the child. This change in perception encouraged judges to leave children where they were, unless they were clearly being exposed to improper influences. The emergence of the private transfer doctrine therefore reflected a more psychological conception of parenthood, a development rooted in the rise of the family as a child-rearing institution and its decline as an economic one. Southern judges, in short, now began to view the parent-child connection as a contractual relationship that had tremendous emotional overtones.

THE TRIUMPH OF STATE PATERNALISM

A profound shift in the distribution of power between southern families and the state accompanied this new understanding of parenthood. The development of external standards of parental evaluation, and the application of these standards to remove children from their parents, led to an unprecedented intrusion of the state into the southern household. Yet the judicial resolution of private controversies did not in itself fully account for the expansion of the state's role in child rearing. Here the primary task of evaluative standards was to guide the judge in the settlement of a private dispute individuals were unable to decide for themselves. The growing influence of the state was thus brought to bear only in those instances where controversies emerged between biological parents and third persons over the possession of a child.[64]

The overwhelming majority of the private disputes that reached the appellate level involved economically self-sufficient households, and for these families the exercise of judicial discretion to settle these disputes was a new development. In the area of child protection, however, southern courts had a long tradition of intervention in families that lacked adequate financial resources to support themselves. Southern judges hesitant to remove children from parental authority in economically well-off households, in other words, demonstrated far less reluctance in apprenticing the offspring of indigent parents.

Following the Civil War, southern judges moved to construct stronger legal standards for child protection that would distinguish more effectively those cases where the state should intrude coercively on family autonomy. Although the judiciary demonstrated great respect for the family as a private institution, state intervention grew significantly in those families that were deemed to have failed in some way. Courts increasingly removed children from their homes not only upon the finding that parents were too poor to support their offspring, but also upon the finding that they were neglectful or abusive in their treatment of children. In a society where contractual ideology was penetrating parent-child relations and re-shaping them, neglect and abuse were now seen as violations of custodial obligations that justified the termination of parental powers.

The 1882 decision of *State v. Grisby* provided an arresting illustration of this developing perspective on child neglect and abuse. An Arkansas district attorney initiated this legal battle when he filed charges against James and Emma Grisby for extreme child abuse, and recommended that the circuit court remove the six-year-old boy in question from their custody. The boy was the husband's by a previous marriage, and apparently the Grisbys had ample financial resources to provide for the child's needs. Yet, according to the district attorney, the wife would refuse to give the boy food and water, and tied him up when he asked the neighbors for something to eat or drink. In the prosecutor's words, "These and many other tortures have been and still are inflicted upon the child, until, without disease, it has become wan, haggard and emaciated, with barely life in its famished body." Despite these accusations, the circuit court judge allowed the Grisbys to retain custody, so the prosecutor brought the case to the Arkansas Supreme Court.

The appellate court justices reversed the decision of the lower court and sent the case back for retrial. Chief Justice E. H. English observed that parents "are intrusted [*sic*] with the custody of the persons, and the education of their children, yet this is done upon the natural presumption that the children will be properly taken care of, and will be brought up with a due education in literature, and morals, and religion, and that they will be treated with kindness and affection." But, asserted English, whenever parents treated their children cruelly, neglected them, or exhibited long-term behavior likely to corrupt their young, the court had the authority to deprive parents of their custodial rights. The Arkansas chief justice admitted that to remove children from the possession of their parents was a matter of "extreme delicay [*sic*], and of no inconsiderable embarrassment and responsibility." Nevertheless, he added, it was a jurisdiction "which seems indispensible to the sound morals, the good order, and the just protection of a civilized society."[65]

The growing judicial tendency in the South to remove children from neglectful or abusive parents was part of a national child-saving movement that gained momentum in the late nineteenth century. This movement mobilized the courts and legislatures to prescribe new standards of child rearing for American households, in sharp contrast to the antebellum tendency to limit governmental intervention into family life. The existence of neglected, abused, and improperly reared children aroused child savers, and drove them to try to assist the family by dictating what its responsibilities were. In this way, reformers hoped to guarantee that the family performed its function as the chief agent of socialization in American society.[66]

The heart of the child-saving movement lay in the urban centers of the North. Child savers, however, made some headway in the South, where they pushed for child-labor regulations and compulsory educations laws.[67] New custody laws in the late nineteenth century also played a central role in the southern movement. State legislatures passed statutes that granted courts the authority to terminate custody rights if parents failed to support their children, abandoned them, or treated them cruelly. An 1861 Georgia act, for example, provided that any person could bring suit against a father who abused his child, and that the court could exercise its discretion in the appointment of a guardian for the child if the charges were substantiated.[68]

In addition, southern child savers helped to sponsor the establishment of orphanages and other child-care institutions for neglected and abandoned children. Such institutions had made a limited appearance on a private basis in the antebellum South, but during the latter half of the century they became increasingly popular as a means to care for dependent and delinquent minors, and many southern states took over responsibility for their administration. Reflecting the racial mores of the Jim Crow South, separate child-care institutions were established for black children.[69]

Nineteenth-century asylums such as orphanages relied heavily on an environmental approach to child rearing. By isolating children completely from their surroundings, asylum managers believed that they could not only shelter the orphan and delinquent but also discipline and reform them. Managers demanded a total, permanent break, and the right to supplant parental authority.[70] This institutional invasion of parental custody rights in the postwar South found expression in statutory enactments that incorporated child-care institutions. These enactments gave orphan asylums and reformatory institutions wide authority to intervene in family life. The 1896 Tennessee code contained a typical provision: "Said board of managers, trustees, or directors may, at their discretion, require the parents of such indigent children to surrender all right and claim to the control of them, and to consent for the said asylum to provide homes for them . . . for the purpose of caring for and educating them, teaching them trades and household duties generally."[71] By wielding this sort of control, reformers hoped to eradicate corrupting influences and overcome parental failure.

Parents rarely contested these statutory powers in court. When they did, southern courts usually supported the custodial authority of child-care institutions. In an 1887 decision, for instance, the Georgia Supreme Court refused to allow a mother accused of prostitution to recover possession of her daughter after the child had been committed to an orphan asylum. The court dismissed the mother's contention that under its charter the asylum could not take any child who had a living parent. In the court's words, "The authorities of the asylum were willing to receive this particular child, and we do not think the question of their legal right to do so is one which can be raised by an outsider, in no way connected with or interested in the management of its affairs." [72] The appellate judges apparently failed to see that the mother might be interested in the management of her child, if not the asylum, and hence had a right to question whether the girl should be committed.

Even in cases where obvious procedural irregularities existed, southern high courts upheld the sweeping power of child-care institutions to take control of a minor from his or her parents. In *State v. Kilvington* (1898), a mother sought to regain custody of her seven-year-old daughter, who had been placed in the Tennessee Industrial School by a county court judge. The state-operated school was established to shelter and train orphaned, delinquent, and neglected children. According to Justice Wilkes of the Tennessee Supreme Court, "It is not a penal nor altogether a reformatory institution, but is rather a place of refuge and school for homeless, penniless children, where they may be received and cared for, taught the different grades of a common school education, and trained in useful trades and branches of industry." County court judges, under an 1891 act, had the power to commit such children to the institution. In addition, any child who "has no proper or sufficient guardianship to care for its physical, moral, and mental welfare, to at least such a degree as will probably save the child from pauperism, lewdness, and crime" could be placed in the industrial school.[73]

In his decision, Justice Wilkes noted that before any child could be committed to the school, a formal inquiry in open court had to be held. The county judge who had committed the girl in dispute conceded that her proceeding "was informal and summary, and without the issuance of any warrant or any formal investigation." Although Wilkes found that the commitment process "was irregular, and not according to the law," he affirmed the action of the lower court on the grounds that it was in the best interests of the girl to leave her in the institution. "Due regard must in every instance be paid to the rights of parents and of the child," observed the appellate jurist, "but this rule must be enforced and construed when the child is brought into Court in the interest and for the benefit of the child; and when the detention is manifestly for the welfare of the child, it will be allowed and required to remain in the institution."

Wilkes argued that the judicial commitment was in the child's welfare because her detention at the industrial school was "not in the nature of punishment." Instead, the goal was "the upbuilding of the inmate by industrial training, by education, and instilling principles of morality and religion, and, above all, by separating them from the corrupting influences of improper associates." Wilkes's resounding endorsement of the environmentalist position gained special force from the circumstances of the girl's previous home life. Both the mother and grandmother were "of ill repute," he asserted. "The girl, if restored to them or either of them, will be subjected to and surrounded by evil associates and corrupting influences."[74]

Public commitments of poor, neglected, and abandoned children embodied the broadest exercise of state custodial power. Not only did open-ended statutory provisions authorize the "rescue" of children from their families, but also these children were sometimes placed in public institutions with little regard for legal procedure. Such actions revealed a serious danger in the state taking on the role of parent: the paternalistic vision of intervention led earnest reformers, legislators, and judges to ignore the coercive nature of public commitments. The efforts of these groups to create a model of parental fitness—a model shaped by middle-class notions and values—clearly represented a new level of state interference with parenthood. In imposing new standards of parenthood, southern elites revealed their underlying fear of the changes transforming postwar society and their yearning to retain control over individuals and households that defied elite conventions. These were the sorts of powerful emotions that fueled the rise of state paternalism.

Although many poor white parents faced the threat of losing custody of their children after the war, the position of newly freed African American parents was even more precarious. With emancipation and the legal recognition of the African American family in the South, former slaves had theoretically gained the right to control their offspring. The desire of white planters to maintain authority over black children, however, significantly undercut these parental rights. Before the Civil War, southern counties had exercised an almost unlimited discretion to apprentice children of free African Americans. Planters hoped to expand this prewar practice now that slavery had collapsed, seeking new ways to wield white authority and preserve labor discipline. Throughout the South in late 1865 and 1866, state legislatures passed laws that gave local judges the power to bind out all African American orphans or minors whose parents could not support them adequately. Such laws provided some planters with a cheap supply of involuntary labor, for the former owner of the minor was given preference as master if deemed a "suitable" person. Moreover, these laws allowed courts to apprentice African American children without their parents' approval.[75]

The new apprenticeship acts empowered courts to step into African American families and use practically any excuse to bind out their children. A South Carolina statute, for example, allowed local authorities to apprentice not only black children who were poor or orphaned but also those "whose parents are not teaching them habits of industry and honesty, or are persons of notoriously bad character, or are vagrants."[76] In part, the readiness of whites to resort to apprenticeship reflected their difficulty in adjusting to the realities of emancipation; it also provided planters with a way to obtain revenge against former slaves who demonstrated their disloyalty during the war. It may be, as planters claimed, that the apprenticeship acts were rooted in some persistent sense of paternal obligation on their part rather than a desire to exert social control, exact revenge, and exploit the labor of African Americans.[77] More likely, however, the motives were mixed, as they clearly were in the case of Thomas McKie, a large landowner in Edgefield, South Carolina. McKie wrote to a Freedmen's Bureau agent in 1867, seeking to have five African American children apprenticed to him. The parents, now dead, had been his slaves and McKie was taking care of the youngsters, who ranged from about five to thirteen years old. In his words, "They have been permitted to stay on the place and have been provided with food and clothing at my expense since the surrender. . . . Thus far they have been a tax and care upon me without compensation, and I am unwilling to bear it longer unless there can be some assurance of reward at some future day."[78]

Regardless of planter motives, surviving African American mothers and fathers showed little appreciation for this sort of paternalism. In fact, of all the protests inspired by the Black Codes, the most bitter objections centered on the apprenticeship laws. Complaints from distressed African American parents and relatives over arbitrary apprenticeship mounted in the postwar years, and former slaves frequently appealed to the local provost marshal or the Freedmen's Bureau for custody rights to their children. The vigorous resistance of African American families garnered significant support from the reconstructed courts and state governments of the South in the late 1860s and eventually this pressure brought about the system's demise.[79]

A small minority of African American parents carried their pleas as far as the state appellate courts, where they generally received a sympathetic hearing. In the 1866 case of *Comas v. Reddish*, the Georgia Supreme Court reversed the order of a lower court that awarded custody of a teenaged African American youth to his former owner. The county judge had apprenticed the boy without consulting either him or his father. Justice Iverson Harris, in the appellate opinion, emphasized the paternalistic motives of state legislators who had enacted a statute in 1866 allowing the public apprenticeship of poor and orphaned African American children. According to Harris, the goal of this new law was "to make provision for that large class of persons in our midst (colored minors) who, by the results of the civil war, have been thrown upon society, helpless from want of parental protection, want of means of support, inability to earn their daily bread, and from age and other causes." But Harris had stern words for those whites who saw in such legislation a substitute for slavery: "It should be borne always in mind, and at all times should regulate the conduct of the white man, that slavery is with the days beyond the flood; that it is prohibited by the Constitution of the State of Georgia, and by that paramount authority, the Constitution of the United States; and that its *continuance will not by any honest public functionary be tolerated under the forms of law or otherwise, directly or indirectly.*" Declaring that the county judge in this case had no jurisdiction to apprentice the youth, Harris granted the father custody.[80]

As this appellate opinion indicated, the effort to apprentice the children of freed blacks harked back to the days of slavery, when African American parents were treated as dependents and denied the rights that would have allowed them to sustain and protect independent households. Protests from northern Republicans and the freedpeople themselves put an end to this method of apprenticeship and the reasoning behind it. In the child-saving movement that emerged in the late nineteenth century, the state mobilized a different kind of rhetoric to support intervention in poor households, one that emphasized the neglectful or abusive behavior of the parents rather than their dependent status.

Despite the considerable inroads that surrogate parents and the state made into the custodial rights of biological parents, the older view of superior parental rights remained influential in the postwar South. Justices still held that a clear and strong case must be made to deny a father custody of his offspring. As a Georgia judge insisted in 1886, "The rights of the father, on the one hand, and the permanent interest and the welfare of the infant, on the other, are both to be regarded, but the right of the father is paramount, and should not be disregarded, except for grave cause." The traditional emphasis on the importance of the blood tie between the father and child lay at the heart of this outlook. Thus, in granting a father custody of his illegitimate child in 1871, a Texas court asserted that the law "should never receive such a construction as would tend to dry up the sources of natural affection."[81]

The custody rights of mothers also continued to receive vigorous support from southern supreme courts during the postwar period. The great faith of judges in maternal care led to many instances in which the best interests of the child guideline worked to the mother's advantage. Even very poor mothers discovered that the court would award them custody in preference to third persons who were wealthier. The right of a mother to the custody of her children, pronounced the Mississippi court in 1879, was "scarcely less sacred than the right to life and liberty."[82]

The most important legislative expression of support for maternal custody rights involved the passage of statutes in the late nineteenth century that recognized the mother as the natural guardian of her children upon the father's death. In their newly recognized status as natural guardians, widows no longer had to depend upon appointments by their husbands' wills or by the courts to assume guardianship of their children. This improved status also meant that widows could retain custody of their children by statute upon remarriage.[83] These postwar laws further ensured the legal position of mothers in disputes with third persons.

Besides these important elements of continuity in southern custody policy, where it was unclear in private custody contests whether the birth parent had voluntarily relinquished control of his or her child, southern justices in the late nineteenth century still frequently supported the right of the parent to regain custody. In North Carolina, judges required a written contract or deed as evidence of a custody transfer. If such documentation did not exist, and the parent was fit to have custody, then he or she could recover control of the child. Georgia judges maintained as well that the terms of the contract depriving a biological parent of control should be "clear, definite and certain."[84]

The main thrust of southern child-custody law after the Civil War was to provide children with the most stable, supportive environment possible. Custody laws in both the North and South, in fact, shared this thrust by the end of the nineteenth century.[85] The settlement of disputes between parents and third parties now required that the state intervene as final arbiter. As a Georgia jurist remarked, "Where there is a conflict of rights . . . the power to settle it must be lodged somewhere, and we think it is wisely lodged in the judge, whose sound discretion under the facts of each case must decide into whose custody the party must go." [86]

Through the expanded use of judicial discretion the state consolidated its power to establish the child's best interests and to evaluate parental fitness, thus intensifying its involvement in family life. For the South, this was especially important because discretionary authority allowed governing elites after the Civil War to begin to replace the older notion of a government relying on a network of patriarchs with a newer paternalistic conception of government in families, a government that subjected parents and children to unprecedented controls. Treating parenthood as a trusteeship rather than a proprietary right, judges developed innovative policies and set new standards for parental behavior that took into consideration the needs of the child and society. Although biological rights remained important, parental supremacy was no longer unchallengeable.

ADOPTION AND THE NEW DOMESTIC ORDER

The growing acceptance of adoption in the postwar South accompanied the changes taking place in custody and guardianship law. Indeed, the law could sanction adoption only in a society that was moving away from a belief in the absolute primacy of the biological link between parent and child. Therefore the expansion of judicial discretion, the voluntary transfer of parental rights, the concept of psychological parenthood, and the preoccupation with the welfare of the child were all developments in custody and guardianship law that could also be discerned in adoption legislation passed during the late nineteenth century. With statutory backing, the courts assumed a central role in the adoption process, ensuring that the welfare of the child and parental qualifications of the adopters came under judicial scrutiny.[87]

The development of child-centered custody rules and the psychological notion of parenthood, then, laid the foundation for the creation of contractual families through legal adoption. The legal recognition of children as individuals also contributed to this development, generating the construction of custody standards that stressed the importance of proper nurture rather than blood bonds. The growing commitment of legal authorities to the belief that children belonged in stable, supportive homes led them to see that biological ties did not always guarantee such an environment. Hence the adoption process that took form after 1865 established new domestic alternatives under the watchful eyes of the courts.[88]

Comprehensive adoption laws, which existed in Georgia and Mississippi during the antebellum period, entered the statute books in North Carolina in 1872–73, Arkansas and Florida in 1885, Virginia in 1891, and South Carolina in 1892.[89] Despite the widespread implementation of judicially supervised adoption in the postwar South, legislators in Alabama, Louisiana, Tennessee, and Texas refrained during the late nineteenth century from significantly revising their earlier adoption laws, which merely required formal evidence of a transfer of parental authority from the birth to adoptive parent. In these four states, adoption did not become a court-monitored process until the twentieth century.[90]

Although few judges in the South objected to making adoption available, the steady growth in the number of adoptive families following the passage of legislation raised several significant legal issues. These included the construction that should be placed on the adoption legislation, the power of adoptive parents over their new children, the nature of the relationship between adopted offspring and their biological parents, and the legal status of adopted children in their new families.

Southern appellate courts struggled in a series of opinions to clarify the rights gained by the adoptive parent. Because adoption was a legal innovation with little precedent, the postbellum judiciary often narrowly construed the provisions of the new adoption statutes, particularly when they conflicted with those of the birth parents. In this sense, by circumscribing the rights of adoptive parents, southern courts during the postwar period continued to display a hesitancy to sever what were seen as natural bonds.

Two cases underscore this reluctance especially well. In *Succession of Forstall* (1873), the Louisiana Supreme Court decided that Oscar Forstall had no right to administer his adopted daughter's property, and the court appointed the girl's biological mother to oversee the estate left by her deceased husband. Forstall was a brother of the deceased, and he had adopted the girl following her father's death. Despite the adoption, the Louisiana high court insisted that the mother still had control over the child's property. In the words of Justice J. G. Taliaferro, "We find nothing in the statutes of the state relative to adoption, construed with the various articles of the Civil Code on the subject of tutorship, that inclines us to believe that the Legislature, in permitting the adoption of children, had any intention to abridge the right of a natural tutor to the personal care and control of his minor child, or to the administration of the child's property." As long as one of the birth parents survived, it seemed, an adoptive parent in Louisiana had little authority over the adopted child.[91]

The Texas Supreme Court adhered to a similarly restricted interpretation of the adoptive parent's rights. The court, in *Taylor v. Deseve* (1891), declared an adoption invalid on the grounds that the proper parental consent had not been secured. More important, Justice D. P. Marr contended that, even if a legal adoption had taken place, it would not have entitled the plaintiff and his wife to the custody or services of the child: "The only effect would have been to have made the child his heir at law, but not an inmate and constituent of his family." Following adoption, "the relation between the parties would not under our statute have been the same as paternity and filiation." Only further legislation, the judge said, could enable Texas courts to grant adoptive parents the right to the custody of a minor child while the child's parents were still alive.[92]

When no conflict between the rights of adoptive and biological parents arose, appellate jurists in the South gave the prerogatives of adoptive parents stronger backing. In an 1889 opinion, for instance, the Tennessee Supreme Court held that an adoptive parent possessed the right to change the domicile of a child whose birth parents were dead. Justice William C. Folkes admitted that there was "certainly a want of authority directly on the point as to the right of one who has adopted a child to change its domicile." But he noted that little doubt existed concerning the right of a biological father or widowed mother to change the residence of his or her child. Surely, an adoptive parent could exercise a similar prerogative, Folkes reasoned. "It is difficult to see, upon any rule of construction, or of policy," he remarked, "why all the powers possessed by a natural father should not be exercised by him, who, by adoption of a minor, assumes the relationship of parent." The Tennessee court thus denied the contention of the child's legal guardian that the adoptive father could not carry her to a new home in Louisiana.[93]

As southern judges became more comfortable with the notion of contractual families in the late nineteenth century, they embraced a significantly broader conception of the rights held by an adoptive parent. The Alabama Supreme Court declared in 1891 that adoption gave the person seeking it the right to the child's services and earnings. The high court conceded that "adoption may not, by operation of the statute, originate and establish all the legal consequences and incidents of the natural relation of parent and child." Nevertheless, the jurists believed that anyone who adopted a minor should have control of the child's services and earnings "as against all persons." The only exception should be when "the true parents" did not consent to the adoption. In this case, of course, the biological parents would also be entitled to custody of the child, because the adoption would not be valid.[94]

In its decision, the Alabama Supreme Court seemed to imply that, if the birth parents consented to an adoption, then the adoptive parents assumed full control of the minor. Six years later, the Louisiana high court confirmed this growing tendency to grant greater consideration to the rights of adoptive parents in contests with birth parents, as long as the latter had given their consent to the adoption. In *Succession of Haley* (1897), Chief Justice Francis T. Nicholls overturned a lower-court decision that appointed Jeannette Prescott as natural tutrix of her eight-year-old son. Nicholls observed that Prescott had consented several years before to the boy's adoption, and that the will of the adoptive mother had appointed Anatole Ker rather than the biological mother as testamentary tutor to the child. It was no longer certain, said the chief justice, whether the right of the birth mother to be appointed tutrix in such a situation was an "incontrovertible legal proposition." In Nicholls's words, "Legislation in respect to adoption has gone forward . . . and recent adjudged cases will indicate that we view the rights of adopting parents as having been broadened by that legislation beyond what it was." In light of these developments, the Louisiana jurist found that the court order appointing Prescott as natural tutrix should be set aside, and the case sent back to the lower court for further proceedings. Nicholls clearly felt that in this dispute the right of the adoptive mother to appoint a testamentary tutor deserved closer attention.[95]

As with other custody contests, southern appellate courts in the late nineteenth century began to employ child-centered rules and standards of parental fitness to settle adoption battles. The Alabama Supreme Court, in considering the conflicting demands of an adoptive father and the child's grandmother, contended in 1874 that the "welfare of the infant is the guiding light by which the discretion of the court must be directed." The fact that the nine-year-old girl, "without hesitation," expressed a preference for remaining with the adoptive father played a significant role in the court's decision to turn down the grandmother's petition for custody. In addition, the greater financial resources of the adoptive father—who was also the girl's uncle—led the court to the conclusion that she should stay with him.[96]

Even when found fit, biological parents by the end of the century could lose their children if the courts believed the children would be better off with the adoptive parents. Most significant, southern justices began to argue that leaving children in the care of adoptive parents for a sustained period of time led to a forfeiture of parental rights. Therefore, when a Texas couple attempted in 1895 to regain custody of their daughter after giving her up for adoption three years before, the Court of Civil Appeals refused their request. Justice N. W. Finley observed that the birth parents in this contest were "people of good moral character," and that they were "kind, indulgent parents," but he also pointed out that since the adoptive parents had taken custody of the child, they had been "assiduous and devoted in their attentions to the child." In fact, they were now "deeply attached to the child as they would be were it their own child." The only child of the marriage, a fourteen-year-old girl, was "also deeply attached to the child." The vitality of the new family bonds, together with the significantly better economic and social position of the adoptive father, convinced Justice Finley that the interests of the girl would be best promoted by leaving her in the custody of the adoptive family. Reflecting the persistent unwillingness of southern judges to sunder biological bonds, however, Finley allowed the birth parents to visit their daughter at "reasonable intervals." [97]

Despite this continued solicitude for the preservation of blood ties, southern courts by the turn of the century had granted the adoptive family significant legal protection. Adoptive parents had gained the right to the custody, services, and earnings of the child, as well as the right to move the child's settlement or residence. The Tennessee Supreme Court made it clear, moreover, that even with the death of one of the adoptive parents, a biological parent would not be allowed to disrupt the contractual family. In 1898 James P. Streight had adopted the three-year-old son of Victoria Baskette with her consent. Streight and his wife had cared for the child several years prior to adoption, and two years after Streight died. At this point, Baskette filed suit to recover custody of her son. Baskette argued that, upon the death of the adoptive father, the natural right of the birth mother to the custody of her child was revived, because the widow of the adoptive father had not been a party to the adoption proceedings.

Justice William K. McAlister agreed with Baskette that James Streight was the exclusive adoptive parent. Mrs. Streight "was a stranger to the adoption proceedings, and can now assert no legal rights to the custody of the child." McAlister, like most other southern jurists, believed that adoption statutes, "being in derogation of the common law," should be "strictly construed," and he could not support the position that these statutes conferred rights "upon persons who are not parties to the record, and who have assumed no legal obligations as adoptive parent." Yet the judge also considered it important to take into account the best interests of the child. From this perspective, it appeared to McAlister that the boy should stay in the possession of Mrs. Streight due to the "strong mutual attachment" between her and the child. Putting aside his misgivings about the adoptive mother's technical lack of rights, the Tennessee judge awarded custody to Mrs. Streight.[98]

In short, when evaluating the rights of adoptive parents, southern courts remained committed for the most part to a narrow construction of adoption statutes. But toward the end of the nineteenth century the courts also became recognizably more sensitive to the welfare of the child. This evolving child-centeredness often led the judiciary to express findings that were at odds with a strict interpretation of the statutes. Southern judges found themselves breaking new legal ground as they attempted to come to grips with the difficult and complex issues posed by adoption. Consequently, the legal status of adoptive families achieved a firmer footing in southern courtrooms.

Although adoptive families experienced a measurable improvement in their legal standing during the late nineteenth century, their status remained distinct from that of biological families. Inheritance battles especially disclosed the extent to which this was true. The resolution of inheritance claims by adopted children inevitably led the courts to confront the issue of the common law's emphasis on blood ties as the basis for inheritance rights. Struggles over the inheritance rights of adopted children, in this sense, posed the fundamental test of adoption. As Michael Grossberg has commented, "Since the law jealously guarded the transmission of family property, inheritance disputes revealed the extent to which adoptive families differed from natural ones." [99]

Most legislatures left the precise determination of inheritance rights to the courts. As a result, the bulk of adoption cases coming before nineteenth-century courts concerned inheritance claims by adopted children. Southern courts, as in other adoption disputes, generally placed a strict construction on the statutes in dealing with the inheritance rights of adopted children. The restrictions that the southern judiciary imposed on the prerogatives granted adopted children stemmed from the fact that the law did not initially consider such children full legal members of their new families.

The majority of these inheritance contests involved challenges by blood relations of the adoptive parents. The relatives in these conflicts commonly called into question the legality of the bond created by adoption, in an attempt to block the inheritance rights of the adopted child. In some cases, where statutory requirements for adoption had not been fully met, the courts upheld the challenges of blood relations and denied the inheritance rights of adopted children. For example, the Arkansas Supreme Court refused to validate an adoption in 1894 because the order issued by the probate court failed to state the girl's place of residence at the time of the adoption, as stipulated by the act of 1885. The court's rigid insistence on compliance with every detail of the statute rested on the contention that the "proceeding to adopt a child as an heir was unknown at common law, and in this State exists only as a special statutory proceeding." Because the adoption papers had not been properly filed, the child forfeited any right to inherit her adoptive father's land.[100]

Even when adoptions were completely valid, many southern courts imposed tight restrictions on the inheritance rights that flowed from the new relationships. The courts, more often than not, limited these rights to the precise language of the statutes and petitions filed by adoptive parents. In *Russell v. Russell* (1868), the Alabama Supreme Court argued that the state's statutory provisions granted the adopted child no right to share an estate with a biological child of the adoptive parent when the parent's will had been executed before the adoption and was left unchanged. Although Chief Justice George W. Stone recognized that the adoptive father in *Russell v. Russell* "intended to place the child of his adoption on a level with his own child," Stone concluded that the parent's failure to alter his will following the adoption made it impossible for the adopted son to receive any part of the estate.[101]

The Mississippi Supreme Court also narrowly interpreted the state's adoption law to limit the inheritance rights of adopted children. The court held in 1898 that the statute regulating adoption granted the adopted child only those property rights that were explicitly outlined in the adoptive parent's petition. "The petitioner may propose much or little," the judges contended, "and the adoption decree can only secure to the infant the particular benefits proposed." Unless the petition detailed such rights, no guarantee existed that the adopted child would receive a share of the estate. In the case before the Mississippi bench, Alice H. Crump claimed a share of her adoptive father's estate. The father had agreed at the adoption proceeding to bequeath his plantation to Crump, who was his great-niece, but instead he conveyed the property to the woman upon her marriage. There was no uncertainty as to the legality of this conveyance. The father later died intestate, however, and the lack of a will cast doubt on the validity of his additional proposal in the adoption petition to leave the adopted daughter all of the other property not devised to others. The court asserted that this promise alone, vague as it was, did not give her any right in the estate, aside from the plantation. Instead, the Mississippi judiciary ordered the balance of the property to be divided solely among the so-called natural heirs.[102] Many southern jurists, then, viewed adoption as a contractual arrangement that transferred custody and gave the child a stable home without conferring full family property rights on the child. In this way, the courts could support the child-welfare aims of adoption, while minimizing the amount of disruption to the common-law rights of natural heirs.[103]

Although the southern judiciary generally protected common-law prerogatives, some judges refused to deny inheritance rights to adopted children on purely technical grounds, even when these rights conflicted with those of natural heirs. The decision of the Alabama Supreme Court in *Abney v. DeLoach* (1887) illustrates the point well. This case involved a dispute over the estate of John K. Sanders that pitted his nephew and two nieces against his adopted son. The nephew and nieces claimed that several violations of the state's adoption statute, including a failure to state the child's age and record the adoption order "on the minutes of the Probate Court," rendered the adoption invalid.

Justice Henderson M. Somerville noted that, in a strict sense, the adoption proceeding had violated statutory provisions. Yet, in his opinion, this did not destroy the legal validity of the proceeding. The Alabama judge had little doubt that adoption statutes should be interpreted precisely, because they were "in derogation of the common law." He warned, however, that the construction placed on these statutes should not "be narrowed so closely as to defeat the legislative intent which may be made obvious by their terms." In this dispute, Justice Somerville held that a "reasonable construction" led inexorably to the conclusion that Sanders had legally adopted the child, and that the nephew and two nieces must therefore share Sanders's estate with the boy.[104]

Other southern courts also began to afford the inheritance rights of adopted children a significant measure of protection against charges that their adoptions were technically invalid. Although jurists continued to construe adoption statutes rigorously, they became more amenable to overlooking procedural irregularities when such violations threatened to undercut the rights of adopted children to inherit from their new parents.[105] Gradually, these rights expanded in the South as adoption became more widespread and courts endorsed the position that certain inheritance rights were a logical outcome of adoption. For example, despite the fact that Mrs. Theodore Lilienthal left a will that devised all of her property to her husband, the Louisiana Supreme Court in 1885 insisted that the adopted son should inherit the bulk of the estate. According to the court, "The adoption produced that effect or it was an idle and barren ceremony."[106] The Georgia Supreme Court issued an even broader endorsement of adopted children's inheritance rights. In *Pace v. Klink* (1874), the Georgia judges decided that not only did adopted children have the right to inherit from their new parents, but also those adopted gained a right that was transferrable to their offspring. In particular, the children of an adopted person had the right to represent their parent in the distribution of the adoptive father's property if the adopted person died first.[107]

Still, the enlargement of adopted children's rights to inherit from their new parents took place slowly and significant limits to these rights persisted. The way in which southern courts treated the question of whether adopted children possessed the same inheritance rights as birth children of the adoptive parent was especially illuminating in this regard. Judges in the South widely agreed that statutory laws giving special protection to the inheritance rights of biological children should be upheld. The Louisiana high court declared in 1885 that the inheritance rights of adopted children were subject to the statutory provision requiring adoption not to impair the rights of any legitimate children or other "forced heirs." [108] Similarly, the Texas Supreme Court gave its backing a year later to legislation that prohibited the adopted heir from sharing equally with the birth children of the deceased. Under this legislation, when there were biological children of the adoptive parent surviving, the adopted child could not inherit more than one-quarter of the new parents' estate.[109]

Southern courts not only imposed restrictions on the right of adopted children to inherit from their new parents but also refused to allow these children to share in the estates of other members of their adoptive families. "As to the estates of other persons than the adopting parent," held the Tennessee Supreme Court, "the law of adoption fixes no right in the adopted child. It is only as to the adopting parent that the adopted child is made 'heir or next of kin' by the statute." Hence adopted children could not inherit from their new siblings, grandparents, aunts and uncles, and nephews and nieces. Because adoption was "purely a creature of statute," any relationship with members of the adoptive family outside that between the adopting parent and adopted child was "limited and qualified." In the words of the Tennessee tribunal, which decided in 1890 against an adopted child who claimed a share in the estate of his new nephew, "It was not a relation of blood, and except as to the adopting parent, it created none of the rights which, by the general law, depend upon blood relationship." [110]

At the same time that southern law placed these constraints on the rights of adopted children, it shied away from ending their natural inheritance ties. A few states outside the South—Connecticut, for example—had legislation explicitly stating that adopted children could not claim the estates of their biological parents. Southern jurists, in the absence of such legislative prohibitions, allowed adopted children to share in the estates of their biological parents, and they also let these parents inherit the estates of children that they placed out for adoption. The Tennessee Supreme Court in 1895 backed the right of Catherine Noe to inherit property from her son, who had been adopted in 1877. The boy had inherited the estate of his adoptive father, and then died unmarried and without any children. Although the adoptive father's next of kin sought a share in the boy's estate, the court contended that they could not inherit from the adopted child, "as it had no inheritable blood as to them and they none to the adopted child." Instead, the estate must go to the biological mother. The Tennessee judiciary thus reflected a continued commitment to blood ties even while it granted legal recognition to contractual families.[111]

Although adopted children steadily gained the right to inherit from their new parents, then, they were not completely incorporated into the new blood line. In the eyes of the law, they remained artificial members of their adoptive parents' families. As Simon Obermeyer argued in an 1875 article for the *Southern Law Review*, the intention of adoption legislation was "to have the adopted child gain a right of inheritance from the adoptive parent, and from him alone, and not to give or take away the right of inheritance naturally belonging to other persons, whether related to the adopting parent or adopted child." Obermeyer maintained, in particular, that adoption did not "sever the natural relation existing between the adopted child and its natural parents."[112] The adopted child therefore came to occupy an anomalous legal position, one which reflected the weight of past preoccupation with blood ties on the present.

Although the status of adopted children continued to be somewhat uncertain, adoption was far less vulnerable to legal challenges. In the Old South, adoption had been unusual and implemented with a discernable lack of enthusiasm, but by the beginning of the twentieth century the creation of contractual families through adoption had become routine, and the courts had taken on the responsibility of monitoring the process to ensure adherence to the child-welfare standard. The rapid spread of modern adoption procedures during the last decades of the nineteenth century, as well as the accompanying changes in custody and guardianship law, underscore the extent to which Reconstruction was a social process that embraced the southern household in its entirety and that lasted well past the end of Republican governments in the South in 1877.

Emancipation and the triumph of free labor helped to bring about a new order of domestic governance in the South, accelerating changes already underway and making these changes irreversible. Judicially supervised adoption was the logical outgrowth of a society that, on the one hand, had come to view social relations in terms of mutual arrangements based on self-ownership and, on the other hand, had become reliant on the paternalistic state rather than the patriarchal household to provide the primary source of authority and order. The South, then, provides a striking, if distinctive, illustration of Morton Keller's observation that the evolution of legal adoption in the United States mirrored "the tension between the extension of individual rights and the pressure for social order, a tension that was not resolved but, if anything, was heightened by the socioeconomic changes of the late nineteenth century."[113]

CHAPTER 6

THE FORCES OF PERSISTENCE:
RACE, BLOOD, AND GENDER

A tremendous surge of change rolled like a swollen river through the South after the Civil War and spilled over its banks, transforming corners of the society far removed from the battlefield and political stump. These changes seeped into social relations within the inner recesses of the household, and yet even as the floodwaters unleashed by war and emancipation swirled over the southern landscape, customs and conventions regarding race, blood, and gender demonstrated remarkable resilience, continuing to persist in the law and life of the former Confederacy. The torrent of political and economic change left its imprint on these entrenched attitudes and beliefs, but they remained largely intact after the war, much like Thomas Sutpen's house in *Absalom, Absalom!*: "square and enormous, with jagged half-toppled chimneys, its roofline sagging a little." [1]

In this sense, the longstanding debate about the extent of continuity and discontinuity in the New South misses the crucial point: these two historical forces were not mutually exclusive but rather existed in tension with each other, creating a distinctive dynamic—profound economic and political alterations with a strong undertow of cultural continuity—that set the South off from the rest of the country even as the region entered the main currents of national development. Change shaped and defined the forces of persistence, while these forces, in turn, shaped and defined the process of transformation. [2] The postwar paradox that lay at the heart of what became known as the "New South" was nowhere better demonstrated than in the legal developments regarding sexuality and marriage.

THE MISCEGENATION DEBATE

The defeat of the Confederacy and the collapse of slavery prompted a reevaluation by southern courts of the legitimacy of the antebellum miscegenation bans. The outcome of this inquiry into the constitutionality of the legal prohibitions proved to be a fateful one for the history of race relations in the South. For this reason, the judicial findings deserve careful consideration. A close analysis of the appellate court decisions reveals a persistent racial hostility among southern judges that compelled them to resist the fullscale adoption of a contractual understanding of matrimony, despite the headway that the precepts of contract made in other areas of domestic-relations law and labor law.[3]

Now that the protective barrier of bondage had collapsed, southern whites exhibited considerable apprehension about their ability to retain control over the former slaves. Racial amalgamation quickly became one of the most volatile legal and social issues as white anxiety over black male sexuality reached unprecedented heights. Feelings of insecurity and the belief that the supposed sexual powers of African American men would be irresistible to white women provoked an intensified obsession with racial purity.[4] As one southern white exclaimed, "If we have intermarriage — we shall degenerate; we shall become a race of mulattoes; we shall be another Mexico; we shall be ruled out from the family of white nations. Sir, it is a matter of life and death with the Southern people to keep their blood pure."[5]

Playing upon white fears of miscegenation, a term popularized during the Civil War, northern and southern opponents of Republican race policies warned that they would lead directly to intermixture.[6] A conservative delegate to the Arkansas Constitutional Convention in 1868, for example, attacked the extension of suffrage rights to blacks on the grounds that the "investing of an inferior race with social and political equality, is the stepping stone to miscegenation." Republicans usually responded to these charges by denying the logic of such reasoning and making clear that they did not support race mixing. Thus in the House debate on black suffrage in the District of Columbia, a Pennsylvania Republican scoffed at Democrats who raised the bugaboo of miscegenation: "It cannot be possible that any man of common sense can bring himself to believe that marriages between any persons, much less between white and colored people, will take place because a colored man is allowed to drop a little bit of paper in a box. . . . It is too trifling for argument."[7]

Despite Republican denials of any intention to legalize interracial marriages, southern critics of Reconstruction continued to make these charges. They did so in part because the miscegenation issue proved to be an effective way to split up white Republican support in the South and mobilize resistance to Radical Reconstruction. At the same time, the rhetorical emphasis on racial purity had the advantage of obscuring the degree to which whites themselves were responsible for the extensive miscegenation that had already taken place.[8] White responsibility for race mixing, though, did not escape the attention of African Americans in the postwar South. At a North Carolina convention of freedmen in 1865, Abraham H. Galloway, a mulatto, remarked pointedly, "The white man says he don't want to be placed on equality with the negro. Why, Sir, if you could only see him slipping around at night, trying to get into negro women's houses, you would be astonished."

Contemporary observers during Reconstruction believed that racial intermixture appeared to take place less often than before the war. "Miscegenation between white men and negro women diminished under the new order of things," a Freedmen's Bureau officer in South Carolina recalled. "Emancipation broke up the close family contact in which slavery held the two races, and, moreover young gentlemen did not want mulatto children sworn to them at a cost of three hundred dollars apiece. In short, the new relations of the two stocks tended to separation rather than fusion."[9]

Despite such observations, the historical evidence regarding actual rates of miscegenation is inconclusive. Clearly, southern whites feared that blacks after emancipation would rush to enter into interracial sexual liaisons or marriages. After generations of masters satisfying their sexual desires at the expense of female slaves, however, many freedmen and freedwomen welcomed a certain degree of racial distance when it came to domestic relationships.[10] In fact, although most African American delegates to state constitutional conventions opposed prohibitions against mixed marriages, a few agreed to support proposals to ban intermarriage if they included a section prohibiting white men from cohabiting with African American women outside of marriage.[11]

Accounts of miscegenation during the postwar years appeared in southern courts and newspapers. Maria Middleton, an African American woman, brought suit in 1870 against a South Carolina physician for failure to support her three children, who he had allegedly fathered. Rather than denying the paternity, the defendant's lawyer sought dismissal on the grounds that the plaintiff had no legal basis for the suit. In New Orleans, the antebellum pattern of concubinage lingered after emancipation, and for a few years the traditional social events for quadroon women and white men continued. The *New Orleans Times* reported in 1867, for example, that the quadroons had held a picnic at City Park for a number of "distinguished" white men from the community.[12]

White women and black men faced especially severe censure for engaging in sexual relations, yet contacts between them also continued to take place during Reconstruction. The change in the sex ratio among whites as a result of the war, according to historian John Blassingame, contributed to an increase in sexual encounters in New Orleans between African American males and white females. Evidence of such liaisons surfaced elsewhere in the South. In Mississippi, a former African American Union soldier and his wife, who was white, woke up early one morning in 1866 to the sound of local county officers carrying out a raid on their home. The couple, tried before the circuit court and found guilty, had to each serve six months in the county jail and pay a fine of five hundred dollars. A freedman in Alabama found himself in similar trouble with the law after his arrest in 1867 for living with a white female who employed him. Sentenced to thirty days in jail and ordered to pay a fine of two hundred dollars, he looked desperately for a way to extricate himself from the situation. He contacted the local Freedmen's Bureau officer for advice. "I proposed to mary hir but the Judge woodent suffer me. I shal loose my crop if you dont do something for me," the convicted man wrote. "I am ignoant of the laws of the Country. I will try to do write in the future."[13]

Following the reorganization of state governments under President Johnson's direction in 1865, southern legislatures moved rapidly on prohibitions against interracial marriage. The South Carolina black code, adopted in 1865, contained the first law ever enacted in the state barring marriage between whites and blacks.[14] In that same year Alabama and Mississippi significantly bolstered their comparatively weak antebellum sanctions. Alabama included a provision in its new state constitution making interracial marriages null and void, and Mississippi's black code stipulated that any person convicted of intermarriage should be confined to the state penitentiary for life.[15] While southern legislatures instituted stern measures to prevent interracial marriage, several states did not take the trouble to make interracial sex outside of marriage a separate crime. In these states, presumably, legislators believed that already existing statutes punishing fornication, cohabitation, and lascivious and lewd conduct sufficiently deterred interracial sexual behavior outside of marriage.[16]

Southern newspapers occasionally reported incidents in which the white community stepped in and administered its own brand of justice before those who violated antimiscegenation bans could be brought to court. In one Alabama community in 1867, the marriage of a white man to an African American attracted the wrath of the citizenry, "who seized the happy bridegroom, tore him from the gentle arms and tender bosom of his dark Alabama bride, and treated his venerable person to a souze in dirty pondwater, afterwards applying some gentle touches of raw hide to his rear. The Miscegenator was then put on the train, and sent off without Madame M."[17] Sometimes newspapers initiated their own campaigns to uphold the prohibition against miscegenation. The *Columbia Daily Register* in South Carolina, for example, attacked "white male adulterers who more or less infest every community in our State," asserting that such men "living unlawfully with negro women must be taught that virtuous society will not endure the evil which the law has especially condemned and provided punishment for."[18] Such campaigns disclosed the enduring reliance on community control when it came to the enforcement of racial etiquette in the rural South, even when whites had recourse to the law to punish infractions.

During the period of Radical Republican dominance, several southern states (including Mississippi and South Carolina) temporarily abandoned the prohibition against miscegenation.[19] This move raised an outcry among conservative whites, who predicted that racial intermixture would bring about the "*extinction* of such descendants of whites and Africans." "Now, there is not a man possessed of true manhood who would not say that death would be preferable at first and at once to such a perpetuation of the races, upon whom would be entailed a legacy of increasing misery and degradation," *De Bow's Review* proclaimed in 1868. For some writers, not even death could keep at bay the forces of social chaos if intermarriage took place. Admitting African Americans into the "family circle by the sacred rites of marriage," the author of "Progress of Amalgamation" warned, would give them the "power to open family vaults in the graveyards, order the white ancestors' bones to be disinterred and removed elsewhere, and their own transferred into these hitherto held sacred white family sepulchres."[20]

With the overthrow of Radical Reconstruction, resurgent white supremacists in the South reenacted antebellum measures or put new statutes on the books outlawing miscegenation. In addition, six southern states followed Alabama in prohibiting intermarriage by constitutional provision.[21] As before the Civil War, these new laws usually pronounced interracial marriages void, making the parties to such marriages subject to prosecution for violation of the laws against fornication and cohabitation. Maximum terms of imprisonment under the antimiscegenation statutes ranged from six months in Georgia to ten years in Florida, Mississippi, and North Carolina. Only Alabama, Georgia, Tennessee, and Texas made it a separate crime for unmarried persons of different races to live together, but many states continued to punish anyone issuing a marriage license to an interracial couple or performing the ceremony for them.[22]

Outside of the South, the hardening of racial caste lines in the late nineteenth century led to a new wave of legislation against interracial marriage, but this took place primarily in western states that entered the

Union after the Civil War. The major innovation of the West during this period was to extend its ban to include the growing number of Asians in the region. In the North, most states continued to rely on customary rather than legal restraints to enforce the color line in matrimony. Four northern states even abolished the prohibition: Rhode Island (1881), Maine (1883), Michigan (1883), and Ohio (1887). By the end of the nineteenth century at least twenty-six states, mainly in the South and West, had laws forbidding interracial marriage.[23]

In the South, the revitalized effort during the late nineteenth century to prevent interracial marriage and cohabitation manifested itself not only in a new round of prohibitory legislation but also in the rigorous treatment that criminal prosecutions under this legislation received in the high courts. Those who sought to escape miscegenation convictions in the state supreme courts had little success. Indictments of individuals who intermarried made up 72 percent of the appellate cases involving miscegenation prosecutions between 1866 and 1899, and 24 percent concerned indictments of persons who violated statutes punishing interracial fornication or cohabitation.[24] The gender of the white and black partners made little difference in the rates of reversal, and southern appellate courts affirmed over two-thirds of all the convictions.[25]

Defendants found guilty of violating the antimiscegenation statutes petitioned the appellate courts on a variety of technical grounds, including alleged flaws in the indictment process, insufficient or inadmissible evidence, improper instructions to the jury, and other procedural irregularities.[26] In the few reversals that did occur, the evidence regarding the racial identity of one or both of the parties was frequently in dispute. In *Moore v. State*, for instance, the Texas Court of Appeals ordered a new trial for a woman accused of intermarriage with an African American. In the court's judgment, it was not at all clear that the female defendant was white, although this was "an essential fact, perhaps the most essential to be established by the prosecution." Given the lack of clear proof, the Texas jurists concluded that sending her to prison for two years "would be an outrage upon law and justice, which the courts cannot tolerate." In another case, which appeared before the Virginia Supreme Court in 1877, members of the bench were convinced that they had more than enough evidence on the racial background of a woman indicted for contracting matrimony with a white man. But, as far as the court was concerned, the evidence showed that "less than one-fourth of her blood is negro blood." Therefore she did not fall within the statutory definition of "Negro," and her conviction for miscegenation could not be sustained.[27]

Although successful in the sense that they received a new trial, defendants in these appeals did not challenge the validity of the antimiscegenation statutes. Far more threatening were those cases that raised questions about the constitutionality of the bans on interracial marriage and sexual relations. In their response to these challenges, southern judges usually expressed an unremitting opposition to racial amalgamation. "The laws of civilization demand that the races be kept apart in this country," intoned the Tennessee Supreme Court in 1871. "The progress of either does not depend upon an admixture of blood. A sound philanthropy, looking to the public peace and the happiness of both races, would regard any effort to intermerge the individuality of the races as a calamity full of the saddest and gloomiest portent to the generations that are to come after us." [28]

Given the widespread adherence to such views among southern jurists following the Civil War, it is not surprising that the judiciary was nearly unanimous in its endorsement of legal sanctions against miscegenation. As members of the North Carolina bench proclaimed in 1869, "Late events, and the emancipation of the slaves, have made no alteration in our policy, or in the sentiments of our people." According to the court, Reconstruction measures were "not intended to enforce social equality, but only civil and political rights. This is plain from their very terms; but if the terms were doubtful, the policy of prohibiting the intermarriage of the two races is so well established, and the wishes of both races so well known, that we should not hesitate to declare the policy paramount to any doubtful construction." [29]

Nonetheless, the expanded legal personality of African Americans brought about by civil rights legislation and constitutional amendments during Reconstruction compelled the courts to rethink the basis for the bans on miscegenation. Antebellum policies had been formulated when most African Americans lived in the shadow of slavery and thus had few legal rights. The new political and civil rights of the former slaves seriously undermined the old legal foundation, and in response, judges devised a more elaborate framework to uphold the color line in domestic affairs. The aim of this revised defense was to narrow the scope of black citizenship and resist the principle of equal rights. In doing so, southern judges employed the institution of marriage to place significant limits on federal interference in the former states of the Confederacy. [30]

The impact of Reconstruction race policy on the thinking of southern jurists could be seen most clearly in Alabama, where the prohibition against miscegenation became a source of conflict among appellate judges. In 1872 the Republican-dominated state court drew on the Civil Rights Act of 1866 and the Fourteenth Amendment to strike down the sanctions against interracial marriage, making Alabama the only state before

1948 whose judiciary invalidated an antimiscegenation law. As the justices pointed out in *Burns v. State*, the granting of citizenship to African Americans included the right to make and enforce contracts. Viewing marriage as "civil contract," the court maintained that the "same right to make a contract as is enjoyed by white citizens means the right to make any contract which a white citizen many make. The law intended to destroy the distinctions of race and color in respect to the rights secured by it."[31]

The Alabama judges dismissed the contention that the ban on intermarriage was nondiscriminatory because it applied equally to both races. As they put it, the Civil Rights Act "did not aim to create an equality of the races in reference to each other. If so, laws prohibiting the races from suing each other, giving evidence for or against, or dealing with one another, would be permissible. The very excess to which such a construction would lead is conclusive against it." Thus no restraints could be imposed on the ability of any citizen to contract matrimony with a person of a different race.[32]

The invalidation of the Alabama antimiscegenation laws proved to be short lived. Five years later, following the fall of Reconstruction, a new court made up of Redeemers overturned the Republican ruling, attacking it as "very narrow" and "illogical." Contrary to the Burns decision, the judges in *Green v. State* asserted that the racial prohibition did not discriminate against African Americans because both races were subject to the same criminal punishment under the law. Expressing their firm belief that the Civil Rights Act of 1866 did not intend to legalize interracial marriage, the justices observed that many of the congressmen voting for the measure lived in states with similar laws on mixed marriages.[33]

Most important, the Alabama court relied on an increasingly accepted view of marriage as a legal status, rather than simply a contract, to uphold the power of each state to determine marital capacity. Rejecting the emphasis of their Republican predecessors on the contractual nature of marriage, the new judges stressed the peculiar character of matrimony and the "undoubted right" of each state to supervise it.[34] In advancing this argument, the members of the Alabama bench cited the work of Joel Bishop, whose writings on American marriage laws contributed in large part to the reclassification of wedlock as a hybrid of status and contract.[35]

The main advantage of this approach, of course, was that it kept the enlarged contractual capacities of African Americans from threatening the validity of racial curbs. Indeed, the justices contended that the state had an obligation to shore up these barriers because interracial unions endangered the social order and family stability. Insisting that homes were "the nurseries of States," the Alabama court asked, "Who can estimate the evil of introducing into their most intimate relations, elements so heterogeneous that they must naturally cause discord, shame, disruption of family circles and estrangement of kindred?" In short, the state did not violate the Civil Rights Act or the Fourteenth Amendment by prohibiting intermarriage.

Interracial households made up of slave owners and their slaves had formed the cornerstone of southern society before the Civil War, but the destruction of slavery necessitated a bolstering of boundaries between whites and blacks. The judges concluded that marriage was a social right rather than a political or civil right, and as such, was subject to state intervention. In an age that increasingly endorsed the principles of the wage contract, the ability to enter into the marriage contract thus became hedged in by regulations and prohibitions.[36]

Other southern courts, seeking to defend prohibitions against inter-racial marriage, also emphasized the noncontractual character of matrimony. The Texas high court mounted this defense of the ban on intermarriage in 1877 when it heard the appeal of Charles Frasher, who had been indicted for entering into wedlock with an African American woman. Frasher claimed that the Reconstruction amendments and legislation at the federal level made the state's antimiscegenation statute unconstitutional because it imposed a penalty upon a white person who violated its provisions, but prescribed no punishment for the black partner. The Texas Court of Appeals, however, held that marriage was "not a contract protected by the Constitution of the United States, or within the meaning of the Civil Rights Bill." Instead, matrimony was a "civil *status*, left solely by the Federal Constitution and the law to the discretion of the states, under their general power to regulate their domestic affairs." Because the states had the authority to prohibit interracial marriages, the Texas jurists continued, "it therefore follows, as the night follows the day, that this state can enforce such laws as she may deem best in regard to the intermarriage of whites and negroes in Texas, provided the punishment for its violation is not cruel or unusual."[37]

Accompanying the redefinition of marriage carved out in late-nineteenth-century decisions like the Frasher case was an increased propensity to defend antimiscegenation statutes on the grounds that interracial unions posed serious social and biological risks to society, and thus states had a responsibility to prevent such unions. The racial prohibition, from this perspective, was part of a broader judicial trend in the postwar period to promote more rigorous tests of marital fitness that supposedly protected the well-being and safety of the public. Included in this development were tightened marital restrictions dealing with age, kin ties, and mental and physical health.[38]

In formulating the social and biological argument, southern courts used pseudoscientific findings drawn from a growing body of racial thinking that was characterized by its pessimistic views of heredity. During the late nineteenth century, most white southerners became convinced that not only were blacks racially inferior but their extinction was all but certain in the struggle for existence.[39] It followed from such contentions that miscegenation would lead to the deterioration of the white race and that the preservation of racial purity was a legitimate object for the exercise of legislative power. The Georgia Supreme Court offered this line of reasoning as early as 1869 in upholding the conviction of Charlotte Scott, who had married a white man. "The amalgamation of the races is not only unnatural, but is always productive of deplorable results," the justices declared. "Our daily observation shows us, that the offspring of these unnatural connections are generally sickly and effeminate, and that they are inferior in physical development and strength, to the full-blood of either race."[40]

The costs allegedly incurred when racial purity was not preserved led southern jurists to support not only the ban on intermarriage but also laws against interracial sexual relations. In *Pace and Cox v. State* (1881), the Alabama appellate court affirmed the legality of imposing stricter penalties on interracial fornication or adultery than on illicit intercourse between members of the same race, pointing out that the penalties were applied equally to both races. "The discrimination is not directed against the person of any particular color or race," said the court, "but against the *offense*, the nature of which is *determined by the opposite color of the cohabiting parties*." According to the Alabama judges, the crime of living together in adultery or fornication was far more serious when it was committed by persons of different races, and therefore required more severe punishment. The result of interracial sexual relations, they insisted, "may be the amalgamation of the two races, producing a mongrel population and a degraded civilization, the prevention of which is dictated by a sound public policy affecting the higher interests of society and government."[41]

Southern appellate jurists, then, developed a twofold defense of anti-miscegenation statutes. On the one hand, they claimed that marriage was more of a legal status than a mere contract, allowing them to forestall the classification of marriage as a political rather than social right. Hence, recent developments under Reconstruction did not affect the power of the states to regulate matrimony as they saw fit. On the other hand, the judges cited the social and physiological consequences of amalgamation to support the legitimacy of sanctions against both interracial marriages and sexual relations. Such sanctions were necessary, in their opinion, to protect the health and welfare of society. Similar arguments found their way into appellate opinions outside the South, but they were deployed most extensively in courts below the Mason-Dixon line.[42]

Having secured the constitutionality of the antimiscegenation laws, southern jurists set out to evaluate the ramifications of these laws. Judges in the late nineteenth century agreed with their antebellum predecessors that statutes making interracial marriages absolutely void necessitated treating the offending parties as unmarried persons. Consequently, the courts upheld the practice of prosecuting individuals of different races who married under the fornication and cohabitation laws.[43]

A simple declaration that a marriage between a white person and an African American was "null and void," however, did not settle the status of children born to parents of different races. Indeed, the issue was much debated at the appellate level in the postwar South. North Carolina was unusual in that its antimiscegenation statute explicitly prevented the father from legitimizing the offspring of a mixed marriage, so the courts there had little difficulty denying such children the right to inherit. In fact, the North Carolina Supreme Court did just this in an 1892 case.[44] The situation was somewhat different in Virginia. The law in this state declared that children of a void marriage were legitimate, but members of the appellate bench could not agree whether this provision applied to the offspring of an interracial couple. Although a majority of the jurists concluded that it did not, Justice Richardson sharply dissented, asserting that "the dominant white race has not yet struck, nor will it likely ever strike at the natural legal rights of unoffending children through the sins of their parents." "The idea of amalgamation is repugnant to the white race," Richardson observed, but this did not mean that "the blight and curse of bastardy" should be inflicted on those who were the product of intermixture.[45]

The Georgia Supreme Court agreed with Justice Richardson, arguing in 1887 that there was nothing in the state's law to prohibit David Dickson, a white man, from making provision in his will for the offspring of his cohabitation with Julia Frances Lewis, who had been his slave before emancipation. A wealthy planter, Dickson left the bulk of his estate, about $300,000, to his daughter, Amanda America Dickson. David Dickson's white relatives hired a battery of lawyers to contest the case, which went all the way to the Georgia high court. The appellate justices upheld the validity of the will, basing its decision on the citizenship rights granted to blacks in the Fourteenth Amendment as well as the inviolability of private property rights. The court recognized that popular sentiment in the white community strongly supported overturning the will. But, in the court's words, "loyalty to the law and rigid adherence to the rules it prescribes, is to the enlightened magistrate the plain path of duty, and in pursuing it he can fall into no error nor run into any kind of danger."[46] Overall, as Mary Frances Berry shows, children of interracial relationships won at least twenty cases involving inheritance disputes in southern state supreme courts between 1868 and 1900; it appears that they lost only eight contests.[47]

Another thorny issue involved couples who contracted matrimony in a state where the marriage was not prohibited and later entered another state where it was. Mississippi, Texas, and Virginia had laws on the books after the Civil War that expressly condemned any attempt to evade the prohibition against miscegenation by marrying out of the state and then returning to it.[48] Although statutes in the other southern states made no direct reference to this problem, postwar judges clearly agreed with the antebellum position that when an interracial couple left the state in which they resided solely for the purpose of evading its ban on intermarriage and later returned to their domicile, the marriage was void even though it was valid where contracted. As the North Carolina Supreme Court explained in 1877, the prohibition against interracial marriage "would be very idle if it could be avoided by merely stepping over an imaginary line."[49]

The application of rules regarding the conflict of laws became more complex when parties dwelling in a state whose laws allowed intermarriage later moved to another state that punished the practice. The record of southern jurists during the late nineteenth century on whether such marriages were valid is murky. In *State v. Bell* (1872), the Tennessee Supreme Court decided to nullify a marriage between a white man and black woman who had contracted matrimony in Mississippi when interracial unions had been permitted there. According to the court, "Each State is sovereign, a government within, of, and for itself, with the inherent and reserve right to declare and maintain its own political economy for the good of its citizens, and cannot be subjected to the recognition of a fact or act contravening its public policy and against good morals, as lawful, because it was made or existed in a State having no prohibition against it or even permitting it." Thus, although the marriage had been valid in Mississippi, the couple became subject to criminal prosecution for miscegenation when they moved to Tennessee. To hold otherwise, the judges warned, left the state open to the danger of "the father living with his daughter, the son with the mother, the brother with the sister, in lawful wedlock, because they had formed such relations in a State or country where they were not prohibited." The dire consequences outlined by the Tennessee justices were highly unlikely, but the extreme nature of the analogy with incest underscored the court's intense hostility toward racial amalgamation, which it viewed as "revolting" and "unnatural." [50]

Not all southern jurists agreed with the emphasis of the Tennessee judiciary on state sovereignty. Although members of the North Carolina bench also denounced miscegenation as "immoral and opposed to public policy," they acknowledged the validity of unions involving interracial couples who moved to the state from other jurisdictions that allowed such marriages. In *State v. Ross* (1877), the appellate judges affirmed the legality of a marriage between a white woman and black man that had been celebrated in South Carolina when interracial unions were not forbidden. Noting that the husband and wife had both established residence in South Carolina before entering into wedlock, the jurists concluded that the marriage "must be regarded as subsisting after their immigration here." [51]

Such findings affected only a small minority of interracial couples and did not in any way indicate support on the part of the North Carolina Supreme Court for the practice of intermarriage. Like their colleagues elsewhere in the South, North Carolina judges had no doubts that the state could prohibit interracial marriages within its own boundaries, and that residents could not elude this prohibition by marrying in another state and then returning to their domicile. Whatever minor disagreements existed over the consequences of antimiscegenation statutes, the southern judiciary in the late nineteenth century shared an unwavering commitment to the preservation of racial distinctions in matters involving marriage or sexual contact.

The arguments in support of the bans on miscegenation revealed a growing inclination among southern judges to enlarge state supervision of the household. Before the Civil War, although southern jurists firmly backed the legal effort to prevent miscegenation, they perceived the racial curbs as merely reinforcing the social controls provided by slavery. Following the defeat of the Confederacy, a rising concern about the impact of emancipation on private life and public order gave added significance to the racial restrictions and led to the forging of a sturdy new legal rationale for this prohibitory legislation. The expanded judicial justification for state intervention was so effective that the sanctions against interracial marriage and sexual relations remained on the statute books in the South until the late twentieth century. [52] The new reliance on the state to define and protect the public welfare, which fueled the revitalization of the racial prohibitions as well as the growing regulation of parenthood, eventually resulted in the legal transformation of the southern household. In this way, persistent beliefs about race in the postwar South encountered changed circumstances and then adjusted to them through the mechanism of legal innovation, preserving the core of the beliefs—a commitment to white supremacy—in the process.

THE POLITICS OF RAPE

This same process of adjustment can be observed in the treatment of rape in southern courts after the Civil War. State statutes no longer explicitly called for the imposition of stiffer sentences on blacks convicted of rape or attempted rape than on whites found guilty of similar crimes. Still, hardened racial attitudes in the wake of emancipation had an unmistakable impact on the outlook of judges in cases involving sexual assaults on white females by black men, and led to a disparity in the treatment of defendants of different races. Southern courts even went so far as to develop special procedural rules that applied only to black defendants on trial for the rape or attempted rape of white women and girls. Furthermore, poor white and black women continued to endure negative stereotypes that underscored their inferior positions and that made rape and attempted rape difficult crimes to prosecute successfully. Despite dramatically changed circumstances, then, the legal treatment of sexual violence after the Civil War maintained class and racial hierarchies in southern society.

During the debates over miscegenation, sex and politics became intertwined to a remarkable degree in the postemancipation South as white anxiety about black male sexuality rose to a fever pitch. The popular mythology about the black rapist that developed during this period also had tremendous political resonance.[53] Rape challenged the power of the male household head to protect the women, children, and other dependents in his family, and damaged his standing in the community. By violently gaining access to another woman's sexuality, the rapist not only exercised control over the woman but also undercut the public authority of her husband or father. Now, with the transformation of the household that took place with emancipation and the subsequent redefinition of who qualified as a household head and citizen, the position of propertied white men in both the private and public spheres came under severe pressure. The collapse of slavery liberated African Americans from their dependent role within the household of their master and created the possibility for former slaves to become heads of their own households and actors in the political process. In this context, black political participation and black male sexuality became closely identified as twin threats to the former dominance of white planter/patriarchs. The rape of white women by black men became a metaphor for this perceived loss of power and prestige, for the overthrow of an old hierarchical order that could never be restored and the establishment of an egalitarianism that would, it was feared, lead inexorably to social chaos. It is this vision that drove men like Ben Tillman, the U.S. senator from South Carolina, to storm, "Whenever the Constitution comes between me and the virtue of the white women of the South, I say to hell with the Constitution!"[54]

The changing legislation of the late nineteenth century reflected the rising concerns regarding rape. A few southern states eliminated the death penalty for rape immediately after the Civil War, but this reform was short lived.[55] By the end of the nineteenth century, every state in the South allowed capital punishment, and some states required it, for those convicted of rape. Most legislatures gave the jury authority to impose either the death sentence or a prison term. The 1884 Code of Tennessee stated, for example, "Whoever is convicted of the rape of a female shall suffer death by hanging; *Provided*, The Jury before whom the offender is tried and convicted, may, if they think proper, commute the punishment for the offense to imprisonment in the penitentiary for life, or for a period of not less than ten years."[56] Rape statutes no longer explicitly stipulated different sentences based on race, but such language clearly left open the possibility of wide disparities in the treatment of white and black men by the legal system.[57] Although the majority of southern states permitted the death penalty for rape, assault with intent to rape was no longer a capital crime; prison terms ran from no more than two years in Louisiana to as much as life in Florida.[58]

Because the criminal statutes after 1865 were race neutral, at least on the surface, the vast majority of the rape cases that reached the appellate level in the South do not indicate the racial background of the parties involved. Indeed, the North Carolina State Supreme Court in an 1883 opinion expressed puzzlement at the designation of the defendant filing the appeal as "a person of color," pointing out that the pertinent statute "makes no distinction as between the races."[59] Nevertheless, thirty-seven of the opinions involving prosecution for rape or attempted rape during the last third of the nineteenth century clearly identify the male as African American and the female as white. Of the thirty-seven appeals, the courts upheld convictions in twenty.[60]

The outcome was quite different when the prosecution involved sexual assaults on African American women and girls. Of the 12 cases in which both the male and female were identified as African American, only 4 convictions were sustained.[61] Out of about 345 appeals by males convicted for rape or attempted rape that appear in the published records of state courts in the South between 1865 and 1899, only 2 identifiable cases involving a white man and black female could be found; in both instances, the appeals by the men were successful.[62] The overall pattern of these appellate decisions underscores the persistence of a rigid racial hierarchy after emancipation and, in particular, the subordinate place of African American women in southern society.

As before the Civil War, the sexual assault of a white female by a black man sparked the most heated public rhetoric. In *Jones v. State* (1876), for example, the Texas Court of Appeals assailed "a stout, able-bodied negro" for perpetrating a "foul deed upon a young, delicate white woman" who was newly married and pregnant. "The result of the dastardly outrage was not only the loss of health and happiness to the young wife, but the destruction, no doubt, of her fondest hopes and anticipations, in the premature loss of her child," the appellate opinion declared. Affirming the death sentence inflicted on the black defendant, the Texas court made clear its paternalistic role in maintaining the purity of white womanhood: "The protection of female virtue—to woman the dearest of earthly possessions—and the inviolability of womanhood are the highest and most sacred trusts which the genius of civilization and the interests of society impose upon the law and those who are charged with the duty and responsibility of its faithful execution."[63]

In many appellate opinions involving the prosecution of African American men even the supposedly factual descriptions of the crime were inflammatory, and some verged on the pornographic in their use of images. In describing the assault of "a negro boy" on a seventeen-year-old white girl, an 1888 opinion detailed how the defendant allegedly "threw the witness down, pulled up her clothes, got on top of her, and by main strength and force, despite her protests, screams and struggles, had carnal knowledge of her person, penetrating her sexual organ with his male member, first having inserted his finger." According to the statement of the case, a doctor who examined the two parties after the attack testified that the girl's "female organ was unusually small for a female of her age," whereas "the defendant's sexual organ" was "of extraordinary large size." Given such a provocative account, it is not surprising that the court had "no doubt" that the evidence warranted conviction and execution of the appellant.[64]

Black defendants convicted in rape cases protested in their appeals against the use of racially charged rhetoric. Genie Brown, found guilty of "assault with intent to ravish" a ten-year-old white girl, took exception to the prosecutor's characterization of him in closing arguments to the jury. Calling on the jury to convict the defendant, the prosecutor declared that a guilty verdict would "protect innocent little girls from such black fiends and demons." The Alabama Supreme Court, in an 1898 opinion, demonstrated little sympathy for Brown's appeal, maintaining that the evidence supported this portrayal. As the court put it, "So long as counsel confine themselves to the evidence in the case and reasonable inferences deducible therefrom, they cannot and should not be controlled by the court as to the language employed by them, if decorous or not offensive to the court trying the cause."[65]

What sort of language was offensive to the courts? Attacks that appellate jurists perceived as undermining respect for the law drew their swiftest condemnation. In an 1894 trial, for example, a Texas prosecutor remarked to the jury that friends of the woman allegedly assaulted by an African American man "had not in their anger taken the law in their own hands and lynched or applied the torch to [the] defendant." Consequently, according to the counsel, "the life of this demon of human flesh on trial should pay the penalty." The state's high court energetically dismissed this line of argument; in its words, the notion that the defendant "should be hanged because a mob had not hanged or burnt him is monstrous indeed." Awarding the man a new trial, the Texas jurists proclaimed, "It is not in the interest of the State to secure the conviction of the accused, though they be guilty, by any method except that which is in accord with the due and proper course of the law of the land."[66]

African American defendants challenged the language used outside as well as inside the courtroom in rape trials in an effort to get a fair hearing. Alfred Thompson, a member of an African American regiment in the U.S. Army, asked for a change of venue after being charged with raping a white woman in Alabama. According to Thompson, local newspapers announced that he was "the villain who committed the deed" before the trial, and these publications depicted him as "the brutal negro who assaulted a respectable white woman." The accusations, as well as the threat of mob violence, made it impossible for him to get an impartial trial in the community, Thompson argued. The lower court refused to grant his request for a trial in another county and, upon his conviction in 1898, the private appealed to the state supreme court. The appellate judiciary supported the decision of the trial judge not to grant a change of venue, but it overturned the conviction on the grounds that evidence identifying him as the attacker had been improperly admitted against the defendant's objection.[67]

As these last two appellate opinions indicate, although emotions could run high at the trial, state supreme courts in the South did not automatically sustain the convictions of black men charged with raping white women. Besides inadmissible evidence, improper instructions to the jury by the trial judge regarding the law of rape led to new trials for several African American men.[68] Other technicalities also led to decisions in favor of the appellant. Joe Warton, a former slave, was indicted for raping a white woman in 1859, and over the course of eight years was convicted three times by a county jury, condemned to die twice, and in 1867 was sentenced to ten years in prison under a new law that repealed the rape statute calling for the execution of blacks who raped white women. The Tennessee Supreme Court asserted, however, that the Act of 1866, which substituted imprisonment in the penitentiary for the death penalty, "operates as a pardon of all crimes or offenses committed before that time, and supersedes the jurisdiction of the Criminal Courts." As a result, Warton did not even have to serve time in prison; he was a free man in the fullest sense of the word.[69]

Not only procedural flaws and legal technicalities but also insufficient evidence led appellate jurists to grant new trials to black men charged with sexually assaulting white females. A key issue in appeals involving convictions for attempted rape was evidence of intent. When the courts believed that the testimony was not sufficient to show that an African American defendant intended to rape the female, they stepped in and reversed the verdict, although appellate jurists tended to shy away from interfering with the jury's conclusions.[70] "There is great danger of improper convictions in cases of this character," the Mississippi Supreme Court maintained, "and, while the court should not for that reason invade the province of the jury, the danger admonishes us of the necessity of standing firmly upon the right and duty of proper supervision and control of them."[71]

Despite such efforts to grant them a fair trial, the judicial treatment of African Americans charged with sexually assaulting white females reflected the intensification of hostile racial attitudes in the postwar South. These attitudes manifested themselves in special rules that applied only to blacks on trial for attempted rape or rape of white women and girls. Southern courts, for example, allowed juries to consider the race of the defendant and victim in determining the defendant's intent in prosecutions for attempted rape. If the accused was black and the victim white, according to this judicial rule, the jury had a reasonable basis for inferring that he intended to rape her. No other evidence was necessary to establish intent. As one judge counseled a jury, "You have the right to consider who the parties were; consider whether one was a black person and the other a white person. You have a perfect right to take in consideration the difference in races, so as to see what the intention of the parties was."[72]

Appellate courts were quick to uphold the rule that "social customs founded on race differences" might be taken into account in assessing the question of intent. Indeed, the Georgia Supreme Court in 1899 went even further, arguing that the race of the parties could be used "to rebut any presumption that might otherwise arise in favor of the accused that his intention was to obtain the consent of the female, upon failure of which he would abandon his purpose to have sexual intercouse with her." Because no African American man could reasonably assume that "a white woman would consent to his lustful embraces," according to the court, he could not claim that he intended to discontinue his effort to have sexual intercourse if he met with resistance.[73] Thus a key procedural protection enjoyed by white defendants could not be employed by blacks accused of attempting to rape a white female.

For most southern judges, it was simply a matter of common sense that a black man, in encountering a white female, would try to rape her, and that a white woman would never assent to sexual intercourse with a black man.[74] Chief Justice Pearson of the North Carolina Supreme Court drew a crude barnyard analogy in an 1876 case that emphasized the racism underlying such assumptions: "I see a chicken cock drop his wings and take after a hen; my experience and observation assure me that his purpose is sexual intercourse, no other evidence is needed." Although Pearson conceded that there might be some doubt whether the cock's pursuit was made "with the expectation that he would be gratified voluntarily" or was made "with the intent to have his will against her will and by force," the chief justice insisted that the jury had the right "to call to their assistance their own experience and observation of the nature of animals and of male and female *instincts*." In the case at hand, Pearson had little doubt, "given the repugnance of a white woman to the embraces of a negro," that there was sufficient evidence to find the defendant guilty of attempted rape.[75]

In prosecutions for rape, the different weight given evidence regarding the woman's chastity when the defendant was an African American also put him at a serious disadvantage. Generally, the courts agreed that a woman's prior sexual history had a direct relation to the likelihood of her having consented to any subsequent sexual intercourse. As the Arkansas Supreme Court observed in 1899, "It is more probable that an unchaste woman assented to such intercourse than one of strict virtue." Furthermore, the woman's overall reputation for immorality had a significant impact on her credibility as a witness.[76]

Before the Civil War, evidence of a white woman's lack of chastity sometimes persuaded the courts to treat black defendants with relative leniency. But not so after the war. In *Barnett v. State* (1887), for example, the Alabama Supreme Court upheld the rape conviction of an African American man on the uncorroborated testimony of a white prostitute. The appellate court acknowledged that the usual rule in rape prosecutions was for "the jury to be exceedingly cautious how they convict a defendant on the uncorroborated testimony of the prosecutrix, expecially when there is evidence tending to impeach her credibility." Although the woman had been "impeached for ill-fame in chastity" and refused to undergo a medical examination, the court found no reason to question the verdict of the jury and, consequently, Will Barnett was sentenced to the penitentiary for life.[77]

While African American men struggled against stereotypes about the black rapist, customary white notions about the promiscuity of black women persisted after the Civil War. In an 1885 trial in Limestone County, Texas, the white employer of a black woman who had brought rape charges against another man characterized her as "a simple, silly-minded, childish negro." The witness testified to her poor reputation for chastity, but added that it was "about on an average with that of other unmarried negro women." Such widely held opinions left African American women vulnerable to sexual assault by white men who believed that they had a right to take advantage of this supposed licentiousness.[78]

Sexual violence against African American women became especially rampant during the racially motivated terror campaign launched during Reconstruction. A Freedman's Bureau agent related in 1866 the ordeal of Rhoda Ann Childs of Henry County, Georgia. In his words, Childs was "taken from her house, in her husband's absence, by eight white men who stripped her, tied her to a log, beat and sexually abused her." Childs's account of the attack, published several weeks later in the *Loyal Georgian*, provided a far more graphic account: Two of the attackers "took hold of my feet and stretched my limbs as far apart as they could while the man standing upon my breast applied the strap to my private parts. . . . Then a man supposed to be an ex-Confederate soldier, as he was on crutches, fell upon me and ravished me. During the whipping one of the men had run his pistol into me, and said he had a great mind to pull the trigger." Unfortunately for African American women, incidents like this were repeated countless times throughout the South as white supremacists sought to reaffirm racial dominance after emancipation.[79]

Confronted with this sort of brutality, many African American women preferred to remain within a world circumscribed by their kin, neighbors, and church congregation. Many women from poorer households, however, had to supplement their family's income by entering into domestic service. Not only did these women work long and hard hours for white families, but they had to run the risk of sexual abuse in their employer's home. As one servant observed at the turn of the century, "I believe that nearly all white men take, and expect to take, undue liberties with their colored female servants—not only the fathers, but in many cases the sons also. Those servants who rebel against such familiarity must either leave or expect a mightily hard time, if they stay."[80]

African American women after the Civil War challenged the violence against them, keeping the issue of sexual abuse in the public eye by bringing charges against black and white men who assaulted them. Cases involving the rape and attempted rape of black women steadily appeared before southern courts throughout the late nineteenth century. In Granville County, North Carolina, about one-half of the cases of rape, attempted rape, and other forms of sexual violence tried between 1865 and 1886 involved African American women. Of course, it was one thing to bring charges and another to get a conviction. Although African American women achieved some degree of success in their prosecutions when the assailant had the same racial background, no white men were convicted in Granville County during this period for attempted rape or rape of a black female.[81]

As mentioned earlier, the only two prosecutions of white men for sexually assaulting black females that reached the southern appellate level in the last third of the nineteenth century did not fare any better. Yet the fact that African American females could get a hearing at all in the courts was an achievement, considering that before the Civil War the rape or attempted rape of a black woman or girl by a white man was generally not a crime. If nothing else, the appearance of such cases in the courts showed that the African American community could compel whites to acknowledge that sexually assaulting a black female was a public matter.

Sometimes juries could even be convinced that a white man was guilty. In the 1889 trial of a white man in Halifax County, North Carolina, for attempted rape of a fourteen-year-old African American girl, the prosecuting attorney was implacable in his effort to gain a conviction, leading him to make a potentially explosive observation. "If the color of the parties was reversed, no doubt the jury would neither have the pleasure, nor displeasure, of trying the defendant," he argued. "This thing of outraging innocent girls, white or black, must be stopped by the Courts, or Judge Lynch will stalk through the land unmolested." Apparently, the jury agreed with him, because it sentenced the white defendant to five years in prison; on appeal, however, the North Carolina Supreme Court threw out the conviction in *State v. Powell* (1890) on the grounds that the indictment was defective.[82]

For African American women, the racial stereotype that depicted them as driven by sexual passion and incapable of rational behavior made it unlikely that courts would take seriously their charges of rape or attempted rape even when the assault involved an African American man.[83] Indeed, cases in which both parties were African American often brought out a paternalistic streak in southern judges that led them to condescend to both the defendant and alleged victim. Thus in 1876 the Georgia Supreme Court, reversing the conviction of a sixteen-year-old black male for the rape of a black girl under the age of ten, commented, "The parties all belong to the colored population of our state, who, owing to their ignorance, as a general rule, should have justice administered to them tempered with much mercy." [84]

The justice that such patronizing attitudes produced could border on the nonsensical. Julia Lagrone testified, for example, that she was walking home from church one Sunday afternoon when Fern Williams, an eighteen-year-old African American, propositioned her. When she declined, Williams "caught hold of her, and threw her down, and ravished her." Lagrone, who was "a year or two older than the defendant," determined not to let the incident pass and complained of the crime to the first person she met afterward. Although Williams was indicted for rape, the jury returned a verdict finding him guilty of a lesser crime, assault with an intent to rape, because of doubts about whether Lagrone had actually consented to sexual intercourse with him. According to Williams, "She asked me for a dollar after I got through"; her request angered him, so he threw her to the ground.

The Arkansas Supreme Court in 1899 upheld the conviction for attempted rape, but lowered the sentence from five to three years.[85] Julia Lagrone managed to get her assailant imprisoned, but for a crime neither of the parties thought he had committed. She claimed that Williams had raped her, Williams's testimony conceded that he had assaulted her after having consensual intercourse with her, and the jury found Williams guilty of assault with intent to rape. The resulting muddle that passed for justice in this case highlighted the uphill battle faced by African American women who sought to challenge the sexual violence perpetrated against them. Despite the long odds, however, these women resolutely contested the assumptions of sexual entitlement that men of both races held, seeking in the courtrooms to overturn these assumptions and thereby improve their position in southern society.

Like black women, poor white women continued to face tremendous disadvantages in the courtroom because of widespread beliefs that they were less worthy of protection from sexual violence. As before the Civil War, lower-class women frequently were as much on trial as the men who attacked them. The stock phrase used to describe many of them was "bad character," a term that referred to a woman's social station as well as to females who refused to conform to societal expectations of proper gender roles. By establishing the bad character of a woman, the defendant sought not only to undermine the credibility of her testimony but also to imply that the female party was somehow responsible for her plight.[86]

The postwar courts, attempting to project an image of objectivity and evenhandedness, insisted that the reputation of the woman should not play a role in the outcome of a rape trial. As the Alabama Supreme Court asserted in 1875, a woman "may be of ill-fame for chastity, but she is still under the protection of the law, and not subject to a forced violation of her person, for the gratification of the propensities of the man who has the strength to overpower her." Yet the Alabama jurists conceded, almost in the same breath, that "her known want of chastity may create a presumption that her testimony is false or feigned."[87]

Underlying this mixed message was a persistent mistrust of female sexuality that reached far beyond the courtroom. Clearly, any woman who ventured outside the bounds of sexual propriety in the late Victorian South did so at her own risk, regardless of her race. In the most extreme instances, white women who engaged in illicit sexual activity could find themselves answering to Klansmen and their supporters, who heaped abuse on those considered to be lacking in virtue. In North Carolina, the Klan attacked a white girl whose poor reputation came to its attention; according to a witness, "they took her clothes off, whipped her very severely, and then lit a match and burned her hair off, and made her cut off herself the part that they did not burn off with the match."[88]

Lacking the necessary social standing, lower-class white women provoked such descriptions in the court records as "a woman without virtue," "a reputed prostitute," or "a common strumpet."[89] Any indication that a white female did not adhere to elite notions of womanhood significantly undercut her chances to convince the court that she had been sexually assaulted. Echoing the sentiments of his antebellum counterparts, Justice McFarland of the Tennessee Supreme Court asserted in 1879, "No impartial mind can resist the conclusion that a female who had been in the recent habit of illicit intercourse with others will not be so likely to resist as one who is spotless and pure."[90] Such reasoning abounded in the appellate opinions of the late nineteenth century, often leading to the reversal of convictions for rape and attempted rape.

A striking expression of the belief that women who were sexually active outside of marriage left themselves open to male violence appeared in a case that came before the Texas Court of Criminal Appeals in 1896. Dick Shell, convicted of assault with intent to rape a fifteen-year-old girl, claimed that he had mistaken Clara Sliwinski for her older sister, "who was a lewd woman." When Shell discovered his error, after taking the girl upstairs to his hotel room, he abandoned his bid to have sexual intercourse with the her. The Texas appellate jurists sympathized with Shell's plight, pointing out that the alleged assault had occurred at night. According to the judges, Shell could have easily confused the identity of the girl with her sister and this helped to excuse his conduct towards Clara. The high court reversed Shell's conviction, explaining, "Men take liberties with prostitutes they would not take with virtuous women without intending to rape them."[91]

Clara Sliwinski was unfortunate enough to live in a jurisdiction in which the age of consent was only ten. Other southern states, however, set the age of consent as high as sixteen by the end of the nineteenth century. In cases involving the prosecution of men charged with carnal knowledge of youngsters under the age of consent, no evidence of force had to be presented.[92] The reasoning underlying this policy was that children below a certain age were incapable of sufficiently understanding the nature of sexual intercourse to consent to it. Even doubts about the chastity of the girl and the absence of physical force could not prevent a conviction for statutory rape.[93]

Above the age of consent, however, the courts insisted on a strict definition of force and they required conclusive evidence that the woman actively resisted the sexual advances of the man charged with rape. As the Georgia Supreme Court noted in 1896, "Opposition by mere words is not enough. . . . A 'mixed' resistance or merely equivocal submission will not do. There may be slight physical resistance even though there is a mental willingness to submit." Without clear indications of a "struggle or attempt at physical resistance," southern appellate courts were reluctant to uphold a rape conviction. They did concede, however, that the threat of physical harm might limit the effort of the woman to withstand her attacker, and that evidence of making such threats could be construed as using force. In the words of the Arkansas high court, "If the woman submitted from terror or dread of greater violence, the intimidation becomes equivalent to force."[94]

The major exception to the judicial policy on force involved the use of fraud to persuade a woman to engage in sexual intercourse. According to Texas law, fraud in this context included administering to a woman, "without her knowledge or consent, some substance producing unnatural sexual desire, or such stupor as prevents or weakens resistance." Fraud also included any "strategem by which the woman is induced to believe that the offender is her husband."[95] Without taking active steps to misrepresent himself, however, a man who had sexual intercourse with a married woman who was not his wife while she was asleep could not be convicted of rape by fraud. In *Mooney v. State* (1890), the defendant climbed on a woman "in the old-fashioned, time-honored way and had carnal knowledge of her without her consent, penetrating her sexual organ with his male member while she was asleep." The Texas Court of Appeals reversed his conviction and awarded him a new trial because he did not employ any artifice to induce her to believe that he was her husband.[96]

More than an obtuse bit of legal reasoning, such appellate opinions underscored the fact that a husband could not be convicted of raping his wife, and that he had no need to secure her consent in order to have sexual intercourse with her. As the Louisiana Supreme Court held in 1899, "*The husband* of a woman cannot himself be guilty of an actual rape upon his wife, on account of the matrimonial consent which she has given, and which she cannot retract."[97] In an 1890 North Carolina case, a white defendant drew on a similar line of reasoning to maintain that he was not guilty of assault with intent to rape his wife. The evidence showed that he had forced a black man to have sexual intercourse with his wife, threatening both of them with a gun. The state supreme court granted that the husband could "enforce sexual connection" with his wife, but contended that the husband could not transfer his right to sexual access to someone else. Sustaining the guilty verdict, the court concluded that, "in respect to this offence, he stands upon the same footing as a stranger."[98]

Whether it was the brutal violation of marriage vows, or the racial dynamics of the sexual triangle set in motion by the husband, the North Carolina court in this case rushed to the protection of the wife, stepping in to repair the rent in the social fabric created by the husband's failure to observe the paternalistic responsibilities that went hand in hand with his rights. Not all women in the Victorian South were so quick to receive the assistance of the courts in cases of sexual assault. What one judge called a woman's "experience and condition in life" clearly shaped the degree to which the legal system granted her protection from male violence, despite protestations to the contrary.[99] In particular, race, class, and adherence to elite standards of sexual propriety played a major role in determining a woman's fate in court.

Although white elites used the prosecution of rape to reinforce racial and class stratification, women did not simply remain passive victims subject to violent assault. Instead, by filing complaints against men who sexually attacked them, at least some women sought to use the courtroom as a way to initiate a debate over southern womanhood and to confront patterns of thinking that placed poor white and black women outside the bounds of proper society. Largely unsuccessful in their efforts, it nevertheless took great courage for these women, who suffered a long history of exploitation and devaluation, to bring charges that almost always set off attacks on their own character.

At the heart of how men constructed the law of rape in the South and elsewhere in Victorian America lay not only an impulse to protect those who were judged worthy of protection; there was also a fear that women could use false accusations of rape to redress the balance of power between the genders. The contention of English legal commentator Lord Hale that the charge of rape "is easily made, hard to be proved and harder to be defended by the party accused, notwithstanding his innocence" captured the tone of most southern appellate opinions in the nineteenth century. The danger of women bringing spurious charges against men, according to the courts, made it necessary to grant defendants in rape trials "privileges which are not always allowed to persons accused of crime." Thus the insistence on a close scrutiny of a woman's social standing and reputation for chastity, as well as the strict standards imposed on the proof necessary to show that the alleged assault took place against her will. Otherwise, as the Georgia Supreme Court remarked in an 1871 opinion reversing the conviction of a doctor indicted for raping one of his patients, "Men . . . are put in the power of abandoned and vindictive women to a great extent." [100] The anxiety reflected in such statements represented the underside of paternalism, the desire of those in power to stay in control. Given the social, political, and economic turmoil of the late-nineteenth-century South, it is not surprising that the emphasis on control rather than protection dominated the thinking of elites.

INCEST AND THE DYNAMICS OF COERCION

The tension between granting protection and maintaining control also characterized judicial attitudes toward the prosecution of incest. Certainly, the courts were quick to point out the perils that incest posed to society. A Texas jurist proclaimed in 1882 that incest was "an outrage upon nature in its dearest and tenderest relations, as well as a crime against humanity itself." The goal of the legal prohibition against such behavior, announced the North Carolina Supreme Court in 1886, was "to preserve the purity of the domestic circle, and prevent alike the physical and moral consequences of the abhorrent and unnatural act inhibited."[101] Despite this forceful rhetoric, the postbellum southern judiciary continued to demonstrate an ambivalent attitude toward criminal punishment as a means to discourage incestuous activity. Indeed, between 1865 and 1900, state courts in the South considered the appeals of thirty-seven individuals convicted of incest and granted new trials to seventeen of these defendants.[102]

Ambivalence about public intervention in the household shaped statutory as well as judicial developments regarding incest. Alterations after the Civil War in the legal rules regarding forbidden degrees of marriage reflected a persistent conflict between competing views of matrimony as private and contractual, on the one hand, and as a public affair involving the preservation of the social order, on the other. The emphasis on individualism and contractual rights could be seen in the unimpeded trend of southern states toward the relaxation of restrictions on affinal marriages. Mississippi in 1871, Virginia in 1873, and Georgia in 1875, for instance, lifted their bans on unions with an uncle's widow. At the same time, Virginia abolished its prohibition against marrying a nephew's widow.[103]

In contrast to this loosening of controls on affinal relationships, preoccupation with marriage as a source of social stability led to tighter regulation of consanguineous unions. Most important, Arkansas and Louisiana imposed bans on first-cousin marriages by the end of the century.[104] Other blood relations also fell within the forbidden degrees during this period. Alabama legislators in 1867 extended their marital prohibitions to unions with the daughter of a half-brother or half-sister, and North Carolina lawmakers in 1883 included half-blood relatives in their list of restrictions. Furthermore, the Mississippi legislature in 1880 banned marriages between uncles and nieces for the first time, and in 1892 it saw fit to state explicitly that grandparents and grandchildren could not contract matrimony.[105]

It is not entirely clear why southern lawmakers moved in the late nineteenth century to expand the number of prohibitions against unions between blood relatives at the same time that they were paring down the number of affinal restrictions. New concerns about the possibility of transmitting hereditary defects through marriage, concerns that also made themselves evident during this period in laws banning interracial marriages, accounted in part for the closer regulation of consanguineous unions. Legal commentators throughout the country began to cite such biological arguments with greater frequency after the middle of the nineteenth century to support their opposition to marriages between persons closely related by blood.[106] The Arkansas Supreme Court reflected these heightened fears in 1886 when it explained the aim of the new state ban on first-cousin unions: "The intention of the legislature was to prohibit the intermarriage of persons nearly related by blood, partly no doubt, on account of the supposed evil consequences to body and mind resulting to the offspring of such marriages."[107]

Besides anxiety about inbreeding, a concern with preserving social ← order during the postwar era also led to new criminal punishments for incest. Most important, lawmakers in North Carolina, South Carolina, and Virginia expanded their incest prohibitions, which before the war dealt only with marriage within the forbidden degrees, to include sexual intercourse between certain near kin. Like the other southern states that made incestuous sexual relations a crime before the Civil War, the penalties varied dramatically among these three jurisdictions. In North Carolina an 1879 act made copulation between a grandparent and grandchild, parent and child, or brother and sister a felony punishable by imprisonment in the county jail or penitentiary for up to five years. Intercourse between an uncle and niece or aunt and nephew, however, was only a misdemeanor, and the convicted parties could be punished by fine or imprisonment, at the discretion of the court.[108] Under South Carolina's act of 1884, all those who had sex within the prohibited degrees were subject to the same punishment: a fine of not less than five hundred dollars and at least one year in the penitentiary. Virginia followed a similar route but exacted an even lighter penalty; its 1887 law stipulated that individuals convicted of incestuous sexual intercourse should be fined a maximum of five hundred dollars or imprisoned not more than six months.[109]

Of the forty criminal cases dealing with incest that reached the appellate level in the South between 1865 and 1900, only one involved marriage within the forbidden degrees.[110] The rest consisted of prosecutions for incestuous fornication or adultery, depending on the marital status of the defendant, or simply for incestuous cohabitation. As before the war, usually the man only was indicted. Southern jurists continued to emphasize that incest was not a joint offense and mutual consent of the parties was not necessary for an incest conviction. As the Alabama Supreme Court pointed out in 1895, "Every element of the crime denounced in our law may well exist against one party to the sexual act though the other did not consent thereto."[111] In such cases charges of either rape or incest could be brought against the defendant. Thus the Supreme Court of Texas, in turning down an 1885 appeal by James Mercer, observed that the father could be found guilty of incestuous intercourse with his daughter regardless of whether she "consented to his carnal knowledge of her. She might be entirely innocent of any crime, and yet he might be guilty of rape or incest, or both, by having carnal knowledge of her."[112]

As in *Mercer v. State*, the most common relationship between the parties in southern incest appeals during the late nineteenth century was that of father and daughter. Forty percent of the state supreme court decisions involved the prosecution of father-daughter incest. Twenty-five percent of the cases dealt with the prosecution of incest between step-fathers and stepdaughters, and 20 percent concerned uncle-niece incest.[113] In short, more than four-fifths of the incest cases that appeared in southern high courts during the latter decades of the nineteenth century involved older men accused of carrying out incestuous relations with subordinate female relatives who were considerably younger. If these cases were at all reflective of the kind of incest occurring in the population at large, then incest in the Victorian South had clear patriarchal overtones. It can at least be said with certainty that in the cases examined here incest usually took place in the context of an unequal distribution of power between the parties in terms of their age, gender, and position in the family.

On balance, the new statutory regulations of incest in the late nine-teenth century created the potential for greater judicial intervention in southern domestic relations. The high rate of reversals during this period, however, indicated the unwillingness of appellate judges to break signifi-cantly with the antebellum argument that statutory punishments for com-mitting incest were in derogation of the common law and thus should be narrowly construed. The strict constructionism of southern jurists, among other factors, seriously limited the intrusiveness of the courts and often led them to order new trials in appeals from incest convictions. In *John-son v. State* (1886), the Texas Supreme Court overturned the conviction of Robert Johnson, who had been indicted for sexual intercourse with his fifteen-year-old stepdaughter, Kinnie. The Texas justices did not dispute evidence that intercourse had occurred between these two individuals and that Johnson may have used force to gain his stepdaughter's compliance. But the judges pointed out that sexual relations between the girl and her stepfather did not take place until after her mother had died. Therefore, according to the court, Johnson could not be charged with incest because the relation of stepfather and stepdaughter, within the meaning of the statute, "had ceased to exist" following the termination of the marriage relation between Johnson and Kinnie's mother, even though the girl con-tinued to live in Johnson's house. "Under the facts of the case, he may be guilty of fornication and of adultery and perhaps of rape," concluded the Texas jurists, "but not of incest."[114] Likewise, the Tennessee Supreme

Court refused in 1898 to uphold the incest conviction of a man charged with impregnating his wife's sister because the sexual relationship had commenced after the wife died. The court contended that the deceased wife's sister was no longer an affinal relative and hence sexual intercourse between them was not incestuous. In its words, "This is the literalism of the statute, and the spirit is not broader than the letter." [115]

Besides a persistent propensity to interpret the incest laws strictly, southern high courts maintained a vigorous commitment to procedural formalism in criminal cases, often awarding new trials to defendants accused of incest on grounds that were quite technical in nature. As a Tennessee judge explained in 1891, "No feeling of abhorrence respecting the crime should obscure the judgment or abate the vigilance of the Court to see that he has the fullest and fairest trial and chance to establish his innocence under the law, which in its best strictness is in its best purity." [116] Appeals from incest convictions after the Civil War raised three major procedural issues: flaws in the indictment process, admissibility and sufficiency of evidence, and corroboration of female testimony. A systematic examination of the way that southern courts handled these issues reveals the extent to which the judiciary sought to ensure the defendant's procedural safeguards in criminal trials. At the same time, it demonstrates the general lack of regard on the part of southern jurists for the victims of incest.

An almost unnerving insistence on procedural niceties was especially evident in the judicial response to flaws in the indictment process. The Mississippi Supreme Court reversed an incest conviction in 1891 because the word "feloniously" had been omitted from the indictment.[117] The Arkansas court exhibited a similar predisposition to quash incest indictments on the basis of technical defects. In an 1886 case, the court held that an indictment was insufficient because it accused the parties of incestuous fornication without making it clear that they were unmarried at the time of the alleged crime. Seven years later, an Arkansas father won his appeal from a conviction for copulation with his daughter on the grounds that the indictment charged him with incestuous adultery but did not state his marital status. "A particular description of the specific act which constitutes the crime of incest, when committed by parties within the prohibited degrees, as well as the status of the party charged" were necessary components for an adequate indictment, the Arkansas court decided, insisting upon adherence to this rule, "however technical it may seem." [118]

As we have seen, southern jurists throughout the nineteenth century commonly ordered new trials because of convictions based on faulty indictments. Even antebellum slaves convicted of felonies were able to take advantage of small mistakes in indictments to gain new trials. This pre-occupation with accurately drawn indictments stemmed from the belief that the accused had the right to know exactly what crime he or she had allegedly committed.[119] Certainly, judicial attention to the form of the indictment was called for when substantial flaws, such as seeking conviction for a nonexistent crime or a truly inadequate description of the offense, were involved.[120] As Daniel Flanigan notes, however, "This quite sensible requirement . . . when too rigidly applied resulted in numerous reversals and new trials because of miniscule drafting errors."[121]

Not only did southern jurists uphold a strict observance of the indictment process, they also adopted tough requirements for the admissibility and sufficiency of evidence. Although southern judges had demanded high standards of proof during the antebellum period, the increased number of incest appeals after the Civil War led to the development of more detailed evidential rules. In order to prosecute for the crime of incest, two main elements had to be established: the relationship of the parties and sexual intercourse between them. On the first issue, southern high courts argued that "the evidence should be clear and unequivocal as to the fact of the relationship." If the evidence fell short of this standard, the courts did not hesitate to overturn an incest conviction because proof of the relationship was "absolutely essential to the establishment of the crime charged." In *McGrew v. State* (1883), for instance, Texas appellate jurists ordered a new trial for William McGrew, who was accused of incestuous intercourse with his stepdaughter, on the grounds that his legal marriage with the girl's mother had not been "proven affirmatively." At issue was whether the mother's original marriage had been legally terminated, either by divorce or death of the first husband, before she married McGrew. "If she was not his lawful wife," observed the court, "then the illicit connection of McGrew with her daughter by the previous marriage, however reprehensible in morals, would not constitute the crime of incest in law."[122]

Crucial for an incest prosecution, proof of relationship was usually not difficult to attain. Establishing the act of sexual intercourse was far more complex, and state supreme courts in the South grappled at length with this knotty legal problem. Generally, southern jurists maintained that in prosecutions for incest evidence could be admitted relating to sexual acts between the parties at any time prior to the indictment charging incestuous intercourse. When attempting to establish that the illicit relations continued, the prosecution also had the right to present proof of sexual intercourse following the act specifically under trial.[123] Nevertheless, because the majority of incest offenses were committed within the privacy of the family home, they remained difficult to prove. Often other family members were the only witnesses, and they were frequently reluctant to testify. In most jurisdictions, moreover, wives were prohibited by law from testifying against their husbands in prosecutions for incest. The Texas Supreme Court in 1882 granted Daniel Compton a new trial because his wife had testified against him, claiming that Compton had engaged in sexual intercourse with her fourteen-year-old daughter by a former marriage. The appellate court in South Carolina took a less restrictive approach, deciding that a wife could act as a witness against her husband in an incest prosecution as long as she was not compelled to disclose "any confidential communication" during the marriage.[124] Any restraints on the testimony of wives, however, made it more difficult to establish the occurrence of incestuous intercourse in the household.

Even more serious as an obstacle to the effective prosecution of incest was the fact that in many cases the uncorroborated testimony of the female party was not enough to bring about the conviction of the accused. Although southern courts usually did not prosecute the female party in incest cases, they held that when she consented to incestuous intercourse she was an accomplice. In Florida, a conviction could be supported on the uncorroborated testimony of an accomplice, but this was not true in other southern states, where accomplice testimony required corroboration.[125]

To authorize an incest conviction on the testimony of an accomplice in these states, corroborating evidence had to connect the accused with the commission of the offense. According to the Georgia Supreme Court, evidence that went "no further than merely to raise a grave suspicion that the accused committed the crime in question" was insufficient. Thus, the court contended, a young woman's pregnancy did not corroborate her testimony against her stepfather to the extent that it warranted his conviction of incestuous adultery. But evidence that the stepfather had tried to bribe the arresting sheriff and, when this proved unsuccessful, "exclaimed that the thing would ruin him and his whole family" was adequate corroboration. Appellate courts elsewhere in the South laid down similar rules on the extent of corroboration necessary to support the testimony of an accomplice to incest.[126]

Failure to instruct the jury on the law of accomplice testimony and the necessary corroboration was a reversible error, and in several late-nineteenth-century cases defendants gained new trials on these grounds.[127] More important, though, the issue of accomplice testimony raised the questions of what constituted consent on the part of the female, and at what point she became an accomplice to incestuous intercourse. In *Mercer v. State* (1885), the Texas Supreme Court defined an accomplice in the following terms: "If the witness, knowingly, voluntarily, and with the same intent which actuated the defendant, united with him in the commission of the crime against him, she was an accomplice." On the other hand, "if in the commission of the incestuous act, she was the victim of force, threats, fraud or undue influence, so that she did not act voluntarily, and did not join in the commission of the act with the same intent which actuated the defendant, then she would not be an accomplice, and a conviction would stand even upon her uncorroborated testimony." [128]

These seem like fairly straightforward and sensible guidelines, yet in the case before it the Texas court appeared to construe the phrase "force, threats, fraud or undue influence" in an extremely restrictive manner. According to the prosecution witness, her father "first forced her to submit to his unnatural desire when she was thirteen years old, and he continued to have sexual intercourse with her from that time until she was twenty years old." The father had impregnated her at that time, and when she was about four-and-a-half months advanced, she revealed the paternity of the child. The court did not believe that "this long continued incestuous intercourse" could have taken place without the consent of the witness, and it contended that she was an accomplice to the crime. The judges noted that she was "a stout, healthy girl" and yet offered "no resistance" during the last sexual encounter in which she became pregnant. The woman, however, said that she "did not cry out, nor did she make any great resistance, simply because she was afraid." And well she might be, for she had tried to resist her father's sexual advances two years earlier and he had "whipped her severely with a board." Following the final copulation, her father told her that "if she ever reported the occurrence to any one, he would beat her to death." Surely, this constituted threatening behavior and the exercise of "undue influence." Why the Texas judges did not think so is difficult to explain, but they obviously demonstrated enormous insensitivity to the woman's ordeal. Fortunately, in this instance, the jurists felt that enough corroborating evidence existed to uphold the father's conviction. [129]

In other cases, however, where the court considered the female party an accomplice and there was insufficient corroboration of her testimony, southern appellate justices overturned the incest convictions of male defendants. In an 1896 case, for example, Ada Coburn testified that her father coerced her into copulating with him, beginning when she was six years old. Despite this testimony, the Texas Supreme Court argued that certain circumstances "were such to indicate that she was consenting." Specifically, the court asserted that "no objection or resistance was interposed when the least act of resistance or objection interposed by her would have prevented the acts of sexual intercourse." Because no corroborating evidence existed outside of the woman's testimony, and because the lower court had failed to instruct the jury on the subject of accomplice testimony, the Texas high court reversed the father's conviction and ordered a new trial.[130]

Apparently, unless there was evidence of actual physical resistance on the part of the female party, she was considered an accomplice to incest. Most southern judges gave little weight to the concept of psychological coercion in their determinations of whether a female had consented to incestuous intercourse. In *Taylor v. State* (1900), Maggie McGuire insisted that "she had never consented to the illicit intercourse" with her stepfather; "in each instance it occurred against her will, and . . . she was forced to submit to his lustful embraces." The Georgia Supreme Court, though, decided that "she in fact consented to it, so doing however with that reluctance and disinclination which would naturally be felt by any young girl in sustaining such relations with her mother's husband." Of course, by acknowledging that she was a "young girl," the court underscored the fact that she lacked the maturity and autonomy to make a real choice respecting sexual relations with her stepfather. It is hard to imagine circumstances under which sexual relations between these two parties would not have been abusive.[131]

Although appellate judges by and large discounted the significance of psychological coercion, not all of them were unaware of the subtler dynamics of incest. At least two jurists from the Georgia Supreme Court recognized that often incest was not consensual and that it almost always involved sexual relations based on power and inequality. According to Judge McKay, "The unnatural crime . . . is generally the act of a man upon a woman, over whom, by the natural ties of kindred, he has almost complete control, and generally he alone is to blame." Unlike most of his colleagues, McKay realized that there was "a *force* used, which, while it cannot be said to be that violence which constitutes rape, is yet of a character that is almost as overpowering." [132]

Judge Crawford seemed to endorse this view of incest dynamics eleven years later in his 1882 decision to uphold the conviction of a man for incestuous fornication with his niece. The young woman had been living with her uncle since the death of her mother thirteen years before, and she had given birth to a child whom she claimed the defendant had fathered. Testifying that the sexual relationship was not voluntary, the niece explained that "she had been taught to obey him, was afraid of him, and gave up to him because she was afraid of him." The appellate court jurist considered her an accomplice, and only the corroborating testimony of a servant made it possible to convict the uncle. Judge Crawford, however, sympathized with the niece's plight, and he censured the uncle for bringing about "the ruin of this young woman," portraying him as a man who had betrayed the trust of a female under his protection:

> Fatherless and motherless, brought up in the house where he stood as the head of the family, taught to obey him, and above all being the very man to whom she would naturally turn to protect her against wrong, we can well imagine the truth of her statement, that the sexual intercourse was not voluntarily indulged in, and that the coercion of which she spoke was but the paralysis of all power to suggest a reason against the terrible wrong, or assert herself against his caresses and apparently loving force until he had accomplished her ruin.[133]

Given the central role of psychological coercion in the exercise of patriarchal authority, it is not surprising that southern judges largely accepted the legitimacy of its use.[134] For the most part, southern jurists assumed that absence of strong physical resistance to the male's sexual advances meant that the woman consented to incestuous intercourse and was thus an accomplice. The predisposition to classify women as accomplices, together with the rule in most jurisdictions prohibiting an incest conviction upon uncorroborated accomplice testimony, made it difficult to prosecute the crime because often there was no other witness to provide sufficient corroboration.[135]

Many northern courts in the nineteenth century appeared to have devised a strikingly different approach to the prosecution of incest cases, especially regarding the issues of psychological coercion and corroboration of female testimony. Appellate jurists in the North more widely embraced the notion that incestuous assaults could take place even in the absence of physical force. In an 1895 case, the Wisconsin Supreme Court upheld the incest conviction of Ernest Porath, who engaged in sexual intercourse with his thirteen-year-old daughter while they were pitching hay in the family's barn. The Wisconsin judges noted that "her resistance was not as strenuous and effective as it might have been." "It does not necessarily follow in all such cases," the court asserted, however, "that the female is to be regarded as an accomplice, and particularly in a case like the present, in view of the relation between the parties, and the coercive authority of her father over her." Likewise, the Michigan high court pointed out that James Burwell did not employ physical force in an assault on his daughter and that she "yielded on account of threats and fear." As a result, the judges contended, "evidence tending to show that he had abused and beaten her before, that he was abusive to his wife and other children, and the language used on these occasions, were competent and important for the jury to consider in determining whether she yielded under those circumstances which under the law are the equivalent of force." Northern jurists, then, more readily recognized that, although a female party might not physically oppose the sexual advances of her father or stepfather, this did not automatically mean she became an accomplice in the commission of the crime.[136]

Even when the woman or girl was considered an accomplice, many northern jurisdictions allowed incest convictions based on her uncorroborated testimony. According to the Vermont Supreme Court, the evaluation of such testimony was "always a question for the jury, who is to pass upon the credibility of the accomplice, as they must upon that of every other witness." In cases where the prosecution of incest rested upon the uncorroborated testimony of an accomplice, warned the Vermont appellate jurists, the court should always "advise great caution on the part of the jury in giving credit to it," but the jury should not be instructed, "as a matter of law, that the prisoner in such a case must be acquitted."[137]

Requiring corroboration of female testimony in circumstances that pitted one person's word against another indicated that southern courts had a basic mistrust of the victim's testimony. It also suggested that although appellate jurists in the nineteenth-century South roundly denounced incest as a crime against nature, they felt conflicted about actually prosecuting men for the crime. Judicial ambivalence stemmed in large part from a continued commitment to the patriarchal ideal. Even the Georgia justices who acknowledged that incest usually occurred within the context of unequal power relations did not abandon this ideal. Rather than attacking the traditional family as an outmoded institution, these jurists focused their criticisms on individual men whom they perceived as misusing their "natural" power to rule. The judges did not mean to imply by their criticism of the males in these cases that patriarchal authority ought to be eliminated or transformed. On the contrary, they continued to assume that inequality and hierarchical control formed the very basis of the family.

In this context, the concept of being an accomplice to incest was a legal fiction that allowed southern judges to express their disapproval of incest while restricting convictions for the crime mainly to those indisputable instances of assault which exposed the coercion inherent in the exercise of patriarchal authority and therefore called into question its legitimacy. The criminalization of incest in this manner actually strengthened the legitimacy of male power in southern households by isolating those patriarchs who used physical violence against female members of their family to gain sexual satisfaction, and labeling these men as "deviants." For those men who employed psychological coercion the chances of successful conviction seemed to be far less. Despite the judicial rhetoric of outrage, then, the reality was that during the late nineteenth century the sexual access of men to women and children in their families remained unchallenged in some important ways. In this sense, legal change led to the reshaping rather than decline of patriarchy, with the state stepping in to monitor the household only in the most extreme cases.

The effort to preserve the legitimacy of male authority in the household that can be discerned in the southern appellate incest cases was not simply a holdover from an antebellum world tolerant of psychological coercion. The reluctance to prosecute men accused of incestuous sexual relations absent clear signs of physical violence should also be viewed in the context of changing modes of racial control. With the abolition of slavery, primary responsibility for the maintenance of racial order shifted from the household to the public arena, a move highlighted by the Black Codes and, after their demise, the emergence of Jim Crow laws. The increased reliance on the state to enforce white supremacy was one more sign of the passing of the old domestic order. The postwar ambivalence about intervening in families to prosecute incest may have stemmed from a desire on the part of southern judges to undergird patriarchal rule in the home during a time of high anxiety about the declining importance of the household in the governance of southern society.

The legal regulation of miscegenation and rape in the postemancipation South also reflected widespread consternation about the profound changes set in motion by the Civil War and Reconstruction, as well as the determination of those in power to retain an upper hand in race, gender, and class relations. Underlying the general commitment to white supremacy and racial separation was an obsession with keeping black men away from white women, and keeping lower-class blacks and whites from mounting a united challenge to elite rule. These preoccupations were readily apparent in the wave of lynchings and related forms of racial violence that swept the region at the end of the century, all of which drew on sexuality to maintain their potency. As Nell Irvin Painter puts it, "Sex was the whip that white supremacists used to reinforce white solidarity, probably the only whip that could cut deeply enough to keep poor blacks in line."[138]

The resort to lynch law revealed not only important dimensions of the racial, gender, and class dynamics of the late-nineteenth-century South, it also underscored the continuing commitment of white southerners to community control and custom even in the face of increased state authority. With the racial controls of slavery dismantled, white dismay about black male sexuality combined with fears about African American political and economic autonomy, forming an inflammatory mixture that exploded at the slightest provocation. Seizing on any infraction by individual black men of the etiquette governing interactions with white women, white men sought to justify retribution against an entire race and to ensure the purity of white women. The myth of the "black beast rapist," in particular, allowed less-affluent white males to portray themselves as defending "their" women at a time when economic uncertainty made it difficult for these men to fulfill their financial responsibilities to the household and when traditional gender roles seemed to be weakening.

The eruption of racial violence thus had its roots in southern ideas about sexuality and gender roles as well as race relations.[139] Southern white women as well as men helped to promote these notions. One of the more popular myths that evolved out of the Lost Cause was that of the valiant female, who in spite of all insults to her dignity during the war and its aftermath, held her head up high and remained a lady in the most dire of circumstances. Evelyn Baker Dodd captured this image perfectly in an 1894 article: "History affords no parallel of like privation, distress and defeat, which have developed a nobler, truer, more heroic, more adorable womanhood, arisen from the ashes of sorrow and desolation." [140]

Now, at the end of the nineteenth century, having done so much to earn the respect and favor of white males, the southern lady had to be protected from the most treacherous menace of all: the black rapist. Just as legislation against miscegenation and rape aimed at preserving racial purity and keeping female whites on their pedestals, so the extralegal employment of the noose sought to protect white womanhood against the alleged hypersexuality of this supposedly subhuman creature. The African American rapist was no distant threat, southern newspapers and common wisdom insisted; whether ensconced in the relative security of the town or isolated in the countryside, every white woman was subject to sexual attack, and only constant vigilance could ensure her safety.[141] Not even the grossest violations of the incest ban seemed to generate as much horror and rage in the white community as rape by an African American man. The outburst of lynching, a movement largely generated by anxiety about the perceived threat of black rape, not only exposed the persistent influence of traditional beliefs about race, gender, and blood but also forced southern elites to reexamine their fundamental assumptions about law and the nature of domestic governance in southern society.

DOMESTIC GOVERNANCE IN
THE NEW SOUTH

Charles W. Chesnutt, a black writer raised in North Carolina, published a collection of short fiction in 1899 about African American life called *The Wife of His Youth and Other Stories of the Color Line*. In one of the stories, "The Sheriff's Children," Chesnutt explores the issue of lynching in the postwar South, deftly probing the complexities of race relations, family dynamics, and the law in rural North Carolina. As in other southern communities, the Civil War in Branson County was "the one historical event that overshadows all others." But "the fierce tide of war," having rushed through the surrounding country, only "slightly disturbed the sluggish current of life in this region, remote from railroads and navigable streams."

Ten years after the surrender at Appomattox, one of the county's prominent white citizens—a former Confederate officer who had fought at Gettysburg—is found murdered. Suspicion centers on "a strange mulatto who had been seen going in the direction of Captain Walker's house," and the sheriff promptly gathers a posse to search for the mulatto and bring him to the county jail. Once the suspect is rounded up, the news of his capture spreads quickly and a growing number of white men in town come to the conclusion that "ordinary justice was too slight a punishment for such a crime." "They had some vague notions of the majesty of the law and the rights of the citizen," according to Chesnutt, "but in the passion of the moment these sunk into oblivion; a white man had been killed by a negro."

LYNCHING AND THE LAW

A crowd soon gathers outside the jail in Troy, the county seat, where they are met by Sheriff Campbell, who is determined to uphold the law. As Campbell announces to the mob, "I'm a white man outside, but in this jail I'm sheriff; and if this nigger's to be hung in this county, I propose to do the hanging." Campbell is a man of substance: before the war he attended the university at Chapel Hill and owned several large estates as well as dozens of slaves. Despite financial setbacks since the war, he is still a member of the town's elite, and he sees it as a matter of personal honor to defend the jail and its prisoner against the mob.

The sheriff finally persuades the lynching party to withdraw, and in the aftermath discovers that he has saved the life of his own son, the offspring of a liaison with a slave woman he had sold, along with the child, when the couple had a falling out years before. Torn between a desire to help his son by allowing him to escape and a sense of duty to his office, the sheriff decides that duty must prevail, and he keeps the prisoner locked up. The story does not end here, however: the mulatto, wounded in an earlier attempt to escape, dies during the night, having pulled off his bandage and bled to death.[1]

Campbell, as father and sheriff, embodies in one person the postwar conflict between the tradition of patriarchy, with its emphasis on personal justice, and the emergence of state authority, with its stress on the abstract rule of law. Faced with a racial crisis that is both domestic and communal, private and public, the sheriff finds that neither the old nor the new system of authority operates very effectively. With slavery no longer in place to ensure the maintenance of social order, the white townspeople demand immediate retribution for what they perceive to be a dire threat to the racial hierarchy. As one of the leaders of the mob tells the sheriff, "We've got to do something to teach the niggers their places, or white people won't be able to live in the county."[2] Although Campbell manages to stave off the resort to extralegal action, in the end he cannot protect his prisoner and son from harm.

Murder sparked the attempted lynching in Chesnutt's story and, in fact, statistics indicated that homicides and attacks on whites by blacks were the most common causes of mob violence in the late-nineteenth-century South. Nevertheless, contemporary observers believed that charges of rape — were the key to the upsurge in racial violence. "While other crimes may renew the lynching fever in the lawless, it is the crime against female virtue that spreads the fever among those who have never had it," remarked Edward Leigh Pell in 1898, "thereby not only feeding the ranks of the lynchers, but weakening the spirit of many who remain on the side of law and order so that their denunciation of lawlessness encourages the mob by its feebleness."[3] Whether prompted by allegations of rape, murder, or other crimes, the highest rates of lynchings took place not in the black belt but in isolated counties of the South where low population density and a rapid rise in black population combined with scattered towns and ineffective law enforcement to generate an explosive mix of anxiety and fear without the restraints of state authority that could keep such emotions from getting out of hand.[4]

The lynching frenzy touched off an intense discussion about its causes among lawyers and judges in the South, who saw themselves as advocates for the rule of law. A deep-seated concern for the impact of lynching on class as well as racial order ran throughout this discussion. Chief Justice L. E. Bleckley of the Georgia Supreme Court spoke for many members of the bench and bar in 1892 when he denounced what he called "emotional justice." Bleckley insisted that mob violence had "no standing in the forum of right reason, and ought to have none anywhere." As he put it, "The mob exercises concurrent jurisdiction with the jury; or rather, the mob makes its own selection of the most flagrant cases, draws to itself exclusive jurisdiction of these, and tolerates the jury in dealing with the rest." The danger was clear: when people no longer respected the law, social chaos resulted, leaving open the possibility of class conflict. "One of the most urgent needs of our time," the chief justice pleaded, "is an earnest, temperate, judicious and persistent remonstrance from the bench, the pulpit, the press and the rostrum, against emotional justice."[5]

Members of the bar were especially sensitive about the extralegal violence because widespread assertions regarding the inefficiency of the courts served as one of the main justifications for lynching.[6] Attorney John J. Strickland of Georgia thought that there might be some merit to the charge that judicial delays in meting out justice to criminals accounted for the upsurge in lynchings. In particular, he suggested, the irregular nature of court sessions in his state undermined respect for judicial proceedings. But the problem was not with individual judges; the real cause of judicial inefficiency was a state statute passed in 1866 that "permitted the court to convene at the pleasure of the judge." The solution was simple: "If speedy trials are desired, establish in every county a court with power to try all criminals and have it set monthly, and have it fixed by law so that it will command the respect and confidence of the people under its influence." Rationalizing the judicial process in this way would restore respect for the law and lead to more sensible behavior on the part of the citizenry.[7]

Other members of the bar in the late nineteenth century echoed Strickland's criticisms of the legal system's cumbersome and erratic mode of operation. Although he did not make an explicit connection with lynching, James Weatherly, an Alabama lawyer, claimed in 1884 that judicial delay in the state's circuit courts had grown to such proportions that "it amounts to a denial of justice." According to Weatherly, the root of the problem was the increasingly commercial character of the Alabama economy and the stepped-up legal activity that accompanied this change. In his words, "We have become a *commercial* people, and as a consequence need ampler facilities for the transaction of all business, the settling of all disputes, the maintenance of law and order, and the preservation of the peace and dignity of the State." His proposed remedies included increasing the terms of court, expanding the number of judicial circuits, and establishing city courts in the larger cities.[8] Other critiques located the source of delayed justice elsewhere in the legal system, from the burden of excessive legislation, which made it difficult for judges to find their way through the thicket of new laws and establish reliable precedents, to the lawyers themselves, who too often asked for a continuance, entered demurrers or objections to evidence, and engaged in other legal maneuvers to gain time for their clients.[9]

In contrast to these assessments of how the administration of justice contributed to the climate of lynching, a number of attorneys vehemently blamed the African American community in the South. These arguments, venomous as they are, make for disturbing reading, but they provide a singular opportunity to gaze through the distorting lens of white supremacy that characterized the professional classes of the South during these years. H. T. Lewis, in a forum at the annual meeting of the Georgia Bar Association in 1897, recognized that lynching was "an evil which every citizen should do all in his power to correct and every official should use all means at his disposal to prevent." But he made no bones about who was responsible, in his view, for the epidemic of extralegal violence: the black rapist himself, who was "more to be dreaded than the most ferocious beast that ever roamed the forest." Reacting to the "horrible outrages perpetrated upon helpless and defenseless women," the public insisted on lynching the alleged culprit "not because the lynchers have less regard for law and order, but because they have more concern for the sanctity of the home and the protection of its inmates." Not just simple lust for white women compelled the black man to commit such crimes, suggested Lewis, noting that the perpetrator selected "a white victim as if his brutal passion was fired with an element of malignity against the Caucasian race."[10]

Other members of the Georgia bar at this 1897 forum offered similar explanations for lynching, placing the burden of blame on the behavior of African American males. "In his proper sphere no one would go further to protect the negro and make him happy than myself," Lewis W. Thomas earnestly announced. Nonetheless, "the white people of the South in the country are surrounded by a race who, in the main, are uneducated and illiterate, who have very little race pride, very little ambition, who to a large extent are lazy and indolent, and who have very little moral character and power to resist temptation, and who are weak mentally, but whose animal passions are highly developed." Speeding up the legal process would have little effect on lynching, Thomas contended, because "the lynching of negroes for assault on white women grows out of the enormity of the crime." When such heinous acts were committed, "no white man stops to consider that the criminal will be punished." Instead, he simply acted instinctively out of a sense of personal outrage and a need to defend his honor.

Like the other attorneys on the panel, G. P. Munro asserted that the increase of lynching was not due to any defects in criminal law or judicial administration. "The lawyers are not responsible for the increase of mob law," he maintained. "There is no class of men whose daily walk, life and conduct do more to promote peace and happiness than the members of our noble profession." [11] Munro overlooked the fact, however, that the very expression of white supremacist beliefs in a public forum helped to create a climate in which lynchings became an acceptable form of behavior in the white community, despite all protestations to the contrary. In this sense, the attempt of southern judges and lawyers to evade responsibility for the acts of racial violence mounting all around them appeared more than a little hollow. The defensive tone sounded by many members of the bar and bench indicated that those who attributed the spread of lynching to flaws within the legal system had struck a raw nerve.

The debate over the role played by the inefficiency of the courts in the outbreak of lynching was only one manifestation of a revitalized self-consciousness in the legal profession during the late nineteenth century. Continuing to operate after Reconstruction as a "strategic elite," to use Gail William O'Brien's apt phrase, lawyers became an important key to the rise of the New South. Not only did attorneys mediate relations between commercial and agricultural interests, they pursued a diverse range of economic activities, retaining their close ties with the land, and becoming deeply involved in the promotion of mills, mines, and railroads as well. While newspaper editors campaigned in their publications for the New South, lawyers negotiated for it, sued for it, and invested in it. [12]

Besides acting as a strategic elite mediating between different groups in the economic sphere, attorneys viewed themselves as architects overseeing the reconstruction of the relationship between society and the state following the war. The bar became especially outspoken about the law's social importance, and it outlined a legal conservatism that reflected the preoccupation of the age with stability and order. W. C. P. Breckinridge of Kentucky, a Confederate veteran and member of Congress, told the

Virginia State Bar Association in 1891 that only "the liberty of the law" protected "day by day the ordinary rights of the people so that they may perform their usual and obscure duties with security to their persons and property and safety to themselves and family." As in the old system of household patriarchy, harmony and hierarchy were the watchwords. Breckinridge, in his address, celebrated the "quiet of family relations, the peace of the community in the highest sense, freedom from strife, confidence in honor, obedience to law, habitual subordination to the dictates of the civil law." Now, however, the state served as the keystone in this vision of the secure society, and the job of the lawyer was to monitor and guide the state's development. As Breckinridge put it, "Our monument is the growing monument of an advancing and noble state—it is a well-ordered commonwealth." [13]

Thomas Cooley, a well-known legal conservative from the North, fleshed out the new postwar association between the family and state for his southern colleagues, making clear the joint responsibility of these two institutions for the preservation of social and political order. In an address to the annual meeting of the Tennessee Bar Association in 1885, Cooley maintained that "duty" constituted the "binding tie alike of family and of the State, and the one, as certainly as the other, must succumb to anarchy if its obligations are not acknowledged. And when family and State dissolve, the race itself must shortly cease to exist, for upon these alone can the helplessness of infancy rely for necessary care and protection." The role of the legal profession, according to Cooley, was to act as "a balance-wheel in the political society," ensuring that "all members of the State may be kept in harmonious and beneficent co-operation." [14]

By no means did every southern lawyer embrace the ideal of the paternalistic state as formulated by Breckinridge and Cooley. I. E. Shumate, in a paper read to the Georgia Bar Association in 1887, criticized the growth of regulatory legislation, contending that these enactments were "affecting the conduct of almost every branch of business and controlling the private conduct of men in all relations of life." "A variety of industries, conflicting interests and different races are asserting, more or less aggressively, their rights and claims of right, and our civilization is becoming more and more complex," noted Shumate, bemoaning the loss of personal freedom that took place with the encroachment of the state. The courts and legislatures were both at fault for having "discovered a wonderful elasticity in those provisions of our written constitutions conferring and limiting legislative powers. Under the pressure of real or apparent necessity or of imperative popular demand, this elasticity is made available." Rather than endorsing the growth of the paternalistic state as a positive development, Shumate sought to rally legal conservatism to the defense of the status quo, arguing that the individual rather than the state should continue to be the main concern of society.[15]

Living in a period of intense political and economic conflict and divisive rhetoric, southern lawyers during the late nineteenth century articulated in the most explicit terms the values and commitments of their profession, including their assumptions about gender. The weight of responsibility placed on the shoulders of lawyers in a time of change and confrontation led to a renewed emphasis on the bar's masculine ideals.[16] Images of combat dominated the professional discourse, not surprising for a generation that came of age during or in the immediate aftermath of war. "Yes! the brave lawyer is ever at his post," proclaimed Samuel Meek, in a speech before the Alabama State Bar Association in 1895. "Morning, noon and night, his watchful eye is ever awake, regardful, at all times, of the true interest of his fellow man, exposing error and vice, and when necessity demands, striking with Herculean power, at the Hidra-headed monster, whose filth and slime and unholy touch would paralize, if not entirely destroy, the holiest instincts of individual virtue, as well as the loftiest aims of governmental policy." Meek had little doubt that "the true, manly, courageous lawyer, with his store of learning, amassed by incessant labor," would successfully carry out his mission.[17]

In the same martial vein, M. A. Spoonts, a Fort Worth attorney, contended that "an independent bar and an incorruptible judiciary" were the "breastworks behind which American institutions repose in safety." At the bar, Spoonts asserted, the lawyer "develops the character, and forges and tempers the weapon, with which his battles are fought when he enters the wide arena where nations fight for supremacy, and contests are waged that furnish the material out of which history is written." The world depicted in this portrait of professional warfare was certainly different from the antebellum legal fraternity, where conviviality and collegiality characterized interaction among lawyers rather than strife and mayhem. Having rejoined the Union on the North's terms, the bar in the South adopted the national rhetoric of competitive struggle that accompanied the triumph of industrial capitalism.[18]

As part of their expanded sense of self-importance, southern lawyers demonstrated a rising concern in the late nineteenth century for the character and standards of their profession. The formation of the state bar associations themselves, beginning in the late 1870s, was one of the most important expressions of this concern. These associations appealed mainly to lawyers in urban areas who made up the profession's elite corps: corporate attorneys, judges, law professors, and appellate practitioners, among others. Rural lawyers, whose practice was generally confined to the lower courts and operated at a much more local level, tended to be less attracted to the bar-association movement. Members of the bar associations drafted bills on subjects of interest to the profession such as judicial administration, and lobbied state legislatures to gain adoption of these proposed reforms. The local and state bar association also served a crucial social function, providing legal practitioners with a place to meet, exchange information, and size each other up.[19]

Besides these political and social activities, southern bar associations sought to deal with what they perceived as a growing problem with professional standards and quality. The increasingly commercial nature of the legal business caused noticeable anxiety among southern attorneys concerned with the image of the profession. Thomas Nelson Page, in a sketch of "The Old Virginia Lawyer" delivered to the Virginia State Bar Association in 1891, recalled the antebellum tradition of the gentleman practitioner: "The profession of the law was to him the highest of all professions. It was a brotherhood; it was sacred; it maintained the rights of man, preserved the government, controlled the administration of the law." In contrast to these noble pursuits, according to W. C. Wear of the Hillsboro Bar in Texas, lawyering had been "permitted to descend to the level of a mere trade, calling or occupation, and is to be estimated solely and alone by reason of the dollars and cents which it affords."[20]

Members of the southern state bars assailed the more mercenary lawyers in their ranks, viewing them as a blot on the profession's public image. Besides the pettifogger, who first made his appearance during the antebellum period, two new categories of undesirables were discovered in the postwar era: the "shyster" and the "razor-back lawyer." Like the pettifogger, the shyster's first priority was personal gain rather than the welfare of his client. In contrast to the pettifogger's lack of education and proper training, though, the shyster often knew a great deal of law. The razor-back lawyer was a subspecies of the shyster; his specialty was drumming up business by initiating lawsuits stemming from personal injuries, especially against larger corporations.[21]

To foster greater professionalism, and rid the bar of these undesirables, the state associations advocated more formal educational requirements and stricter standards of admission to the bar. In the words of W. S. Parkerson, a Louisiana attorney, the profession "must be willing to expose the cancer and apply the knife." Of course, there was more than a little self-interest involved in such surgical efforts. As the *Southern Law Review* put it, "The legal profession is a good deal overstocked," and reducing the number of new lawyers entering the profession would clearly provide some relief.[22] The increasing complexity of the law also provided the impetus for more formal educational prerequisites and tighter admission requirements. While differences existed among members of the bar associations over whether law-school training should be demanded, there was a strong consensus that it was too easy to set up as a lawyer and that action needed to be taken. Most important, as the president of the South Carolina Bar Association stressed in 1889, whatever the standards and regardless of their uniformity, they "must be established and enforced in and by the profession itself, and not by the outside community."[23]

THE ORIGINS OF SOUTHERN PROGRESSIVISM

Many of the lawyers who engaged in these far-reaching debates participated in a coalition of like-minded moderate conservatives that wielded extensive influence in the South. This coalition, which included other professionals, newspaper editors, educators, and politicians, sought to forge the notions of the interventionist state and the rule of law into instruments for countering a dual menace: the populists, on the one hand, who agitated for a redistribution of power in southern society, and extreme racists, on the other hand, who openly advocated lynching. Although the bar associations taken together lagged far behind the vanguard of the progressive movement, reform-oriented lawyers individually became involved in important efforts to stabilize the New South.

Progressive lawyers and their allies embraced a dynamic view of the law, seeing in such an approach a way to reconstruct the relationship between society and the state, as well as restore social and political order, while preserving the power and influence of elites like themselves. "Adapted, as the laws are intended to be, to the condition of man at the time the system is formed," the *Southern Review* pointed out as early as 1869, "they must of necessity change or be changed, according as society and civilization advance." Laws suitable to the people of Stuart England would be as out of touch with the conditions of their American descendants at the present time as "the education and habits of the Squires of the seventeenth century would be unsuited to the position and duties of the American gentleman of the nineteenth century." According to the *Southern Review*, "symmetry of proportion" or "unity of design" might be pleasing to the eye, but it made for ineffective law. Instead, laws should evolve in response to "public necessity" and "private need."[24]

To the more democratic elements of the bar, these ideas for guiding social reform from above seemed like pretty tame stuff. Seymour D. Thompson, a leading critic of legal conservatism, delivered a sharp denunciation of what he called "government by lawyers" to the Texas Bar Association in 1896. Assailing the power that lawyers exerted in American society, the former Missouri judge and editor of the *American Law Review* argued that "the general trend of this irresponsible government, by lawyers, is in favor of the rich and powerful classes, and against the scattered and segregated people." Unless the bar became more responsive to the people, Thompson warned, there was danger that "the furies will then break loose, and that all hell will ride on their wings."[25]

This radical attack on the bar's social influence, as well as the apocalyptic admonition issued by Thompson, no doubt shocked most of the Texas lawyers in the audience. The origins of southern progressivism, rather than developing out of Thompson's more militant approach, stemmed from the efforts of pragmatic, middle-class elites who believed in the efficacy of gradual change and who saw the law as a bulwark to social order. Southern reformers, by and large a more conservative group than their counterparts in the North, sought during the late nineteenth century to employ state interventionism and legal reform as a means to channel discontent and anxiety, and to avoid what they perceived as the twin dangers of class warfare and racial chaos. Sharing a "yearning for a more orderly and cohesive community," as historian Dewey Grantham Jr. puts it, the professionals and experts who made up the ranks of southern reformers at the turn of the century believed that expanding the regulatory powers of the state and strengthening social controls should be the top priority. Rather than viewing law as a philosophical system based on immutable principles of right and wrong, these pragmatists considered law to be an experimental science in which the exercise of "lawmaking-power" was "tested by experience" in order to determine its usefulness.[26]

Whether it be public schools, agricultural reform, child labor, the convict lease system, or public health, southern reformers turned to the law for solutions. Evangelicals pushed for the passage of legislation to prohibit the drinking of alcohol, swearing, and blood sports in an effort to improve the moral tone of their communities. Another strain of legal interventionism represented a far less benign use of state power: the imposition of Jim Crow laws that enforced racial segregation in public facilities, and the employment of voting requirements such as literacy tests and poll taxes that restricted the participation of blacks and poor whites in electoral politics. All in all, an elite governing style had emerged by the turn of the century that emphasized social welfare, economic development, and political control.[27]

Reflecting the southern predilection for decentralized authority, those who supported expanding the sphere of governmental activity generally expressed hostility toward the use of federal power. Hannis Taylor, president of the Alabama State Bar Association, insisted in 1891 that "the State, and only the State, can be, under our system of government, the home of anything like paternalism." But, if the state government was to perform its new responsibilities properly, he declared, then its powers needed to be enlarged. In Taylor's words, "Nothing brings either an individual or an institution quicker into contempt than to be burdened with duties which neither he nor it has the capacity to fulfill."[28]

The inadequacy of governmental and legal power at the state and local levels generated surprisingly widespread complaints among southern reformers in the late nineteenth century, who viewed the tools at hand as seriously deficient given the extent of social change and conflict. Although suspicious of federal intrusion, these moderate elites sought to reinvigorate state government. The initiatives that they carried out beginning in the late 1880s in the area of social welfare and public education promoted a significant increase in governmental responsibility and expenditures, developments that marked the earliest stirrings of progressivism in the South.[29]

Perhaps more than any other phenomenon in the New South, the outburst of lynching and the debate that it precipitated among those who held power and influence disclosed the transitional nature of the social and political order at the turn of the century. The emerging system of state paternalism had not yet completely supplanted the traditional order of household patriarchy; consequently, with one system of governance undercut by the collapse of slavery and the other still gearing up, neither worked very well, especially when it came to enforcing racial and gender norms. Caught between two worlds, southern elites less honorable than Sheriff Campbell often decided to capitulate to the bloodlust of lynching parties; sometimes those in power even helped to facilitate lynching as a way to bolster their exercise of authority.[30]

The tension between the forces of change and persistence that manifested itself so starkly in the lynching outbreak reflected the slow and halting character of the legal transformation of the southern household and its relationship to the state. Two main characteristics marked the new legal order in domestic, sexual, and racial relations that southerners created by the end of the nineteenth century. First, the law now recognized that wives, children, and former slaves possessed important legal interests and rights as family members, if not as autonomous individuals. The male head of household still maintained a position of authority, but the traditional concept of the household had given way in large part to the division of the household into separate legal personalities whose bond with each other was more contractual than organic. Second, state intervention in southern private life expanded dramatically. As women, children, and former slaves acquired limited individual rights, they became directly linked to the state. In this way, the paternalistic notion of government regulating the relations between husbands and wives, parents and children, and blacks and whites sought to replace the older model of domestic governance based on a network of white patriarchs who exercised unchallenged authority in the household. These developments were part of a larger process at work in the postwar South: the growing responsibility of public institutions rather than individual households for the regulation of gender and racial mores.[31]

James Roark has observed, in his study of southern planters during the Civil War and Reconstruction, that slavery was "a kind of log jam behind which forces of social and cultural change had stacked up, and with emancipation, the South moved toward the mainstream of American development."[32] This movement, of course, took place gradually and unevenly. The impact of postwar legal change, in particular, varied within the different subregions of the South. Although the statutory and appellate case data employed in this study do not allow one to draw distinctions between rural and urban areas, evidence from other investigations of the southern legal system in the nineteenth century indicates that in relatively isolated counties where there were few towns local customs and values continued to play a more important role than formal law.

Likewise, those areas of the South that underwent urbanization during this period seem to have experienced the greatest degree of legal growth and development.[33] If such a pattern held true for domestic-relations law, then households in southern towns and cities probably had much more direct and extensive interaction with the legal system than those in the countryside, where the tradition of noninterference in family matters appears to have prevailed. Suggestive in this regard is a recent analysis of three counties in North Carolina during Reconstruction revealing that the most rural of them had the fewest divorce petitions filed in the superior court.[34] Conclusive evidence about these matters awaits more systematic research in the local court records, and until then we can only speculate.[35] Still, it would not be surprising if urban centers accounted for the bulk of the legal activity that took place at the local level in the postwar South.

Even in rural areas of the South lawyers were widely available, and individuals with sufficient financial resources could always gain access to the legal system.[36] For these persons, statutory law and judicial precedent remained at their disposal, ready to be mobilized whenever the need arose. Thus developments in these bodies of law were important even where custom and convention held sway over formal law in the daily life of the community.

Although we lack a detailed understanding of how the legal system operated at the local level in the South during the nineteenth century, the evolution of legal attitudes toward the household captured in the appellate court opinions and state statutes underscores the extent to which Reconstruction was an ideological and social as well as political and economic undertaking.[37] Overall, the process of reconstructing the household went hand in hand with the larger project of national unification and nation building, what Stephen Hahn has referred to as "the absorption of regional elites and labor systems into capitalist nation-states." Indeed, the legal transformation of the household—a process that continued throughout the United States well past the end of Radical Reconstruction in 1877— was itself a crucial stage in the consolidation of the nation-state.[38] In the South, courts and legislatures carried out domestic Reconstruction predominantly in response to the destruction of the war and the collapse of slavery. In the North and West, on the other hand, the swelling tide of immigration, the explosion of urban growth, and the triumph of industrial capitalism proved to be the main catalysts for increased state involvement in family life.[39]

This is not to say that industrialization and urbanization failed to shape the legal regulation of families in the New South. One need look no further than the movement to reform child labor during the late nineteenth and early twentieth centuries to understand the connection between the rise of factories and mill towns in the South and expanded state intervention in families. The campaign to keep children out of the mills and mines, which gained increasing momentum after 1880, reflected the confidence of urban, middle-class reformers in the promise of the paternalistic state to establish new standards of family behavior. The zeal with which these reformers pursued the regulation of child labor frequently led them to overlook the needs and desires of working-class households and to downplay the resentment that reform efforts often inspired in these households. Nevertheless, there was no mistaking the fervent faith in the redeeming power of laws and regulations that participants in the child labor crusade exhibited, a faith that served as the cement in the ideological edifice of state paternalism.[40]

As we have seen, significant differences between the North and South existed during the nineteenth century in the timing, pace, and sources of change regarding the transition from a system of domestic governance primarily reliant on patriarchal households to one grounded in the exercise of state authority. At the end of the period and well into the twentieth century, pronounced disparities in the political and legal cultures of the two regions endured. The distinguishing elements of southern public culture, including the emphasis on local government, insistence on community control, and hostility to outside interference, can be accounted for largely by the uniqueness of the South's historical experience with slavery, race relations, military defeat, and economic underdevelopment. These persistent legal and political traditions came into conflict with the new forces of intrusive government, coercive bureaucracy, and middle-class paternalism that accompanied the rise of the progressive movement, and they imposed serious constraints on the ability of this movement to implement its reform agenda in the South.[41]

Thus the South entered the mainstream of American legal development by the end of the nineteenth century, but in a way that preserved its distinctiveness. In the regulation of domestic and sexual relations, as in the North, a household-centered patriarchy had yielded for the most part to an emergent state paternalism. But although southern courts adopted certain legal innovations, such as a contractual understanding of parenthood and the best interest of the child standard, when it came to other changes that challenged the core of sexual dynamics in a patriarchal society, such as recognizing the role of psychological coercion in incest between father and daughter and dropping the corroboration of female testimony requirement, they refused to endorse these new legal doctrines. Despite the increasingly national vision that took hold in much of American public life after the Civil War, then, regional variations in the approach to domestic governance continued.[42]

Striking as these variations were, however, domestic Reconstruction in both the North and South shared a common focus on order and stability; the attainment of justice and equity in the household was only a secondary consideration, if that. Like political Reconstruction, in other words, the legacy of domestic Reconstruction has been mixed.[43] Its most laudable achievement was the legal recognition of former slave families. Also important were the child-centered custody rules and judicial backing of adoption, as well as reforms in divorce and married women's property rights. Too often, though, the limited protections that women received against rape and incestuous assault simply consolidated rather than challenged gender as a category in the law. In addition, the new supervisory powers of the state frequently singled out for high-handed treatment families that did not meet the norms of middle-class legal authorities and charity workers. State interventionism, moreover, upheld the ideology of white supremacy by bolstering the effort to curb interracial marriage and cohabitation. It is a troubling balance sheet, to be sure. The question of ultimate success or failure, however, remains open. Wherever poor families face economic hardship in their struggle to stay together, wherever women encounter sexual violence in their homes and on the streets, and wherever children get caught in a web of agencies, courts, and institutions, domestic Reconstruction continues to be a contest that can be won or lost.[44]

APPENDIX: TABLES

The following tables summarize information garnered from southern appellate court opinions relating to child custody, miscegenation, and incest. They have been constructed on the basis of all the relevant cases that could be discovered in the published appellate records. As such, they provide a helpful if somewhat crude guide to the contours of appellate behavior in the southern state courts, and the types of disputes and prosecutions that reached the high courts in these three areas of the law. They should not, however, be employed to make any generalizations about the workings of the southern legal system as a whole because appellate cases are, by their very nature, inherently unrepresentative.

TABLE I. *Child Custody Disputes between Parents Decided by Southern High Courts, 1800–1900*

Period	Number of Cases	Father Granted Custody	Mother Granted Custody	Custody Split	Other
1800–1865	24	10 (42%)	9 (38%)	4 (17%)	1 [a] (4%) [b]
1866–1900	42	15 (36%)	20 (48%)	5 (12%)	2 (5%)
1800–1900	66	25 (38%)	29 (44%)	9 (14%)	3 (5%)

Note: Of the sixty-six custody contests between parents that appear in the nineteenth-century appellate records of the southern states, 47 percent involved parents who were divorced, 8 percent who were legally separated, and 21 percent who were informally separated. Another 9 percent involved parents who were never legally married or whose status is unknown.

Fathers initiated only 35 percent of the custody disputes in lower court; mothers initiated 65 percent. Of the suits that they initiated, fathers ultimately won 35 percent in appellate courts and mothers won 47 percent. Only two of the custody disputes between parents involved black mothers and fathers: *Hansford v. Hansford*, 10 Ala. 561 (1846); and *Pascal v. Jones*, 41 Ga. 220 (1870). The former case involved free blacks, and the latter former slaves; in both instances the father gained custody.

[a] In two Other cases, the suit was remanded, that is, sent back to the lower court for a new trial. In the third case, custody was given to the maternal grandfather due to the unfitness of both parents.

[b] Percentages do not total 100 horizontally due to rounding.

TABLE 2. *Child Custody Disputes between Parents and Third Parties Decided by Southern High Courts, 1800–1900*

Period	Number of Cases	Custody Granted Parent(s)	Custody Granted Third Party	Remanded (New Trial)
1800–1865	18	14 (78%)	3 (17%)	1 (6%)[a]
1866–1900	43	20 (47%)	20 (47%)	3 (7%)
1800–1900	61	34 (56%)	23 (38%)	4 (7%)

Note: Of the sixty-one custody suits involving parents and third parties that reached southern appellate courts in the nineteenth century, parents initiated 72 percent in the lower courts and third parties initiated 28 percent. Of the suits that they initiated, parents won 45 percent in appellate courts and third parties won a mere 6 percent.
[a] Percentages do not total 100 horizontally due to rounding.

TABLE 3. *Third Parties Seeking Custody in Disputes with Parents in Southern High Courts, 1800–1900*

Relation to Child	Number of Cases	Percentage
Grandparent(s)	15	25
Aunt and/or uncle	14	23
Other relative(s)	5	8
Nonrelative(s)	18	29
State/institution	6	10
Unknown	3	5
Total	61	100

TABLE 4. *Rates of Success in Southern High Courts for Relatives and Nonrelatives in Custody Disputes with Parents, 1800–1900*

	Relatives		Nonrelatives	
Period	Number of Contests	Granted Custody	Number of Contests	Granted Custody
1800–1865	9	1 (11%)	6	2 (33%)
1866–1900	25	13 (52%)	18	7 (39%)
1800–1900	34	14 (41%)	24	9 (37%)

Note: Nonrelatives are defined here as persons not related to the children in dispute, as well as the state and various institutions such as orphan asylums.

MISCEGENATION CASES IN THE POSTWAR SOUTH

TABLE 5. *Prosecutions Involving Miscegenation before Southern High Courts, 1865–1899*

Type of Case	Number of Cases	Percentage
Intermarriage	18	72
Interracial fornication	6	24
Performing illegal marriage	1	4
Total	25	100

Note: In the course of my research I uncovered six other appellate cases during the postwar period in which individuals were indicted for violating laws against illicit intercourse or cohabitation when the other party was of a different race. These cases are not included in table 5 because they did not involve prosecutions under antimiscegenation statutes. See *Richardson v. State*, 34 Tex. 142 (1871); *Kinard v. State*, 57 Miss. 132 (1879); *Scott v. Commonwealth*, 77 Va. 344 (1883); *Mulling v. State*, 74 Ga. 10 (1884); *Stewart v. State*, 64 Miss. 626 (1887); and *State v. Chancy*, 110 N.C. 507 (1892). Mary Frances Berry also has discovered two late-nineteenth-century appeals from convictions for cohabitation, rather than miscegenation, that involved interracial couples: *Sullivan v. State*, 32 Ark. 187 (1877); and *Smelser v. State*, 31 Tex. 96 (1868). See Berry, "Judging Morality," 839 n. 14.

TABLE 6. *Appeals from Miscegenation Convictions before*
Southern High Courts, 1865–1899

Type of Miscegenation	Number of Cases	Reversals	Rate of Reversal
White male/ black female	7	2	29%
Black male/ white female	13	4	31%
Total	20	6	30%

Note: One other appeal from conviction, *Burns v. State*, 48 Ala. 195 (1872), dealt with the indictment of a justice of the peace for performing an interracial marriage. Since the appellate opinion did not provide any information about the parties who contracted marriage, beyond the obvious fact that they were not of the same race, it is not included in table 6.

INCEST CASES IN THE POSTWAR SOUTH

TABLE 7. *Appeals from Incest Convictions before*
Southern High Courts, 1866–1900

Party Convicted	Number of Appeals	Reversals
Father	14	5
Stepfather	9	6
Uncle	8	4
Brother	2	0
Brother-in-law	1	1
Niece	1	1
Nephew	1	0
First cousin (male)	1	0
Total	37	17

TABLE 8. *Types of Incest before Southern High Courts, 1866–1900*

Type of Incest	Number of Cases	Percentage
Father-daughter	16	40
Stepfather-stepdaughter	10	25
Uncle-niece	8	20
First cousin	2	5
Brother-sister	2	5
Brother- and sister-in-law	1	2
Aunt-nephew	1	2
Total	40	99[a]

[a] Percentages do not total 100 due to rounding.

NOTES

PREFACE

1. See, for example, Ala., *Code* (Ormond, Bagby, and Goldthwaite 1852), p. 375; Ga., *Code* (Clark, Cobb, and Irwin 1861), p. 330; and Tenn., *Code* (Meigs and Cooper 1858), p. 480.

2. Among the works that have opened up an examination of sexuality and the law in the nineteenth-century South are Bardaglio, " 'Outrage upon Nature' "; Berry, "Judging Morality"; Edwards, "Sexual Violence, Gender, Reconstruction, and the Extension of Patriarchy"; and Bynum, *Unruly Women*.

3. The best introduction to southern legal history is the section entitled "Law," edited by Maxwell Bloomfield, in Wilson and Ferris, *Encyclopedia of Southern Culture* 2:667–736. A sampling of recent work in the area can be found in "Symposium: The Legal History of the South"; Bodenhamer and Ely, *Ambivalent Legacy*; and Hall and Ely, *Uncertain Tradition*.

4. The most significant exception to the lack of focus on the question of regionalism in the development of American domestic relations law is Salmon, *Women and the Law of Property*. See also two additional studies by Salmon, "Women and Property in South Carolina" and " 'Life, Liberty, and Dower.' "

Other notable contributions to the legal history of southern women include Censer, " 'Smiling through Her Tears,' " and Lebsock, "Radical Reconstruction." Important discussions can also be encountered in Lebsock, *Free Women of Petersburg*; and Wyatt-Brown, *Southern Honor*. Much of this literature is assessed in Hall and Scott, "Women in the South."

5. Bloomfield, "Law and Southern Society," p. 669.

6. Grossberg, *Governing the Hearth*, pp. xi, 8, 9. Grossberg's book is the starting point for any study of American family law in the nineteenth century. Recent overviews of the legal history of American families include Mintz, "Regulating the American Family"; Boris and Bardaglio, "Gender, Race, and Class"; and Grossberg, "Crossing Boundaries." On American women and the law, see Basch, "Emerging Legal History of Women"; and Hoff, *Law, Gender, and Injustice*.

7. Two recent essays make clear the distinctive nature of the southern slaveholding household: Clinton, " 'Southern Dishonor' "; and Genovese, " 'Our Family, White and Black.' "

8. Quoted in Whites, "Civil War as a Crisis in Gender," p. 7.

9. My thinking about the impact of regionalism on the development of southern

law has been influenced Ely and Bodenhamer, "Regionalism and American Legal History"; Friedman, "Law between the States"; and Wiecek, " 'Old Times There Are Not Forgotten.' "

10. Fox-Genovese, *Within the Plantation Household*, pp. 62–64; Lewis, *Pursuit of Happiness*, pp. 216–30; Stowe, *Intimacy and Power*, pp. 164–91.

11. *Ex parte Boaz*, 31 Ala. 425 (1858), p. 426; *Ex parte Hewitt*, 11 Rich. 326 (S.C. 1858), pp. 329–30.

12. "The Black Race in North America; Why Was Their Introduction Permitted?" *De Bow's Review* 20 (May 1856): 291.

13. Recent evaluations of southern distinctiveness include Degler, "Thesis, Antithesis, Synthesis"; and McPherson, "Antebellum Southern Exceptionalism."

14. *Comas v. Reddish*, 35 Ga. 236 (1866), p. 238.

15. Grossberg stresses the dominant role of the courts in taking over patriarchal control from individual fathers. I would argue that, at least for the South, an examination of not only appellate court opinions, but also state statutes, the state bar association reports, and the writings of lawyers in state and regional law journals, suggests that the legislatures and the bar also assumed important roles as agents of the expanding state. One of the advantages of this approach is that it allows us to make connections between social and political history that would otherwise remain overlooked. Hence my preference for the term "state paternalism" rather than Grossberg's "judicial patriarchy." See *Governing the Hearth*, pp. 289–307.

16. Foner, *Reconstruction*, p. xxvii.

17. Thompson, *Whigs and Hunters*, pp. 260–62; Tigar and Levy, *Law and the Rise of Capitalism*, p. xiii.

18. On the issue of relative autonomy, see Tushnet, "Marxist Analysis of American Law"; and Kairys, *Politics of Law*. A sense of the issues at stake in the debate over the critical legal studies movement can be garnered from "Exchange on Critical Legal Studies."

19. Genovese, *Roll, Jordan, Roll*, pp. 26–27. For a similar approach, see Hay, "Property, Authority and the Criminal Law."

20. My understanding of how to analyze a legal system has been aided by Friedman, "Legal Culture and Social Development."

21. Jordan, *White Over Black*, pp. 587–88; Wiecek, "Statutory Law of Slavery and Race," pp. 279–80.

22. Tushnet, "American Law of Slavery," pp. 125–31; White, "Appellate Opinion," pp. 492–93.

23. Nash, "Reason of Slavery," p. 24 n. 65; Censer, " 'Smiling through Her Tears,' " pp. 25–26. Cases involving domestic relations law and the regulation of sexuality made up only a small fraction of the workload handled by the state supreme courts in the nineteenth century. The bulk of appellate decisions dealt with property, debt, and other commercial disputes. See Kagan et al., "Business of State Supreme Courts."

CHAPTER ONE

1. Bleser, *Secret and Sacred*, pp. 173, 175.
2. For descriptions of the incident involving Hammond and the Hampton sisters,

see ibid., pp. xi–xii, 164–76; and Faust, *Hammond and the Old South*, pp. 241–5, 287–92, 338–39. I have relied heavily on Faust's outstanding biography for the account here. The quotation from the state legislator can be found on p. 290. See also Bleser, *Hammonds of Redcliffe*, pp. 9–10, 32–33 n. 3; and Faust, *Sacred Circle*, pp. 41–42, 108–9.

3. Studies of gender in the antebellum South that have helped me to understand the larger cultural significance of the Hammond affair include Scott, *Southern Lady*; Johnson, "Planters and Patriarchy"; Clinton, *Plantation Mistress*; Wyatt-Brown, *Southern Honor*; Fox-Genovese, *Within the Plantation Household*; and Bynum, *Unruly Women*.

4. [Thomas R. Dew], "Dissertation on the Characteristics Between the Sexes," *Southern Literary Messenger* 1 (May 1835): 498. But see Collins, *White Society*, pp. 132–33, for an argument that questions the prevalence of a sexual double standard in the antebellum South.

5. Quoted in Wyatt-Brown, *Southern Honor*, p. 199.

6. For an interesting cross-cultural analysis of the ideological connection between the purity of women and the honor and status of families, see Ortner, "Virgin and the State." On the South, see Clinton, *Plantation Mistress*, pp. 88–89.

7. Bleser, *Secret and Sacred*, p. 174; Burton, *In My Father's House*, p. 140.

8. Hindus, *Prison and Plantation*, pp. 42–53; Lewis, *Pursuit of Happiness*, pp. 19–20; Williams, *Vogues in Villainy*, pp. 53–59. These studies emphasize the lack of interest southerners had in using the law to enforce the private morality of their neighbors. Recent investigations of antebellum Georgia, however, show that cases of sexual misconduct appeared with surprising frequency on the local criminal dockets. See, for example, Bodenhamer, "Law and Disorder in the Old South," pp. 113–14.

9. Wyatt-Brown, *Southern Honor*, pp. xv, 14–15, 298–99, 383–85; Ayers, *Vengeance and Justice*, pp. 13–14, 18–19; Greenberg, *Masters and Statesmen*, pp. x–xi, 21–22; Stowe, *Intimacy and Power*, pp. 48–49.

10. Samuel H. Hempstead to William Hempstead, July 12, 1836, Samuel H. Hempstead Letters, Southern Historical Collection, University of North Carolina, Chapel Hill, N.C. (hereafter cited as SHC); Twain, *Pudd'nhead Wilson*, p. 96.

11. "Recollections of a Retired Lawyer," *Southern Literary Messenger* 5 (March 1839): 219. See also Hindus, *Prison and Plantation*, p. 47.

12. Quoted in Bruce, *Violence and Culture*, p. 81. On attitudes toward law in Victorian America generally, consult Armao, "In Search of a New God."

13. [J. D. B. De Bow], "Law and Lawyers," *Southern Quarterly Review* 6 (October 1844): 374. This piece reappeared as a series of articles in *De Bow's Review* 19 (September–December 1855).

14. Sydnor, "Southerner and the Laws"; Ayers, *Vengeance and Justice*, pp. 15–16, 21–22; Gorn, "'Gouge and Bite,'" pp. 38–42; Greenberg, "The Nose, the Lie, and the Duel," pp. 57–58; Greenberg, *Masters and Statesmen*, pp. 23–41; Stowe, *Intimacy and Power*, p. 49.

For other recent discussions of the social and cultural significance of dueling in the slave South, see Wyatt-Brown, *Southern Honor*, pp. 350–61; Bruce, *Violence and Culture*, chap. 1; and Stowe, "'Touchiness' of the Gentleman Planter."

15. Twain, *Pudd'nhead Wilson*, p. 93.

16. Easterly, "Common Law"; Davis, *Intellectual Life* 3 : 1589, 1592–93; Hall, *Magic*

Mirror, pp. 9–12, 17–19; Roeber, *Faithful Magistrates*, pp. 44–45. On the appellate role of the Privy Council, see Friedman, *History of American Law*, pp. 49–50.

17. Greene, *Pursuits of Happiness*, p. 17; Davis, *Intellectual Life* 3:1597–98; Roeber, *Faithful Magistrates*, pp. 41–43.

18. On the social and cultural significance of the county court and court day in the colonial Chesapeake, see Isaac, *Transformation of Virginia*, pp. 88–94; Roeber, "Authority, Law, and Custom"; and Konig, "Country Justice." T. H. Breen discusses the centrality of tobacco in the lives of Chesapeake planters in *Tobacco Culture*.

19. Morgan, "Law and Social Change"; Roeber, *Faithful Magistrates*, pp. 86–89, 140–44, 179–88; Wiecek, "Statutory Law of Slavery and Race," p. 276; Spindel and Thomas, "Crime and Society in North Carolina"; Hoffer, "Disorder and Deference." For a thorough examination of one colony's criminal justice system, see Spindel, *Crime and Society in North Carolina*.

20. Davis, *Intellectual Life* 3:1601–9; Shepard, "Lawyers Look at Themselves," pp. 2, 11; Roeber, *Faithful Magistrates*, pp. 48–71. On the legal profession in colonial America, in general, see Friedman, *History of American Law*, pp. 94–102.

21. Shepard, "Lawyers Look at Themselves," p. 3; Henretta and Nobles, *Evolution and Revolution*, p. 215; Hall, *Magic Mirror*, pp. 63–64; Senese, "Building the Pyramid," pp. 357–59.

22. Bloomfield, *American Lawyers*, pp. 39–51; Zainaldin, *Law in Antebellum Society*, pp. 8–10; Ely, "Law in a Republican Society," pp. 59–63. For a close look at antilawyer sentiment in postrevolutionary Virginia, see Roeber, *Faithful Magistrates*, pp. 231–32, 240–51.

23. Quoted in Shepard, "Lawyers Look at Themselves," p. 10.

24. Wooster, *People in Power*, pp. 64–70, 84–85; Wooster, *Politicians, Planters, and Plain Folk*, pp. 79–87, 99–100; Escott, *Many Excellent People*, pp. 15–19; Wallenstein, *From Slave South to New South*, p. 19.

For detailed examinations of the county courts, consult Ireland, *County Courts in Antebellum Kentucky*; and Brown, "Tennessee County Courts," pp. 349–412. Roeber analyzes the establishment in postrevolutionary Virginia of a district court system and its impact on the justice of the peace courts in *Faithful Magistrates*, pp. 203–30. Fourteen superior courts replaced the district court system in 1809 (pp. 241–42).

25. Wooster, *People in Power*, pp. 70–80; Wooster, *Politicians, Planters, and Plain Folk*, pp. 87–96; Zainaldin, *Law in Antebellum Society*, pp. 14–15; Hall, *Magic Mirror*, p. 80; Ely, "Law in a Republican Society," pp. 63–64. The evolution of the court system of South Carolina is outlined in Senese, "Building the Pyramid," pp. 357–79; and that of North Carolina in Johnson, *Ante-Bellum North Carolina*, pp. 613–43.

26. "The Black Race in North America; Why Was Their Introduction Permitted?" *De Bow's Review* 20 (May 1856): 294; Cash, *Mind of the South*, p. 34.

27. Ayers, *Vengeance and Justice*, pp. 31–32; Farmer, "Legal Practice and Ethics," pp. 334–37; Phifer, "Slavery in Microcosm," p. 143; Kennedy, *Swallow Barn*, p. 167.

28. "Memoir of the Ambitious Lawyer," *Southern Literary Messenger* 1 (July 1835): 645; Eaton, *Growth of Southern Civilization*, p. 277 (Micajah Clark quotation).

29. Studies that emphasize the ineffectiveness of southern justice include Franklin, *Militant South*, pp. 14–32; Ireland, "Law and Disorder," pp. 281–99; Hindus, *Prison and Plantation*; and Collins, *White Society*, pp. 169–71.

30. Bodenhamer, "Efficiency of Criminal Justice"; Bodenhamer, "Law and Dis-

order," pp. 112–16; Preyer, "Crime, the Criminal Law and Reform," pp. 53–85; Ayers, *Vengeance and Justice*, pp. 34–72. For a summary of recent findings regarding southern criminal justice, see Ely and Bodenhamer, "Regionalism and American Legal History," pp. 558–62; and Bodenhamer, "Criminal Justice."

31. Wyatt-Brown, *Southern Honor*, pp. 365–66, 391, 390; Ayers, *Vengeance and Justice*, pp. 109–13, 137; Escott, *Many Excellent People*, pp. 23–24. See also Wyatt-Brown, "Community, Class, and Snopesian Crime"; and Paludan, *Victims*, pp. 23–25.

32. Roeber discusses the ambivalent attitude of southerners in the early nineteenth century toward lawyers in *Faithful Magistrates*, pp. 258–61. On antebellum stereotypes regarding lawyers, see Maxwell Bloomfield, "Law and Lawyers in American Popular Culture," in Smith, McWilliams, and Bloomfield, *Law and American Literature*, pp. 129–43; and Bloomfield, "Image of Lawyer," pp. 698–99.

33. Kennedy, *Swallow Barn*, p. 185.

34. Thorpe, *Master's House*, p. 228. Thorpe, although a northerner, was a close observer of southern mores. Interestingly, the slave in this episode is the property of a planter, Graham Mildmay, who has moved to Louisiana from the North. In contrast to Bledsoe and the others, Mildmay expresses a deep faith in the rule of law and tries to persuade his fellow slaveholders to let "the laws have their sway" (p. 233). A better symbolic representation of the different regional attitudes toward the law would be difficult to find.

35. Baldwin, *Flush Times*, pp. 96, 100.

36. Shepard, "Breaking into the Profession"; David Schenck Books, May 4, 1854, and October 3, 1856, SHC. Schenck, after the Civil War, became a superior court judge and general counsel for the Richmond and Danville Railroad.

37. See, for example, "Study of the Law," *Southern Literary Messenger* 3 (January 1837): 25–31; "Story's Commentaries," *Southern Quarterly Review* 2 (October 1842): 416–22; and "Legal Education," *Southern Quarterly Review* 14 (October 1848): 432–48.

38. Cashin, "Structure of Antebellum Families," p. 69. On the bar in antebellum America generally, see Bloomfield, *American Lawyers*, pp. 136–63; and Friedman, *History of American Law*, pp. 303–33. For contemporary criticism of attempts in the South to form bar associations, see "Bar Associations," *Southern Literary Messenger* 4 (September 1838): 581–84.

39. James Graham to Thomas Ruffin, November 9, 1817, in Hamilton, *Papers of Thomas Ruffin* 1:198. For a sense of the difficulties one faced in establishing a legal practice on the southern frontier, see Bloomfield, "Texas Bar in the Nineteenth Century."

40. John W. Brown Diary, October 2, 1821, and August 20, 1822, SHC; Samuel Hempstead to William Hempstead, December 3, 1836, Hempstead Letters, SHC. Unless otherwise noted, emphasis in all quotations is in the original document and is not added.

41. "The County Court Attorney," *Southern Literary Messenger* 12 (February 1846): 120; O'Brien, *Legal Fraternity*, pp. 68–72, 79–89.

42. Shepard, "Lawyers Look at Themselves," pp. 17–23.

43. [B. F. Porter], "The Utility, Studies, and Duties of the Profession of Law," *De Bow's Review* 2 (September 1846): 151; "The Study of the Law," *Carolina Law Journal* 1 (1830): 12. See also [De Bow], "Law and Lawyers," pp. 389–93.

It should be noted that the appearance of law journals in the South such as the *Carolina Law Journal* was itself another indicator of the increased self-awareness of the legal profession. See Shephard, "First Law Journals in Virginia."

44. Lucian Minor, "The Model Lawyer," *Southern Literary Messenger* 20 (October 1854): 635–36. See also "Christianity in the Legal Profession," *Southern Literary Messenger* 27 (July 1858): 66–75.

45. Jeremiah Battle to William H. Battle, March 13, [1820?], Battle Family Papers, SHC. William went on to a distinguished legal career, holding positions in the state legislature and Superior and Supreme Courts of North Carolina, and teaching law at the University of North Carolina.

46. Twain, *Pudd'nhead Wilson*, p. 23; Kennedy, *Swallow Barn*, p. 170. But, for complaints about the quality of the judiciary in antebellum South Carolina, see Hindus, *Prison and Plantation*, pp. 19–20.

47. Hall, " 'Route to Hell' Retraced," pp. 235–37, 245; Wooster, *Politicians, Planters, and Plain Folk*, pp. 92–93; Wooster, *People in Power*, p. 78. On the political careers of judges in the early nineteenth century, see Friedman, *History of American Law*, pp. 137–38.

48. Yanuck, "Thomas Ruffin and North Carolina Slave Law"; Francis Nash, "Chief Justice Ruffin," in Hamilton, *Papers of Thomas Ruffin* 1: 35–43. For an extensive treatment of the appellate judiciary in the antebellum South, see Nash, "Negro Rights and Judicial Behavior."

49. Griswold, "Adultery and Divorce in Victorian America," pp. 12–15; Grossberg, *Governing the Hearth*, pp. 290–91.

50. William D. Valentine Diary, June 4, 1848, SHC; Augustin Harris Hansell Memoirs (1905), p. 19, SHC; Grossberg, "Institutionalizing Masculinity."

51. Beverly Tucker, "Valedictory Address to his Class," *Southern Literary Messenger* 1 (July 1835): 600.

52. Andrews, *Old Georgia Lawyer*, pp. 20–21, 24–26; Farmer, "Legal Practice and Ethics," pp. 329–34; Frederick Nash to Susan Nash, April 11, 1819, Francis Nash Papers, SHC. See also the unpublished account of circuit riding by Francis Nash in this collection, entitled "A Phase of Judicial History in North Carolina"; and William H. Battle to Lucy M. Battle, September 14, 1840, Battle Family Papers, SHC.

53. Tushnet, "Approaches to the Study of the Law of Slavery," pp. 332–33; Nash, "A More Equitable Past?" pp. 235–40. Ayers (*Vengeance and Justice*, p. 55) presents a similar analysis of southern governors, legislators, and newspaper editors regarding the issue of the penitentiary.

54. Hall, "Judiciary on Trial"; Hall, " 'Route to Hell' Retraced," p. 229. In the latter work, Hall presents evidence that the trend toward popular election of appellate jurists appears to have had little effect on their social origins, and most members of the high state courts continued to come from moderately well off families with kinship ties to the bench (pp. 245–50). Wooster discusses the various methods for choosing judges in the antebellum South in *People in Power*, pp. 64–80, 114; and *Politicians, Planters, and Plain Folk*, pp. 79–96, 122.

55. Alexander A. Allen to George W. Allen, June 2, 1855, and March 12, 1856, George Washington Allen Papers, SHC.

56. Ely, "Judicial Impeachments." On the need to streamline the judicial system in South Carolina and make it more responsive, see "The Judiciary System of South-Carolina," *Southern Quarterly Review* 18 (November 1850): 464–86.

57. Ruffin to B. F. Moore, November 10, 1852, in Hamilton, *Papers of Thomas Ruffin* 2:347; "The Judicial Tenure," *Southern Quarterly Review* 7 (April 1845): 449.

58. Tucker, *Valley of the Shenandoah*, p. 236; Wyatt-Brown, *Southern Honor*, pp. 392–93.

59. Ayers, *Vengeance and Justice*, pp. 41–42; Shalhope, "Thomas Jefferson's Republicanism"; Thornton, *Politics and Power*, pp. 443–45; Cash, *Mind of the South*, p. 35.

60. "The Doctrine of the 'Higher Law,'" *Southern Literary Messenger* 17 (March 1851): 136–37.

61. Wallenstein, *From Slave South to New South*, pp. 23–96; Ayers, *Vengeance and Justice*, pp. 64–69; Thornton, *Politics and Power*, pp. 54–58, 98–100; Ely, "Poor Laws of the Antebellum South"; Collins, *White Society*, pp. 101–14, 122–23.

62. "Reflections on the Duty of a Magistrate," *Carolina Law Repository* 1 (September 1814): 452. On ambivalent attitudes in South Carolina toward the concept of an independent judiciary, see Hindus, *Prison and Plantation*, pp. 15, 20–21.

63. Hurst, *Law and the Conditions of Freedom*, chap. 1; Horwitz, *Transformation of American Law*, esp. chaps. 1–2; Ely and Bodenhamer, "Regionalism and American Legal History," pp. 554–55; Freyer, "Law and the Antebellum Southern Economy," pp. 49–68. The Horwitz thesis about legal change has been the subject of much criticism, in no small part because of its dependence on examples from New England and Middle Atlantic states.

64. [George Fitzhugh], "Law Reports—Multiplicity of Law-Books," *De Bow's Review* 27 (July 1859): 76–77, 79, 80.

65. Gaston quoted in Schauinger, "William Gaston," p. 115. The role of southern appellate jurists in formulating a law of slavery is explored in a number of studies, many of which are cited in note 93 below. See also the discussion in chapter 2 of how the commitment to formal legal process shaped judicial policy in antebellum incest and rape cases.

66. On the growth of judicial power in antebellum America, see Grossberg, *Governing the Hearth*, p. 14; Hall, *Magic Mirror*, pp. 106–8; Friedman, *History of American Law*, p. 133.

67. Cooper, *Liberty and Slavery*, p. 180; Greenberg, *Masters and Statesmen*, pp. xi, 146.

68. Ayers, *Vengeance and Justice*, pp. 26–27; Greenberg, *Masters and Statesmen*, pp. 85–88; Cooper, *Liberty and Slavery*, pp. 30–32, 179; Morgan, *American Slavery*, pp. 380–86.

69. Sydnor, "Southerner and the Laws," p. 8.

70. This study adopts Gerder Lerner's definition of patriarchy in its broadest sense as "the manifestation and institutionalization of male dominance over women and children in the family and the extension of male dominance over women in society in general." Lerner notes that patriarchy also has a narrow, traditional meaning, referring to the system rooted in Greek and Roman law in which the male head of the household exercised absolute legal and economic power over the dependent members of his family. In Lerner's formulation, paternalism is a modified form of patriarchy: it is "the relationship of a dominant group, considered superior, to a subordinate group, considered inferior, in which the dominance is mitigated by mutual obligations and reciprocal rights." Lerner, *Creation of Patriarchy*, pp. 238–39. For a somewhat different approach, see Sennett, *Authority*.

There is considerable debate over the question of patriarchy and the southern household. For studies of antebellum southern society that stress its patriarchal nature, see Johnson, "Planters and Patriarchy"; Wyatt-Brown, *Southern Honor*; Clinton, *Plantation Mistress*; Scott, *Southern Lady*; Burton, *In My Father's House*; Cashin, *Family Venture*; and Peterson, *Ham and Japeth*. Willie Lee Rose contends that "the slaveholder presided over not one, but three interlocking domesticities—his blood family, the slave families, and the larger family of the plantation community." Rose views the planter's blood family as a matriarchy "because of the paramount role of his wife in child-rearing, in household management, and in religious and social matters." There is little doubt that the planter's wife was influential in these areas, but such influence did not pose a serious challenge to the economic, political, and legal power that formed the basis of the planter's patriarchal authority over the members of his biological family. See "The Domestication of Domestic Slavery," in Rose, *Slavery and Freedom*, pp. 28–29.

Studies that downplay the patriarchal character of family relations among southern whites and instead stress the affectionate character of the family include Smith, *Inside the Great House*; Lewis, *Pursuit of Happiness*, esp. chap. 5; Censer, *North Carolina Planters*; and Blake, "Ties of Intimacy." Rhys Issac, Steven Stowe, Elizabeth Fox-Genovese, and Eugene Genovese underscore the commitment of southern society to male domination, but they prefer paternalism to patriarchy as a description of southern social relations. In particular, Isaac emphasizes the role of republicanism and sentimentalism after the American Revolution in bringing about a more individualistic and contractual conception of social relations. As Isaac observes, however, "Patriarchy, and its adaptation, paternalism, continued to be a powerful principle in a thoroughly agrarian society where households small and great were still the social units of production." See Isaac, *Transformation of Virginia*, pp. 308–10, 320–22; Stowe, *Intimacy and Power*, pp. 165–66, 190–91, 237–38; Fox-Genovese, *Within the Plantation Household*, pp. 63–64; and Genovese, " 'Our Family, White and Black.' "

The key point here is that paternalism did not represent a sharp break with "genuine" patriarchy, but rather was a new variant of patriarchy that emerged in response to social pressures and demands. Patriarchy, in other words, was not a static social system; simply because it did not assume ancient Roman form in the nineteenth-century South is no reason to deny its existence in a more modern guise. Indeed, I would argue that although patriarchy in the South changed in crucial ways before and after the Civil War, it persisted alongside, and in tension with, competing forces of individualism, contractualism, and domesticity. Much of the present study aims at illuminating the ways in which these changes and tensions manifested themselves in the legal sphere, leading to the state's increasingly important role in mediating relations between men and women, parents and children, and blacks and whites, a form of patriarchy that I call state paternalism. Household patriarchy, in this context, is the form of patriarchy in which the male head of the household governed in a largely autonomous fashion with the support of the state, and in which economic, political, and legal power is channeled through a network of patriarchs. It is this kind of patriarchy that predominated in the slave South, although state paternalism began to make inroads in the 1840s and 1850s.

71. Burton, *In My Father's House*, pp. 104–9, 117–18; Cashin, *Family Venture*, pp. 10–20, 29–30; Collins, *White Society*, pp. 125–26; Richards, "All Our Connections"; Owsley, *Plain Folk of the Old South*, pp. 94–95; Kenzer, *Kinship and Neighborhood*,

pp. 6, 29; Wyatt-Brown, "Ideal Typology," pp. 4–6; Friedman, *Enclosed Garden*, pp. 3, 9–10.

Orville Vernon Burton finds that wealthier households in Edgefield, South Carolina, were much more likely to swell beyond the nuclear core than the poorer households. While only 18 percent of the poorest household heads under thirty years of age had nonnuclear households, 48 percent of the wealthiest household heads from this same age group had nonnuclear households. See Burton, *In My Father's House*, pp. 109–10.

72. Hundley, *Social Relations*, p. 75.

73. On the ideology of separate spheres and domesticity in Victorian America, see Welter, "Cult of True Womanhood"; Smith-Rosenberg, *Disorderly Conduct*; Cott, *Bonds of Womanhood*; Sklar, *Catharine Beecher*; Ryan, *Cradle of the Middle Class*; Mintz and Kellogg, *Domestic Revolutions*, pp. 43–65; and Degler, *At Odds*, pp. 26–51.

For a superb collection of writings on the ideology of domesticity in the North, see Boydston, Kelley, and Margolis, *Limits of Sisterhood*, esp. pp. 114–221; and for Victorian England, see Murray, *Strong-Minded Women*, esp. pp. 21–39. On the emergence of the bourgeois ideology of domesticity and womanhood in western Europe, see Fox-Genovese and Genovese, *Fruits of Merchant Capital*, pp. 299–336.

74. Fox-Genovese, *Within the Plantation Household*, pp. 61–63, 66–68, 98–99; Friedman, *Enclosed Garden*, pp. 21–38; Hahn, *Roots of Southern Populism*, pp. 29–30; McCurry, "Politics of Yeoman Households in South Carolina," pp. 28–31.

Although Fox-Genovese emphasizes regional differences in the relationship between the market and the household, differences in the relationship between the state and the household were just as important: hence the need to examine the ideological structure of the laws dealing with domestic and sexual relations in the Old South, and how this structure underwent transformation following the collapse of slavery.

75. On patriarchal ideals in premodern England and the relationship between the family and the social order, see Amussen, *An Ordered Society*; Stone, *Family, Sex, and Marriage*; and Schochet, *Patriarchalism in Political Thought*.

76. The data on the demographic environment of the colonial Chesapeake and its impact on family relations is summarized in Kulikoff, *Tobacco and Slaves*, pp. 167–74. See also Walsh, " 'Till Death Us Do Part' "; Rutman and Rutman, " 'Now-Wives and Sons-in-Law' "; and Smith, "Mortality and Family in the Colonial Chesapeake."

On the development of kinship networks in the colonial South, see Rutman and Rutman, *A Place in Time*, pp. 95–127; Kulikoff, *Tobacco and Slaves*, pp. 240–60; and Greene, *Pursuits of Happiness*, pp. 94–95. For a contrasting analysis that questions the intensity and scope of southern kin networks, see Smith, *Inside the Great House*, pp. 175–77, 186–87, 224–30.

77. Treckel, " 'To Comfort the Heart.' "

78. William Byrd II quoted in Isaac, *Transformation of Virginia*, pp. 39–40; Lewis, *Pursuit of Happiness*, p. 12. For an astute analysis of Byrd and his understanding of family, see Zuckerman, "William Byrd's Family," esp. pp. 274–81.

Drew Gilpin Faust illuminates the effort of another planter, James Henry Hammond, to achieve mastery over his slaves and to gain their allegiance within the framework of this patriarchal ideal in "Culture, Conflict, and Community."

79. Rutman and Rutman, *A Place in Time*, pp. 171–73; Genovese, " 'Our Family, White and Black,' " pp. 69, 72–73; Fox-Genovese, "Family and Female Identity in the Antebellum South," p. 19. For a contrasting view that downplays the extent to which

planters considered slaves as part of their family, see Censer, *North Carolina Planters*, pp. 135–49.

80. Faust, "Southern Stewardship"; Greenberg, *Masters and Statesmen*, pp. 92–102; Genovese, "'Our Family, White and Black,'" pp. 75–78.

81. Address delivered before the State Agricultural Society of North Carolina, October 18, 1855, in Hamilton, *Papers of Thomas Ruffin* 4:333–34.

82. Johnson, "Planters and Patriarchy," pp. 46, 55–72; Cashin, *Family Venture*, chaps. 4–5.

83. Jan Lewis explores the problematic aspects of romantic love for white Virginians in the eighteenth and early nineteenth century in *Pursuit of Happiness*, pp. 169–208, and Steven Stowe analyzes the struggles over authority, autonomy, and intimacy in the domestic relations of the antebellum planter class in *Intimacy and Power*, pp. 106–28, 164–91. Also useful is Stowe, "Rhetoric of Authority." For a perceptive discussion of the role of romantic love in the transformation of patriarchy, see Lystra, *Searching the Heart*, pp. 229–37.

84. Richards, "All Our Connections," pp. 145–46, 149–50.

85. Wallenstein, *From Slave South to New South*, pp. 86–88; "Woman Physiologically Considered," p. 297.

86. Fitzhugh, *Sociology for the South*, p. 105. As Eugene Genovese has pointed out, George Fitzhugh feared that bourgeois society would destroy the patriarchal ideal of the family because the bourgeois state placed great emphasis upon the recognition of individual rights, and hence would undermine the authority of the father. Fitzhugh, however, defined the outer limits of southern thinking on the matter of patriarchal authority, and did not necessarily represent mainstream opinion in his unwavering opposition to granting household subordinates any individual rights. See Genovese, *World the Slaveholders Made*, p. 199; Degler, *Place Over Time*, pp. 88–89; and Faust, *Sacred Circle*, pp. 127–30.

87. Wyatt-Brown, "Ideal Typology," p. 15; Burton, *In My Father's House*, p. 102; McCurry, "Politics of Yeoman Households," pp. 26–27, 35; McCurry, "Two Faces of Republicanism"; Williamson, *Crucible of Race*, pp. 24–35.

88. Helpful theoretical analyses of how the law perpetuates patriarchy can be found in MacKinnon, *Toward a Feminist Theory of the State*, pp. 157–70; Rifkin, "Toward a Theory of Law and Patriarchy"; Taub and Schneider, "Perspectives on Women's Subordination and the Role of Law"; and Polan, "Toward a Theory of Law and Patriarchy."

A review of feminist debates over gender and the law, as well as a perceptive critique of "liberal legalism," can be found in Hoff, *Law, Gender, and Injustice*, pp. 350–75. For a wide-ranging discussion of how gender has played a crucial historical role in organizing equality and inequality, see Scott, "Gender: A Useful Category."

89. Victoria Bynum analyzes the efforts of North Carolina courts to define the limits of patriarchal power regarding physical abuse of slaves and wives in *Unruly Women*, pp. 70–72.

90. Sydnor, "Southerner and the Laws," pp. 9–10; De Bow, quoted in Elkins, *Slavery*, p. 56.

91. Quoted in Stampp, *Peculiar Institution*, p. 207.

92. Wyatt-Brown, *Southern Honor*, pp. 363, 371–77; Rose, "Domestic Slavery," pp. 20–23, 25–27; Genovese, *Roll, Jordan, Roll*, pp. 3–7, 31–43. In contrast to Rose and

Genovese, James Oakes argues that slavery became less paternalistic over the course of the antebellum period, although he does concede that a portion of the slaveholding class continued to adhere to a paternalistic ideology. See Oakes, *Ruling Race*, pp. xii–xiii, 192–224.

93. Leading discussions of slave law in the antebellum South include Tushnet, *American Law of Slavery*; Hindus, "Black Justice Under White Law"; Howington, "'Not in the Condition of a Horse or an Ox'"; Flanigan, "Criminal Procedure in Slave Trials"; and Nash, "Texas Supreme Court and Trial Rights of Blacks." The latter work is one of a series of four articles by Nash, all of which are cited in Hindus, "Black Justice Under White Law," p. 576n.

Hindus is significantly less impressed with the effectiveness of the legal constraints on the behavior of slaveholders and other whites. In contrast to many of the other studies cited here, which rely heavily on appellate opinions, Hindus uses trial records. As he properly points out, the findings of the high courts often had little impact on the operation of slave justice at the local level. Nash surveys the debate about the legal character of slavery in "Reason of Slavery."

94. Stampp, *Peculiar Institution*, p. 206; Hall, *Magic Mirror*, p. 131.

95. Genovese, *Roll, Jordan, Roll*, pp. 28–29; Tushnet, *American Law of Slavery*, pp. 111–21; Hall, *Magic Mirror*, pp. 132–33. See McLaurin, *Celia*, esp. chaps. 5–7, for a penetrating examination of the dilemmas faced by southern legal authorities in prosecuting a female slave who killed her master following years of sexual abuse.

96. Quoted in Howington, "'Not in the Condition of a Horse or an Ox,'" p. 258.

97. Quoted in Genovese, *Roll, Jordan, Roll*, p. 30.

98. Bloomfield, "Law and Southern Society," pp. 669–70; Tushnet, *American Law of Slavery*, pp. 157–58, 229–31; Genovese and Fox-Genovese, "Slavery, Economic Development, and the Law."

99. Oakes, *Slavery and Freedom*, pp. 156–58, 160; Younger, "Southern Grand Juries and Slavery"; Wyatt-Brown, *Southern Honor*, pp. 377–80.

100. For a valuable analysis of how slaves challenged Virginia's criminal justice system and managed to secure a degree of autonomy, see Schwarz, "Forging the Shackles," and his larger study, *Twice Condemned*, esp. pt. 3.

101. Genovese, *Roll, Jordan, Roll*, pp. 45–49; Rose, "Domestic Slavery," pp. 24–25; Burnham, "Impossible Marriage."

102. McKnight, "Family Law," p. 687. See also his "Texas Community Property Law," pp. 31–35.

103. On the legal concept of marital unity, see Basch, "Invisible Women"; and Kerber, *Women of the Republic*, pp. 119–20, 139–55.

104. Lebsock, *Free Women of Petersburg*, pp. 23–24. A good discussion of the constraints southern women confronted in the area of property rights can be found in Wyatt-Brown, *Southern Honor*, pp. 254–69. For a more optimistic view of married women's legal rights, see Gundersen and Gampel, "Married Women's Legal Status."

Lebsock points out that many free black women in antebellum Petersburg sought to avoid the common-law disabilities of married women by remaining single, thus retaining control over their property and wages. See *Free Women of Petersburg*, pp. 104–9; and "Free Black Women and the Question of Matriarchy," pp. 282–85.

105. Salmon, *Women and the Law of Property*, pp. 90–116; Salmon, "Women and Property in South Carolina." See also the important discussions of separate estates in

Lebsock, *Free Women of Petersburg*, pp. 54–86; and Bynum, *Unruly Women*, pp. 64–67. Theodore Rosengarten examines a tangled legal dispute over a marriage settlement in a South Carolina planter family in *Tombe*, pp. 100–110.

Besides a judicial tendency to support marriage settlements in the postrevolutionary South, Salmon finds legislative improvements for women in the laws governing a widow's right to dower and the distribution of estates left by husbands who died intestate. See Salmon, *Women and the Law of Property*, pp. 168–72; and " 'Life, Liberty, and Dower,' " pp. 92–96.

106. Chused, "Married Women's Property Law," pp. 1398–99; Hall, *Magic Mirror*, p. 159.

107. On the passage of the Mississippi Act, consult Brown, "Husband and Wife"; Warbasse, *Changing Legal Rights of Married Women*, pp. 138–54; and Moncrief, "Mississippi Married Women's Property Act of 1839."

108. McMillen, *Southern Women*, pp. 43–45; Lebsock, "Radical Reconstruction"; Chused, "Married Women's Property Law," pp. 1398–1412, 1423–25; Salmon, "Republican Sentiment," pp. 474–75. Other recent examinations of married women's property rights in antebellum America include Basch, *In the Eyes of the Law*; and Rabkin, *Fathers to Daughters*.

109. On the distinction between equity and equality as it pertained to the status of American women during the early nineteenth century, see Basch, "Equity vs. Equality."

110. Spruill, *Women's Life and Work*, pp. 342–44; Friedman, *History of American Law*, pp. 204–5; Bloomfield, *American Lawyers*, pp. 97, 120–22; Clinton, *Plantation Mistress*, pp. 79–86; Salmon, *Women and the Law of Property*, pp. 58–66. For a survey of divorce legislation in the nineteenth-century South, see Howard, *Matrimonial Institutions* 3 : 31–95.

111. On the role of cruelty in English divorce law, see Stone, *Road to Divorce*, pp. 192–93, 198–206; and Perkin, *Women and Marriage*, pp. 22–24.

112. Censer, " 'Smiling through Her Tears,' " pp. 27, 29 (Scott quotation); Wyatt-Brown, *Southern Honor*, pp. 286–87. Robert Griswold discusses the expanded definition of marital cruelty in American divorce cases in "Evolution of the Doctrine of Mental Cruelty," and "Sexual Cruelty and the Case for Divorce."

113. McMillen, *Southern Women*, p. 46; Censer, " 'Smiling through Her Tears,' " p. 28 (Ruffin quotation).

114. Quoted in Bynum, *Unruly Women*, p. 61. Although Ruffin and Pearson shared a consensus on the undesirability of divorce, Ruffin adopted a more liberal position on separate estates for married women (pp. 66–72).

115. Ibid., pp. 72–74; Censer, " 'Smiling through Her Tears,' " pp. 37–40. Robert Griswold also finds that similar Victorian ideals of womanhood and manhood shaped the nineteenth-century divorce process in *Family and Divorce in California*, pp. 39–140; and "Divorce and the Legal Redefinition of Victorian Manhood."

116. James Oakes points to the rise of individualism in planter households during the antebellum period, seeing it as the result of inroads made by liberal political culture into slaveholding society. But, in my judgment, he overstates the degree to which individualism undercut the structure of patriarchal power in southern households and in the society at large. Furthermore, what is crucial in understanding why the South went to war is not so much the extent of the change itself, but the reaction of those in power (in both the domestic and political arenas) to the change. See Oakes, *Slavery and Freedom*, pp. 88–90.

117. Tushnet, "Approaches to the Study of the Law of Slavery," pp. 335–38; Tushnet, *American Law of Slavery*, pp. 5–8, 36–37; Wright, *Political Economy*, pp. 7, 45, 87–88. See also the discussion of Tushnet's work in Genovese, "Slavery in the Legal History of the South and the Nation."

118. On southern economic developments in the 1850s, see Wright, *Political Economy*, esp. chaps. 2, 5; Reidy, *From Slavery to Agrarian Capitalism*, chap. 4; and Thornton, *Politics and Power*, pp. 268–91.

119. Grossberg, *Governing the Hearth*, pp. 17–30. Eileen Boris and I first discussed how "the nineteenth and early twentieth centuries . . . saw not the decline of patriarchy but its transformation from a familial to a state form" in a 1983 essay. See Boris and Bardaglio, "Transformation of Patriarchy."

CHAPTER TWO

1. *Stephen v. State*, 11 Ga. 225 (1852), pp. 234, 229.

2. Ibid., pp. 233, 230, 234, 242. For an assessment of Justice Lumpkin, see Stephenson and Stephenson, " 'To Protect and Defend.' "

3. The most recent analyses of sexual dynamics in the Old South and the implications for understanding the power relations of slave society are Clinton, " 'Southern Dishonor,' " pp. 52–68; Bynum, *Unruly Women*; and Painter, "Of *Lily*, Linda Brent, and Freud." See also Clinton, *Plantation Mistress*, chap. 11; and Wyatt-Brown, *Southern Honor*, chap. 12.

Helpful discussions of sexuality in nineteenth-century America include D'Emilio and Freedman, *Intimate Matters*, chaps. 4–6; Smith-Rosenberg, *Disorderly Conduct*, pp. 90–108, 182–96; Cott, "Passionlessness"; Barker-Benfield, *Horrors of the Half-Known Life*; and Rosenberg, "Sexuality, Class and Role." See also Estelle Freedman's survey of the relevant literature in "Sexuality in Nineteenth-Century America." To place American developments in a transatlantic context, consult Weeks, *Sex, Politics and Society*.

4. For a provocative analysis of the connection between patriarchy and the rise of the state, see Lerner, *Creation of Patriarchy*, esp. pp. 121–22; 208–9; 216–19.

5. Hall, " 'The Mind That Burns in Each Body,' " p. 331.

6. For a fascinating study of how the treatment of sex crimes in Venice during the fourteenth and fifteenth centuries provides a fuller understanding of Renaissance culture and society, see Ruggiero, *Boundaries of Eros*.

7. Wyatt-Brown, *Southern Honor*, p. 293. For important analyses of sexuality as a social construction, see MacKinnon, *Toward a Feminist Theory of the State*, pp. 127–54; Ross and Rapp, "Sex and Society"; Weeks, *Sex, Politics and Society*, pp. 1–16; Padgug, "Sexual Matters"; and Walters, "Sexual Matters as Historical Problems."

8. Gay, *Education of the Senses*, p. 444; Anderson, " 'Marriage with a Deceased Wife's Sister Bill' Controversy"; Anderson, "Cousin Marriage in Victorian England"; and Wohl, "Sex and the Single Room." Other historical investigations dealing with incest in Victorian society include Strong, "Toward a History of the Experiential Family"; and Kern, "Explosive Intimacy." Like the analysis here, these studies focus on public beliefs about incest rather than incest behavior. For a sophisticated historical consideration of incest behavior, one that views it as a kind of family violence, see Gordon, *Heroes of Their Own Lives*, pp. 204–49.

9. *Morgan v. State*, 11 Ala. 289 (1847), p. 291; *Ward v. Dulaney*, 23 Miss. 410 (1852), p. 426.

10. *Tuberville v. State*, 4 Tex. 128 (1849), p. 130.

11. *Ex parte Hewitt*, 11 Rich. 326 (S.C. 1858), p. 329. The South Carolina court made this declaration in justifying its decision to award custody of a child to the father in a dispute between the parents.

12. "One practical result of the 'hands-off' rhetorical stance of the law toward activities within the 'private realm of the family,'" feminist legal scholar Diane Polan points out, "has been to license men's exploitation of women within the family unit." See "Toward a Theory of Law and Patriarchy," p. 298. I would only add that this license has some limits: the courts intervened in the nineteenth-century South when the abuse by the male head of the household was so excessive that it threatened to undermine the legitimacy of patriarchal authority as a system.

13. Seligman, "Incest Barrier"; Parsons, "Incest Taboo"; and Lévi-Strauss, *Elementary Structures of Kinship*. On Lévi-Strauss and his theory of the incest taboo, see Poster, *Critical Theory of the Family*, pp. 97–102. Other significant studies by social scientists of incest include Fox, *Red Lamp of Incest*; Shepher, *Incest*; Herman, *Father-Daughter Incest*; and Begus and Armstrong, "Daddy's Right." The latter two studies, like Gordon's *Heroes of Their Own Lives*, recognize the importance of an analysis based on gender, and they place incest in the context of family violence.

14. Lévi-Strauss, "Family," p. 276; Lloyd, "Management of Incest," p. 17; Manchester, "Incest and the Law," pp. 487–88; Storke, "Incestuous Marriage," pp. 473–74.

15. Wolfram, *In-Laws and Outlaws*, pp. 21–27; Trumbach, *Rise of the Egalitarian Family*, p. 18; Einbinder, "Legal Family," p. 782, 782 n. 7; Schouler, *Law of Domestic Relations*, pp. 26–28; Bishop, *Law of Marriage and Divorce*, p. 171; Grossberg, *Governing the Hearth*, p. 111. For a detailed discussion of canon law and its treatment of incestuous marriages, see Kelly, "Kinship, Incest, and the Dictates of Law."

16. Spruill, *Women's Life and Work*, pp. 141–42; Va., *Statutes at Large* (Hening 1809–23), 4:245–46 (Act of 1730); S.C., *Statutes at Large* (Cooper and McCord 1836–41), 2:241, 243, 475–76. For North Carolina legislation, see N.C., *Colonial Records* (Saunders 1886–90), 2:212–13. Discussions of colonial incest laws in the South include Howard, *Matrimonial Institutions* 2:234, 251, 260; Calhoun, *American Family* 1:264, 304, 315; and Semonche, "Common-Law Marriage in North Carolina," pp. 330–31. For colonial cases dealing with the prohibited degrees of marriage, see *Dr. Strahan's Opinion*, 2 Va. Col. Dec. Baradall's Rep. B20 (1724); *Dr. Paul's Opinion* (1724), Carolina Law Repository 1 (September 1814): 424–26; and Parker, *North Carolina Higher-Court Records*, pp. 468–69.

17. Ga., *Code* (Clarke, Cobb, and Irwin 1861), sec. 1655, p. 331; Ga., *Acts of the General Assembly* (1865–66), p. 244.

18. Ala., *Digest of the Laws* (Toulmin 1823), p. 578; Ark., *Revised Statutes* (Ball and Roane 1838), ch. 94, sec. 3, p. 535; La., *Digest of the Civil Laws* (1808), title 4, ch. 2, arts. 9–10, pp. 24–26; Miss., *Revised Code* (Poindexter 1824), ch. 102, sec. 8, pp. 447–48; N.C., *Revised Code* (Moore and Biggs 1855), ch. 68, sec. 9, p. 392; Tenn., *Compilation of the Statutes* (Caruthers and Nicholson 1836), ch. 23, sec. 18, pp. 318–19; Tex., *Digest of the Laws* (Dallam 1845), p. 103; and Va., *Revised Code* (Leigh 1819), vol. 1, ch. 106, sec. 17, p. 399.

19. Ala., *Code* (Ormond, Bagby, and Goldthwaite 1852), secs. 1942–43, p. 375; Ark., *Revised Statutes* (1838), ch. 94, sec. 3, p. 535; La., *Digest* (1808), title 4, ch.

2, arts. 9–10, pp. 24–26; and Tex., *Digest of the General Statute Laws* (Oldham and White 1859), p. 503. The Texas restrictions dealt solely with half-blood relatives. In addition, Virginia and Mississippi had antebellum legislation specifically banning marriages between half-brothers and half-sisters. See Va., *Revised Code* (1819), vol. 1, ch. 106, sec. 17, p. 399; and Miss., *Revised Code* (1824), ch. 102, sec. 8, pp. 447–48.

20. Louisiana abolished all such barriers in 1827. La., *Civil Code* (Upton and Jennings 1838), title 4, ch. 1, art. 98. For the lack of affinal prohibitions in the other three states, consult Ark., *Digest of the Statutes* (Gould 1858), ch. 51, pt. 8, art. 1, sec. 6, p. 368; Fla., *Manual or Digest of the Statute Law* (Thompson 1847), p. 499; and N.C., *Revised Code* (1855), ch. 68, sec. 9, p. 392.

21. Va., *Revised Code* (1819), vol. 1, ch. 106, sec. 17, p. 399.

22. For a detailed description of a wedding in the eighteenth-century Chesapeake that displayed these traditional values, see Kulikoff, " 'Throwing the Stocking.' "

23. Farber, *Kinship and Class*, pp. 14–16; Grossberg, "Law and the Family," p. 125; Trumbach, *Rise of the Egalitarian Family*, pp. 18–19. For a full examination of the debate in England over the prohibition against marriage with a wife's sister, see Anderson, " 'Marriage with a Deceased Wife's Sister Bill' Controversy," pp. 74–84; and Wolfram, *In-Laws and Outlaws*, pp. 30–40.

See also "Affinity in Marriage," *Carolina Law Repository* 1 (September 1814): 448–50, which condemns this prohibition "as an absurdity consistent only with the narrow ideas of Britain's legislators in past ages, or the artificial blindness produced by quibbling lawyers," and provides an interesting account of an English case in which a marriage with a deceased wife's sister is declared null and void.

Despite the traditional stricture against marriages between a widower and his deceased wife's sister or a widow and her late husband's brother, it appears that such unions were actually not uncommon in the antebellum South. See Clinton, *Plantation Mistress*, pp. 78–79; Censer, *North Carolina Planters*, p. 88; and Wyatt-Brown, *Southern Honor*, p. 219.

24. Virginia finally lifted its legal sanction against contracting matrimony with a deceased wife's sister in 1849. In its 1859–60 session, the Virginia legislature also abolished the prohibition against marriage with a brother's widow. Georgia, another southern state that had followed English tradition closely on these matters, dropped the two marital bans in 1861. Compare Va., *Digest of the Laws*, 2d ed. (Tate 1841), pp. 500–501 with *Code* (Patton and Robinson 1849), ch. 108, sec. 10, pp. 470–71, where the prohibition against marrying a deceased wife's sister does not appear. For the dropping of the ban on marrying a brother's widow, see Va., *Code*, 2d ed. (Munford 1860), ch. 108, sec. 9, p. 524. For Georgia, see Ga., *Code* (1861), sec. 1655, p. 331.

25. Grossberg, "Guarding the Altar," p. 213; Howard, *Matrimonial Institutions* 2:397–98, 473–75; Clarke, *Social Legislation*, p. 97.

26. *Kelly v. Neely*, 12 Ark. 657 (1852), p. 660. See also *State v. Shaw*, 25 N.C. 532 (1843).

27. On the growing role of voluntary consent and mutual affection in influencing marital decisions, see Lystra, *Searching the Heart*, pp. 159–64; Mintz and Kellogg, *Domestic Revolutions*, pp. 46–48; Degler, *At Odds*, pp. 9–14; Norton, *Liberty's Daughters*, pp. 229–30; and Fliegelman, *Prodigals and Pilgrims*, pp. 132–37. Analyses of southern marriage that emphasize free choice and affection include Smith, *Inside the Great House*, pp. 140–50; Lewis, *Pursuit of Happiness*, pp. 188–91; Censer, *North Carolina Planters*, pp. 68, 72, 79–81; and Blake, "Ties of Intimacy," pp. 64–70,

81–82. Bleser, "Perrys of Greenville," presents an interesting case study of a southern marriage based on voluntary consent and romantic love.

Steven Stowe and Suzanne Lebsock make the important point that, despite the inroads made by the ideal of romantic love in the Old South, the traditional concern for wealth and kinship remained a critical part of courtship. See Stowe, *Intimacy and Power*, pp. 104–6, 214–18; and Lebsock, *Free Women of Petersburg*, pp. 15–23. For other studies that give significant weight to familial and financial considerations, consult Wyatt-Brown, *Southern Honor*, pp. 207–13; Clinton, *Plantation Mistress*, pp. 59–60, 64–65; Johnson, "Planters and Patriarchy," pp. 65–66; and Johnson, "Courtship and Marriage Customs," pp. 384–87.

28. See Ala., *Code* (1852), sec. 1942, p. 375; Ga., *Code* (1861), sec. 1655, p. 331; Miss., *Revised Code* (Sharkey, Harris, and Ellett 1857), ch. 40, art. 8, p. 333; Tenn., *Code* (Meigs and Cooper 1858), secs. 4836–37, p. 867; Tex., *Digest* (1859), p. 503; and Va., *Code* (1860), ch. 108, sec. 9, p. 524.

29. Farber, *Kinship and Class*, pp. 40–41. See the discussion of Farber's analysis in Grossberg, *Governing the Hearth*, p. 112.

30. Wyatt-Brown, *Southern Honor*, pp. 217–21; Clinton, *Plantation Mistress*, pp. 57–58, 61; Censer, *North Carolina Planters*, pp. 84–87. On the tabooo against cousin unions in the slave community, see Gutman, *Black Family*, pp. 880–90. Of course, seventeenth-century Chesapeake society had provided few opportunities for kin marriages as a result of the preponderance of immigrants and short adult life expectancies. But by the mid-eighteenth century, with the growth of a native population and improved mortality rates, marriages in the Chesapeake area between first cousins and other blood relations were on the upswing. See Walsh, " 'Till Death Us Do Part,' " pp. 127–29; Rutman and Rutman, " 'Now-Wives and Sons-in-Law,' " pp. 168–69; Smith, *Inside the Great House*, pp. 151, 177; and Kulikoff, *Tobacco and Slaves*, pp. 206, 252–55.

31. Degler, *At Odds*, pp. 104–6; Berthoff, *Unsettled People*, p. 205. The major exception to this weakening of kin bonds outside the South was among New England elites. See Hall, "Marital Selection and Business."

32. Cashin, "Structure of Antebellum Families," pp. 65–67; Clinton, *Plantation Mistress*, pp. 36–37; Owsley, *Plain Folk of the Old South*, pp. 94–95. According to Jane Censer, nearly one-tenth of the marriages among planters' sons and daughters in antebellum North Carolina involved matches with first or second cousins. See Censer, *North Carolina Planters*, p. 84. Burton, *In My Father's House*, pp. 119–23, provides evidence that cousin marriage occurred more often among wealthier white families in the Old South than among those not so well off. On the frequency of cousin marriage among the middle and upper classes in Victorian England, see Anderson, "Cousin Marriage in Victorian England," pp. 287–91.

33. Weeks, *Sex, Politics and Society*, p. 31; Hughes, "Crime of Incest," pp. 322–23; Royce and Waits, "Crime of Incest," pp. 191–92. The Matrimonial Causes Act of 1857 transferred jurisdiction over matrimonial cases to other courts, but failed to make provision for the punishment of incest. As a result, for half a century between 1857 and 1908, no sanctions whatsoever against incest existed in England. See Wolfram, *In-Laws and Outlaws*, pp. 42–43.

34. Georgia and Louisiana in 1817, Tennessee in 1829, Florida in 1832, Arkansas in 1837, Mississippi in 1839, Alabama in 1841, and Texas in 1848 all passed legislation imposing criminal penalties for incestuous marriages and sexual relations. See Ga.,

Digest of the Laws (Prince 1822), p. 365; La., *Consolidation and Revision of the Statutes* (Peirce, Taylor, and King 1852), p. 188; Tenn., *Compilation* (1836), ch. 23, sec. 18, pp. 318–19; Fla., *Compilation of the Public Acts* (Duval 1839), p. 120; Ark., *Revised Statutes* (1838), ch. 44, art. 7, sec. 5, p. 254; Miss., *Code* (Hutchinson 1848), ch. 64, title 7, sec. 5, p. 978; Ala., *Supplement to Aikin's Digest* (Meek 1841), ch. 6, sec. 6, p. 239; and Tex., *Digest of the Laws* (Hartley 1850), art. 557, p. 212.

In Mississippi, only persons within the prohibited degrees of consanguinity who had sex could be convicted of incest. No penalties existed in the state's incest regulations for close affines who engaged in intercourse, even though some of these affines were not allowed to contract matrimony. In other words, a stepfather who had sexual intercourse with his stepdaughter could not be punished for incest in Mississippi, despite the fact that marriage between them was considered incestuous. Compare ch. 64, title 7, sec. 5, p. 978, with ch. 34, art. 1, sec. 8, p. 494, in Miss., *Code* (1848). See also *Chancellor v. State*, 47 Miss. 278 (1872), in which the Mississippi Supreme Court decried its inability under the state's incest laws to punish a man who had sex with his stepdaughter.

Virginia's act of 1730 gave colonial courts the power to fine at their discretion any person who copulated within the prohibited degrees, but this law was repealed and replaced by the act of 1788, which did not provide any punishment for incestuous intercourse. Va., *Statutes at Large* (1809–23), 4:246, 12:688–89. Virginia, as well as North Carolina and South Carolina, did not enact legislation until the late nineteenth century classifying incestuous sexual relations as a crime. See chapter 6 in this volume.

35. Fla., *Manual* (1847), p. 499; La., *Statutes* (1852), p. 188. For legislation declaring marriages within the forbidden degrees void, see Ala., *Code* (1852), sec. 1945, p. 376; Ark., *Digest* (1858), ch. 109, sec. 3, p. 760; Ga., *Code* (1861), sec. 4418, p. 860; Miss., *Revised Code* (1857), ch. 64, art. 184, p. 603; N.C., *Revised Code* (1855), ch. 68, sec. 9, p. 392; and Va., *Code* (1860), ch. 109, sec. 1, p. 529.

36. For discussions of the distinction between void and voidable, see Goda, "Void and Voidable Marriages"; Schouler, *Law of Domestic Relations*, pp. 24–25; and Bishop, *Law of Marriage and Divorce*, pp. 37–46.

37. Only two antebellum cases involved the indictment of the female party: *Hutchins v. Commonwealth*, 2 Va. Cas. 331 (1823), in which Nancy Hutchins was convicted of marrying her uncle; and *Commonwealth v. Perryman*, 29 Va. 717 (1830), in which the woman was convicted of marrying her deceased husband's brother.

38. See, for example, *State v. Cone*, 46 N.C. 18 (1853), and *Williams v. State*, 27 Tenn. 585 (1848), in which fathers are indicted for the rape of their teen-aged daughters. See also *Turney v. State*, 16 Miss. 104 (1847), which involves an indictment for the rape of a sixteen-year-old girl who was the defendant's stepdaughter. In all three cases the lower-court convictions were reversed and new trials ordered.

39. For an example of strict constructionism vis-à-vis the incest statutes, consult *Commonwealth v. Leftwich*, 5 Rand. 83 (Va. 1827), in which the General Court of Virginia overturned the conviction of a man who had married his deceased wife's sister. The act under which the widower had been indicted in 1822 was repealed by the time his case reached the appellate level, and it was replaced with a more lenient statute. The new act, passed in 1827, no longer required the court to separate a man and his late wife's sister upon conviction for marrying within the forbidden degrees, although the man could still be fined or imprisoned for this misdemeanor. In this case, however, the widower escaped criminal punishment completely because the 1827 statute

contained no proviso requiring offenses committed before the implementation of the new law to be prosecuted under the old one. As a result of this legislative oversight, the appellate court ruled that there was no law in force by which the remarried man could be punished. See also Va., *Digest* (1841), pp. 500–501 n. 2, which provides a statement of the 1827 act.

40. *State v. Barefoot*, 2 Rich. 209 (S.C. 1845), pp. 213, 218.

41. Ibid., pp. 221, 227, 223.

42. *Bowers v. Bowers*, 10 Rich. Eq. 551 (S.C. 1858), p. 555.

43. The major exception to this approval of judicial power was *Attorney General v. Broaddus*, 20 Va. 116 (1818), in which the Virginia appellate court declared that the state statute punishing marriage within the prohibited degrees was unconstitutional because it directed prosecution to be instituted in the chancery court, which did not have jurisdiction in criminal cases. The Supreme Court of Appeals thus upheld the lower court's dismissal of an indictment charging Andrew Broaddus and his wife for marrying because she was a sister of his former wife.

With the passage of new legislation, however, Virginia appellate judges in 1823 affirmed the criminal conviction of a woman who had married her uncle. But the high court made certain that its decision had sufficient legislative basis: "Upon examination of the Act of the Assembly it is seen that the offence is . . . laid in the very words of the Act" and "it seems to all the Judges that there is all the certainty which reason, or the Law of the Case requires." *Hutchins v. Commonwealth*, 2 Va. Cas. 331 (1823), p. 259. For the new legislation stipulating that the superior court should handle such prosecutions, consult Va., *Revised Code* (1819), vol. 1, ch. 106, sec. 17, p. 399.

For other cases in which the Virginia court employed its power to punish those who contracted incestuous marriages, see *Commonwealth v. Perryman*, 29 Va. 717 (1830), in which the court declared a union between a man and his brother's widow void; and *Kelly v. Scott*, 46 Va. 479 (1849), in which the court upheld the invalidation of a union between a man and his deceased wife's sister.

44. *Ewell v. State*, 14 Tenn. 364 (1834), p. 376.

45. *Cook v. State*, 11 Ga. 53 (1852), p. 57.

46. But see *Morgan v. State*, 11 Ala. 289 (1847) and *Baker v. State*, 30 Ala. 521 (1857) for examples of southern jurists who refused to impose the narrowest possible construction on incest statutes. In these two cases the Alabama Supreme Court decided that the state's incest statute applied to illegitimate as well as legitimate relations within the forbidden degrees, even though the statute did not explicitly state so.

47. *Morgan v. State*, 11 Ala. 289 (1847), p. 292; *Tuberville v. State*, 4 Tex. 128 (1849), p. 130.

48. [W. W. Wright], "Amalgamation," *De Bow's Review* 29 (July 1860): 13.

49. Mencke, *Mulattoes and Race Mixture*, pp. 7–8; Jordan, *White Over Black*, pp. 136–38, 167–68, 178, 475; Fredrickson, *White Supremacy*, pp. 95–99; Williamson, *New People*, pp. 63, 71, 73–75.

50. Twain, *Pudd'nhead Wilson*, p. 29. Susan Gillman, in " 'Sure Identifiers,' " explores the theme of racial identity in Twain's novel. She makes the important point that it tells us as much about the intensifying racism of the 1890s as it does about the antebellum era.

51. Wyatt-Brown, *Southern Honor*, pp. 296–97, 307–8; Bynum, *Unruly Women*, pp. 36–37, 96–98; Clinton, *Plantation Mistress*, pp. 204–5, 209–10; Smith, *Inside the*

Great House, p. 138; Higginbotham, *In the Matter of Color*, pp. 40–41; Brownmiller, *Against Our Will*, pp. 165–66, 177–78.

52. [Wright], "Amalgamation," p. 14.

53. Catherine Clinton vividly underscores the extent to which the "social constellation" of the slave South centered around race and gender. As she puts it, "Ante-bellum patriarchs simultaneously emasculated male slaves, dehumanized female slaves, and desexualized their own wives. The imposition of this difficult and twisted balance had become the indispensable counterpoint to a racial dynamic of sexuality that was of the white masters' own creation." See Clinton, *Plantation Mistress*, pp. 221–22.

54. On regional variations in southern attitudes toward miscegenation, see Williamson, *New People*, pp. 14–24, 33–42; Jordan, *White Over Black*, pp. 144–50; and Mills, "Miscegenation and the Free Negro." Joan Cashin suggests that planter men in the Southwest may have been more open about their sexual relations with slave women than were men in the seaboard. See *Family Venture*, pp. 102, 105–6.

55. Calhoun, *American Family* 1:323–26; Jordan, "Modern Tensions," pp. 27–29; Morgan, *American Slavery*, pp. 333–34; Getman, "Sexual Control," pp. 121–24; Williamson, *New People*, pp. 7–8. Jordan and Morgan question, in particular, whether there was any racial feeling involved in the famous 1630 case of Hugh Davis, who was ordered by Virginia authorities to be whipped "before an assembly of Negroes and others for abusing himself to the dishonor of God and shame of Christians, by defiling his body in lying with a negro." The wording of these charges, however, clearly indicates the extent to which the issue was a matter of racial as well as sexual misconduct.

56. Quoted in Jordan, *White Over Black*, pp. 34–35, 158.

57. Mencke, *Mulattoes and Race Mixture*, pp. 5–6; Jordan, *White Over Black*, pp. 141–42, 175–76; Degler, *Neither Black nor White*, pp. 226–39; Nash, *Red, White, and Black*, p. 281.

58. Johnston, *Race Relations*, pp. 165–90; Spruill, *Women's Life and Work*, pp. 176–77; Calhoun, *American Family* 1:210–11, 325; Jordan, *White Over Black*, pp. 138–39; Morgan, *American Slavery*, p. 334; Wood, *Black Majority*, pp. 98–99, 233–36; Breen and Innes, *"Myne Owne Ground,"* p. 107.

59. Clarke, *Social Legislation*, p. 102; Applebaum, "Miscegenation Statutes," pp. 49–50; Grossberg, "Guarding the Altar," p. 200.

60. The following discussion of antimiscegenation statutes in colonial Maryland and Virginia owes much to Fredrickson, *White Supremacy*, pp. 101–7; Higginbotham, *In the Matter of Color*, pp. 40–47; and Getman, "Sexual Control," pp. 125–31.

61. The quotations from the act of 1664, as well as those from the acts of 1681 and 1692 in the following paragraphs, can be found in Alpert, "Origin of Slavery," pp. 195, 209, 211.

62. The new act stipulated that any master who encouraged or merely allowed a white woman servant to marry a black slave should be fined ten thousand pounds of tobacco, and the woman and her children immediately discharged from their indentures. In addition, any minister who performed such marriages was fined ten thousand pounds of tobacco. See Getman, "Sexual Control," p. 129; and Alpert, "Origin of Slavery," pp. 209–10.

63. Under the act of 1692 any white woman who married a black was subject to a period of servitude for seven years, unless she was a servant and the master had in-

stigated the marriage; under these circumstances, the woman was to be released from servitude. If the marriage took place "without the Connivance or procurement of her master," however, then the female servant's indenture was increased by seven years and any offspring were to be bound out until the age of twenty-one. Alpert, "Origin of Slavery," p. 210.

64. Fredrickson, *White Supremacy*, p. 106.

65. Va., *Statutes at Large* (1809–23), 2:170 (Act of 1662); Clinton, *Plantation Mistress*, p. 203. As George Fredrickson observes in *White Supremacy* (p. 101), the act of 1662 was "the first clear-cut example of statutory racial discrimination in American history." For other discussions of the 1662 statute, see Degler, "Genesis of American Race Prejudice," p. 61; Billings, "Fernando and Elizabeth Key," p. 473; and Palmer, "Servant into Slave," p. 360.

66. Under the law of 1691, a free white woman who had an illegitimate child by a black or mulatto father was to be fined fifteen pounds. If she could not pay, she was to be sold for a five-year term. The "abominable mixture and spurious issue" of this interracial union, though free because its mother was free, was to be bound out until the age of thirty. If the woman was a servant, she was to serve her master an additional two years, as the law provided for servants having bastards, and then she was to be sold for another five years. Va., *Statutes at Large* (1809–23), 3:86–87 (Act of 1691). Emphasis added in quotation.

The best discussions of the 1691 act are Higginbotham, *In the Matter of Color*, p. 45; and Morgan, *American Slavery*, p. 335. The statute probably did not include a punishment for white servants who intermarried because they were not allowed to marry without their master's permission. Furthermore, to banish such servants would have meant a serious financial loss for their masters. See Wadlington, "*Loving* Case," p. 1192 n. 18.

Apparently, the threat of banishment from the colony did not work as an effective deterrent against interracial marriage because the general assembly enacted new measures in 1705. The 1705 statute required any white person, having "christian white" servants, who married a black, mulatto, Indian, or non-Christian to free such servants. The statute also authorized a fine of ten pounds and imprisonment for six months. In addition, ministers who performed the prohibited ceremony were subject to a penalty of ten thousand pounds of tobacco. Although this act overhauled the punishments for interracial marriage, it left untouched the sanctions to be applied against women who had a bastard by a black or mulatto. Va., *Statutes at Large* (1809–23), 3:450, 453–54 (Act of 1705).

67. North Carolina's act of 1715 banned intermarriage and punished white women who bore mulatto children. Georgia pronounced all interracial marriages "absolutely null and void" in 1750, when blacks were first admitted to the colony. Although South Carolina did not act on the issue of intermarriage, it passed a statute in 1717 that exacted serious penalties for interracial fornication that ended in pregnancy. See N.C., *State Records* (Clark 1886–1907), 23:65 (Act of 1715); Ga., *Colonial Records* (Candler 1904–16), 1:59 (Act of 1750); and S.C., *Statutes at Large* (1836–41), 3:20 (Act of 1717).

On antimiscegenation laws in colonial North Carolina, consult Padgett, "Status of Slaves," p. 324; and Semonche, "Common-Law Marriage," p. 331. Of all the colonies only North Carolina (and briefly Virginia) included Indians in its antimiscegenation legislation. Discussions of the historical and cultural forces that discouraged marriage between Native Americans and whites, and thus made legal sanctions largely unnecessary, can be found in Smits, " 'Abominable Mixture' "; and Grossberg, "Law and the Family," pp. 144–46.

68. The Massachusetts statute prohibited intermarriage between a white person and a black or mulatto, and imposed a fine of fifty pounds upon any person officiating at such a marriage. Blacks or mulattoes convicted of illicit intercourse with whites were to be sold out of the colony. In Pennsylvania, a free black who intermarried was to be sold into slavery, whereas a white person violating the 1725–26 law was to forfeit thirty pounds or be indentured for a period not to exceed seven years. The children from an interracial marriage were bound out until they reached the age of thirty-one, and the minister who performed the ceremony was fined one hundred pounds. In cases of interracial fornication, a free black was to serve a term of seven years, and the guilty white was subject to imprisonment for one year and payment of a fifty-pound fine, the penalty for illicit intercourse between persons of the same race. See Calhoun, *American Family* 1:65, 149, 211; Higginbotham, *In the Matter of Color*, pp. 81, 285–86; Jordan, *White Over Black*, p. 139; and Fredrickson, *White Supremacy*, p. 101.

69. Getman, "Sexual Control," p. 125; Morgan, *American Slavery*, pp. 328–33; Fredrickson, *White Supremacy*, p. 107. See also Breen, "Changing Labor Force."

70. Getman, "Sexual Control," p. 126; Higginbotham, *In the Matter of Color*, p. 44; Clinton, *Plantation Mistress*, p. 203; Jordan, *White Over Black*, p. 141.

71. Morgan, *American Slavery*, p. 336; Williamson, *Crucible of Race*, p. 32; Alexander, *Ambiguous Lives*, p. 36; *Howell v. Netherland*, Jefferson 90 (Va. 1770), p. 90.

72. See, for example, *Gwinn v. Bugg*, Jefferson 87 (Va. 1769), as well as the cases examined in Johnston, *Race Relations*, pp. 178–81.

73. Berlin, *Slaves without Masters*, pp. 86–89; Genovese, *Roll, Jordan, Roll*, pp. 50–58; Williamson, *New People*, pp. 13–14.

74. Clinton, *Plantation Mistress*, pp. 204, 210–11; Toplin, "Between Black and White," pp. 191–92; Taylor, *Antebellum South Carolina*, p. 22.

75. Quoted in Genovese, *Roll, Jordan, Roll*, p. 418. For a discussion of Hughes's career and social thought, see Takaki, *Iron Cages*, pp. 128–36.

76. Genovese, *Roll, Jordan, Roll*, p. 422; Clinton, *Plantation Mistress*, p. 210; Bynum, *Unruly Women*, pp. 41–45, 92–93. For appellate cases disclosing sexual relations between white women and black men in the antebellum South, see *State v. Hayes*, 1 Bailey 275 (S.C. 1829); *Scroggins v. Scroggins*, 14 N.C. 535 (1832); *Barden v. Barden*, 14 N.C. 548 (1832); *Watkins v. Carlton*, 37 Va. 560 (1840); *State v. Fore*, 23 N.C. 378 (1841); *State v. Watters*, 25 N.C. 455 (1843); *Johnson v. Boon*, 1 Spears 268 (S.C. 1843); *State v. Hooper*, 27 N.C. 201 (1844); and *State v. Brady*, 28 Tenn. 74 (1848).

Additional evidence can be found in Johnston, *Race Relations*, pp. 250–68; Berlin, *Slaves without Masters*, p. 266; Johnson, *Ante-Bellum North Carolina*, p. 588; Franklin, *Free Negro in North Carolina*, pp. 37–39; Blassingame, *Black New Orleans*, pp. 19–20; and Williams, *Vogues in Villainy*, p. 56.

77. Boles, *Black Southerners*, p. 132; Blassingame, *Black New Orleans*, pp. 17–19; Gehman, "Quadroon Society of New Orleans"; McMillen, *Southern Women*, pp. 27–28.

78. Stampp, *Peculiar Institution*, pp. 353–56; Genovese, *Roll, Jordan, Roll*, pp. 418–19; Clinton, *Plantation Mistress*, pp. 213–14; Alexander, *Ambiguous Lives*, p. 66.

79. Jacobs, *Incidents in the Life of a Slave Girl*, pp. 54–55. On the issue of dis-

tinguishing Harriet Jacobs the author from her fictional self, Linda Brent, see Fox-Genovese, *Within the Plantation Household*, pp. 374–76, 462 n. 5.

80. Walters, "Erotic South," pp. 182–83; Blassingame, *Slave Community*, pp. 82–85; Calhoun, *American Family* 2:290–92; Stampp, *Peculiar Institution*, pp. 359–61; Genovese, *Roll, Jordan, Roll*, pp. 422, 428; Jones, *Labor of Love*, pp. 28, 37–38; Burton, *In My Father's House*, pp. 185–89. For a compelling study of one black woman's plight under slavery, see McLaurin, *Celia*.

81. Clinton, "Caught in the Web," pp. 28–32; Woodward, *Mary Chesnut's Civil War*, p. 168; Fox-Genovese, *Within the Plantation Household*, pp. 325–26. In addition, Carl Degler has pointed out in *Neither Black nor White* (pp. 232–39) the objections of white women in antebellum New Orleans to the liaisons between white husbands and black mistresses.

82. Clinton, *Other Civil War*, pp. 37–38; McMillen, *Southern Women*, pp. 24–26; Martineau, *Society in America*, p. 225.

83. For a detailed account of one planter's self-imposed predicament and his efforts to resolve it, see Faust, *Hammond and the Old South*, pp. 314–20.

84. Alexander, *Ambiguous Lives*, pp. 80–87.

85. Guido Ruggiero makes this point regarding sexuality in Renaissance society. See *Boundaries of Eros*, pp. 158–59.

86. Stampp, *Peculiar Institution*, pp. 357–59; Clinton, *Plantation Mistress*, pp. 214–17; Genovese, *Roll, Jordan, Roll*, pp. 415–16; Johnson, *Ante-Bellum North Carolina*, pp. 591–92; Johnston, *Race Relations*, pp. 217–36; Schafer, " 'Open and Notorious Concubinage.' "

87. Peterson, *Ham and Japeth*, pp. 52–53, 76–77; Johnson, "Planters and Patriarchy," pp. 70–71; Duvall, "*Uncle Tom's Cabin*," pp. 9–12.

88. Scott, *Southern Lady*, pp. 4–21; Clinton, *Plantation Mistress*, pp. 87–89, 93–94; Fox-Genovese, *Within the Plantation Household*, pp. 196–97, 203; Leslie, "Myth of the Southern Lady"; Cash, *Mind of the South*, pp. 87–89; Taylor, *Cavalier and Yankee*, pp. 165–76.

89. [Wright], "Amalgamation," pp. 3–8.

90. Mencke, *Mulattoes and Race Mixture*, pp. 7–8; Berlin, *Slaves without Masters*, pp. 97–99; Jordan, *White Over Black*, pp. 168–70. For an excellent analysis of antebellum attitudes toward mulattoes, see Toplin, "Between Black and White."

91. Va., *Statutes at Large* (1809–23), 12:184 (Act of 1785); Berlin, *Slaves without Masters*, pp. 161–62 n. 39. In North Carolina an individual with one African ancestor in the previous two generations was a mulatto, except for marriage to a white person, when the line was drawn at three generations.

92. On the importance of placing ideas about race in their historical context and not viewing race simply as a biological fact, see Fields, "Ideology and Race."

93. Grossberg, "Guarding the Altar," pp. 200–201; Bloomfield, *American Lawyers*, pp. 104–9. See also Grossberg, *Governing the Hearth*, pp. 69–83. For a revealing example of how American legal commentators attempted to incorporate the ban on interracial marriages into the common-law tradition, see Bishop, *Law of Marriage and Divorce*, 2d ed., pp. 74–75, 183.

94. Following the American Revolution, the three states that had enacted colonial legislation prohibiting miscegenation—Virginia, North Carolina, and Georgia—amended their laws in several important respects. Virginia's 1792 act imposed a jail

sentence of six months and a fine of thirty dollars on any white person who married a black or mulatto; this punishment was increased in an 1847–48 statute to a maximum of one year in prison and a fine of one hundred dollars. The 1849 code provided that "all marriages between a white person and a negro" were "absolutely void, without any decree of divorce, or other legal process." Va., *Statutes at Large* (Shepherd 1835–36), vol. 1, ch. 42, sec. 17, pp. 134–35; *Code* (1849), ch. 196, sec. 8, p. 740 and ch. 109, sec. 1, p. 471.

North Carolina included Indians and "mustees" in its ban on interracial unions, and stipulated that white men and women who violated this prohibition were to pay a fine of one hundred dollars. Under an act passed in 1838, all marriages in the state between "a white person and a free negro, or person of color to the third generation" were void, thus making both parties to an interracial union liable to prosecution for cohabitation or fornication. N.C., *Revised Statutes* (Nash, Iredell, and Battle 1837), vol. 1, ch. 71, sec. 5, pp. 386–87; *Revised Code* (1855), ch. 68, sec. 7, p. 391.

The Georgia code of 1861 prohibited marriages between white persons and blacks or mulattoes. Furthermore, any white man who lived in "a state of adultery or fornication" with a woman "of color, free or slave" was punishable by fine and imprisonment at the discretion of the court. The penalty for couples of the same race who lived together "in a state of adultery or fornication" was a maximum fine of five hundred dollars and a jail sentence of sixty days. Ga., *Code* (1861), sec. 1664, p. 333; sec. 4445, p. 866; and sec. 4419, p. 860.

New legislation also appeared on the books elsewhere in the South between the Revolution and the Civil War. The Louisiana code of 1808 proclaimed that "marriages contracted by free white persons with free people of color" were void; in addition, free persons and slaves were "incapable of contracting marriage together." La., *Digest* (1808), title 4, ch. 2, art. 8, p. 24. This provision was slightly reworded in the 1838 code. See *Civil Code* (1838), title 4, ch. 2, art. 95, p. 17. Arkansas also insisted in 1838 that marriages between whites and blacks or mulattoes were "illegal and void," but left the penalty for such unions up to the discretion of the jury or the court. Ark., *Revised Statutes* (1838), ch. 94, secs. 4 and 9, p. 536.

In Tennessee, whites who entered into matrimony with blacks, mustees, mulattoes, or "any person of colored blood, bond or free, to the third generation inclusive" were subject to a penalty of five hundred dollars, and such marriages were considered "null and void, to all intents and purposes." Moreover, the 1822 statute provided that, if any white person lived with "any negro, mustee or mulatto man or woman, as man and wife," the offending party was punishable by a fine of five hundred dollars. Tenn., *Compilation* (1836), ch. 19, secs. 1 and 3, p. 451. See also *Code* (1858), sec. 2437, p. 481, and secs. 4924–27, p. 880.

Florida in 1832 not only pronounced every marriage between a white and black or mulatto "utterly void and null," it also explicitly stated that the issue of such illegal unions were illegitimate and thus unable to inherit. All white males who married or lived with a black or mulatto female were to be fined one thousand dollars, and they were disqualified from holding public office, serving as a juror, or testifying in court except where blacks or mulattoes were parties to the case. The penalty in Florida for a couple living together "in an open state of adultery or fornication" when the parties were of the same race was only a maximum fine of five hundred dollars for the first conviction, seven hundred dollars for the second, and eight hundred dollars for every subsequent conviction. In no instance did the male suffer any civil disabilities as a result of his being found guilty of illegal cohabitation. Fla., *Compilation* (1839), pp. 88–89, 120.

Under its 1837 law, Texas prohibited "persons of European blood or their descendants" from marrying "Africans or descendants of Africans," and such marriages were deemed "null and void." In 1858 the state legislature further stipulated that any white person who contracted matrimony with a black or "person of mixed blood, descended from negro ancestry, to the third generation inclusive" should be punished by imprisonment for a term of two to five years. Those whites who lived "in adultery or fornication" with a black were to be fined not less than one hundred dollars and not more than one thousand dollars. The punishment for interracial couples who lived together out of wedlock was the same as that for intraracial couples. Tex., *Digest* (1845), p. 168; *Digest* (1859), art. 386, p. 503; art. 395a, p. 504; and art. 392, p. 504.

95. The five states were Florida, North Carolina, Tennessee, Alabama, and Virginia. In Florida, anyone who "knowingly" granted a license or celebrated a marriage in violation of the state's laws against miscegenation faced a fine of one thousand dollars. North Carolina's act of 1830 made such a person guilty of a misdemeanor and subject to fine and imprisonment at the discretion of the court. Tennessee also declared issuing a license or performing a ceremony that involved parties of different races a misdemeanor, in this instance punishable by a fine of five hundred dollars. See Fla., *Compilation* (1839), p. 89; N.C., *Revised Statutes* (1837), vol. 1, ch. 34, sec. 72, pp. 108–9; and Tenn., *Code* (1858), secs. 4926–27, p. 880. On North Carolina, see also *Revised Statutes* (1837), vol. 1, ch. 71, sec. 6, p. 387; and *Revised Code* (1855) ch. 68, sec. 8, p. 392, which provided that any minister or justice of the peace who performed an interracial marriage was to be fined one hundred dollars.

Alabama and Virginia punished only the person who married an interracial couple, not the clerk who granted the license. In Alabama, anyone solemnizing the rites of matrimony when one of the parties was black and the other white was subject to a fine of not less than one thousand dollars. An 1847–48 law in Virginia reduced the penalty from two hundred and fifty dollars to two hundred dollars for every such marriage. See Ala., *Code* (1852) sec. 1956, p. 377; and compare Va., *Revised Code* (1819), vol. 1, ch. 106, sec. 23, p. 401 with *Code* (1849), ch. 196, sec. 9, p. 740.

96. During the period between Independence and the Civil War, several legislatures in the North and Midwest also implemented bans on intermarriage. A few northeastern states, however, turned back efforts to pass prohibitory legislation. Furthermore, Massachusetts in 1840, Iowa in 1851, and Kansas in 1857 repealed their statutes. As Grossberg observes, "These actions, while they did little to alleviate customary barriers to interracial unions, helped turn formal prohibition into a sectional phenomenon." See Applebaum, "Miscegenation Statutes," p. 50 n. 10; Jordan, *White Over Black*, pp. 471–72; and Grossberg, "Law and the Family," p. 141. See also Grossberg, *Governing the Hearth*, pp. 127–29.

97. Berlin, *Slaves without Masters*, pp. 163–65; Mencke, *Mulattoes and Race Mixture*, pp. 11–13. The best introduction to the intricacies of race relations in South Carolina is the fascinating account of William Ellison and his free mulatto family in Johnson and Roark, *Black Masters*.

98. *Johnson v. Boon*, 1 Spears 268 (S.C. 1843), p. 270. See also *State v. Hayes*, 1 Bailey 275 (S.C. 1829).

99. Quoted in Johnson and Roark, *No Chariot Let Down*, p. 112 n. 6.

100. The only law in Mississippi that touched on this question before the Civil War was an 1822 act authorizing designated officials to "solemnize the rites of matrimony between any free white persons" who presented a valid license. The act implied that interracial marriages were illegal, but no explicit prohibition existed against blacks contracting matrimony with whites. Miss., *Revised Code* (1824), ch. 102, sec. 1, pp. 445–46.

In Alabama, an 1805 statute permitted unions "between any free persons," leaving open the possibility of marriage between whites and free blacks. This loophole was not closed until the publication of the 1852 code, which stated that "marriages may be solemnized between free white persons, or between free persons of color." The code also provided that any person who performed a marriage "when one of the parties is a negro and the other a white person" was guilty of a misdemeanor and subject to a minimum fine of one thousand dollars. Although Alabama law severely punished the individual who performed the ceremony, it did not pronounce interracial marriages null and void, and it established no penalty for those who intermarried. Ala., *Digest* (1823), p. 576; *Code* (1852), secs. 1946 and 1956, pp. 376–77. See also *Black v. Oliver*, 1 Ala. 449 (1840).

101. Williamson, *New People*, pp. 2–3, 14–24; Berlin, *Slaves without Masters*, pp. 196–99, 214–16, 343–80; Johnson and Roark, *Black Masters*, pp. 160–68, 187–94, 236–48, 256–62. On Louisiana, see Domínguez, *White by Definition*, esp. pp. 23–26. The letters that Johnson and Roark have collected and annotated in *No Chariot Let Down* starkly document the harassment and repression of free blacks and mulattoes in Charleston during the deepening sectional crisis.

102. Johnson and Roark, *Black Masters*, p. 53; Fredrickson, *White Supremacy*, p. 108. Gary Mills sees the lack of vigorous legal sanctions against intermarriage in antebellum Alabama as evidence of a "wide variance in southern attitudes toward miscegenation." Yet his own statistics fail to demonstrate much enthusiasm among Alabamians for interracial unions: an exhaustive search of antebellum records in forty-eight counties turned up only six legal marriages and eighty-three acknowledged cohabitations between a free black and white. See Mills, "Miscegenation and the Free Negro," pp. 18, 21.

103. "Coloured Marriages," *Charleston Mercury*, October 29, 1823; reprinted in *Carolina Law Journal* 1 (1830): 92–106. The quotations can be found on pp. 99, 105.

104. Quoted in Nash, "Negro Rights, Unionism, and Greatness," p. 181. Although social sanctions against intermarriage may have been effective in South Carolina, those against interracial sex were not as rigidly observed, leading some whites in the state to call for the passage of laws against miscegenation. In 1812, for example, responding to what they perceived as an increase in sexual intercourse between black men and white women, citizens in Orangeburg District petitioned the state legislature to impose legal penalities against miscegenation. According to the petitioners, the "softening" conditions of slavery had emboldened slaves to attempt "to exercise among some of the lower classes of white peoples freedom and familiarities which are degrading to them and dangerous to society. We allude to attempts which are made and some of them with success at sexual intercourse with white females." Johnson and Roark, *Black Masters*, p. 356 n. 63. On social sanctions against intermarriage in South Carolina and Mississippi, see Wikramanayake, *A World in Shadow*, pp. 13, 176; and Wharton, *Negro in Mississippi*, p. 227.

105. *Bowers v. Newman*, 2 McMull. 472 (S.C. 1842), pp. 481, 480.

106. Ibid., pp. 486, 492. See also *Wells v. Thompson*, 13 Ala. 793 (1848), in which the Alabama Supreme Court upheld the validity of a marriage between a white man and a woman of "mixed white and Indian blood." According to the court, "There is no law of this State, which inhibits the marriage of a white man and a woman whose blood partakes of the white and Indian races; and if such a marriage is consummated between persons able and willing to contract, the parties become subject to all the disabilities, and are entitled to all the rights and privileges incident to such a relation."

It is interesting to note the lack of hostility expressed by the court toward this particular interracial marriage, a reflection of the less intense racial antipathies that most antebellum southern whites felt toward Native Americans. Only North Carolina during this period banned marriages between Native Americans and whites. See Grossberg, "Law and the Family," pp. 144–46.

107. *Succession of Minvielle*, 15 La. An. 342 (1860), pp. 342–43.

108. *State v. Melton*, 44 N.C. 49 (1852), p. 51. In this case, which involved a white woman and a man of Native American descent, the North Carolina Supreme Court found the defendants innocent of fornication because there was no clear proof that the husband fell within the statutory definition of an Indian. See also *State v. Fore*, 23 N.C. 378 (1841); *State v. Hooper*, 27 N.C. 201 (1844); and *State v. Brady*, 28 Tenn. 74 (1848). These three cases involved white women who married black men. Although the appellate judges found the white women guilty of illegal cohabitation in all of these cases, the Tennessee Supreme Court arrested judgment against the male defendant in *State v. Brady* on the grounds that blacks were not liable to indictment under the state's statute prohibiting intermarriage.

109. *Succession of Minvielle*, 15 La. An. 342 (1860).

110. *Dupre v. Boulard*, 10 La. An. 411 (1855), p. 412.

111. *Scroggins v. Scroggins*, 14 N.C. 535 (1832), pp. 545, 546.

112. *Barden v. Barden*, 14 N.C. 548 (1832), p. 550. For other cases dealing with interracial fornication before the Civil War, see *Commonwealth v. Isaacs*, 5 Rand. 634 (Va. 1826); and *Commonwealth v. Jones*, 43 Va. 555 (1845). Both decisions involved indictments of white men for cohabiting with black women; in the first instance, the indictment was quashed on a technicality, and in the second, the conviction of the man was overturned because of procedural errors in the lower court trial. Apparently, southern judges saw no pressing need to override common-law traditions when interracial sex between white men and black women was involved, another indication of the lesser seriousness with which this form of miscegenation was viewed.

113. On the due process accorded slaves accused of raping white women, see Genovese, *Roll, Jordan, Roll*, pp. 33–34; and Wyatt-Brown, *Southern Honor*, pp. 387–90.

114. The class dimension of sexual violence in the nineteenth-century South is explored in Bynum, *Unruly Women*; and Edwards, "Sexual Violence, Gender, Reconstruction, and the Extension of Patriarchy."

115. Jordan, *White Over Black*, pp. 151–52.

116. For an example of early rape legislation, see Va., *Statutes at Large* (1809–23), 8:358 (Act of 1769). The 1769 statute prohibited the castration of any slave except when convicted of an attempt to rape a white woman. Philip Schwarz examines several eighteenth-century trials of Virginia blacks accused of raping or attempting to rape a white woman in *Twice Condemned*, pp. 150–52, 155–64.

117. Jordan, *White Over Black*, pp. 154–55; Oakes, *Slavery and Freedom*, p. 164;

Getman, "Sexual Control," pp. 134–35; Va., *Revised Code* (1819), vol. 1, ch. 158, sec. 4, pp. 585–86. Not until 1823 did the legislature disallow castration for slaves convicted of attempted rape. Instead, they were to "suffer death as in other cases of felony, by hanging by the neck; any law, custom, or usage, to the contrary notwithstanding." See Va., *Digest of the Laws* (Tate 1823), pp. 127–28 (Act of 1823).

In colonial Georgia and North Carolina, blacks who were convicted for rape or attempted rape of a white woman were sentenced to death. See Ga., *Digest of the Laws* (Marbury and Crawford 1802), p. 430 (Act of 1770); and N.C., *State Records* (1886–1907), 23:489 (Act of 1758).

118. Ala., *Digest of the Laws* (Clay 1843), p. 472; Ark., *Revised Statutes* (1838), ch. 44, art. 4, sec. 8, p. 245; Fla., *Manual* (1847), p. 538; Ga., *Digest of the Laws*, 2d ed. (Prince 1837), p. 791; La., *Digest of the Penal Law* (Robinson 1841), ch. 8, art. 230, p. 140; Miss., *Revised Code* (1857), ch. 33, art. 58, p. 248; N.C., *Revised Statutes* (1837), vol. 1, ch. 111, sec. 78, p. 590; Tenn., *Code* (1858), sec. 2625, p. 509; Tex., *Digest* (1850), art. 2539, p. 777. In Virginia, a free black convicted of rape or attempted rape of a white female could be executed or imprisoned for five to twenty years at the discretion of the jury. The law demanded the execution, however, of slaves convicted of either offense. See Va., *Code* (1849), ch. 200, secs. 1 and 4, p. 753.

Although most of them were passed in the South, statutes providing castration or the death penalty for blacks convicted of raping or attempting to rape a white woman appeared on the books of other states as well. See Wriggins, "Rape, Racism, and the Law," p. 105 n. 8.

119. *Stephen v. State*, 11 Ga. 225 (1852), p. 239. For other cases in which blacks were sentenced to death for the rape or attempted rape of a white female, see *Dennis v. State*, 5 Ark. 230 (1843) (slave sentenced to death for rape of white woman); *State v. Bill*, 8 Rob. 527 (La. 1844) (slave sentenced to death for attempted rape of white female under age of ten); *State v. Joshua*, 15 La. An. 118 (1860) (slave sentenced to death for rape of white woman); *Wash v. State*, 22 Miss. 120 (1850) (slave sentenced to death for attempted rape of white female under age of twelve); *State v. Jefferson*, 28 N.C. 305 (1846) (slave sentenced to death for rape of white woman); *State v. Tom*, 47 N.C. 414 (1855) (slave sentenced to death for attempted rape of white woman); *State v. Elick*, 52 N.C. 68 (1859) (slave sentenced to death for attempted rape of white woman); *State v. Peter*, 53 N.C. 19 (1860) (slave sentenced to death for rape of white woman); *Bill v. State*, 24 Tenn. 155 (1844) (slave sentenced to death for attempted rape of white woman); *Ellick v. State*, 31 Tenn. 325 (1851) (slave sentenced to death for attempted rape of white woman); *Isham v. State*, 33 Tenn. 111 (1853) (slave sentenced to death for attempted rape of white female); *Thompson v. Commonwealth*, 31 Va. 652 (1833) (free black sentenced to death for attempted rape of white woman); *Commonwealth v. Watts*, 31 Va. 672 (1833) (free black sentenced to death for attempted rape of white woman); and *Smith v. Commonwealth*, 51 Va. 734 (1853) (free black sentenced to death for rape of white girl).

120. William D. Valentine Diary, February 17, 1838, SHC. Two months later Valentine noted the execution of the black man, remarking that although it was the first hanging that he had ever witnessed, because "my imagination had often pictured to me this magic scene it seemed no novelty to me." See the entry for April 20, 1838. For other accounts of southern trials involving black men accused of raping a white female, consult Johnson, *Ante-Bellum North Carolina*, pp. 508–10; and Franklin, *Free Negro in North Carolina*, p. 98.

121. Painter, "'Social Equality,'" p. 49; Fox-Genovese, *Within the Plantation Household*, pp. 235–38; Clinton, *Plantation Mistress*, pp. 110–11, 121–22.

122. C. R. C[arroll], "Woman," *Southern Literary Journal* 3 (November 1836): 181–82.

123. Bynum, *Unruly Women*, p. 118; Wyatt-Brown, *Southern Honor*, p. 53; Schwarz, *Twice Condemned*, p. 210. For a similar analysis regarding the law of adultery and seduction in Victorian America, see Ireland, "Libertine Must Die." Ireland contends that "an unwritten law" existed in the nineteenth century that "forgave men and women who killed to avenge sexual dishonor." As he shows in another study ("Frenzied and Fallen Females"), however, women who took matters into their own hands received a far less sympathetic hearing in the courtroom.

124. For early laws designating rape as punishable by death when committed by white men, see Ala., *Digest* (1823), p. 207 (Act of 1807); Miss., *Revised Code* (1824), ch. 54, sec. 11, p. 298 (Act of 1822); S.C., *Digest of the Laws* (James 1822), p. 87 (Act of 1792); and Va., *Statutes at Large* (1835–36), 1:178 (Act of 1792).

Southern states that retained the death penalty for white men convicted of rape during the late antebellum years include Arkansas, Florida, Louisiana, and North Carolina. See Ark., *Digest* (1858), ch. 51, art. 4, sec. 2, p. 334; Fla., *Manual* (1847), p. 490; La., *Consolidation* (1852), p. 184; and N.C., *Revised Code* (1855), ch. 34, sec. 5, p. 203. For cases in which white men were condemned for rape, see *State v. Terry*, 20 N.C. 289 (1839); and *State v. Farmer*, 26 N.C. 224 (1844). The defendants in these two decisions were charged with raping female children.

125. *State v. Le Blanc*, 3 Brev. 339 (S.C. 1813), p. 342. For other cases in which white men were condemned for raping female children, see *State v. Terry*, 20 N.C. 289 (1839); and *State v. Farmer*, 26 N.C. 224 (1844). Generally, proof of penetration and emission was necessary for a rape conviction. See *State v. Gray*, 53 N.C. 170 (1860).

126. Before the Civil War, Alabama, Mississippi, Texas, and Virginia eliminated capital punishment for white males convicted of rape. See Ala., *Digest* (1843), p. 414 (life imprisonment); Miss., *Statutes* (Howard and Hutchinson 1840), ch. 50, title 3, sec. 22, pp. 696–97 (not less than ten years); Tex., *Digest* (1859), art. 529, p. 523 (five to fifteen years); and Va., *Revised Code* (1819), vol. 1, ch. 158, art. 1, p. 585 (ten to twenty-one years).

The Mississippi legislature increased the penalty for rape to life imprisonment in the late antebellum period. See *Revised Code* (1857), ch. 46, art. 218, p. 608. Other states that imposed prison sentences on white men who committed rape were Georgia (two to twenty years) and Tennessee (ten to twenty-one years). Ga., *Digest* (1837), p. 625; and Tenn., *Compilation* (1836), ch. 23, sec. 14, p. 318.

127. For the punishment of white men who committed assault with intent to rape in the antebellum South, see Ala., *Digest* (1823), pp. 206–7 (not more than one year); Ark., *Digest of the Statutes* (English 1848), ch. 51, art. 5, sec. 1, p. 331 (three to twenty-one years in prison); Ga., *Digest* (1837), p. 625 (one to five years); La., *Digest* (1841), ch. 8, art. 240, p. 143 (not more than two years); Tenn., *Code* (1858), sec. 4615, p. 830 (two to ten years); and Tex., *Digest* (1859), art. 494, p. 520 (two to seven years). In all of these states attempted rape of white women by black men was punishable by death. See note 118 above.

128. *Charles v. State*, 11 Ark. 389 (1850), pp. 397, 404–5. This was the only constitutional challenge to the statutes imposing capital punishment on blacks convicted for

attempted rape of a white woman that appeared in the published appellate opinions from the nineteenth-century South.

129. Wriggins, "Rape, Racism, and the Law," pp. 106, 118; D'Emilio and Freedman, *Intimate Matters*, p. 101; Burnham, "Impossible Marriage," p. 221.

130. Brownmiller, *Against Our Will*, p. 176; Getman, "Sexual Control," p. 146; Cobb, *Law of Negro Slavery* 2:99; Tushnet, *American Law of Slavery*, p. 82.

131. Alexander, *Ambiguous Lives*, p. 65. Although it was not considered rape for a master to engage in this sort of sexual behavior with one of his slaves, it violated laws against fornication, miscegenation, and, if he was married, adultery. These laws could have been enforced but were not, which further underscored the double standards of southern slave society. In a similar fashion, the legal system of Renaissance Venice largely overlooked rape when it involved members of the nobility sexually assaulting their female servants. See Ruggiero, *Boundaries of Eros*, pp. 99, 107–8.

132. Davis, "Legacy of Slavery," in *Women, Race, and Class*, pp. 6–7; Hall, "'The Mind That Burns in Each Body,'" p. 332; Burnham, "Impossible Marriage," pp. 198–99; Fox-Genovese, *Within the Plantation Household*, p. 294.

133. White, *Ar'n't I a Woman?*, pp. 38, 78–79; Gutman, *Black Family*, pp. 83–84; Clinton, "Caught in the Web," pp. 22–25; Jones, *Labor of Love*, p. 20.

134. Kemble, *Residence on a Georgian Plantation*, p. 270; Jacobs, *Life of a Slave Girl*, p. 27. Darlene Clark Hine suggests that rape and the threat of rape fostered "a culture of dissemblance" among black women, in which they developed secret personae to counteract the negative sexual stereotypes imposed on them by whites. See Hine, "Rape and the Inner Lives of Black Women."

135. McLaurin, *Celia*, pp. 95–96; Bynum, *Unruly Women*, pp. 5, 17–18. For a concise overview of how the double burden of race and gender shaped the lives of slave women, see Jones, "'My Mother Was Much of a Woman.'"

136. Grimké, *Equality of the Sexes*, p. 59. See also Goodell, *American Slave Code*, pp. 85–86.

137. *George v. State*, 37 Miss. 316 (1859), pp. 317, 319, 320.

138. Tushnet, *American Law of Slavery*, pp. 84–86; *George v. State*, 37 Miss. 316 (1859), p. 320; White, *Ar'n't I A Woman?*, pp. 152–53. On the Jezebel image of black women in the Old South, see White, *Ar'n't I A Woman?*, pp. 29–46.

139. Fox-Genovese, *Within the Plantation Household*, p. 326; Cobb, *Law of Negro Slavery*, 2:99–100 (quotation on p. 100).

140. Ga., *Code* (1861), secs. 4248–49, p. 824, and sec. 4704, p. 918. Emphasis added. No case involving a white man convicted of sexually assaulting a slave woman appears in the published appellate court records for Georgia after the enactment of this law.

141. Hindus, "Black Justice Under White Law," p. 587; Schwarz, *Twice Condemned*, pp. 208–9, 291–93.

142. Hall, *Magic Mirror*, p. 134. Michael Hindus makes the same point about procedural irregularities in the lower courts in "Black Justice Under White Law," pp. 591–92.

143. Flanigan, "Criminal Procedure in Slave Trials," p. 553.

144. Hindus, "Black Justice Under White Law," p. 578; Flanigan, "Criminal Procedure in Slave Trials," pp. 556, 540–45, 550–51. In Virginia, slaves charged with capital crimes were subject to trial by magistrates without any right of appeal. State law,

however, allowed the governor to sell and transport a condemned slave if the executive believed, based on a review of the case, that the slave had been unfairly tried. Of course, if no one petitioned the governor to consider the case, he had no way of telling whether the slave had been granted a fair trial.

South Carolina established a tribunal made up of two justices and three to five freeholders for such slaves, and appeals were allowed in certain instances. Similar arrangements existed in Louisiana, where one magistrate and ten slaveholders tried slaves, who had the right of appeal. See Flanigan, "Criminal Procedure in Slave Trials," pp. 541, 544–45.

145. *Major v. State*, 34 Tenn. 7 (1854); *Major v. State*, 36 Tenn. 597 (1857), p. 603.

146. *Major v. State*, 36 Tenn. 597 (1857), p. 613. In only one other antebellum decision dealing with the conviction of a slave for rape or attempted rape did southern appellate courts directly challenge the jury's verdict and acquit the defendant due to insufficient evidence. See *Peter v. State*, 24 Tenn. 436 (1844).

Most state appellate courts were not allowed to review the facts, and jury verdicts were seldom aborted. Generally, if the high courts were upset by a jury verdict, they resorted to attacking the trial judge's charge to the jury or to discovering some other procedural flaw. See Flanigan, "Criminal Procedure in Slave Trials," p. 552.

147. Slaves had no right of appeal in Virginia. See note 144.

148. Overall, five of the defendants were free blacks, one was a quadroon, and the rest were slaves. A total of fifty-seven appellate court opinions regarding rape or attempted rape were found in the published records before the Civil War. Besides the thirty-seven appeals by African American men convicted of sexually assaulting a white female, thirteen were appeals by white men convicted of rape or attempted rape, four were appeals by states that had failed to gain a conviction of the accused (three of whom were black) at the trial, and two involved petitions from lower courts to consider a point of law. The remaining case (see note 137 above) involved the prosecution of a slave for attempting to rape a female slave.

149. *Cato v. State*, 9 Fla. 163 (1860), pp. 173–74. For similar statements, see *Pleasant v. State*, 13 Ark. 360 (1853), p. 370; and *Stephen v. State*, 11 Ga. 225 (1852), p. 230.

150. Genovese, *Roll, Jordan, Roll*, pp. 26–27; Flanigan, "Criminal Procedure in Slave Trials," pp. 547–48. Judges in the lower courts also demonstrated a sensitivity to these issues. See, for example, the account of a slave's murder trial in McLaurin, *Celia*, chap. 5.

151. *State v. Martin*, 14 N.C. 329 (1832), pp. 329, 330. Other rape cases in which inaccurate indictments against black men were thrown out include *Sullivant v. State*, 8 Ark. 400 (1848); *State v. Jim*, 12 N.C. 142 (1828); and *State v. Jesse*, 19 N.C. 297 (1832). See *Nugent v. State*, 19 Ala. 540 (1851); and *Williams v. State*, 27 Tenn. 585 (1848) for similar cases involving white men accused of attempted rape.

152. *Grandison v. State*, 21 Tenn. 451 (1841), p. 452 (conviction reversed and arrested). See also *Commonwealth v. Mann*, 2 Va. Cas. 210 (1820), in which an indictment of a black man for attempted rape was dismissed because it did not explicitly state the woman's race; *Henry v. State*, 23 Tenn. 270 (1843), in which the court record did not show that the woman involved in an attempted rape was white (conviction reversed and new trial awarded); and *Pleasant v. State*, 13 Ark. 360 (1853), in which the trial judge refused to instruct the jury that it could not convict a slave for attempted

rape unless the state proved that the female victim of the assault was white (conviction reversed and new trial awarded).

In *State v. Charles*, 1 Fla. 298 (1847) the circuit court, unable to reach a decision on whether to dismiss an indictment of a slave for attempted rape of a white woman because it did not state her race, called on the Florida Supreme Court to consider the matter. The high court, however, believed that it did not have jurisdiction to decide a point of law put to it by the court below, and it dismissed the case.

153. *Thurman v. State*, 18 Ala. 276 (1850), p. 279. See also *Dick v. State*, 30 Miss. 631 (1856), in which the appellate court threw out a conviction for attempted rape of a white woman because the indictment had designated the defendant a Negro and the evidence did not settle the question of whether he was a mulatto or black slave.

In *Commonwealth v. Tyree*, 2 Va. Cas. 262 (1821) questions about whether the defendant was a free mulatto or slave also emerged. After the arraignment and plea were entered, a white man objected to the proceedings, claiming to be the prisoner's master. Despite strong evidence indicating that the defendant was, in fact, a runaway slave, the court denied the challenge and accepted the assertion in the indictment that the defendant was a free mulatto on the grounds that, if convicted for rape of a white woman as a slave, he would face capital punishment rather than imprisonment. Sustaining the challenge, in the court's words, would "convert a principle dictated by humanity into an instrument of cruelty." See ibid., p. 266.

154. For other cases in which slaves or free blacks gained new trials because of errors in criminal procedure, see *State v. Phil*, 1 Stew. 31 (Ala. 1827); *Lewis v. State*, 35 Ala. 380 (1860); *Pleasant v. State*, 15 Ark. 624 (1855); *State v. Peter*, 14 La. An. 521 (1859); *State v. Henry*, 50 N.C. 65 (1857); and *Day v. Commonwealth*, 44 Va. 629 (1846). The Tennessee high court in an 1842 decision quashed the indictment of a slave for assault with intent to commit rape upon "a free white woman of the age of six years" because a female less than ten years old was not a woman "within the meaning of the statute." See *Sydney v. State*, 22 Tenn. 478 (1842), p. 479.

Attempts of slaves to escape conviction through legal loopholes, of course, did not always succeed. In *State v. Peter*, 53 N.C. 19 (1860), the slave appealed his rape conviction, arguing that the slave code only punished attempted rape, and that since the statute covering rape referred to "persons" committing the crime, it did not include slaves. The North Carolina court, however, determined that the failure of the relevant rape statute to state explicitly that it covered slaves was not cause to reverse the conviction. See also *Isham v. State*, 33 Tenn. 111 (1853), in which the Tennessee Supreme Court upheld the death sentence for a slave convicted of attempting to rape a white female. In the court's words, "The day has now passed for rescuing the guilty upon mere technicalities."

155. Besides Flanigan, "Criminal Procedure in Slave Trials," see his "Criminal Law of Slavery and Freedom"; Nash, "Negro Rights and Judicial Behavior"; and two important articles by Nash: "Fairness and Formalism" and "Texas Supreme Court and Trial Rights of Blacks."

156. Hindus, "Black Justice Under White Law," pp. 595–96; Hall, *Magic Mirror*, p. 132; Schwarz, *Twice Condemned*, pp. 52–53. I am grateful to Paul Finkelman for drawing my attention to these points.

157. Besides the cases examined here, see Bynum, *Unruly Women*, pp. 109–10, 118.

158. Tenn., *Compilation* (1836), ch. 23, sec. 13, p. 318. See also the definitions of

rape in Ark., *Revised Statutes* (1838), ch. 44, art. 4, sec. 1, p. 245; Ga., *Digest* (1837), p. 625; and Tex., *Digest* (1845), p. 198.

159. *Camp v. State*, 3 Ga. 417 (1847), pp. 422. The conviction was reversed and a new trial ordered on the grounds that the judge failed to instruct the jury that the reputation of the alleged victim, who was shown to be a prostitute, could be impeached in order to challenge the credibility of her testimony.

160. *Pleasant v. State*, 15 Ark. 624 (1855), p. 644.

161. Wyatt-Brown, *Southern Honor*, pp. 293–94; Stowe, *Intimacy and Power*, pp. 54–55; Fox-Genovese, *Within the Plantation Household*, pp. 235–36.

162. [Thomas R. Dew], "Dissertation on the Characteristic Differences Between the Sexes," *Southern Literary Messenger* 1 (May 1835): 497.

163. *Camp v. State*, 3 Ga. 417 (1847), p. 422.

164. For a concise discussion of the effect of the "lying temptress" image on rape law, and recent efforts to reform the evidentiary rules of rape law, consult Tong, *Women, Sex, and the Law,* pp. 99–109. The roots of the close association between a woman's sexual reputation and her credibility as a witness can be traced to early modern England. See Amussen, *An Ordered Society*, pp. 99–100.

165. *Brogy v. Commonwealth*, 51 Va. 722 (1853), pp. 725–26; *Turney v. State*, 16 Miss. 104 (1847), p. 118. See also *State v. Cone*, 46 N.C. 18 (1853); and *Phillips v. State*, 28 Tenn. 246 (1848) for discussions about the passage of time before disclosure.

166. *Pleasant v. State*, 15 Ark. 624 (1855), p. 644.

167. Ibid. For discussions of how poor women were vulnerable to rape in the North, see Arnold, " 'Life of a Citizen,' " pp. 35–56; and Stansell, *City of Women*, pp. 23–27, 96–99.

168. Johnston, *Race Relations*, pp. 257–63 (quotation on p. 260). Johnston's data is drawn from reports between 1789 and 1833 of blacks condemned for rape, most of whom were slaves, in the executive papers of Virginia governors. See also a similar account of a case from North Carolina in Franklin, *Free Negro in North Carolina*, p. 37.

169. Getman, "Sexual Control," p. 137. Getman discusses Johnston's data in some detail on pp. 136–38.

170. Johnston, *Race Relations*, pp. 260–61.

171. *Cato v. State*, 9 Fla. 163 (1860), pp. 181, 184, 185.

172. *Commonwealth v. Fields*, 31 Va. 648 (1832), p. 649. See also *Charles v. State*, 11 Ark. 389 (1850), in which the Arkansas Supreme Court cited the Fields case in its decision to reverse the conviction of a slave charged with attempted rape of a fourteen-year-old white girl. According to the Arkansas court (p. 410), "The accused in this case used no force, nor is it probable, from all the surrounding circumstances, that the idea of force entered into his original design, and in case his intention was to effect his purpose while she was asleep, the authority cited shows that he is not guilty of the offence charged against him."

173. *Lewis v. State*, 30 Ala. 54 (1857), p. 57. For a similar case in which the conviction of a slave for attempted rape of a white woman was overturned, see *Wyatt v. State*, 32 Tenn. 394 (1852).

174. Ala., *Digest* (1843), p. 414; Ark., *Revised Statutes* (1838), ch. 44, art. 4, sec. 4, p. 245; Miss., *Statutes* (1840), ch. 50, title 3, sec. 23, p. 697; Tenn., *Code* (1858), secs. 4612–13, p. 830; Tex., *Digest* (1859), art. 526, p. 523. Only the Tennessee and Texas statutes punished those who pretended to be the woman's husband.

175. *Lewis v. State*, 35 Ala. 380 (1860), p. 388. In this case the Alabama Supreme Court reversed the conviction of a slave for attempted rape.

176. Tex., *Digest* (1859), arts. 524–525, p. 523 (Act of 1856). It should be noted that when the female victim was under the age of ten years old, it was not necessary to prove the use of force or lack of consent to gain a rape conviction in most southern states. See Ala., *Digest* (1843), p. 415; Miss., *Statutes* (1840), ch. 50, title 3, sec. 22, p. 697; N.C., *Revised Statutes* (1837), vol. 1, ch. 34, art. 5, p. 192; S.C., *Digest* (1822), p. 87; Tenn., *Code* (1858), sec. 4614, p. 830; Tex., *Digest* (1859), art. 523, p. 523; and Va., *Revised Code* (1819), vol. 1, ch. 158, sec. 3, p. 585.

Virginia raised the age to twelve in 1849, and in Arkansas an 1838 act proclaimed that a person could be convicted of rape without proof of force when the victim was a "female child under the age of puberty." See Va., *Code* (1849), ch. 191, sec. 15, p. 725; and Ark., *Digest* (1848), ch. 51, art. 4, sec. 4, p. 330.

A Mississippi statute made it a crime for a slave to have, or attempt to have, "carnal connexion with any white female child under fourteen years old, with or without her consent," although in all other cases a person could be convicted of rape without evidence of consent only when the female was under the age of ten. See Miss., *Revised Code* (1857), ch. 33, art. 58, p. 248.

The reasoning behind such laws was that children under a certain age were incapable of consenting to any sexual act regardless of whether force was used. For cases involving the prosecution of white men for attempting to rape a female child, see *Nugent v. State*, 19 Ala. 540 (1851); *State v. Terry*, 20 N.C. 289 (1839); *State v. Farmer*, 26 N.C. 224 (1844); *State v. Gray*, 53 N.C. 170 (1860); *State v. Le Blanc*, 3 Brev. 339 (S.C. 1813); *Wright v. State*, 23 Tenn. 194 (1843); *Rhodes v. State*, 41 Tenn. 351 (1860); and *Commonwealth v. Bennet*, 2 Va. Cas. 235 (1820).

177. Mark Tushnet analyzes the difficulty of constructing a separate body of slave law in *American Law of Slavery*.

178. Stampp, *Peculiar Institution*, pp. 190–91; Wyatt-Brown, *Southern Honor*, pp. 387–89 (Barrow quoted on p. 389). See also the report of a similar lynching in Johnson, *Ante-Bellum North Carolina*, p. 508.

179. Ayers, *Vengeance and Justice*, p. 135.

180. MacKinnon, *Toward a Feminist Theory of the State*, pp. 172–83 (quotation on p. 172).

181. Gordon, *Heroes of Their Own Lives*, pp. 218–26; Pleck, *Domestic Tyranny*, pp. 184–86. Besides rape, the prosecution of adultery and seduction during the nineteenth century also reflected the persistence of patriarchal attitudes. See Ireland, "Libertine Must Die," pp. 33–37. On nineteenth-century divorce cases involving adultery, consult Griswold, "Adultery and Divorce in Victorian America."

CHAPTER THREE

1. For a discussion of these developments, see Mintz, *Prison of Expectations*, pp. 10, 29–35; Grossberg, *Governing the Hearth*, pp. 19–20, 24–27; and Fliegelman, *Prodigals and Pilgrims*, esp. pp. 197–206.

2. For general discussions of child custody law, see Foster and Freed, "Child Custody"; Goldstein, Freud, and Solnit, *Beyond the Best Interests*, esp. pp. 3–28; Mnookin, "Child-Custody Adjudication"; and Oster, "Custody Proceeding."

3. Roman law had given the father absolute control over his offspring, and he could even sell his children or condemn them to death. This concept of absolute right, somewhat modified, carried over into English law and remained largely intact until the fourteenth century. Forsyth, *Custody of Infants*, pp. 2–3; Derdeyn, "Child Custody Contests," p. 1369; Inker and Perretta, "Child's Right to Counsel," p. 109.

4. Trumbach, *Rise of the Egalitarian Family*, pp. 52–54, 160–63; Grossberg, *Governing the Hearth*, p. 235; Marcus, "Equal Protection," pp. 8–9.

5. Blackstone, *Commentaries* 1:452; Spruill, *Women's Life and Work*, p. 344.

6. Grossberg, "Law and the Family," pp. 259–60; Marcus, "Equal Protection," p. 9.

7. Blackstone, *Commentaries* 1:446–51; McGough and Shindell, "Coming of Age," pp. 209 n. 2, 220–21. The precise date of the doctrine's earliest application in infant cases is disputed, but it was clear by the mid-eighteenth century that English courts under parens patriae would assume greater jurisdiction than they had previously. In 1817 Percy Shelley was one of the first men in England to lose custody of his children under the parens patriae doctrine. The court removed Shelley's children from his custody because he was an atheist; it ruled that his "vicious and immoral" beliefs made him unfit to be a parent. Cogan, "Juvenile Law"; Custer, "Origins of the Doctrine of 'Parens Patriae' "; Derdeyn, "Child Custody Contests," p. 1369.

8. Roberts, *Paternalism in Early Victorian England*, pp. 22, 190–91.

9. *State v. Paine*, 23 Tenn. 523 (1843), p. 533. For an overview of developments during the late eighteenth and nineteenth centuries in English child-custody law, see Stone, *Road to Divorce*, pp. 170–80.

10. Spruill, *Women's Life and Work*, pp. 344–46; Walsh, "Child Custody in the Early Colonial Chesapeake." The lack of maternal custody rights reflected the subordinate status of married women in colonial southern society. In contrast to Puritan New England, the southern colonies of Maryland, Virginia, and South Carolina followed English practices, creating chancery courts and retaining common-law ideas of dower interest, separate estates, prenuptial contracts, and suits in equity that provided married women with some legal protection. Nevertheless, women did not experience a significant improvement in their legal rights during the colonial period, and their legal position was not an enviable one, for they gave up much of their legal existence in marriage. Salmon, *Women and the Law of Property*; Carr and Walsh, "Planter's Wife"; Walsh, "Experience and Status of Women in the Chesapeake." Older discussions of women's legal status in the colonial South, besides Spruill's classic work, include Bartlett, "Eighteenth Century Georgian Women," pp. 41–52; and Morgan, *Virginians at Home*, pp. 44–45.

For concise summaries of women's legal status in colonial America generally, see Norton, *Liberty's Daughters*, pp. 45–51; and DePauw, "Women and the Law." Until recently, historians emphasized the improvement of women's rights in the colonial period, arguing that social and economic conditions, especially the shortage of women and labor, helped to bolster the legal powers of married women in several notable respects. This argument was first advanced in studies such as Morris, *Studies in the History of American Law*, pp. 126–200; Benson, *Women in Eighteenth-Century America*; and Beard, *Woman as Force in History*. The so-called golden-age thesis has been effectively dismantled by newer and more sophisticated studies by Salmon, Carr, Walsh and others. For overviews of the debate on women's status in colonial America, see Salmon, "Legal Status of Women in Early America"; and Norton, "Evolution of White Women's Experience."

11. Zainaldin, "Modern American Family Law," p. 1052; Bloomfield, *American Lawyers*, pp. 118–19; Grossberg, *Governing the Hearth*, pp. 237–38; Brown, "Mothers, Fathers, and Children," pp. 250–53. See also Grossberg, "Who Gets the Child?"

12. At common law, the court would grant a writ of habeas corpus on the application of a husband, parent, guardian, or mother in order to look into any alleged illegal restraint. The writ of habeas corpus was originally designed as a protection against illegal imprisonment. In the case of infants, any unauthorized absence from legal custody was treated as the legal equivalent to imprisonment. Hurd, *Personal Liberty*, pp. 450–54.

13. Zainaldin, "Modern American Family Law," pp. 1053–54; Grossberg, *Governing the Hearth*, pp. 209, 236–37. For nineteenth-century commentaries on *Rex v. Delaval*, 97 Eng. Rep. 913, see Hurd, *Personal Liberty*, pp. 465–67; Forsyth, *Custody of Infants*, pp. 58–61; and Hocheimer, *Custody of Infants*, pp. 75–76, 96.

14. Zainaldin, "Modern American Family Law," pp. 1053–59; and Grossberg, *Governing the Hearth*, pp. 237–42.

15. On the southern cult of ladyhood, see Taylor, *Cavalier and Yankee*, pp. 146–76; Scott, *Southern Lady*, pp. 4–21; Clinton, *Plantation Mistress*, pp. 87–109; Wyatt-Brown, *Southern Honor*, pp. 226–36; Burton, *In My Father's House*, pp. 127–33; and Fox-Genovese, *Within the Plantation Household*, pp. 196–99, 202–3, 235–36. The agricultural press in the antebellum South also celebrated the virtues of the hardworking farm wife. See Hagler, "Ideal Woman in the Antebellum South."

16. [Thomas R. Dew], "Dissertation on the Characteristic Differences between the Sexes," *Southern Literary Messenger* 1 (May 1835): 495.

17. C. R. C[arroll], "Woman," *Southern Literary Journal* 3 (November 1836): 182–83. See also "Woman and Her Needs," *De Bow's Review* 13 (September 1852): 272–74, 286–89.

18. On changes in the new Republic regarding attitudes toward childhood and child rearing, see Greven, *Protestant Temperament*; Kerber, *Women of the Republic*, pp. 199–200, 283–88; Norton, *Liberty's Daughters*, pp. 235–38, 247–49; Wishy, *Child and the Republic*; McLoughlin, "Evangelical Childrearing"; Sunley, "Literature on Child Rearing"; Cott, "Antebellum Childrearing"; Degler, *At Odds*, pp. 66–85; and Mintz and Kellogg, *Domestic Revolutions*, pp. 58–60.

19. "Female Education," *Southern Literary Journal* 1 (December 1835): 277. On child rearing in southern white households, see Smith, *Inside the Great House*, chap. 1; Lewis, *Pursuit of Happiness*, pp. 174–87; Bruce, *Violence and Culture*, chap. 2; Censer, *North Carolina Planters*, chap. 2; Stowe, *Intimacy and Power*, chaps. 4–5; McMillen, *Motherhood in the Old South*, chap. 6; Wyatt-Brown, *Southern Honor*, pp. 125–48; Friedman, *Enclosed Garden*, pp. 36–37; Burton, *In My Father's House*, pp. 105–9; and Clinton, *Plantation Mistress*, pp. 46–50.

All of these studies of southern child-rearing beliefs and practices acknowledge the inroads made during the late eighteenth and early nineteenth centuries by the new, mother-centered form of child rearing that emphasized affection and automony, but Wyatt-Brown in *Southern Honor* argues that the traditional style, stressing fatherly authority, discipline, and deference, continued to play an important role in the South.

20. "Female Education," *Southern Literary Messenger* 6 (June 1840): 453.

21. On antebellum reforms related to children and the family, see Axinn and Levin, *Social Welfare*, pp. 45–50; Rothman, *Discovery of the Asylum*, pp. 65–78, 120–29,

206–36; Trattner, *From Poor Law to Welfare State*, pp. 93–102; and Walters, "Family and Ante-Bellum Reform."

22. Zainaldin, "Modern American Family Law," pp. 1059–68; Bloomfield, *American Lawyers*, p. 119; and Grossberg, "Law and the Family," pp. 261, 269, 273.

23. Fox-Genovese, *Within the Plantation Household*, p. 195; Friedman, *Enclosed Garden*, pp. xii–xiii, 29–31, 33–36.

24. *Bermudez v. Bermudez*, 2 Mart. O.S. 180 (La. 1812), pp. 180, 182.

25. *Ex parte Ralston*, R. M. Charlt. 119 (Ga. 1821), p. 119.

26. *State v. Fraser*, Dud. 42 (Ga. 1831), p. 45. This case involved a black woman, Winey Stephens, who had been jailed in a dispute over whether she was free or slave, and who sought a writ of habeas corpus to be released from jail and returned to the custody of her guardian, Dr. William Savage. The woman's counsel requested, in addition, that the court decide the question of her status. The court released Stephens from jail and allowed her to return to Savage, but it refused either to award custody or to decide whether she was free or slave. The court noted that the institution of slavery made it especially important for it to adhere to the stricter view of judicial discretion, but insisted that Stephen's race did not relieve it of the obligation to release her from any illegal restraint. Upon her discharge, the court observed, she would be free to seek further legal remedies to decide her status.

27. Boatwright, "Political and Civil Status," p. 316; and Ga., *Compilation of the Laws* (Dawson 1831), pp. 223, 219, 212. Other southern states also gave fathers the power to award custody of their children by will. For early statutes relating to this right, see Ala., *Digest of the Laws* (Toulmin 1823), p. 386; Ark., *Revised Statutes* (Ball and Roane 1838), ch. 72, sec. 6, p. 429; Fla., *Compilation of the Public Acts* (Duval 1839), p. 181; Miss., *Revised Code* (Poindexter 1824), ch. 9, sec. 122, pp. 64–65; N.C., *Manual of the Laws*, 2d ed. (Haywood 1808), 1:191–92; Tenn., *Laws* (Scott 1821), 1:97; and Va., *Collection of Acts* (1803), p. 172.

28. *In re Kottman*, 2 Hill 363 (S.C. 1834), p. 365.

29. *In re Mitchell*, R. M. Charlt. 489 (Ga. 1836), pp. 493, 495.

30. Besides the evidence presented here, see Censer, " 'Smiling through Her Tears,' " pp. 43–46; Wyatt-Brown, *Southern Honor*, pp. 243–44; and Clinton, *Plantation Mistress*, pp. 84–85.

31. *Ex parte Boaz*, 31 Ala. 425 (1858), pp. 426–27.

32. *Bryan v. Bryan*, 34 Ala. 516 (1859), pp. 517–19, 521–22.

33. *J.F.C. v. M.E.*, 6 Rob. 135 (La. 1843), pp. 137–38.

34. *Lindsey v. Lindsey*, 14 Ga. 657 (1854), pp. 657, 661.

35. Ibid., p. 660.

36. Other antebellum southern cases that awarded custody to the father in disputes between parents include Anonymous, 4 Desaus. 94 (S.C. 1810); *Hansford v. Hansford*, 10 Ala. 561 (1846); *Ex parte Hewitt*, 11 Rich 326 (S.C. 1858); *Fitts v. Fitts*, 21 Tex. 511 (1858); and *Faulk v. Faulk*, 23 Tex. 653 (1859). Arkansas, Florida, North Carolina, and Virginia supreme court records reveal no custody contests between fathers and mothers before the Civil War.

37. *Goodrich v. Goodrich*, 44 Ala. 670 (1870), p. 677.

38. Johnson, "Planters and Patriarchy," pp. 57–66. See also Wyatt-Brown, *Southern Honor*, pp. 117–25, 195–98; and Stowe, *Intimacy and Power*, pp. 179–91.

39. See table 1 in the appendix.

40. There was, of course, no divorce in South Carolina before the Civil War, but the state's chancery court did grant legal separations. See Salmon, *Women and the Law of Property*, pp. 64–65, 74–76.

41. *Prather v. Prather*, 4 Desaus. Eq. 33 (S.C. 1809), pp. 34, 39, 44.

42. *Williams v. Williams*, 4 Desaus. 183 (S.C. 1811), p. 184; *Threewits v. Threewits*, 4 Desaus. 560 (S.C. 1815), pp. 571, 575. For somewhat different interpretations of these cases and *Prather v. Prather*, see Salmon, " 'Life, Liberty, and Dower,' " pp. 98–99.

43. Lasok, "Virginia Bastardy Laws," pp. 405–7; Marcus, "Equal Protection," pp. 17–19; Trumbach, *Rise of the Egalitarian Family*, pp. 160–63; Grossberg, *Governing the Hearth*, pp. 197–200.

44. Grossberg, *Governing the Hearth*, pp. 207–10.

45. *Lawson v. Scott*, 9 Tenn. 92 (1825), p. 94. The Louisiana Supreme Court in 1829 employed the Spanish civil law to reach the same conclusion: illegitimate children "are not in the power of the father as legitimate children are"; instead, the mother had the right to guardianship. By 1838, this position had gained statutory backing in the state's civil code. *Acosta v. Robin*, 7 Mart. 387 (La. 1829), p. 390; La., *Civil Code* (Upton and Jennings 1838), art. 274, p. 40.

The right of women to the possession of their bastard children also achieved statutory recognition in Georgia. "Being the only recognized parent," the 1861 code declared, the mother of an illegitimate child "may exercise all the paternal power." Ga., *Code* (Clark, Cobb, and Irwin 1861), sec. 1750, p. 347.

46. Miss., *Statutes* (Turner 1816), p. 69; *Byrne v. Love*, 14 Tex. 81 (1855), p. 95. Besides the article by Lasok (cited in note 43), other discussions of bastardy in the South include Spruill, *Women's Life and Work*, pp. 314–25; Boatwright, "Political and Civil Status," pp. 317–18; and Johnson, *Ante-Bellum North Carolina*, pp. 209–15.

47. *Ex parte Hewitt*, 11 Rich. 326 (S.C. 1858), p. 330.

48. *Cocke v. Hannum*, 39 Miss. 423 (1860), pp. 441, 438–39. See also *Robinson v. Robinson*, 26 Tenn. 440 (1846). Other antebellum cases in which the mother received custody upon gaining her divorce due to the father's lack of fitness include *Ledoux v. Boyd*, 10 La. An. 663 (1855); and *Trimble v. Trimble*, 15 Tex. 19 (1855).

49. *In re Mitchell*, R. M. Charlt. 489 (Ga. 1836), p. 491.

50. The South Carolina court in *Prather v. Prather* (see note 41 and the accompanying text) was the first southern bench to grant custody to the mother in a dispute between parents, but it did not cite the best interests of the child standard as justification for its decision.

51. *State v. King*, 1 Ga. Dec. 93 (1842), pp. 93, 94, 95. Other antebellum disputes between parents in which mothers gained custody of all the children include *Ex parte Schumpert*, 6 Rich. 344 (S.C. 1853); and *Cornelius v. Cornelius*, 31 Ala. 479 (1858).

52. Degler, *At Odds*, pp. 73–74. See also Zelizer, *Pricing the Priceless Child*, pp. 5–12.

53. "Female Education" (1835), p. 279.

54. *Foster v. Alston*, 7 Miss. 406 (1842), pp. 414, 426, 456.

55. Ibid., pp. 466, 462, 463.

56. *Ex parte Schumpert*, 6 Rich. 344 (S.C. 1853), p. 347. See also *State v. Paine*, 23 Tenn. 523 (1843); *Hansford v. Hansford*, 10 Ala. 561 (1846); *Armstrong v. Stone*, 50 Va. 102 (1852); and *Ex parte Williams*, 11 Rich. (S.C. 1858), p. 452.

57. *In re Mitchell*, R. M. Charlt. 489 (Ga. 1836); *Foster v. Alston*, 7 Miss. 406

(1842); *State v. Paine*, 23 Tenn. 523 (1843); *Armstrong v. Stone*, 50 Va. 102 (1852); *Ex parte Schumpert*, 6 Rich. 344 (S.C. 1853); *Cornelius v. Cornelius*, 31 Ala. 479 (1858); *Rice v. Rice*, 21 Tex. 58 (1858).

58. La., *Civil Code* (1838), arts. 82–84, p. 15; Tenn., *Code* (Meigs and Cooper 1858), sec. 2490, p. 489.

59. Ala., *Digest of the Laws* (Aiken 1833), p. 132; Ala., *Code* (Ormond, Bagby, and Goldthwaite 1852), secs. 1977, 1980, pp. 379–80; Ga., *Digest of the Statute Laws* (Cobb 1851), ch. 149, p. 335; Miss., *Revised Code* (Sharkey, Harris, and Ellet 1857), ch. 40, art. 17, pp. 334–35; Tenn., *Code* (1858), sec. 2490, p. 489; Tex., *Digest of the Laws* (Dallam 1845), p. 81; Va., *Digest of the Laws*, 2d ed. (Tate 1841), p. 288; Va., *Code* (Patton and Robinson 1849), ch. 109, secs. 10 and 12, p. 473.

60. Ga., *Digest* (1851), ch. 149, p. 335. The act of 1845 also gave widows the right to the guardianship of the children when the father died without appointing a testamentary guardian, as well as the power to appoint testamentary guardians for their offspring who had no guardian.

Despite the significant changes in maternal custody rights that this act brought about, it apparently passed both the house and senate in Georgia with little opposition. Representative John W. Anderson of Chatham County introduced the bill on November 28, 1845, and the bill passed with no amendments on December 19. In the senate, Sen. Robert V. Hardeman from the Twenty-fifth District offered an amendment that gave the justices of the inferior court jurisdiction, in the absence of the judge of the superior court, to exercise their discretionary authority to award custody. The bill as amended passed the senate on December 23, and the house agreed to the amendment on December 24, when the president of the senate signed the act and passed it on to the governor for his approval. The *Federal Union*, published in Milledgeville (the capital of Georgia at the time), reported the passage of the new law without comment on December 30, 1845. See *Journal of the House of Representatives of the State of Georgia* (Columbia, 1846), pp. 130, 157, 316, 384, 393, 417; *Journal of the Senate of the State of Georgia* (Columbia, 1846), pp. 324, 327, 352, 376, 385, 413; and *Federal Union* (Milledgeville, Ga.), December 30, 1845, p. 2.

61. Ala., *Code* (1852), sec. 1977, pp. 379–80; Va., *Code* (1849), ch. 109, sec. 10, p. 473.

62. "Woman Physiologically Considered," *Southern Quarterly Review* 2 (October 1842): 309–11.

63. *Ex parte Hewitt*, 11 Rich. 326 (S.C. 1858), pp. 329–30.

64. Zainaldin, "Modern American Family Law," p. 1075; Grossberg, "Law and the Family," pp. 259–60; McGough and Shindell, "Coming of Age," pp. 217–21.

65. Spruill, *Women's Life and Work*, pp. 344–46; Johnson, *Ante-Bellum North Carolina*, pp. 256–57; Carr, "Maryland Orphan's Court." See also Walsh, "Child Custody in the Early Colonial Chesapeake."

66. Burnham, "Impossible Marriage," pp. 203–5, 215–19; Rosengarten, *Tombee*, pp. 109–10; Gutman, *Black Family*, pp. 17, 35–36, 131–33, 148–49, 318–19. Antebellum Louisiana, however, prohibited the separation of slave mothers and infant children. State law stipulated that no child under ten could be sold away from his or her mother nor the mother from her offspring. See Burnham, "Impossible Marriage," p. 203 n. 69.

67. Franklin, *Free Negro in North Carolina*, pp. 122–23; Johnson, *Ante-Bellum North Carolina*, p. 703; Spruill, *Women's Life and Work*, pp. 58–59; Wisner, *Social*

Welfare in the South, pp. 12–13; Calhoun, *American Family* 1:306–8; Bloomfield, *American Lawyers*, pp. 99–104.

68. For general discussions of the issues involved in parent–third party disputes, see Note, "Alternatives to 'Parental Right' "; Marcus, "Equal Protection," pp. 12–15; and McGough and Shindell, "Coming of Age," pp. 209–45. On state intervention in child abuse and neglect cases, see Areen, "Intervention between Parent and Child"; Wald, "State Intervention on Behalf of 'Neglected' Children"; and Levine, "Caveat Parens."

69. Grossberg, *Governing the Hearth*, p. 255.

70. *In re Waldron*, 13 Johns. 418 (N.Y. 1816), p. 420.

71. See *Commonwealth v. Hamilton*, 6 Mass. 273 (1810); In re McDowle, 8 Johns. 328 (N.Y. 1811); *U.S. v. Green*, 3 Mas. 482 (1st. Cir. 1824); *Commonwealth v. Hammond*, 27 Mass. 274 (1830); *State v. Hand*, 1 Ohio Dec. 238 (1848); *Commonwealth v. Gilkeson*, 1 Phila. 194 (Penn. 1851); *Pool v. Gott*, 14 Mon. L. Rep. 269 (Mass. 1851); and *In re Murphy*, 12 How. Pr. 513 (N.Y. 1856).

72. See *People v. Cooper*, 8 How. Pr. 288 (N.Y. 1853); *State v. Richardson*, 40 N.H. 272 (1860); and *State v. Libbey*, 44 N.H. 321 (1862) for cases in which northern judges upheld the superiority of parental custody rights.

73. See table 2 in the appendix. In *Brewer v. Harris*, 46 Va. 285 (1848), a free black woman attempted to recover custody of her three children, bound out by county officials to a white man. *Midgett v. McBryde*, 48 N.C. 22 (1855) involved a custody dispute between a white mother and the master to whom her two children, fathered by a black man, had been apprenticed by the county court. In both cases, the mothers failed in their efforts to challenge the validity of the indentures. The judicial response in such cases reflected the inferior status of women who contradicted the sexual and racial norms of southern society. For further discussion of these matters, consult Bynum, "On the Lowest Rung." See also notes 95–96 and the accompanying text below.

74. *Tutorship of Virginia Kershaw*, 5 Rob. 488 (La. 1843), pp. 488, 489. Tutorship was the term in Louisiana law for guardian. See also *In re Celina*, 7 La. An. 162 (1852), in which the Louisiana Supreme Court again returned custody of a daughter to a father accused of child neglect.

75. *In re Mitchell*, R. M. Charlt. 489 (Ga. 1836), pp. 493, 491, 495. See also *In re Kottman*, 2 Hill 363 (S.C. 1834); *Hutson v. Townsend*, 6 Rich. Eq. 249 (S.C. 1854); *Ex parte Williams*, 11 Rich. 452 (S.C. 1858); and *Taylor v. Jeter*, 33 Ga. 195 (1862).

76. Although antebellum courts strongly backed the common-law rights of fathers to custody of their children, the courts gradually imposed restrictions on the father's power to control the property of his child without regulation. See *Hall v. Lay*, 2 Ala. 529 (1841); and *Faulk v. Faulk*, 23 Tex. 653 (1859). See also *Anderson v. Darby*, 1 Nott & McCord 369 (S.C. 1818); *Miles v. Kaigler*, 10 Yerg. 10 (Tenn. 1836); *Wood v. Wood*, 3 Ala. 756 (1842); and *Ex parte Atkinson*, 40 Miss. 17 (1864) for discussions of paternal rights to child services and custody.

77. Grossberg, "Law and the Family," pp. 285–87; Spruill, *Women's Life and Work*, pp. 345–46; Boatwright, "Political and Civil Status," p. 316. Louisiana, with its civil-law heritage, offered the sole exception at the outset of the nineteenth century to this scheme of guardianship. Under the influence of French law, the Louisiana Civil Code stipulated that the mother could retain her status as guardian (known as a tutor in the state's law) upon remarriage. To do so, however, she had to call a meeting of family members beforehand, and gain their approval to remain tutor. If a widow remarried without requesting a family meeting, she lost her tutorship. The Louisiana Supreme

Court, in several antebellum cases, upheld the revocation of maternal tutorship rights in such instances. See La., *Digest of the Civil Laws* (1808), title 8, ch. 1, arts. 6–7, 10, pp. 58, 60; *Robin v. Weeks*, 5 Mart. N.S. 379 (La. 1827); and *Webb v. Webb*, 5 La. An. 595 (1850). Louisiana decisions supporting a widow's rights after remarriage include *Delacroix v. Boisblanc*, 4 Mart. O.S. 715 (La. 1817); *Bailey v. Morrison*, 4 La. An. 523 (1849); and *Lea v. Richardson*, 8 La. An. 94 (1853). For a fuller discussion of these issues, Sachse, "Tutorship in Louisiana."

78. On this point generally, see Grossberg, *Governing the Hearth*, pp. 242–43.

79. *Armstrong v. Stone*, 50 Va. 102 (1852), pp. 107, 108. On the other hand, see *Huie v. Nixon*, 6 Port. 77 (Ala. 1837), in which the guardianship of a widow who remarried was revoked.

80. *Striplin v. Ware*, 36 Ala. 87 (1860), p. 91; *Foster v. Alston*, 7 Miss. 406 (1842), p. 459. See also *Heyward v. Cuthbert*, 4 Desaus. Eq. 445 (S.C. 1814); *Carlisle v. Tuttle*, 30 Ala. 613 (1857); and *Wheeler v. Hollis*, 19 Tex. 522 (1857).

81. *Byrne v. Love*, 14 Tex. 81 (1855), pp. 91–92. See also *Gates v. Renfroe*, 7 La. An. 569 (1852).

82. *Cook v. Bybee*, 24 Tex. 278 (1859), p. 281. See also *Lea v. Richardson*, 8 La. An. 94 (1853).

83. *In re Murphy*, 12 How. Pr. 513 (N.Y. 1856), p. 515.

84. Grossberg, *Governing the Hearth*, pp. 259–60; Presser, "American Law of Adoption," pp. 456–59; Thurston, *Dependent Child*, pp. 11–18; Bloomfield, *American Lawyers*, p. 99.

85. Rutman and Rutman, *Place in Time*, p. 172; Morgan, *Virginians at Home*, pp. 22–25; Smith, *Inside the Great House*, pp. 90–91, 184–85; Spruill, *Women's Life and Work*, pp. 58–59.

86. Ala., *Digest* (1823), p. 651; Ark., *Laws of the Arkansas Territory* (Steele and M'Campbell, 1835), p. 74; Ark., *Revised Statutes* (1838), ch. 8, secs. 6–10, p. 102; Fla., *Compilation* (1839), p. 168; La., *Digest* (1808), title 6, ch. 2, arts. 7–10, pp. 36–38; La., *Civil Code* (1838), art. 158, p. 25; Miss., *Statutes of the Mississippi Territory* (Toulmin 1807), pp. 420–21; N.C., *Revised Code* (Moore and Biggs 1855) ch. 5, sec. 3, p. 78; S.C., *Statutes at Large* (1873–75), 11:21–22 (Act of 1839); Tenn., *Laws* (1821), 1:102; Va., *Collection of Acts* (1803), p. 174; Va., *Code* (1849), ch. 126, sec. 5, p. 530.

See *Owens v. Chaplain*, 48 N.C. 323 (1856), p. 324, where Chief Justice Nash of the North Carolina Supreme Court explained that if an apprentice "is ill-used, or not taught the trade, profession or employment to which he is bound," the county court could "cancel the indenture, and bind the infant to some other person."

87. *Pierce v. Massenburg*, 4 Leigh 493 (Va. 1833), p. 495. But in *Stewart v. Rickets*, 2 Hump. 151 (Tenn. 1840) the court suggested that a father might be able to bind his son as an apprentice without the son's assent.

Following the Civil War, at least two southern states passed laws that required children to sign indentures of apprenticeship as evidence of their assent. See Fla., *Digest of the Statute Law* (Bush 1872), ch. 5, sec. 5, p. 82; and S.C., *Statutes at Large* (1873–75), Act of 1865, p. 271.

88. See, for instance, the act of 1740 in S.C., *Statutes at Large* (Cooper and McCord 1836–41), 3:545.

89. *Stringfield v. Heiskell*, 10 Tenn. 546 (1831), p. 552.

90. *Versailles v. Hall*, 5 La. 281 (1833), pp. 282–83.

91. *Morrill v. Kennedy*, 22 Ark. 324 (1860), p. 328.

92. Ala., *Digest* (1823), pp. 651–52; Ark., *Revised Statutes* (1838), ch. 8, secs. 2–4, p. 101; Fla., *Compilation* (1839), p. 168; Ga., *Digest of the Laws* (Watkins 1800), p. 497; Miss., *Statutes* (1807), p. 420; Miss., *Statutes* (Howard and Hutchinson 1840), ch. 10, sec. 32, p. 152; N.C., *Manual* (1808), 1:19–20; S.C., *Statutes at Large* (1836–41), 5:410 (Act of 1830); Tenn., *Laws* (1821), 1:102; Tex., *Digest* (1845), p. 180; and Va., *Collection* (1803), pp. 173, 181–82; and Va., *Code* (1849), ch. 126, sec. 3, p. 530.

For discussions of child placement in the Old South, see Ely, "Poor Laws of the Post-Revolutionary South," pp. 13–16; Ely, "Poor Laws of the Antebellum South," pp. 863–71; Johnson, *Ante-Bellum North Carolina*, pp. 703–08; and Eaton, *Growth of Southern Civilization*, p. 288. On antebellum America in general, see Grossberg, *Governing the Hearth*, pp. 263–68; and Bloomfield, *American Lawyers*, pp. 130–31.

93. Ala., *Digest* (1823), pp. 652–53; Miss., *Statutes* (1816), p. 366; S.C., *Statutes at Large* (1836–41), 5:410 (Act of 1830); Tenn., *Laws* (1821), 1:102; Va., *Collection* (1803), p. 184. In addition, North Carolina and Tennessee courts had the power to apprentice children whose fathers had abandoned them and left them without sufficient financial support. The agreement of the mother was required in Tennessee before the children could be apprenticed. See N.C., *Manual* (1808), 1:20; and Tenn., *Compilation of the Statutes* (Caruthers and Nicholson 1836), ch. 46, pp. 98–99.

Appellate courts, especially in cases involving orphans and illegitimate children, tended to defer to the discretion that state statutes conferred on local magistrates. See *Dowd v. Davis*, 15 N.C. 61 (1833). In 1825, however, the Tennessee Supreme Court stressed that county courts had no power to bind out either an orphan or an illegitimate child unless he or she was a pauper. See *Lawson v. Scott*, 9 Tenn. 92 (1825).

94. In antebellum North Carolina and Virginia, for example, the law exempted masters from the requirement to teach their apprentice reading and writing when the apprentice was a free black. N.C., *Revised Statutes*, (Nash, Iredell, and Battle 1837), vol. 1, ch. 5, sec. 6, p. 68; and Va., *Code* (1849), ch. 126, sec. 5, p. 530. See also Bloomfield, *American Lawyers*, p. 132; Franklin, *Free Negro in North Carolina*, pp. 123–30; and Berlin, *Slaves without Masters*, pp. 226–27.

95. Bynum, *Unruly Women*, pp. 99–101; Ely, "Poor Laws of the Post-Revolutionary South," pp. 14–15; *Midgett v. McBryde*, 48 N.C. 22 (1855), p. 22; *Prue v. Hight*, 6 Jones 265 (N.C. 1859), p. 267.

96. Butler, "Exploitation and Opportunity"; Bynum, *Unruly Women*, p. 103; Ely, "Poor Laws of the Antebellum South," p. 868. On the unsuccessful efforts of free black parents to regain custody of their apprenticed children, see *Brewer v. Harris*, 46 Va. 285 (1848).

97. *Johnson v. State*, 21 Tenn. 282 (1840), p. 283; Pleck, *Domestic Tyranny*, pp. 76–77. See also *Tutorship of Virginia Kershaw*, 5 Rob. 488 (La. 1843); and *In re Celina*, 7 La. An. 162 (1852).

98. *In re Mitchell*, R. M. Charlt. 489 (Ga. 1836), pp. 494–95.

99. Wyatt-Brown, *Southern Honor*, pp. 118–25 (quotation on p. 119). See also Wyatt-Brown, "Ideal Typology," pp. 4–6; Johnson, "Planters and Patriarchy," pp. 45–72; and Brown, *Modernization*, pp. 142–44.

100. On the legal effect of adoption, see Peck, *Adoption Laws*, pp. 1–4; Grossberg, *Governing the Hearth*, p. 268; Kadushin, *Child Welfare Services*, p. 465; Mnookin, "Child Custody Adjudication," pp. 244–45; and Clarke, *Social Legislation*, p. 291.

101. The fullest discussion of the origins of adoption is in Presser, "American Law of Adoption." On adoption among the Romans and other early civilizations, see ibid.,

pp. 445–48; Brosnan, "Law of Adoption," pp. 332–35; Huard, "Law of Adoption," pp. 743–45; Benet, *Politics of Adoption*, pp. 22–39; Howard, *Matrimonial Institutions* 1:12–13; Clarke, *Social Legislation*, pp. 291–92; and Kadushin, *Child Welfare Services*, pp. 465–66.

102. Presser, "American Law of Adoption," pp. 448–55; Zainaldin, "Modern American Family Law," p. 1045; Grossberg, *Governing the Hearth*, p. 268; Brosnan, "Law of Adoption," p. 335; Huard, "Law of Adoption," pp. 745–47; Benet, *Politics of Adoption*, pp. 58–65; Witmer et al., *Independent Adoptions*, pp. 21–23.

103. Kadushin, *Child Welfare Services*, p. 466; Presser, "American Law of Adoption," pp. 456–59; Rothman, *Discovery of the Asylum*, pp. 206–07; Thurston, *Dependent Child*, pp. 10–19; Kawashima, "Adoption in Early America."

104. Huard, "Law of Adoption," pp. 747–48; Calhoun, *American Family* 1:335; Sims, "Adoption by Estoppel," p. 162; Babier, "Adoption Law of Louisiana," p. 298; Wadlington, "Adoption in Louisiana," p. 202. The civil code of 1808 held that "adoption which was authorized by the laws heretofore in force, shall be and is hereby abolished." La., *Digest* (1808), title 7, ch. 4, art. 35, p. 50.

105. Witmer et al., *Independent Adoptions*, p. 29; Presser, "American Law of Adoption," pp. 463–64; Grossberg, *Governing the Hearth*, pp. 269–70; Zainaldin, "Modern American Family Law," p. 1043.

106. Hubert, "Rights of the Descendants," p. 432; Snellings, "Civil Effects of Adoption," pp. 287–88; Bugea, "Adoption," pp. 196–97; Babier, "Adoption Law of Louisiana," p. 298.

107. *Vidal v. Commagère*, 13 La. An. 516 (1858), pp. 519, 517.

108. Presser, "American Law of Adoption," p. 461; Grossberg, *Governing the Hearth*, p. 271.

109. In an earlier Louisiana case, for example, the supreme court refused to uphold an adoption by notarial act because the husband and wife, who were free blacks, had failed to follow proper procedure. The Texas Supreme Court in 1863 also declared a private adoption act invalid. In this case, the court found that the act—which had been obtained in 1832—failed because the Spanish law then in force prohibited a person who had a legitimate child from adopting a stranger as co-heir with such a child. See *Fuselier v. Masse*, 4 La. 423 (1832); and *Teal v. Sevier*, 26 Tex. 516 (1863).

110. *In re Upton*, 16 La. An. 175 (1861), p. 176.

111. The acts of Vermont (1850), Missouri (1857), and Iowa (1858) also fell into this category. See Witmer et al., *Independent Adoptions*, pp. 29–30; Presser, "American Law of Adoption," pp. 465–66; Grossberg, *Governing the Hearth*, p. 271; and Wadlington, "Adoption in Louisiana," p. 202.

112. Ala., *Code* (1852) sec. 2011, p. 385; Miss., *Code* (Hutchinson 1848) ch. 35., arts. 3 and 5, p. 501. See also McFarlane, "Mississippi Law on Adoptions," p. 240.

113. Tex., *Digest of the Laws* (Hartley 1850), art. 5, p. 89. Similar statutes imposing some constraints were passed in Tennessee and Louisiana after the war. In Tennessee, the adoption law conferred full inheritance rights upon the adopted child, but gave to the person seeking the adoption "no mutual rights of inheritance and succession nor any interest whatever in the estate of the person adopted." The Louisiana civil code of 1870 declared that adoption "shall not interfere with the rights of forced heirs." In other words, in the division of an adoptive parent's estate, the rights of adopted children could not interfere with those of legitimate children. The person adopting in

Louisiana also had to be at least forty years old and fifteen years older than the person adopted. Finally, married persons had to concur in any adoption; one spouse could not adopt without the consent of the other. Tenn., *Compilation of the Statute Laws*, (Thompson and Steger 1873), vol. 1, sec. 3645, p. 1508; La., *Revised Civil Code* (1870), art. 214, p. 28. On adoption statutes in Texas and Tennessee, see Sims, "Adoption by Estoppel," pp. 162–63; and Merlin, "Tennessee Law of Adoption," p. 629 n. 23.

114. Whitmore, *Law of Adoption*, pp. 1–3. See also Note, "Law of Adoption"; and Ben-Or, "Law of Adoption."

115. These states included Pennsylvannia (1855), Indiana (1855), Wisconsin (1858), and Ohio (1859). See Witmer et al., *Independent Adoptions*, pp. 30–31; Presser, "American Law of Adoption," p. 465; Zainaldin, "Modern American Family Law," pp. 1042–43; and Grossberg, "Law and the Family," pp. 319–20.

116. Ga., *Code* (1861), sec. 1739, p. 345. The dates of passage are provided in Ga., *Code*, 2d ed. (Irwin, Lester, and Hill 1873), sec. 1788, p. 310. The Georgia Supreme Court upheld the legality of adoption under this legislation in *Rives v. Sneed*, 25 Ga. 612 (1858); and *Massee v. Snead*, 29 Ga. 51 (1859).

117. Miss., *Revised Code* (1857), ch. 61, art. 41, p. 484. See also McFarlane, "Mississippi Law on Adoptions," pp. 240–41.

118. Grossberg, "Law and the Family," pp. 320–21; Presser, "American Law of Adoption," pp. 470–89; Zainaldin, "Modern American Family Law," pp. 1083–86; Thurston, *Dependent Child*, pp. 28–38; Witmer et al., *Independent Adoptions*, pp. 33–34; Bloomfield, *American Lawyers*, p. 134. On the fit between apprenticeship and plantation society, see Ely, "Poor Laws of the Antebellum South," p. 873.

119. *Rives v. Sneed*, 25 Ga. 612 (1858), pp. 613, 620. In 1859, Sneed faced another challenge to the adoption, this time from the boy's grandfather. Again, the Georgia Supreme Court affirmed the legality of the adoption. See *Massee v. Snead*, 29 Ga. 51 (1859).

CHAPTER FOUR

1. Berlin et al., *Black Military Experience*, pp. 689–90. On the experience of slave children during the Civil War, see Bardaglio, "Children of Jubilee."

2. Litwack, *Been in the Storm So Long*, pp. 52–59; Ripley, *Slaves and Freedmen*, pp, 14, 16–21; Mohr, *On the Threshold of Freedom*, pp. 72–75; Jimerson, *Private Civil War*, pp. 61–62, 65–67.

3. Myers, *Children of Pride*, pp. 935, 940.

4. Bardaglio, "Children of Jubilee," pp. 226–27 (Barbour quotation on p. 227); Litwack, *Been in the Storm So Long*, pp. 229–31. For other discussions of African American family life during the Civil War, see Ripley, "Black Family in Transition"; Berlin et al., "Family and Freedom"; and Berlin, Miller, and Rowland, "Afro-American Families."

5. "The South and the Union," *De Bow's Review* 19 (July 1855): 47, 43.

6. Ibid., pp. 42–43.

7. Wright, *Political Economy*, pp. 34–35, 41–42, 140–41; Cashin, *Family Venture*, pp. 91–93; Thornton, *Politics and Power*, pp. 268–91. Steven Hahn, in *Roots of Southern Populism*, pp. 40–49, finds similar developments taking place in the upcountry,

but the overall impact of such economic changes was to widen the gap between these two subregions of the South.

8. Whites, "Civil War as a Crisis in Gender," p. 6.

9. Document no. 54, in Boydston, Kelley, and Margolis, *Limits of Sisterhood*, p. 173. For an astute discussion of how the ideology of domesticity shaped Stowe's approach to slavery, see "Harriet Beecher Stowe: 'My Life's Blood,'" in Boydston, Kelley, and Margolis, *Limits of Sisterhood*, pp. 155–65.

10. Document no. 56, in Boydston, Kelley, and Margolis, *Limits of Sisterhood*, pp. 180, 181.

11. Quoted in "Harriet Beecher Stowe," p. 159.

12. "Marriage and Divorce," *Southern Quarterly Review* 26 (October 1854): 50. Thornton has found that, in fact, divorce rates in Alabama skyrocketed during the 1850s. See *Politics and Power*, pp. 306–7.

13. "The Relative Moral and Social Status of the North and the South," *De Bow's Review* 22 (March 1857): 246, 230–33. Other antebellum southern writings that attacked reforms in marriage and divorce law include "The Effect of Foreign Divorces on South Carolina Marriages," *Carolina Law Journal* 1 (January 1831): 377–83; [Wheelock S. Upton], "Divorce," *De Bow's Review* 2 (September 1846): 155–64; and "The Contract of Marriage," *De Bow's Review* 2 (October 1846): 238–42.

14. McCurry, "Politics of Yeoman Households," p. 35; Wiecek, "'Old Times There Are Not Forgotten,'" p. 169; Jimerson, *Private Civil War*, pp. 12–18; Johnson, *Toward a Patriarchal Republic*, pp. xx–xxi, 85–101.

15. Thomas Settle to R. M. Pearson, August 8, 1868, Thomas Settle Papers, Group Number 2, SHC.

16. Thomas, *Confederacy as a Revolutionary Experience*, pp. 58–71, 73–78; Escott, *After Secession*, chap. 3.

17. Robinson, *Justice in Grey*, pp. 435–36; Thomas, *Confederate Nation*, pp. 194–95. For an intriguing comparative analysis of the growth of central authority in the Union and Confederacy, see Bensel, *Yankee Leviathan*, chap. 3.

18. Wallenstein, *From Slave South to New South*, pp. 102–5; Escott, "Poverty and Government Aid for the Poor in Confederate North Carolina"; Thomas, *Confederacy as a Revolutionary Experience*, pp. 71–73 (Smith quotation on p. 72).

19. Ayers, *Vengeance and Justice*, pp. 144–46; Thomas, *Confederacy as a Revolutionary Experience*, pp. 102–3; Escott, *Many Excellent People*, pp. 64–67.

20. Ayers, *Vengeance and Justice*, pp. 146–47; Bynum, "On the Lowest Rung," p. 42; Bynum, *Unruly Women*, p. 149.

21. Roark, *Masters without Slaves*, p. 64 (Watson quotation); Escott, *Many Excellent People*, pp. 67–69; Carter, *When the War Was Over*, pp. 6–10; Ash, *Middle Tennessee Society Transformed*, pp. 163–67 (Nimrod quotation on p. 164). For a vivid account of Confederate attempts to crack down on outlaw bands in the mountain South, see Paludan, *Victims*.

22. Helis, "Of Generals and Jurists"; Ash, *Middle Tennessee Society Transformed*, pp. 96–100.

23. Ash, *Middle Tennessee Society Transformed*, pp. 176–77, 180–82; St. Clair, "Judicial Machinery in North Carolina in 1865"; Carter, *When the War Was Over*, pp. 10–23; Ash, "Poor Whites in the Occupied South."

24. John W. Brown Diary, June 9, 1865, SHC.

25. Wayne, *Reshaping of Plantation Society*, pp. 144–47; Escott, *Many Excellent People*, pp. 120–22; Ash, *Middle Tennessee Society Transformed*, pp. 195, 200; Roark, *Masters without Slaves*, pp. 144–47 (Virginia planter quotation on p. 145); Myers, *Children of Pride*, p. 1341.

26. Litwack, *Been in the Storm So Long*, pp. 408–20; Foner, *Reconstruction*, pp. 164–67; Reidy, *From Slavery to Agrarian Capitalism*, pp. 143–46. On the development of the contract labor system during the war, see Gerteis, *From Contraband to Freedman*, pp. 65–82; and Rose, *Rehearsal for Reconstruction*, pp. 203–5, 224–25, 298–313.

27. De Forest, *Miss Ravenel's Conversion*, p. 230; Stanley, "Beggars Can't Be Choosers."

28. Wilson, *Black Codes*, pp. 66–75; Nieman, *To Set the Law in Motion*, pp. 73–98; Carter, *When the War Was Over*, pp. 177–83, 216–20, 226–28; Litwack, *Been in the Storm So Long*, pp. 366–71; Foner, *Reconstruction*, pp. 199–201, 208–9.

29. Ibid., pp. 204–5; Bryant, "Market Revolution in Black and White," pp. 6–7; Ash, *Middle Tennessee Society Transformed*, pp. 198–200 (Freedmen's Bureau agent quotation on p. 198).

30. Jonathan Worth, Governor of North Carolina, to Hon. David A. Barnes, Judge of the Superior Court, August 22, 1866, David Alexander Barnes Papers, SHC.

31. Ayers, *Vengeance and Justice*, pp. 150, 169–79, 190–98; Reidy, *From Slavery to Agrarian Capitalism*, p. 225.

32. Foner, *Reconstruction*, pp. 364 (Alcorn quotation), 370–73; Keller, *Affairs of State*, pp. 213–15; Wallenstein, *From Slave South to New South*, pp. 144–45; Escott, *Many Excellent People*, pp. 142–44.

33. Foner, *Nothing But Freedom*, pp. 52–53; Robinson, *Justice in Grey*, pp. 610–19; Nieman, "Black Political Power and Criminal Justice"; Norvell, "Reconstruction Courts of Texas."

34. Ayers, *Vengeance and Justice*, pp. 151–61 (quotation on p. 152); Nieman, *To Set the Law in Motion*, pp. 156–90, 196–222; Bryant, "Market Revolution in Black and White," p. 8 (Colby quotation).

35. R. C. Lawrence, "Chief Justice Pearson," magazine clipping (n.d.), Richard M. Pearson Papers, SHC; Thomas Settle to R. M. Pearson, August 8, 1868, Thomas Settle Papers, Group Number 2, SHC; Benedict, "Problem of Constitutionalism and Constitutional Liberty."

36. Keller, *Affairs of State*, pp. 222–25; Escott, *Many Excellent People*, pp. 147–56; Tourgée, *A Fool's Errand*, p. 137.

37. David Schenck Diary, August 12, 1867, SHC; A. W. Dozier to Richard Dozier, March 13, 1870, Richard Dozier Papers, SHC.

38. Thomas Settle Papers, Group II, A. W. Tourgée to Thomas Settle, June 24, 1869, SHC.

39. Foner, *Reconstruction*, pp. 365–66, 379–80, 588–89; Foner, *Nothing But Freedom*, pp. 53, 68–71.

40. Scott, *Southern Lady*, pp. 81–102; Cashin, " 'Since the War Broke Out,' " pp. 200–212; Bleser and Heath, "Clays of Alabama"; Faust, " 'Trying to Do a Man's Business.' "

41. [George Fitzhugh], "The Women of the South," *De Bow's Review* 31 (August 1861): 151; Tillett, "Southern Womanhood as Affected by the War." Scholarly

literature that emphasizes the dedication of Confederate women to the war effort includes Simkins and Patton, *Women of the Confederacy*; Massey, *Bonnet Brigades*; and Sterkx, *Partners in Rebellion*.

42. Woodward, *Mary Chesnut's Civil War*, p. 625. For studies that stress the key role of women in the decline of southern morale during the war, see Rable, *Civil Wars*; Faust, "Altars of Sacrifice"; Bynum, *Unruly Women*, pp. 130–50; McKinney, "Women's Role in Civil War Western North Carolina."

43. East, *Civil War Diary of Sarah Morgan*, p. 610; Wiener, "Female Planters and Planters' Wives in Civil War and Reconstruction," pp. 146–47.

44. Friedman, *Enclosed Garden*, pp. 92–94; Burton, *In My Fathers House*, p. 226; Kenzer, *Kinship and Neighborhood*, pp. 97–99.

45. Fields, "Nineteenth-Century American South"; Reidy, *From Slavery to Agrarian Capitalism*, pp. 137–38, 245–46; Hahn, *Roots of Southern Populism*, pp. 137–203; Wright, *Old South, New South*, pp. 47–50; Woodman, "Sequel to Slavery," p. 554.

Michael Wayne (*Reshaping of Plantation Society*, esp. pp. 202–4) also stresses the transformation of planters from masters to landlords. Studies that emphasize planter persistence in the postwar South include Wiener, *Social Origins of the New South*; and Billings, *Planters and the Making of a "New South."*

46. Thomas, *Confederacy as a Revolutionary Experience*, pp. 66–68, 87–93; Cobb, *Industrialization and Southern Society*, pp. 5–26; Eller, *Miners, Millhands, and Mountaineers*, pp. 28–32, 235–37; Hall et al., *Like a Family*, pp. 14–19, 152–63.

47. Woodman, "Post–Civil War Southern Agriculture and the Law"; Reidy, "Unfinished Revolution"; Hahn, "Hunting, Fishing, and Foraging"; Flynn, *White Land, Black Labor*, pp. 84–149.

On the debate over fence laws in the postwar South, see Kantor and Kousser, "Common Sense or Commonwealth?" as well as Steven Hahn's response and Kantor and Kousser's rejoinder in the same issue. What threatens to get lost in this intense debate over who supported the fence laws and why is the significance of the legislation itself: it was part of a broader effort among southern whites to reconstruct the relationship between the state and society following the collapse of household-centered patriarchy.

48. Foner, *Reconstruction*, pp. 82, 84; George L. Christian and Frank W. Christian, "Slave Marriages," *Virginia Law Journal* 1 (November 1877): 644.

49. Berlin et al., *Black Military Experience*, pp. 660, 672, 712.

50. Blassingame, *Black New Orleans*, pp. 85–87; Berlin et al., *Black Military Experience*, pp. 623–24; Litwack, *Been in the Storm So Long*, p. 240.

51. Grossberg, *Governing the Hearth*, pp. 133–34; Gutman, *Black Family*, pp. 414–18. In July 1865, Bedford County, Tennessee, 406 out of 422 marriage licenses issued that month were to blacks. See Ash, *Middle Tennessee Society Transformed*, p. 210.

52. Litwack, *Been in the Storm So Long*, pp. 241–42; Gutman, *Black Family*, pp. 419–20.

53. Quoted in Grossberg, *Governing the Hearth*, pp. 134, 135.

54. Bynum, "Reshaping the Bonds of Womanhood," pp. 321–22. For a survey of postwar divorce laws, see "Marriage and Divorce," *Southern Review*, n.s., 9 (January 1871): 135–40.

55. George F. Holmes, "Milton's Domestic Life—His Ethics of Divorce," *De Bow's Review* 36 (January 1867): 12; Holmes, "Milton's Domestic Life—His Ethics of Divorce," *De Bow's Review* 36 (February 1867): 124. See also M. F. Taylor, "Marriage and Divorce," *Southern Magazine* 11 (October 1872): 447–52.

56. Bynum, "Reshaping the Bonds of Womanhood," pp. 321, 324 (Pearson quotation). It should be noted that Bynum finds a remarkable shift in the sex ratio of the litigants in divorce cases from the antebellum to postbellum periods. Her research into three Piedmont counties in North Carolina reveals that while twice as many women as men sought divorce before the war, three times as many men as women petitioned for divorce during and after the war. The superior court records suggest that these men were escaping marriages "crippled by war, social chaos, and economic depression," according to Bynum. See ibid., pp. 326, 332.

57. Lebsock, "Radical Reconstruction," pp. 195–98 (James Allen quotation on p. 198).

58. Ibid., pp. 201–4. For a brief survey of American developments in married women's property rights in the late nineteenth century, see Henry Hitchcock, "Modern Legislation Touching Marital Property Rights," *Southern Law Review*, n.s., 6 (December 1880): 633–62. On Virginia, consult John O. Steger, "The Virginia Married Woman's Acts," *Virginia Law Journal* 4 (February 1880): 65–75.

59. *Huff v. Wright*, 39 Ga. 41 (1869), quoted in Lebsock, "Radical Reconstruction," p. 209; and H. A. Matthews, "The Property Rights of Married Women: Is Additional Legislation Needed?" *Georgia Bar Association Proceedings* 8 (1891): 76. For an insightful analysis of the contradiction between the expansion of contract rights and the denial of the wife's title to her own wages during the postwar years, see Stanley, "Conjugal Bonds and Wage Labor."

60. R. L. Dabney, "Women's Rights Women," *Southern Magazine* 8 (March 1871): 325, 326–27. See also John Randolph Tucker, "Property Rights of Baron and Femme," *Report of the Virginia State Bar Association* 4 (1891): 189–210.

CHAPTER FIVE

1. See table 1 in the appendix.

2. Southworth, *Ishmael*, p. 590. For an interesting discussion of this novel in the context of nineteenth-century American legal culture, see Bloomfield, *American Lawyers*, pp. 186–89.

3. On the development of the tender years doctrine in nineteenth-century America, see Grossberg, *Governing the Hearth*, pp. 248–49; Zainaldin, "Modern American Family Law," pp. 1072–73; Derdeyn, "Child Custody Contests," p. 1371; and Marcus, "Equal Protection," pp. 10–11.

4. *Taylor v. Jeter*, 33 Ga. 195 (1862), p. 199. "Tender age" usually meant under twelve years of age. Early appearances of the tender-age approach to resolving custody disputes between parents include *Threewits v. Threewits*, 4 Desaus. 560 (S.C. 1815); *State v. King*, 1 Ga. Dec. 93 (1842); *State v. Paine*, 23 Tenn. 523 (1843); and *Ex parte Schumpert*, 6 Rich. 344 (S.C. 1853).

5. Ginzberg, *Women and the Work of Benevolence*, pp. 11–12; [George Fitzhugh], "The Women of the South," *De Bow's Review* 31 (August 1861): 147; Ownby, *Subduing Satan*, pp. 10–12, 15 (quotation).

6. Chopin, *Awakening*, p. 57.

7. Anonymous, 55 Ala. 428 (1876), p. 432. See also *McShan v. McShan*, 56 Miss. 413 (1879).

8. *Cornelius v. Cornelius*, 31 Ala. 479 (1858), p. 482; *Bryan v. Bryan*, 34 Ala. 516 (1859), p. 521; *Carr v. Carr*, 63 Va. 168 (1872), p. 174.

9. *Beene v. Beene*, 64 Ark. 518 (1898), p. 522. Custody of the children was also split between parents in *State v. Paine*, 23 Tenn. 523 (1843); *Scoggins v. Scoggins*, 80 N.C. 318 (1879); *Norris v. Norris*, 46 S.W. 405 (Tex. 1898); *Lowrey v. Lowrey*, 108 Ga. 766 (1899); and *Defee v. Defee*, 51 S.W. 274 (Tex. 1899).

Other custody decisions based in part on the tender-years doctrine were *Goodrich v. Goodrich*, 44 Ala. 670 (1870); *Holt v. Holt*, 42 Ark. 495 (1883); *Lyle v. Lyle*, 86 Tenn. 372 (1888); and *Trimble v. Trimble*, 97 Va. 217 (1899).

10. Hurd, *Personal Liberty*, pp. 527–36; Hochheimer, *Custody of Infants*, p. 137.

11. *Harris v. Harris*, 115 N.C. 587 (1894), p. 589.

12. *Williams v. Williams*, 23 Fla. 324 (1887), p. 325.

13. *Haymond v. Haymond*, 74 Tex. 414 (1889), pp. 415, 420, 421.

14. *Jordan v. Jordan*, 4 Tex. Civ. App. 559 (1893).

15. Ga., *Code* (Clark, Cobb, and Irwin 1861), sec. 1685, pp. 335–36; La., *Revised Civil Code*, (Saunders 1888), art. 157, p. 72. In addition, Florida, Georgia, and North Carolina joined Alabama and Virginia after the war in giving the courts power to determine custody of the children pending the outcome of the divorce suit. See Fla., *Revised Statutes* (Blount, Cooper, and Massey 1892), sec. 1489, p. 506; Ga., *Code* (Clark, Cobb, and Irwin 1873), sec. 1741, p. 301; and N.C., *Revisal of the Public Statutes* (Battle 1873), ch. 37, sec. 18, p. 367.

16. *Goodrich v. Goodrich*, 44 Ala. 670 (1870), p. 674.

17. Elton Eliot, "Women and Women," *Southern Magazine* (Louisville) 5 (September 1894): 200.

18. Besides *Goodrich v. Goodrich*, see *Johns v. Johns*, 57 Miss. 530 (1879); *McGill v. McGill*, 19 Fla. 341 (1882); *Ex parte Reed*, 19 S.C. 604 (1883); and *Myers v. Myers*, 83 Va. 806 (1887). Nineteenth-century courts outside the region also depicted similar images of mothers and fathers in child-custody disputes. See Griswold, *Family and Divorce in California*, pp. 155–69.

19. Robert Griswold discusses a similar process of redefining manhood in late-nineteenth-century divorce trials in rural California. See "Divorce and the Legal Redefinition of Victorian Manhood." On the evangelical campaign in the South, see Ownby, *Subduing Satan*, pp. 133–36, 170–73, 191–93.

20. *Owens v. Owens*, 96 Va. 191, p. 196.

21. *Evans v. Evans*, 57 S.W. 367 (Tenn. 1900), pp. 370, 369.

22. *Carr v. Carr*, 63 Va. 168 (1872), pp. 174–75.

23. *Latham v. Latham*, 71 Va. 307 (1878), pp. 310, 326, 328.

24. Ibid., pp. 387, 388, 397.

25. *Miller v. Miller*, 38 Fla. 227 (1896), p. 232. See also *Gahn v. Darby*, 36 La. An. 70 (1884); *Tuggle v. Tuggle*, 97 Ga. 658 (1896); and *Randall v. Randall*, 28 So. 19 (Miss. 1900).

26. Grossberg, *Governing the Hearth*, pp. 252–53; and Grossberg, "Law and the Family," pp. 608–9.

27. *Slater v. Slater*, 90 Va. 845 (1894), p. 847. See also *In re D'Anna*, 117 N.C. 462 (1895); and *Tuggle v. Tuggle*, 97 Ga. 658 (1896).

28. Berlin et al., *Black Military Experience*, pp. 660, 673–79.

29. Frankel, "Federal and State Policy in Mississippi," pp. 12–13. Only one dispute between former slaves reached southern high courts in the postwar years—*Pascal v. Jones*, 41 Ga. 220 (1870)—and there is no indication that the jurists in this case evaluated the financial resources of the parents. The court awarded custody to the father on

the basis of statutes passed in 1865 and 1866 that made fathers who were former slaves the natural guardians of children acknowledged by them.

30. *McShan v. McShan*, 56 Miss. 413 (1879), pp. 416, 418.

31. See, for example, *Lemunier v. McCearly*, 37 La. An. 133 (1885); and *Lyle v. Lyle*, 86 Tenn. 372 (1888). Other postwar southern disputes between parents in which the mother received custody include *Moore v. Moore*, 66 Ga. 336 (1881); *Hammond v. Hammond*, 90 Ga. 527 (1892); *Lawson v. Lawson*, 111 Ga. 825 (1900); *Howard v. Walker*, 111 Ga. 862 (1900); and *Wills v. Wills*, 58 S.W. 301 (Tenn. 1900).

32. Laws granting the courts such authority first entered southern statute books in the early nineteenth century. See Ala., *Digest of the Laws* (Toulmin 1823), pp. 252–53; Ark., *Laws* (Steele and M'Campbell 1835), pp. 220–21; Fla., *Compilation of the Public Acts* (Duval 1839), p. 81; Miss., *Revised Code* (Poindexter 1824), ch. 36, sec. 7, p. 229; Tenn., *Code* (Meigs and Cooper 1858), sec. 2468, p. 485; and Tex., *Digest of the Laws* (Hartley 1850), art. 849, p. 283.

For antebellum cases involving court-ordered maintenance, see *Williams v. Williams*, 4 Desaus. Eq. 183 (S.C. 1811); *Threewits v. Threewits*, 4 Desaus. Eq. 560 (S.C. 1815); and *Harris v. Davis*, 1 Ala. 259 (1840).

33. *Holt v. Holt*, 42 Ark. 495 (1883), p. 499. See also *Trimble v. Trimble*, 15 Tex. 19 (1855); and *Nicely v. Nicely*, 40 Tenn. 184 (1859).

34. *Pape v. Pape*, 35 S.W. 479 (Tex. 1896), pp. 481, 480.

35. *Phelan v. Phelan*, 12 Fla. 449 (1869); *Heninger v. Heninger*, 18 S.E. 193 (Va. 1893).

36. *Myer v. Myer*, 83 Va. 806 (1887).

37. *Rice v. Rice*, 21 Tex. 58 (1858).

38. *Defee v. Defee*, 51 S.W. 274 (1899), p. 274.

39. *Bowles v. Dixon*, 32 Ark. 92 (1877), p. 96. Other postwar southern contests between parents in which the father gained control of the children include *Keppel v. Keppel*, 92 Ga. 506 (1893); and *Brown v. Brown*, 2 Va. Dec. 308 (1896).

40. On these developments generally in American custody law, consult Grossberg, "Law and the Family," pp. 598–99, 611–12; and Brown, "Mothers, Fathers, and Children," p. 19. Nine northern and western states, as well as the District of Columbia, gave mothers the statutory right to equal guardianship. See Grossberg, *Governing the Hearth*, p. 247.

41. Ga., *Code* (1861), sec. 1700, p. 338. On the father as natural guardian in the late-nineteenth-century South, see Ark., *Digest of the Statutes* (Sandels and Hill 1894), sec. 3568, pp. 874–75; Ga., *Code* (Hopkins, Anderson, and Lamar 1896), vol. 2, sec. 2513, p. 260; La., *Revised Civil Code* (1888), art. 256, p. 87; and Tex., *Revised Civil Statutes* (1895) art. 2575, p. 514.

42. Some states also gave widows the power to appoint testamentary guardians if their husbands had not yet done so. On the power of fathers and mothers to appoint guardians by will in the postwar South, see Ala., *Code* (Martin 1897), sec. 2250, p. 690; Ark., *Digest of the Statutes* (Sandels and Hill 1894), sec. 3574, p. 875; Fla., *Revised Statutes* (1892), sec. 2086, p. 687; Ga., *Code* (Hopkins, Anderson, and Lamen 1896), vol. 2, secs. 2514–15, p. 261; Miss., *Annotated Code* (Thompson, Dillard, and Campbell 1892), sec. 2184, p. 552; N.C., *Code* (Dortch, Manning, and Henderson 1883), vol. 1, sec. 1562, p. 609; S.C., *Revised Statutes* (Breazeale 1894), vol. 1, sec. 2189, p. 763; Tenn., *Annotated Code* (Shannon 1896), art. 4258, pp. 1062–63; Tex., *Revised Civil Statutes* (1895), art. 2578, p. 514; and Va., *Code* (Burks, Staples, and Riely 1887),

sec. 2597, p. 629. See also *Taylor v. Jeter*, 33 Ga. 195 (1862); *McKinney v. Noble*, 38 Tex. 195 (1873); and *Ex parte Bell*, 2 Tenn. Chan. 327 (1878).

43. Hoff, *Law, Gender, and Injustice*, p. 133, notes correctly that the evolution in American child-custody law by the end of the nineteenth century "should not be viewed as unqualified linear progress in women's legal status but rather the cooptation of gender into constitutional jurisprudence as a natural, rather than a suspect, classification, thus empowering women to take legal action only within very circumscribed limits of their private sphere of activities."

44. *Gardenhire v. Hinds*, 38 Tenn. 402 (1858), pp. 410–11.

45. See table 2 in the appendix.

46. See table 3 in the appendix. On the role of kin in providing child care upon parental death or abandonment in the nineteenth-century South, see Richards, "All Our Connections," pp. 147–48; and Kenzer, *Kinship and Neighborhood*, p. 22. Joan Cashin, in "Structure of Antebellum Planter Families" (pp. 61–63), also makes the point that kin outside the nuclear core played an important part in child rearing among planter families.

47. See table 4 in the appendix.

48. For a general discussion of this judicial attitude toward parental custody rights in late-nineteenth-century America, see Grossberg, *Governing the Hearth*, pp. 257–59.

49. *Legate v. Legate*, 87 Tex. 248 (1894), pp. 252, 253. The foster parents in this case had formally adopted the child after her natural parents voluntarily relinquished custody of her.

50. *Verser v. Ford*, 37 Ark. 27 (1881), pp. 30, 31.

51. *Ex parte Murphy*, 75 Ala. 409 (1883). p. 411. In *Verser v. Ford*, the Arkansas court also noted that the father could again apply to obtain the custody of his daughter once she became "more advanced in years."

52. *Payne v. Payne*, 39 Ga. 174 (1869), p. 177.

53. *Maples v. Maples*, 49 Miss. 393 (1873), p. 403; *Spears v. Snell*, 74 N.C. 210 (1876), p. 216.

54. *Fullilove v. Banks*, 62 Miss. 11 (1884), p. 12.

55. *Spears v. Snell*, 74 N.C. 210 (1876), p. 216; *Latham v. Ellis*, 116 N.C. 30 (1895), p. 31; *Casanover v. Massengale*, 54 S.W. 317 (Tex. 1899), p. 318.

56. *State v. Deaton*, 52 S.W. 591 (Tex. 1899), p. 592; *Merritt v. Swimley*, 82 Va. 433 (1886), p. 439. On the other hand, several southern justices expressed the belief that a parent should not be denied custody simply because he or she was poorer than the nonparent in the dispute. See *Moore v. Christian*, 56 Miss. 408 (1879); *Verser v. Ford*, 37 Ark. 27 (1881); and *Stringfellow v. Somerville*, 95 Va. 701 (1898).

57. *Spears v. Snell*, 74 N.C. 210 (1876), p. 215. Other cases in which the court consulted the wishes of the child and at least in part rested its decision on this inquiry included *Maples v. Maples*, 49 Miss. 393 (1873); and *Merritt v. Swimley*, 82 Va. 433 (1886).

58. For cases in which the court did not follow the child's preference in deciding custody battles, see *Beard v. Dean*, 64 Ga. 258 (1879); and *Moore v. Christian*, 56 Miss. 408 (1879).

59. *Smith v. Bragg*, 68 Ga. 650 (1882), p. 653.

60. *Merritt v. Swimley*, 82 Va. 433 (1886), pp. 437, 438–39. Southern courts also took into account the formed attachments of children to their surrogate parents in the following cases: *Spears v. Snell*, 74 N.C. 210 (1876); *Bently v. Terry*, 59 Ga. 555 (1877);

Verser v. Ford, 37 Ark. 27 (1881); *Coffee v. Black*, 82 Va. 567 (1886); and *State v. Deaton*, 52 S.W. 591 (Tex. 1899). The Texas Supreme Court reversed the decision of the court of civil appeals in the last case and awarded control of the child to the mother. See *State v. Deaton*, 54 S.W. 901 (Tex. 1900).

61. *Coffee v. Black*, 82 Va. 567 (1886), pp. 569, 570; *Stringfellow v. Somerville*, 95 Va. 70 (1898), p. 707.

62. *Washaw v. Gimble*, 50 Ark. 351 (1887), pp. 354, 356.

63. *Bently v. Terry*, 59 Ga. 555 (1877), pp. 556, 557. Other cases in which the southern judiciary based its decision to leave a child with a third party at least in part on a parental agreement to transfer custody include *Smith v. Bragg*, 68 Ga. 650 (1882); *Fullilove v. Banks*, 62 Miss. 11 (1884); *Townsend v. Warren*, 99 Ga. 105 (1896); *Anderson v. Young*, 54 S.C. 388 (1898); and *State v. Deaton*, 52 S.W. (Tex. 1899).

64. For a discussion of these matters, see Mnookin, "Child-Custody Adjudication," p. 265.

65. *State v. Grisby*, 38 Ark. 406 (1882), pp. 407, 409, 410. See also Succession of LeBlanc, 37 La. An. 546 (1885), in which the court denied a mother's custodial claim on the grounds that her cohabitation with a man after her husband's death posed a threat to the morals of her two sons; and *Brinster v. Compton*, 68 Ala. 299 (1880), in which the court refused custody to a father on the grounds that he had abandoned his two sons.

66. Platt, *Child Savers*; Hawes, *Children in Urban Society*; Zuckerman, "Children's Rights," pp. 382–83; Pleck, *Domestic Tyranny*, pp. 69–87; Gordon, *Heroes of Their Own Lives*, pp. 27–58.

67. Wisner, *Social Welfare in the South*, pp. 105–6; Woodward, *Origins of the New South*, pp. 400–406, 416–20.

68. Ga., *Code* (1861), secs. 1744, 1746, p. 346. See also Ark., *Statutes* (Gantt, 1874), secs. 3036, 3038, p. 577.

69. Sydnor, *Development of Southern Sectionalism*, pp. 93–94; Ely, "Poor Laws of the Antebellum South," pp. 865–67; Eaton, *Growth of Southern Civilization*, pp. 288–89; Wisner, *Social Welfare in the South*, pp. 118–23; Rabinowitz, *Race Relations in the Urban South*, pp. 128–29, 143–48. See also Tenn., *Code* (1896), ch. 4352, p. 1084.

70. Rothman, *Discovery of the Asylum*, chap. 9; Thurston, *Dependent Child*, chap. 5.

71. Tenn., *Code* (1896), art. 4346, p. 1083.

72. *Hunter v. Dowdy*, 100 Ga. 644 (1897), p. 645.

73. *State v. Kilvington*, 100 Tenn. 227 (1898), pp. 229, 230.

74. Ibid., pp. 233, 234, 235, 236.

75. On the postwar apprenticeship of black children, consult Scott, "Battle over the Child"; Kolchin, *First Freedom*, pp. 63–64; Litwack, *Been in the Storm So Long*, p. 366; and Myers, "Freedman and the Law," pp. 62–63.

76. S.C., *Statutes at Large* (1873–75), 13:271. See also Ala., *Revised Code* (Walker 1867), sec. 1454, p. 347.

77. Fields, *Slavery and Freedom*, pp. 140–41; Scott, "Battle over the Child," p. 203.

78. Quoted in Burton, *In My Father's House*, p. 273. See also Berlin et al., *Destruction of Slavery*, pp. 314–17.

79. Foner, *Reconstruction*, p. 201; Bynum, "On the Lowest Rung," p. 43; Fuke, "Planters, Apprenticeship, and Forced Labor"; Fields, *Slavery and Freedom*, pp. 153–

56; Litwack, *Been in the Storm So Long*, pp. 191, 237–38; Kolchin, *First Freedom*, pp. 64–67. For other discussions of black attempts to claim custodial rights in the postwar South, see Gutman, *Black Family*, pp. 402–12; Reidy, *From Slavery to Agrarian Capitalism*, pp. 154–55; and Frankel, "Federal and State Policy in Mississippi," pp. 10–11.

80. *Comas v. Reddish*, 35 Ga. 236 (1866), pp. 237–38. Other appellate cases in which black parents regained custody of their offspring after they had been subjected to public apprenticeships include *Adams v. Adams*, 36 Ga. 236 (1867); *Adams v. McKay*, 36 Ga. 440 (1867); *Hatcher v. Cutts*, 42 Ga. 616 (1871); *Mitchell v. McElvin*, 45 Ga. 558 (1872); and *Mitchell v. Mitchell*, 67 N.C. 307 (1872). See *Lowry v. Holden*, 41 Miss. 410 (1867) for a case in which the parents failed to recover custody.

81. *Miller v. Wallace*, 76 Ga. 479 (1886), p. 487; *Barela v. Roberts*, 34 Tex. 554 (1871), p. 557. For other postwar discussions of father's custody rights in disputes with nonparents, see *McKinney v. Noble*, 38 Tex. 195 (1873); *Ely v. Gammel*, 52 Ala. 584 (1875); *McDowell v. Bonner*, 62 Miss. 278 (1884); and *Stirman v. Turner*, 16 S.W. 787 (Tex. 1890).

82. *Moore v. Christian*, 56 Miss. 408 (1879). For other postwar cases involving third parties in which mothers received custody, see *Payne v. Payne*, 39 Ga. 174 (1869); *Thompson v. Thompson*, 72 N.C. 32 (1875); *Beard v. Dean*, 64 Ga. 258 (1879); *Ashby v. Page*, 106 N.C. 328 (1890); and *Prieto v. St. Alphonsus Convent of Mercy*, 52 La. An. 631 (1900).

83. Ark., *Statutes* (1874), sec. 3035, p. 577; Ga., *Code* (1861), sec. 1754, p. 348; Miss., *Revised Code* (Campbell 1880), sec. 2099, p. 575; N.C., *Code* (1883), vol. 1, sec. 1565, pp. 609–10. For judicial discussions of a mother's rights as natural guardian, see *Keene v. Guier*, 27 La. An. 232 (1875); *Hood v. Perry*, 73 Ga. 319 (1884); and *Byrom v. Gunn*, 102 Ga. 565 (1897).

84. *Latham v. Ellis*, 116 N.C. 30 (1895), pp. 33–34; *Miller v. Wallace*, 76 Ga. 479 (1886), p. 487. See also *Franklin v. Carswell*, 103 Ga. 553 (1897); *Casanover v. Massengale*, 54 S.W. 317 (Tex. 1899); *Hibbette v. Baines*, 78 Miss. 695 (1900); and *State v. Deaton*, 54 S.W. 901 (Tex. 1900) for other postwar decisions supporting the rights of parents to recover custody after a voluntary transfer.

85. Grossberg, "Law and the Family," p. 659.

86. *Gibbs v. Brown*, 68 Ga. 803 (1882), pp. 804–5.

87. On these developments for nineteenth-century America generally, see Zainaldin, "Modern American Family Law," pp. 1046, 1052–84.

88. Grossberg, "Law and the Family," pp. 320–21; Presser, "American Law of Adoption," pp. 470–89; Zainaldin, "Modern American Family Law," pp. 1083–86.

89. N.C., *Revisal of the Public Statutes* (Battle 1873), ch. 1, pp. 72–73; Ark., *Digest* (1894), secs. 1142–47, p. 436; Fla., *Revised Statutes* (1892), secs. 1536–41, pp. 520–21; Va., *Supplement to the Code* (Polland 1898), sec. 2614, p. 277; S.C., *Revised Statutes* (1894), vol. 1, sec. 2204, p. 766. See also Long, "Adoption in South Carolina"; and Note, "Adoption in Virginia."

90. This finding is based on an extensive examination of published collections of statutes passed in these states during the nineteenth century. See also Bugea, "Adoption in Louisiana," p. 3; Wadlington, "Adoption in Louisiana," pp. 203–5; Merlin, "Tennessee Law of Adoption," p. 629 n. 23; and Sims, "Adoption by Estoppel," pp. 162–64.

Interestingly enough, when Louisiana and Texas passed new adoption laws in the twentieth century implementing judicial supervision they also included provisions that expressly prohibited interracial adoption. Texas did so in 1907 and Louisiana in 1948. No other southern state banned interracial adoption by statute. Few courts, however, in any southern or northern state before 1965 approved adoptions between whites and blacks. See La., *Revised Statutes* (West 1950), vol. 1, sec. 422, p. 472; and Tex., *Revised Civil Statutes* (1912) art. 8, p. 4.

On interracial adoption and the law, see Vernier, *American Family Laws* 4:281–92; Greenberg, *Race Relations and American Law*, pp. 351–53; Cohen, *Race, Creed, and Color*, pp. 1–4; Grossman, "Child of a Different Color"; and Dorsey, "Race in Adoption and Custody Proceedings."

91. *Succession of Forstall*, 25 La. An. 430 (1873), p. 431.

92. *Taylor v. Deseve*, 81 Tex. 246 (1891), p. 249. See Sims, "Adoption By Estoppel," p. 163.

93. *Woodward v. Woodward*, 87 Tenn. 644 (1889), pp. 657, 659. In an earlier case, the Tennessee Supreme Court contended that even when a person did not formally adopt a child, and stood merely in loco parentis to the child, this person could sometimes gain the right to the custody and services of the child. Hence when a husband received his wife's daughter by a previous marriage into his own home, he became responsible for the maintenance and education of the girl, and assumed the corresponding right to the service and control of the child. See *Maguinay v. Saudek*, 37 Tenn. 146 (1857).

94. *Tilley v. Harrison*, 91 Ala. 295 (1891), p. 297. See also *Cofer v. Scroggins*, 98 Ala. 342 (1892–93).

95. *Succession of Haley*, 49 La. An. 709 (1897), p. 714. This case reached the Louisiana Supreme Court again in 1898. At this point, it appeared that the boy had never been formally adopted. Yet the state tribunal reversed the lower court's appointment of the natural mother as tutrix of the child on the grounds that she was unfit. In the supreme court's words, "It is our duty to look after the good of the child, rather than the wishes or feelings of the mother." See *Succession of Haley*, 50 La. An. 840 (1898), p. 845.

96. *Woodruff v. Conley*, 50 Ala. 504 (1874), pp. 305, 306.

97. *Legate v. Legate*, 29 S.W. 212 (Tex. 1895), pp. 213, 214. See also *Legate v. Legate*, 87 Tex. 248 (1894).

98. *Baskette v. Streight*, 106 Tenn. 549 (1901), pp. 555, 556, 557. Tennessee law allowed for a joint application by husband and wife for the adoption of a child, but in this case the Streights did not join in the proceedings.

99. Grossberg, *Governing the Hearth*, p. 275.

100. *Morris v. Dooley*, 59 Ark. 483 (1894), p. 486. Justice Riddick dissented from this opinion, contending that the statute did not expressly require the residence of the child to be named in the adoption declaration.

101. *Russell v. Russell*, 84 Ala. 48 (1888), p. 52.

102. *Beaver v. Crump*, 76 Miss. 34 (1898), p. 58. See McFarlane, "Mississippi Law on Adoptions," pp. 240, 242.

103. On this point in general, see Grossberg, *Governing the Hearth*, p. 276.

104. *Abney v. DeLoach*, 84 Ala. 393 (1888), pp. 395, 399, 402.

105. *Ortiz v. DeBenavides*, 61 Tex. 60 (1884); *Succession of Vollmer*, 40 La. An.

593 (1888); *Moore v. Bryant*, 10 Tex. Civ. App. 131 (1895); *Bland v. Gollaher*, 48 S.W. 320 (Tenn. 1898); *Crocker v. Balch*, 104 Tenn. 6 (1900). See also Sims, "Adoption by Estoppel," pp. 164–65; and Merlin, "Tennessee Law of Adoption," p. 637.

106. *Succession of Hosser*, 37 La. An. 839 (1885), p. 842. See also *Succession of Teller*, 49 La. An. 281 (1897); *Balch v. Johnson*, 106 Tenn. 249 (1901); and *White v. Holman*, 25 Tex. Civ. App. 152 (1901).

107. *Pace v. Klink*, 51 Ga. 220 (1874).

108. *Succession of Hosser*, 37 La. An. 839 (1885), p. 840.

109. *Eckford v. Knox*, 67 Tex. 200 (1886).

110. *Helms v. Elliott*, 89 Tenn. 446 (1890), pp. 449, 447, 449–50. In this regard, adoption and legitimation had very different effects. While by adoption a child gained only the right to succeed to the estate of the adopting parent, by legitimation the child acquire the right to inherit from the parent's next of kin as well. See *McKamie v. Baskerville*, 86 Tenn. 459 (1887); and *Murphy v. Portrum*, 95 Tenn. 605 (1895).

111. Grossberg, *Governing the Hearth*, p. 278; *Murphy v. Portrum*, 95 Tenn. 605 (1895), p. 610. See also *Succession of Unforsake*, 48 La. An. 546 (1896). In the absence of explicit legislation prohibiting adopted children from claiming the estates of their natural parents, other courts outside the South also granted them that right. The point here, though, is that such legislation did not exist in any southern state, while it did exist in the North. Other discussions of the inheritance rights of adopted children in the South include Merlin, "Tennessee Law of Adoption," pp. 639–40; Snellings, "Civil Effects of Adoption"; and Hubert, "Rights of the Descendants," p. 434 n. 29.

112. Simon Obermeyer, "The Effect of the Law of Adoption Upon Rights of Inheritance," *Southern Law Review*, n.s., 1 (April 1875): 79, 75.

113. Keller, *Affairs of State*, p. 464.

CHAPTER SIX

1. Faulkner, *Absalom, Absalom!*, pp. 261, 366.

2. The most recent round of exchanges in the long and venerable controversy over the relationship between the Old and New South involves Ayers, *Promise of the New South*, and Rabinowitz, "Origins of a Poststructural New South." For an earlier assessment of this issue, see Degler, *Place Over Time*, pp. 113–26.

3. On the growing importance of contract in the development of postbellum labor law, see Stanley, "Conjugal Bonds and Wage Labor."

4. Roark, *Masters without Slaves*, pp. 94–108; Litwack, *Been in the Storm So Long*, p. 265; Wood, *Black Scare*, pp. 143–44. For an insightful analysis of how Mark Twain's *Pudd'nhead Wilson* addresses the growing concerns of the late nineteenth century with racial purity, see Gillman, "'Sure Identifiers.'"

5. Quoted in Litwack, *Been in the Storm So Long*, p. 265.

6. Wood, *Black Scare*, pp. 53–79, 148–52; Fredrickson, *Black Image in the White Mind*, pp. 171–93; Baker, *Affairs of Party*, pp. 252–53.

7. Palmer, "Miscegenation," p. 117; Avins, "Anti-Miscegenation Laws," p. 1230. See also Pittman, "Fourteenth Amendment."

8. Grossberg, *Governing the Hearth*, p. 136; Avins, "Anti-Miscegenation Laws," p. 1227; Litwack, *Been in the Storm So Long*, p. 267.

9. Abraham Galloway quoted in ibid., p. 266; Freedmen's Bureau officer quoted in Williamson, *After Slavery*, p. 295.

10. Williamson, *New People*, pp. 88–91, argues that miscegenation decreased significantly after emancipation, whereas Berry and Blassingame, *Long Memory*, pp. 120–21, contend that miscegenation did not decrease, "it simply changed in character." On southern white fears regarding miscegenation during Reconstruction, see Wood, *Black Scare*, pp. 150–51.

11. Palmer, "Miscegenation," pp. 102–5; Wharton, *Negro in Mississippi*, p. 150; Kolchin, *First Freedom*, pp. 170–71. Blacks also sought to make white fathers responsible for the offspring of their cohabitation with African American women, but bastardy laws passed during Reconstruction were repealed following the takeover by the Redeemers. See D'Emilio and Freedman, *Intimate Matters*, pp. 106–7.

12. Williamson, *After Slavery*, p. 297; Blassingame, *Black New Orleans*, pp. 202–3.

13. Ibid., p. 203; Wharton, *Negro in Mississippi*, p. 228; Kolchin, *First Freedom*, p. 62. For a fascinating glimpse of sexual relations between African American men and white women in the Civil War South, see Hodes, "Wartime Dialogues on Illicit Sex," pp. 230–42.

14. Williamson, *New People*, pp. 91–92; Stephenson, *Race Distinctions*, p. 79.

15. Ala., *Revised Code* (Walker 1867), p. 38 (Constitution of 1865, art. 4, sec. 31); Miss., *Session Laws* (1865), ch. 4, sec. 3, p. 82. See also Wharton, *Negro in Mississippi*, p. 227.

16. Berry, "Judging Morality," p. 839.

17. Quoted in Kolchin, *First Freedom*, p. 61.

18. Quoted in Tindall, *South Carolina Negroes*, p. 298.

19. Arkansas, Florida, Louisiana, Mississippi, and South Carolina dispensed with the ban for varying periods of time during Reconstruction, but all five states reintroduced stringent prohibitions by the end of the nineteenth century. See Ark., *Digest of the Statutes* (Gantt 1874), in which the 1838 statute declaring interracial marriages illegal and void does not appear; and *Digest of the Statutes* (Mansfield 1884), sec. 4593, p. 911, which reaffirms the 1838 act. Fla., *Digest of Statute Law* (Bush 1872), p. 578 n. q notes that the "various provisions of the statutes in relation to marriages between white and colored persons are omitted out of deference to the opinion of those who think that they are opposed to our Constitution and to the legislation of Congress." New prohibitory legislation appeared, however, in *Digest of Laws* (McClellan 1881), ch. 59, sec. 13, p. 376.

In addition, Louisiana was without a statutory ban on interracial marriages from 1870 to 1894, and Mississippi lacked such a ban between 1870 and 1880. For Louisiana, see Act 54 of 1894 in *Revised Civil Code* (Merrick 1900), title 4, ch. 2, art. 94, p. 23; and Dagget, "Legal Aspect of Amalgamation in Louisiana," in *Legal Essays on Family Law*, p. 15. For Mississippi, see *Revised Code* (Campbell 1880), ch. 1147, p. 335; and Wharton, *Negro in Mississippi*, pp. 228–29.

Radical Republicans in South Carolina repealed the prohibition against intermarriage after they assumed power in 1868, but Redeemers enacted new legal sanctions in 1879. See act of 1879 in S.C., *Revised Statutes* (Breazeale 1894), vol. 1, ch. 2163, p. 753; Williamson, *After Slavery*, p. 297; and Tindall, *South Carolina Negroes*, pp. 296–97.

20. "The Negro Problem," *De Bow's Review* 38 (March 1868): 253, 252; "Progress of Amalgamation," *De Bow's Review* 38 (August 1868): 600.

21. The six states besides Alabama that prohibited intermarriage by constitutional provision were Florida, Georgia, Mississippi, North Carolina, South Carolina, and

Tennessee. See Fla., *Revised Statutes* (Blount, Cooper, and Massey 1892), p. 69 (Constitution of 1885, art. 16, sec. 24); Ga. *Code* (Clark, Cobb, and Irwin 1867), p. 983 (Constitution of 1865, art. 5, sec. 1, par. 9); Miss., *Code* (Whitfield, Catchings, and Hardy 1906), p. 106 (Constitution of 1890, sec. 263); N.C., *Code* (Dortch, Manning, Henderson 1883), 2:723 (Constitution of 1868, art. 14, sec. 8, 1875 provision); S.C., *Code* (Bethea 1912), 2:613–14 (Constitution of 1895, art. 3, sec. 33); and Tenn., *Compilation of the Statute Laws* (Thompson and Steger 1873), 1:118 (Constitution of 1870, art. 11, sec. 14).

22. Consult the following for details of this late-nineteenth-century legislation in the South: Ala., *Revised Code* (1867), secs. 3602–3, p. 690. Ark., *Digest* (1884), sec. 4593, p. 911; sec. 4601, p. 912; sec. 4617, p. 914. Fla., *Digest* (1881), ch. 59, sec. 13, p. 376; ch. 149, secs. 8–11, p. 753. Ga., *Code* (1867), sec. 1707, p. 344; sec. 4483, p. 881; sec. 4487, p. 882. La., *Revised Civil Code* (1900), title 4, ch. 2, art. 94, p. 23. Miss., *Revised Code* (1880), sec. 1147, p. 335. N.C., *Code* (1883), vol. 1, secs. 1084–85, pp. 437–38; sec. 1284, pp. 513–14. S.C., *Revised Statutes* (1894), vol. 1, sec. 2163, p. 753. Tenn., *Compilation* (1873), vol. 1, secs. 2437a–b, p. 1097; secs. 2445–47, p. 1098. Tex., *Digest of the Laws* (Paschal 1866), art. 2016, p. 429; art. 2026, p. 430; art. 4670, p. 783. Va., *Code* (Munford 1873), ch. 192, secs. 8–9, p. 1208. Mary Frances Berry, working with a summary of antimiscegenation legislation rather than the codes themselves, has identified Alabama and Georgia as the only two states that made interracial, nonmarital sex a separate crime. See Berry, "Judging Morality," p. 839.

23. Grossberg, "Law and the Family," pp. 464–65; Fredrickson, *White Supremacy*, p. 130; Stephenson, *Race Distinctions*, pp. 81–83; Applebaum, "Miscegenation Statutes," p. 50 n. 10. In addition, Applebaum notes that Washington in 1867 and New Mexico in 1886 repealed their statutes prohibiting interracial marriages.

24. See table 5 in the appendix. Only one of the appellate cases pertained to the prosecution of an official who solemnized a mixed marriage. See *Burns v. State*, 48 Ala. 195 (1872). Nearly all of these appeals reached the state supreme courts as the result of convictions handed down at the lower level. Two cases dealt with motions to quash indictments: *Robeson v. State*, 50 Tenn. 266 (1871); and *State v. Bell*, 66 Tenn. 9 (1872). In the first decision, the Tennessee court contended that an indictment charging illegal cohabitation between a white woman and black man had been improperly drawn up, and the court ordered it quashed. In the second opinion, members of the Tennessee bench overturned a lower court decision to quash the indictment of a white man and black woman.

Besides these two cases, *State v. Reinhardt*, 63 N.C. 547 (1869); and *State v. Ross*, 76 N.C. 242 (1877) concerned petitions by the state to overturn acquittals. In these appeals, marriages between a black man and white woman were at issue. In *State v. Reinhardt*, the North Carolina Supreme Court reversed the lower court verdict of not guilty, and in *State v. Ross* the court upheld the acquittal. Aside from these four cases, all of the postwar miscegenation cases in southern high courts involved appeals from convictions.

25. See table 6 in the appendix.

26. See, for example, *Linton v. State*, 88 Ala. 216 (1889); *Bell v. State*, 33 Tex. Cr. R. 163 (1894); and *Frasher v. State*, 3 Tex. App. 263 (1877).

27. *Moore v. State*, 7 Tex. App. 608 (1880), pp. 609–10; *McPherson v. Commonwealth*, 69 Va. 939 (1877), p. 940. Besides *Moore v. State*, serious problems existed

with the evidence regarding the racial identities of the parties in *Jones v. Common-wealth*, 79 Va. 213 (1884) and *Jones v. Commonwealth*, 80 Va. 538 (1885). For other reversals, see *Ellis v. State*, 42 Ala. 525 (1868) and *Frasher v. State*, 3 Tex. App. 263 (1877). In *Ellis v. State*, a new trial was ordered because the jury had not imposed a harsh enough punishment on the black male and white female convicted of inter-racial adultery, a punishment required by the state's antimiscegenation statute. Such an outcome hardly reflected tolerance for this form of race mixing.

28. *Lonas v. State*, 50 Tenn. 287 (1871), pp. 310–11.

29. *State v. Hairston*, 63 N.C. 451 (1869), pp. 452, 453. The North Carolina court upheld this decision in *State v. Reinhardt*, 63 N.C. 547 (1869).

30. Grossberg, "Law and the Family," pp. 448, 455–56; Keller, *Affairs of State*, pp. 149–50; 451–52.

31. *Burns v. State*, 48 Ala. 195 (1872), p. 197; Grossberg, "Law and the Family," pp. 462–63.

32. *Burns v. State*, 48 Ala. 195 (1872), p. 197. For a view that took exception to the Burns decision before it was overturned in 1877, see D. D. Shelby, "The Thirteenth and Fourteenth Amendments," *Southern Law Review* 3 (July 1874): 524–32.

The Alabama Supreme Court had outlawed interracial marriages before the Repub-licans took over. See *Ellis v. State*, 42 Ala. 525 (1868). In *Ford v. State*, 53 Ala. 150 (1875), the court upheld the legality of the state's statute punishing whites and blacks who cohabited, arguing that the Burns decision covered only the unconstitutionality of laws prohibiting interracial marriage.

33. *Green v. State*, 58 Ala. 190 (1877), p. 192.

34. Ibid., p. 195.

35. On Bishop's contribution to American marriage law, see Grossberg, "Guard-ing the Altar," pp. 201, 204. Other nineteenth-century legal commentators who em-phasized the noncontractual nature of marriage include Schouler, *Law of Domestic Relations*, pp. 22–24; and Tyler, *Law of Infancy*, pp. 805–9.

36. *Green v. State*, 58 Ala. 190 (1877), p. 194; Stanley, "Conjugal Bonds and Wage Labor," pp. 477, 480–81.

37. *Frasher v. State*, 3 Tex. App. 263 (1877), pp. 276, 277. Despite this harsh and far-reaching opinion, Frasher escaped a four-year term in the penitentiary (at least temporarily) because the appellate judges found that the lower court had erred in its instructions to the jury, making it necessary to grant the defendant a new trial.

The constitutionality of the state's antimiscegenation statute was affirmed in *François v. State*, 9 Tex. App. 144 (1880). The legislature, however, in 1879 extended criminal penalties to offenders of both races. See Tex., *Revised Penal Code* (1879), art. 326, p. 44. Other cases advancing the position that marriage was more than a civil contract and thus subject to state regulation include *Lonas v. State*, 50 Tenn. 287 (1871); and *Dodson v. State*, 61 Ark. 57 (1895). As Mary Frances Berry points out, however, in an 1876 bigamy case involving whites, the Alabama Supreme Court refers repeatedly to marriage as a contract. See Berry, "Judging Morality," p. 840; and *Beggs v. State*, 55 Ala. 108 (1876).

38. Michael Grossberg discusses the development of this trend in both northern and southern courts in "Guarding the Altar," pp. 206–26. Berry evidently disagrees that the courts placed restrictions on interracial marriage within the broader category of state efforts to protect public health by monitoring matrimony more closely. Ac-

cording to her, this line of thinking would have made little sense because "some of the persons convicted of sexual offenses already had children" and "there was no evidence that they were unhealthy." See Berry, "Judging Morality," pp. 838–39 n. 11.

Berry seems to have missed the point here. On an issue as volatile as interracial marriage, racial ideology rather than empirical evidence dictated the court's stance. Southern judges in the late nineteenth century commonly justified the ban on mixed marriages based on the belief that such unions posed a threat to public health. For a striking example of pseudoscientific thinking clearly influenced by this sort of racial outlook, see *Scott v. State*, 39 Ga. 321 (1869), discussed in the text. See also *Kinney v. Commonwealth*, 71 Va. 858 (1878), p. 869, where the Virginia appellate court insisted that "the moral and physical development of both races" made it necessary to enforce the legal prohibitions against intermarriage.

39. A more paternalistic strain of thinking viewed blacks as inferior but believed that individuals were capable of uplifting themselves. On developments in late-nineteenth-century thinking about race, consult Mencke, *Mulattoes and Race Mixture*, pp. 99–123; Fredrickson, *Black Image in the White Mind*, pp. 198–255; Williamson, *Crucible of Race*, pp. 85–139; and Takaki, *Iron Cages*, pp. 194–214.

40. *Scott v. State*, 39 Ga. 321 (1869), p. 323. For an excellent example of how this growing pseudoscientific thinking found its way into divorce cases as well, see Justice William Blount Rodman's dissent in *Long v. Long*, 77 N.C. 287 (1877), discussed in Bynum, "Reshaping the Bonds of Womanhood," p. 325.

41. *Pace and Cox v. State*, 69 Ala. 231 (1881), p. 232. The penalty for conviction of interracial fornication or adultery was imprisonment for two to seven years, whereas those convicted of illicit intercourse with a person of the same race were subject upon the first offense to a minimum fine of one hundred dollars and no more than six months in jail. See Ala., *Revised Code* (1867), sec. 3598, p. 689, and sec. 3602, p. 690. The U.S. Supreme Court upheld the constitutionality of the state's antimiscegenation statute in *Pace v. Alabama*, 106 U.S. 583 (1883).

42. Discussions of miscegenation cases before state supreme court cases outside the South can be found in Applebaum, "Miscegenation Statutes," pp. 56–62; Grossberg, "Law and the Family," pp. 458–61; and Keller, *Affairs of State*, pp. 150, 451–52. See also Phillips, "Miscegenation," pp. 135–39; and Schuhmann, "Miscegenation," pp. 72–78.

43. *Hoover v. State*, 59 Ala. 57 (1877); *Kinney v. Commonwealth*, 71 Va. 858 (1878). See also *Carter v. Montgomery*, 2 Tenn. Ch. 216 (1875), in which the Tennessee court held that an interracial marriage was void even though the statute simply prohibited the marriage and contained no nullifying clause. For the relevant statute, consult Tenn., *Compilation* (1873), vol. 1, sec. 2437a, p. 1097.

In Mississippi, the temporary lifting of the ban on intermarriage allowed a white man and black woman to legalize their union. Although the couple commenced their cohabitation at a time when marriage between them was prohibited, the court decided in 1873 that the constitution in force removed all "former impediments to marriage between blacks and whites," and thus their cohabitation as husband and wife at the time of the constitution's adoption consummated their marriage. Of course, the ban on intermarriages was reinstituted in 1880. See *Dickerson v. Brown*, 49 Miss. 357 (1873); and Wharton, *Negro in Mississippi*, pp. 150, 228–29.

Although marriages between blacks and whites were void in Georgia, the court there maintained that a husband could not prevent his wife from suing him for alimony by raising questions about her racial background and thus challenging the legality of the marriage. See *Dillon v. Dillon*, 60 Ga. 204 (1878).

44. N.C., *Code* (1883), vol. 1, sec. 1284, pp. 513–14; *Hopkins v. Bowers*, 111 N.C. 175 (1892). Florida had a similar statute. See Fla., *Digest* (1881), ch. 149, sec. 9, p. 753.

45. *Greenhow v. James' Ex'r*, 80 Va. 636 (1885), pp. 648–49.

46. *Smith v. DuBose*, 78 Ga. 413 (1887), p. 442; Alexander, *Ambiguous Lives*, pp. 185–88.

47. Berry, "Judging Morality," pp. 843 n. 26. Berry lists seven cases in which the offspring of interracial couples lost inheritance disputes, but she fails to include *Hopkins v. Bowers*, 111 N.C. 175 (1892), discussed above.

48. Miss., *Revised Code* (1880), sec. 1147, p. 335; Tex., *Revised Penal Code* (1879), art. 326, p. 44; Va., *Code* (Burks, Staples, and Riely 1887), sec. 3783, pp. 898–99.

49. *State v. Kennedy*, 76 N.C. 251 (1877), p. 253. This decision was affirmed in *Kinney v. Commonwealth*, 71 Va. 858 (1878); and *Greenhow v. James' Ex'r*, 80 Va. 636 (1885). See also *Dupre v. Boulard*, 10 La. An. 411 (1855), in which the Louisiana Supreme Court refused to recognize the validity of an interracial marriage when the parties went to France to contract matrimony and then returned to Louisiana.

50. *State v. Bell*, 66 Tenn. 9 (1872), pp. 10–11.

51. *State v. Ross*, 76 N.C. 242 (1877), pp. 244, 246, 247. In this case, the woman had been a resident of North Carolina before moving to South Carolina to live with her husband. The North Carolina Supreme Court, however, noted that she had gone to South Carolina with no intention of returning; thus she did not leave North Carolina for the purpose of evading its laws against miscegenation.

For a similar case, see *Succession of Caballero*, 24 La. Ann. 573 (1872), in which the Louisiana Supreme Court granted the validity of a marriage contracted by a white man and black woman who had been living together in Louisiana, but then moved to Spain and married there. They and their children later returned to Louisiana, where the parents died. The court ruled that the marriage in Spain legitimated the children, although such a marriage was not allowed in Louisiana, and thus made the offspring lawful heirs.

In both cases, the courts made a clear distinction between those marriages in which the couple left the state for the purpose of evading the laws and those marriages in which the couple moved with no intention of returning. It should also be pointed out that dissenting opinions were issued in these two decisions. The dissenting judges sided with the Tennessee Supreme Court in arguing that the policy of the state and the welfare of its citizens were "considerations paramount to the courtesy due to laws of other countries or contracts made in conformity therewith." Ibid., pp. 581–88 (quotation on p. 582); *State v. Ross*, 76 N.C. 242 (1877), pp. 248–50.

For further discussion of these issues, see Stephenson, *Race Distinctions*, pp. 92–95; Hamilton, "Miscegenetic Marriages," p. 124; and Note, "Intermarriage with Negroes—A Survey of State Statutes," *Virginia Law Register*, n.s., 13 (September 1927): 316–17.

52. In 1967, the U.S. Supreme Court declared Virginia's antimiscegenation statute unconstitutional in *Loving v. Virginia*, 388 U.S. 1 (1967). See Schuhmann, "Miscegenation," pp. 69–70, 76–78.

53. For amplification of the issues raised in the following discussion, see Wriggins, "Rape, Racism, and the Law"; Painter, " 'Social Equality,' Miscegenation, Labor, and Power"; Clinton, "Bloody Terrain"; Edwards, "Sexual Violence and the Politics of

Reconstruction"; Hodes, "Sexualization of Reconstruction Politics"; and Edwards, "Sexual Violence, Gender, Reconstruction, and the Extension of Patriarchy."

54. Quoted in Burton, *In My Father's House*, p. 227.

55. For punishments in states where rape was not a capital crime, see S.C., *Statutes At Large* (1873), 14:175 (Act of 1869) (ten years to life); Tenn., *Compilation* (1873), vol. 2, sec. 4611, p. 48 (ten to twenty-one years); and Tex., *Digest* (1866), art. 2190, p. 447 (five to fifteen years). See also *Wharton v. State*, 45 Tenn. 1 (1867).

56. Tenn., *Code* (Milliken and Vertrees 1884), sec. 5362, p. 1030. For similar statutes in other states, see Ala., *Code* (Keyes, Wood, and Roquemore 1877), sec. 4304, p. 912; Fla., *Digest* (1872), ch. 43, sec. 41, p. 217; Ga., *Code* (1867), sec. 4284, p. 841; Miss., *Revised Code* (1880), sec. 2942, p. 768; S.C., *Revised Statutes* (1894), vol. 2, sec. 114, p. 302; Tex. *Revised Statutes* (1887), art. 534, p. 73; and Va., *Code* (1887), sec. 3680, p. 881. In Arkansas, Louisiana, and North Carolina, all those convicted of rape faced execution. See Ark., *Digest* (1884), sec. 1570, p. 433; La., *Revised Statute Laws* (1870), sec. 787, p. 160; and N.C., *Code* (1883), vol. 1, sec. 1101, p. 444.

57. Identifiable rape cases in southern state supreme courts during the late nineteenth century involving a black man and white female that led to the imposition of the death penalty include *Witherby v. State*, 39 Ala. 702 (1866); *Berry v. State*, 87 Ga. 579 (1891); *State v. Johnson*, 67 N.C. 55 (1872); *Jones v. State*, 1 Tex. App. 87 (1876); *Wilson v. State*, 17 Tex. App. 525 (1885); *Johnson v. State*, 17 Tex. App. 565 (1885); *Bruce v. State*, 31 Tex. Cr. R. 590 (1893); and *Wilcox v. State*, 33 Tex. Cr. R. 392 (1894).

58. La., *Revised Statute Laws* (1870), sec. 792, p. 161; Fla., *Digest* (1872), ch. 43, sec. 42, p. 217. For penalties imposed in cases of assault with intent to rape in other southern states, see Ala., *Code* (1877), sec. 4314, p. 914 (two to twenty years); Ark., *Digest* (1884), sec. 1572, p. 433 (three to twenty-one years); Ga., *Code* (1867), sec. 4285 (one to twenty years); Miss., *Revised Code* (1880), sec. 2711, p. 728 (not more than ten years); N.C., *Code* (1883), vol. 1, sec. 1102, p. 444 (five to fifteen years); Tenn., *Code* (1884), sec. 5367, p. 1030 (ten to twenty-one years); Tex., *Revised Statutes* (1887), art. 503, p. 70 (two to seven years); and Va., *Code* (1887), sec. 3888, p. 916 (three to eighteen years).

59. *State v. Staton*, 88 N.C. 654 (1883), p. 655.

60. One of the cases included here—*Irving v. State*, 9 Tex. App. 66 (1880)—involves an African American male convicted of assault with intent to rape a female identified as "Mexican." The Texas Supreme Court reversed the conviction in this appeal. The postwar results are in striking contrast to the antebellum appeals by African American men in which the high courts reversed a significant majority of the convictions for rape or attempted rape of a white female. See chapter 2 in this volume.

61. There are another twenty-five cases from the late nineteenth century in which black men petitioned southern appellate courts to overturn convictions for rape or attempted rape, but in which the race of the female is unspecified or not easily identified. Fifteen of these appeals were successful.

62. *Anschicks v. State*, 6 Tex. App. 524 (1879) (white male indicted for rape of black girl of indeterminate age, probably around nine to eleven years old); *State v. Powell*, 106 N.C. 635 (white male indicted for assault with intent to commit rape on a fourteen-year-old black girl).

63. *Jones v. State*, 1 Tex. App. 87 (1876), pp. 88, 89. See also *Bruce v. State*, 31 Tex. Cr. R. 590 (1893), p. 593, where the Texas court commends "the presence of a womanhood outraged and wronged, but instinctively true to race and self."

64. *Johnson v. State*, 26 Tex. App. 399 (1888), 399, 402, 404. See also the description of a sexual assault of a white woman by a black male in *Wilcox v. State*, 32 Tex. Cr. R. 284 (1893). Although the black defendant was granted a new trial in this case, based on doubts about his age, the Texas Supreme Court upheld his subsequent conviction and death sentence in *Wilcox v. State*, 33 Tex. Cr. R. 392 (1894).

65. *Brown v. State*, 121 Ala. 9 (1899), pp. 11, 12. See also *Young v. State*, 65 Ga. 525 (1880).

66. *Thompson v. State*, 33 Tex. Cr. R. 472 (1894), pp. 475–76.

67. *Thompson v. State*, 122 Ala. 12 (1899), p. 15.

68. *Dawkins v. State*, 58 Ala. 376 (1877); *Irving v. State*, 9 Tex. App. 66 (1880); *Burney v. State*, 21 Tex. App. 565 (1886); *Porter v. State*, 33 Tex. Cr. R. 385 (1894); *Reddick v. State*, 35 Tex. Cr. R. 463 (1895); *Oxsheer v. State*, 38 Tex. Cr. R. 499 (1897).

69. *Wharton v. State*, 45 Tenn. 1 (1867), p. 7. See also *Gordon v. State*, 93 Ga. 531 (1893), in which an African American boy who was a few months shy of fourteen years old was released after being convicted for assault with intent to rape a ten-year-old white girl. As the Georgia high court pointed out (p. 533), according to English common law, "a boy under fourteen years of age cannot be convicted of rape" because he is presumed to be physically incapable of sexual intercourse.

70. For a discussion of the respective roles of the judge and jury in matters of evidence presented in rape trials, see *Griffin v. State*, 76 Ala. (1884).

71. *Green v. State*, 67 Miss. 356 (1889). See also *Gaskin v. State*, 105 Ga. 631 (1898); *House v. State*, 9 Tex. App. 53 (1880); *Johnson v. State*, 17 Tex. App. 565 (1885); and *Jones v. State*, 18 Tex. App. 485 (1885).

72. *Jackson v. State*, 91 Ga. 322 (1892), p. 325. See the discussion of this rule in Wriggins, "Rape, Racism, and the Law," pp. 111–12.

73. *Jackson v. State*, 91 Ga. 322 (1892), p. 330; *Dorsey v. State*, 108 Ga. 477 (1899), p. 480. See also *Darden v. State*, 97 Ga. (1896).

74. See, for example., *Carter v. State*, 35 Ga. 263 (1866); *Sharpe v. State*, 48 Ga. 16 (1873); *Stout v. State*, 22 Tex. App. 339 (1886); and *Cunningham v. Commonwealth*, 88 Va. 37 (1891).

75. *State v. Neely*, 74 N.C. 425 (1876), pp. 427, 428, 429. But see Justice Rodman's dissent, in which he objects to Pearson's assumption that "the prisoner is a brute, or so like a brute that it is safe to reason from one to the other" (p. 430).

76. *Maxey v. State*, 66 Ark. 523 (1899), p. 528.

77. *Barnett v. State*, 83 Ala. 40 (1887), p. 45. For other cases in which evidence regarding the white woman's lack of chastity did not persuade courts to overturn the rape convictions of black men, see *Young v. State*. 65 Ga. 525 (1880); and *Wilson v. State*, 17 Tex. App. 525 (1885).

78. *Favors v. State*, 20 Tex. App. 155 (1886), p. 159. On the continued perception of black women as sexually promiscuous after emancipation, see White, *Ar'n't I a Woman?*, pp. 164–65.

79. Clinton, "Bloody Terrain," pp. 328–29. See also Hodes, "Sexualization of Reconstruction Politics," p. 409.

80. Jones, *Labor of Love*, pp. 127–34, 149–50; Mann, "Slavery, Sharecropping, and Sexual Inequality," pp. 788–89 (servant quotation on p. 789).

81. Edwards, "Sexual Violence, Gender, Reconstruction, and the Extension of Patriarchy," pp. 242, 248. For appellate cases in which convictions for the attempted rape or rape of black females were upheld, see *Williams v. State*, 66 Ark. 264 (1899); *Rogers v.*

State, 1 Tex. App. 187 (1876); *Doyle v. State*, 5 Tex. App. 442 (1879); *Comer v. State*, 20 S.W. 547 (Tex. 1892); *McGee v. State*, 39 Tex. Cr. R. 190 (1898); and *Mings v. Commonwealth*, 85 Va. 638 (1889).

82. *State v. Powell*, 106 N.C. 635 (1890), p. 637. See also *Anschicks v. State*, 6 Tex. App. 524 (1879), p. 531, in which the prosecuting attorney declared, in his closing argument to the jury, that "the defendant, though his skin is white, his heart is blacker than the midnight of hell." Convicted in the lower court of raping a young black girl, the defendant successfully appealed his conviction on the grounds of jury misconduct.

83. Besides the evidence presented here, consult Wriggins, "Rape, Racism, and the Law," pp. 120–21.

84. *Gosha v. State*, 56 Ga. 36 (1876), p. 37.

85. *Williams v. State*, 66 Ark. 264 (1899), pp. 265, 266, 270. See also *Mings v. Commonwealth*, 85 Va. 638 (1889), p. 641, in which a man indicted for raping a sixteen-year-old black female was convicted of attempted rape, despite the testimony of the girl that the defendant "succeeded in accomplishing his purpose" against her will and that of a witness who heard outcries from the girl and observed the couple struggling on the ground.

86. Bynum, *Unruly Women*, pp. 109–10, 118; Edwards, "Sexual Violence, Gender, Reconstruction, and the Extension of Patriarchy," pp. 243–44. See also Bynum, "On the Lowest Rung."

87. *Boddie v. State*, 52 Ala. 395 (1875), p. 398. See also *State v. Long*, 93 N.C. 542 (1885).

88. Hodes, "Sexualization of Reconstruction Politics," pp. 410–11.

89. *Leoni v. State*, 44 Ala. 110 (1870), p. 113; *State v. Daniel*, 87 N.C. 507 (1882); *State v. Long*, 93 N.C. 542 (1885), p. 544.

90. *Benstine v. State*, 70 Tenn. 169 (1879), pp. 172–73.

91. *Shell v. State*, 38 S.W. 207 (Tex. 1896), p. 208. Other cases where the "bad character" of the woman played an important part in the reversal of convictions for rape and attempted rape include *Hollis v. State*, 27 Fla. 387 (1891); *Hunter v. State*, 29 Fla. 486 (1892); *State v. Murray*, 63 N.C. 31 (1868); *State v. Daniel*, 87 N.C. 507 (1882); *Titus v. State*, 66 Tenn. 132 (1874); and *Benstine v. State*, 70 Tenn. 169 (1879).

92. Tex., *Revised Penal Code*, 2d ed. (1889), art. 528, p. 178. For statutory rape laws in other states, see Ala., *Code* (Martin 1897), vol. 2, sec. 5447, p. 460 (under fourteen years); Ark., *Digest of the Statutes* (Sandels and Hill 1894), sec. 1865, p. 572 (under sixteen years); Fla., *Revised Statutes* (1892), sec. 2396, p. 777 (under ten years); Miss., *Revised Code* (1880), sec. 2942, p. 768 (under ten years); N.C., *Code* (1883), vol. 1, sec. 1101, p. 444 (under ten years); S.C., *Revised Statutes* (1894), vol. 2, sec. 115, p. 302 (under ten years); Tenn., *Annotated Code* (Shannon 1896), sec. 6456, p. 1593 (under twelve years); and Va., *Supplement to the Code* (Pollard 1898), sec. 3680, p. 369 (under fourteen years).

93. For examples of cases involving the prosecution of men for rape and attempted rape of a female child under the age of consent, see *Dawkins v. State*, 58 Ala. 376 (1877); *Gosha v. State*, 56 Ga. 36 (1876); *Williams v. State*, 47 Miss. 609 (1873); *State v. Smith*, 61 N.C. 302 (1867); *Comer v. State*, 20 S.W. 547 (Tex. 1892); and *Givens v. Commonwealth*, 70 Va. 830 (1878).

94. *Simmons v. State*, 99 Ga. 699 (1896), pp. 700–701; *Davis v. State*, 63 Ark. 470 (1897), p. 472. For other discussions of what constituted force in a case of rape, see

McQuirk v. State, 84 Ala. 435 (1882); *Hollis v. State*, 27 Fla. 386 (1891); *Rhea v. State*, 30 Tex. App. 483 (1891); and *Brown v. Commonwealth*, 82 Va. 653 (1886).

In order to convict a defendant on the charge of attempted rape, proof of both force and intent was necessary. As the North Carolina Supreme Court stated, "The evidence should show not only an assault, but that the defendant intended to gratify his passion on the person of the woman, and that he intended to do so, at all events, notwithstanding any resistance on her part." *State v. Massey*, 86 N.C. 658 (1882). But see *Dibrell v. State*, 3 Tex. App. 456 (1878), where the only violence used by the defendant involved pulling at the bedclothes of the woman. Although the assailant ran off when the woman awoke, the court held that this was sufficient evidence to sustain a conviction for attempted rape.

95. Tex., *Revised Statutes* (1887), art. 531, p. 73. For similar laws in other states, see Ala., *Code* (1877), secs. 4305, 4307, p. 913; Ark., *Digest* (1884), sec. 1573, p. 433; La., *Revised Laws*, 2d ed. (Voorhies 1884), sec. 787, p. 132; Miss., *Revised Code* (1880), sec. 2943, p. 768; N.C., *Code* (1883), vol. 1, secs. 1103–4, p. 445; and Tenn., *Code* (1884), secs. 5363–5464, p. 1030. The Arkansas, Louisiana, and Mississippi statutes did not cover the punishment of men who pretended to be the woman's husband.

96. *Mooney v. State*, 29 Tex. App. 257 (1890), p. 258. See also *King v. State*, 22 Tex. App. 650 (1887); *Ledbetter v. State*, 33 Tex. Cr. R. 400 (1894); *Franklin v. State*, 34 Tex. Cr. App. 203 (1895); *Payne v. State*, 38 Tex. Cr. R. 494 (1897); and *Ford v. State*, 41 Tex. Cr. R. 270 (1899).

97. *State v. Haines*, 51 La. An. 731 (1899), p. 732. On reform efforts outside the South to protect women from marital sexual assault during the late nineteenth century, see Pleck, *Domestic Tyranny*, pp. 92–98.

98. *State v. Duwell*, 106 N.C. 722 (1890), pp. 724, 723. But see the dissenting opinion of Chief Justice Merrimon, who argued that the husband could not be convicted of attempted rape, but rather was "chargeable with an assault upon his wife with a deadly weapon and with the intent to kill, and a like assault upon the negro" (p. 727).

99. *Kennon v. State*, 42 S.W. 376 (Tex. 1897), p. 378.

100. *Innis v. State*, 42 Ga. 473 (1870), p. 481. See also *Simmons v. State*, 99 Ga. (1896), p. 703, where the Georgia high court again quotes Lord Hale, asserting that "there is much greater danger that injustice may be done to the defendant in cases of this kind than there is in prosecutions of any other character."

101. *Compton v. State*, 13 Tex. App. 271 (1882), p. 275; *State v. Laurence*, 95 N.C. 659 (1886), p. 660. See also *Beggs v. State*, 55 Ala. 108 (1876) at 112, in which the Alabama Supreme Court in 1876 asserted that incest not only "contravenes the voice of nature" and "offends decency and morals" but also "degrades the family."

102. See table 7 in the appendix. There were actually thirty-six cases dealing with appeals from incest convictions, but one of them—*Newman v. State*, 69 Miss. 393 (1891)—involved an appeal on the part of both parties.

103. Compare Miss., *Revised Code* (Campbell, Johnston, and Lovering 1871), sec. 1762, p. 373 with *Revised Code* (Sharkey, Harris, and Ellett 1857), ch. 40, art. 8, p. 333. For Virginia and Georgia, see Va., *Code* (1873), title 31, ch. 104, sec. 9, p. 844; and Ga., *Code*, 4th ed. (Lester, Rowell, and Hill 1882), sec. 1700, p. 392. In contrast, England maintained tight restrictions on affinal unions, maintaining its ban against marriage with a deceased wife's sister until 1907. See Anderson, " 'Marriage with a Deceased Wife's Sister Bill' Controversy," pp. 67–68, 84–85.

104. Ark., *Digest* (1884), sec. 4592, p. 911; La., *Acts* (1900), p. 188. Although the

Arkansas Supreme Court upheld the ban on first-cousin marriages, and argued that intercourse between first cousins could also be punished as incest, the Louisiana high court struck down the first-cousin prohibition on a technicality. See *Nations v. State*, 64 Ark. 467 (1897); and *State v. Couvillion*, 117 La. 935 (1906).

105. Compare Ala., *Code* (Ormond, Bagby, and Goldthwaite 1852), sec. 1942, p. 375 with *Revised Code* (1867), sec. 2331, p. 481; and consult N.C., *Code* (1883), vol. 1, sec. 1811, p. 689. On the uncle-niece ban in Mississippi, contrast *Revised Code* (1871), sec. 1763, p. 373 with *Revised Code* (1880), sec. 1146, p. 335. On the prohibition against marrying one's grandparent, compare *Revised Code* (1880), ch. 1145, p. 335 with *Annotated Code* (Thompson, Dillard, and Campbell 1892), secs. 2857–58, p. 677.

106. Grossberg, "Guarding the Altar," pp. 214–17. See also Grossberg, *Governing the Hearth*, pp. 144–46. For the scientific debate over inbreeding in Victorian England, consult Anderson, "Cousin Marriage in Victorian England," pp. 291–96.

107. *State v. Fritts and Phillips*, 48 Ark. 66 (1886), pp. 68–69.

108. N.C., *Code* (1883), vol. 1, secs. 1060–61, p. 429. Apparently, the North Carolina statute was passed on the urging of the state supreme court, which in a case the year before had declared that an indictment for incest could not be maintained because the offense was not indictable at common law and there was no state statute making it a criminal offense. Following passage of the act, the state court held that the incest statute affected illegitimate as well as legitimate persons. See *State v. Keesler*, 78 N.C. 469 (1878); and *State v. Laurence*, 95 N.C. 659 (1886).

109. S.C., *Revised Statutes* (1894), vol. 2, sec. 258, pp. 349–50; Va., *Code* (1887), sec. 3786, p. 899. Other alterations in the criminal law of incest after the Civil War were relatively minor. In 1878 the Louisiana State Supreme Court overturned a conviction for incest under the 1817 law on the grounds that the statute did not provide a definition of what constituted the crime of incest. In response, the legislators passed a bill in 1884 that pronounced cohabitation and marriage within the forbidden degrees as incest. See *State v. Smith*, 30 La. An. 846 (1878); and *Revised Laws* (Wolff 1897), p. 189. The Louisiana Supreme Court, in *State v. Guiton*, 51 La. An. 155 (1898) and *State v. DeHart*, 109 La. 570 (1903), held that the 1884 definition of incest was legally sufficient, and it affirmed incest convictions under the new legislation. In Alabama, the minimum penalty for committing incest was reduced, from two years to one, but the maximum sentence remained at seven years. Finally, Florida raised the maximum punishment in 1868 from twelve months in jail to twenty years in the state pentitentiary. See Ala., *Code* (1877), sec. 4187, p. 894; and Fla., *Digest* (1872), ch. 48, sec. 7, p. 247.

110. In *Simon v. State*, 31 Tex. Cr. R. 186 (1892), Theodore Simon appealed a conviction for incestuous marriage with the daughter of his half-sister. The Texas Supreme Court upheld his conviction and he was sentenced to three years in the state penitentiary.

Unfortunately, appellate court opinions in these forty criminal cases provide little if any information on the social background of the legal parties. In only one instance is race mentioned: the uncle whose incest conviction is upheld in an 1898 Louisiana opinion and his niece are referred to as a "colored man and . . . a colored woman." See *State v. Guiton*, 51 La. An. 155 (1898), p. 159. There is also little indication of socioeconomic position in these cases. The only exceptions are five state supreme court decisions in late-nineteenth-century Texas that involved small-farm and farm-laborer households. See *McGrew v. State*, 13 Tex. App. 340 (1883); *Mercer v. State*, 17 Tex.

App. 452 (1885); *Johnson v. State*, 20 Tex. App. 609 (1886); *Clements v. State*, 34 Tex. Cr. R. 616 (1895); and *Waggoner v. State*, 35 Tex. Cr. R. 199 (1895).

111. *Smith v. State*, 108 Ala. 1 (1895), p. 3. Besides *Newman v. State*, 69 Miss. 393 (1891) (see note 117), there were only two appellate cases in the postwar South in which a woman was indicted for incest. *Burnett v. State*, 32 Tex. Cr. R. 86 (1893) stemmed from an indictment of the father and daughter for incest. But only the father was found guilty at the trial, so he was the only party in the appellate decision, which affirmed his conviction. In *State v. Fritts and Phillips*, 48 Ark. 66 (1886), both parties (first cousins) were indicted for incest, but the court quashed the indictment, a decision that was upheld by the Arkansas Supreme Court on appeal from the state. Two other late-nineteenth-century cases involved appeals by the state: *State v. Ratcliffe*, 61 Ark. 62 (1895); and *State v. Keesler*, 78 N.C. 469 (1878).

112. *Mercer v. State*, 17 Tex. App. 452 (1885), p. 464. For similar cases, see *Powers v. State*, 44 Ga. 209 (1871); *Raiford v. State*, 68 Ga. 672 (1882); *Schoenfeldt v. State*, 30 Tex. App. 695 (1892); and *Stewart v. State*, 35 Tex. Cr. R. 174 (1895). The Texas high court also made this point in *Alonzo v. State*, 15 Tex. App. 378 (1884), an adultery case: "While the criminal intent may exist in the mind of one of the parties to the physical act, there may be no such intent in the mind of the other party. One may be guilty, the other innocent, and yet the joint physical act necessary to constitute adultery may be complete."
A helpful discussion regarding prosecutions for incest when force was used, and whether incest was a joint offense, can be found in Blackburn, "Incest." I would like to thank Mary Block for bringing this article to my attention. Indictments of men for rape or attempted rape of their daughter or stepdaughter were not at all unusual in the late nineteenth century South. See, for example, *Smith v. State*, 47 Ala. 540 (1872); *Coates v. State*, 50 Ark. 330 (1887); *Rice v. State*, 35 Fla. 236 (1895); *State v. Parish*, 104 N.C. 679 (1889); *Lawson v. State*, 17 Tex. App. 292 (1884); and *Fry v. Commonwealth*, 82 Va. 334 (1886).

113. See table 8 in the appendix. These patterns of incestuous relationships closely resemble those found by Linda Gordon in the records of three child welfare agencies in Boston between 1880 and 1960. As she points out, the proportion of fathers involved in these incest cases makes it difficult to speak of a sociobiological taboo against incest. Instead, incest must be understood within the context of power and dependency relationships in families. See Gordon, *Heroes of Their Own Lives*, pp. 210–12.

114. *Johnson v. State*, 20 Tex. App. 609 (1886), p. 615. See also *Compton v. State*, 13 Tex. App. 271 (1882).

115. *Wilson v. State*, 100 Tenn. 596 (1898), p. 597. For another case in which strict constructionism played a major role in the reversal of an incest conviction, see *State v. Smith*, 30 La. An. 846 (1878).

116. *Owen v. State*, 89 Tenn. 698 (1891), p. 703.

117. *Newman v. State*, 69 Miss. 393 (1891).

118. *State v. Fritts and Phillips*, 48 Ark. 66 (1886); *Martin v. State*, 58 Ark. 3 (1893), p. 6. See also *State v. Ratcliffe*, 61 Ark. 62 (1895).

119. Flanigan, "Criminal Procedure in Slave Trials," pp. 549–50. See also Nash, "Fairness and Formalism," pp. 79–81; and Nash, "Texas Supreme Court and Trial Rights of Blacks," pp. 628–29.

120. See, for example, *Chancellor v. State*, 47 Miss. 278 (1872); and *State v. Keesler*, 78 N.C. 469 (1878).

121. Flanigan, "Criminal Procedure in Slave Trials," p. 549.

122. *Clark v. State*, 39 Tex. Cr. R. 179 (1898), p. 182; *McGrew v. State*, 13 Tex. App. 340 (1883), p. 343. For other cases dealing with proof of relationship, see *Simon v. State*, 31 Tex. Cr. R. 186 (1892); *Cummings v. State*, 36 Tex. Cr. R. 256 (1896); and *Elder v. State*, 123 Ala. 35 (1898).

123. *Burnett v. State*, 32 Tex. Cr. R. 86 (1893); *State v. Reynolds*, 48 S.C. 384 (1897); *Taylor v. State*, 110 Ga. 150 (1900).

124. *Compton v. State*, 13 Tex. App. 271 (1882); *State v. Reynolds*, 48 S.C. 384 (1896), p. 388. See also *Owen v. State*, 89 Tenn. 698 (1891); and *Stewart v. State*, 35 Tex. Cr. R. 174 (1895). On the the restriction of husband and wife testimony in Virginia, see S. S. P. Patteson, "Incompetency of Husband and Wife as Witnesses for or Against Each Other," *Virginia Law Journal* 11 (February 1887): 65–58.

125. See, for example, *Brown v. State*, 27 So. 869 (Fla. 1900); *Powers v. State*, 44 Ga. 209 (1871); *Jones v. State*, 23 Tex. App. 501 (1887); *Shelly v. State*, 95 Tenn. 152 (1895); and *Waggoner v. State*, 35 Tex. Cr. R. 199 (1895). For a discussion regarding corroboration of accomplice testimony in incest cases, see Blackburn, "Incest," pp. 395–97.

126. *Taylor v. State*, 110 Ga. 150 (1900), pp. 154, 157. For other discussions of corroborative evidence, see *Powers v. State*, 44 Ga. 209 (1871); *Mercer v. State*, 17 Tex. App. 452 (1885); *Sauls v. State*, 30 Tex. App. 496 (1891); *Schoenfeldt v. State*, 30 Tex. App. 695 (1892); *Clements v. State*, 34 Tex. Cr. R. 616 (1895); *Jackson v. State*, 40 S.W. 998 (1897); *Bales v. State*, 44 S.W. 517 (1898); *Kilpatrick v. State*, 39 Tex. Cr. R. 10 (1898); *Poyner v. State*, 48 S.W. 516 (1898); and *Adcock v. State*, 41 Tex. Cr. R. 288 (1899).

127. *Freeman v. State*, 11 Tex. App. 92 (1881); *Stewart v. State*, 35 Tex. Cr. R. 174 (1895); *Coburn v. State*, 36 Tex. Cr. R. 257 (1896); *Clark v. State*, 39 Tex. Cr. R. 179 (1898); *Taylor v. State*, 110 Ga. 150 (1900).

128. *Mercer v. State*, 17 Tex. App. 452 (1885), p. 465. See also *Freeman v. State*, 11 Tex. App. 92 (1881).

129. *Mercer v. State*, 17 Tex. App. 452 (1885), pp. 465–66, 455, 457.

130. *Coburn v. State*, 36 Tex. Cr. R. 257 (1896), p. 258. See also *Shelly v. State*, 95 Tenn. 152 (1895); *Stewart v. State*, 35 Tex. Cr. R. 174 (1895); and *Clark v. State*, 39 Tex. Cr. R. 179 (1898).

131. *Taylor v. State*, 110 Ga. 150 (1900), pp. 155–56. The age of the girl was not stated in the facts of the case, but elsewhere in the appellate opinion the judges referred to her as a "female of tender years," indicating that she was in her early teens, at most.

132. *Powers v. State*, 44 Ga. 209 (1871), p. 214.

133. *Raiford v. State*, 68 Ga. 672 (1882), p. 674.

134. Psychological coercion was important in the employment of patriarchal control over subordinate males as well as female members of the household. See Johnson, "Planters and Patriarchy," pp. 56–60.

135. For a recent discussion of how the accomplice testimony rule hinders the successful prosecution of incest, see Wood, "Characterization of the Daughter as an Accomplice."

136. *Porath v. State*, 63 N.W. 1061 (Wis. 1895), p. 1064; *People v. Burwell*, 63 N.W. 986 (Mich. 1895), pp. 987–88. See also *State v. Chambers*, 53 N.W. 1090 (Iowa 1893).

137. *State v. Dana*, 10 Atl. 727 (Vt. 1887), p. 729. See also *State v. Kouhns*, 73 N.W. 353 (Iowa 1897); and *People v. Jenness*, 5 Mich. 305 (1858).

138. Painter, " 'Social Equality,' " p. 49.

139. Williamson, *Crucible of Race*, pp. 115–19, 183–89; Wood, *Black Scare*, pp. 145–48; Hall, " 'The Mind That Burns in Each Body' "; D'Emilio and Freedman, *Intimate Matters*, pp. 215–21; Brundage, *Lynching in the New South*, pp. 58–62. Brundage's analysis of lynching data from Georgia and Virginia during the 1880–1930 period shows that there was a noticeable decline over time in lynchings for alleged sexual offenses, suggesting a lessening of anxiety during the early twentieth century about the black rapist and a transformation in attitudes toward women and the southern code of honor (pp. 68–72).

140. Evelyn Baker Dodd, "The White Woman of the South—Then and Now," *Southern Magazine* (Louisville) 4 (March 1894): 166.

141. Ayers, *Vengeance and Justice*, pp. 241–45; Brundage, *Lynching in the New South*, p. 60. For other examinations of racial lynchings in the late-nineteenth-century South, see Berry and Blassingame, *Long Memory*, pp. 122–25; Fredrickson, *Black Image in the White Mind*, pp. 271–82; and Wyatt-Brown, *Southern Honor*, pp. 435–37, 453–61.

CHAPTER SEVEN

1. Chesnutt, "The Sheriff's Children," in *The Wife of His Youth*, pp. 60–61, 63, 65, 66, 76. On Chesnutt's life and work, see Ayers, *Promise of the New South*, pp. 366–70.

2. Chesnutt, "The Sheriff's Children," p. 76.

3. Brundage, *Lynching in the New South*, p. 72; Ayers, *Vengeance and Justice*, p. 240 (Pell quotation).

4. Ayers, *Promise of the New South*, pp. 156–57. But see Brundage, *Lynching in the New South*, pp. 105–8, which insists that most lynchings in Georgia took place in the black belt counties. Brundage, however, is looking at overall numbers rather than rates.

5. Link, *Paradox of Southern Progressivism*, pp. 59–63; Chief Justice L. E. Bleckley, "Emotional Justice," *Georgia Bar Association Proceedings* 9 (1892): 54–55. See also *Miles v. State*, 93 Ga. 117 (1893), p. 122, in which Judge Lumpkin attacks those who take "the law into their own hands." In his words, if these persons "would appeal to the courts for protection, there would be less of lynch law, the prevalence of which throughout the land is so deplorable."

6. For examples of such charges, see Ayers, *Vengeance and Justice*, p. 246.

7. John J. Strickland, "Are the Courts Responsible for Lynchings, and If So, Why?" *Georgia Bar Proceedings* 16 (1899): 188, 189.

8. James Weatherly, "Judicial Delay in Alabama," *Proceedings of the Alabama State Bar Association* 7 (1884): 47, 48. See also James C. Lamb, "The Virginia Judicial System," *Virginia Law Journal* 12 (February 1888): 65–69.

9. Claud Estes, "Excessive Legislation a Cause of Judicial Inefficiency and an Element of Political Weakness," *Georgia Bar Association Proceedings* 7 (1890): 80–84; T. A. Jones, "Report of the Committee on Judicial Administration and Remedial Procedure," *Report of the Alabama State Bar Association* 3 (1881): 224–41.

10. H. T. Lewis, Lewis W. Thomas, John C. McDonald, and G. P. Munro, "Is Lynch Law Due to Defects in the Criminal Law, or Its Administration?" *Georgia Bar Association Proceedings* 14 (1897): 168, 167, 166.

11. Ibid., pp. 173, 175, 182.

12. O'Brien, *Legal Fraternity*, pp. 90–92; Escott, *Many Excellent People*, pp. 217–19. A recent study of the textile industry in upcountry South Carolina during the late nineteenth century found that about 12 percent of the directors residing in the region were attorneys. See Carlton, " 'Builders of a New State,' " pp. 49–50.

13. W. C. P. Breckinridge, "The Lawyer; His Influence in Creating Public Opinion," *Report of the Virginia State Bar Association* 4 (1891): 156, 171. Despite his emphasis on the importance of family harmony, Breckinridge found himself in the midst of a domestic scandal two years after giving this address. Madeleine Pollard sued the fifth-term congressmen for breach of promise after he failed to marry her when his wife died. Pollard, who was twenty-eight years old at the time, charged that she and Breckinridge, fifty-six years old, had been involved in an affair for nine years. The jury found Breckinridge guilty and awarded Pollard fifteen thousand dollars. The episode turned out to be one of the major reasons for the congressman's defeat in the Democratic primary in 1894. See Ayers, *Promise of the New South*, p. 318.

14. Thomas M. Cooley, "The Lawyer's Duty to the State," *Proceedings of the Bar Association of Tennessee* 4 (1885): 79, 84.

15. I. E. Shumate, "Professional Responsibility," *Georgia Bar Association Proceedings* 4 (1887): 103, 104–5. For a general treatment of the bench and bar as the chief bulwark of conservatism in late-nineteenth-century America, see Paul, *Conservative Crisis*.

16. Michael Grossberg discusses the development of masculine ideals in the American legal profession after the war in "Institutionalizing Masculinity," pp. 143–44.

17. Samuel M. Meek, "The Power and Influence of the Bar," *Proceedings of the Alabama State Bar Associations* 18 (1895): xii.

18. M. A. Spoonts, "A Divided Allegiance," *Proceedings of the Texas Bar Association* 16 (1897): 107–9. For other discussions regarding the role and influence of lawyers in late-nineteenth-century society, see B. H. Bassett, "The Lawyer as a Citizen," *Proceedings of the Texas Bar Association* 3 (1885): 35–42; George W. Croft, "Presidential Address," *Transactions of the South Carolina Bar Association* 7 (1891): 33–48; and Judge Edwin Hobby, "The Legal Profession, Its Value, Importance and Influence," *Proceedings of the Texas Bar Association* 13 (1894): 81–92.

19. Bloomfield, "Texas Bar in the Nineteenth Century," pp. 268–69; Lurie, *Law and the Nation*, p. 53. On the organization of the bar in the United States during the second half of the nineteenth century, see Friedman, *History of American Law*, pp. 648–52; and Hall, *Magic Mirror*, pp. 214–16.

20. Thomas Nelson Page, "The Old Virginia Lawyer," *Report of the Virginia State Bar Association* 4 (1891): 216; W. C. Wear, "Admission to the Bar," *Proceedings of the Texas Bar Association*, 18 (1899): 108. See also Joseph B. Cumming, "Lawyers, the Trustees of Public Opinion," *Georgia Bar Association Proceedings* 3 (1886): 88–97; and Amos E. Goodhue, "The Ideal Lawyer," *Proceedings of the Alabama State Bar Association* 12 (1890): 88–95.

21. Examples of late-nineteenth-century attacks on mercenary lawyers include W. S. Fleming, "The Lawyer," *Proceedings of the Bar Association of Tennessee* 4 (1885): 146–57; R. L. Harmon, "The Lawyer and the Shyster," *Proceedings of the Alabama*

State Bar Association 20 (1897): 39–51; Henry M. Wiltse, "Who Is the Shyster?" *Proceedings of the Bar Association of Tennessee* 16 (1897): 133–42; and W. L. Granberry, "'Razor-Back' Lawyers," *Proceedings of the Bar Association of Tennessee* 12 (1893): 146–51.

22. W. S. Parkerson, "Fellowship of the Profession," *Proceedings of the Louisiana Bar Association* 1 (1898): 75; "About the Profession and Practice of the Law," *Southern Law Review* 1 (April 1872): 250.

23. J. A. Webb, "The Standard of Admission to the Bar in Tennessee," *Proceedings of the Bar Association of Tennessee* 14 (1895): 136–43; A. J. Crovatt, L. Z. Rosser, and R. R. Arnold, "Symposium on What Qualifications Should Be Required for Admission to the Bar," *Georgia Bar Association Proceedings* 11 (1894): 115–27; T. M. Raysor, "Necessity of Preparation for the Bar," *Transactions of the South Carolina Bar Association* 7 (1891): 57–61; Charles Richardson Miles, "Presidential Address," *Transactions of the South Carolina Bar Association* 5 (1889): 31–44.

24. "American and English Law," *Southern Review* (Baltimore), n.s., 5 (April 1869): 404.

25. Seymour D. Thompson, "Government of Lawyers," *Proceedings of the Texas Bar Association* 15 (1896): 72, 73, 84. See Paul, *Conservative Crisis*, p. 43 n. 11, for a discussion of Thompson's career.

26. Grantham, *Southern Progressivism*, pp. xv–xvi, xvii; "American and English Law," p. 405.

27. Woodward, *Origins of the New South*, pp. 396–428; Ownby, *Subduing Satan*, pp. 169–76; Escott, *Many Excellent People*, pp. 171–79, 241, 260–61; Billings, *Planters and the Making of a "New South,"* pp. 198, 202–3, 207–10. I agree with Escott, in contrast to Billings, that merchants, bankers, lawyers, and other professionals gained an influential position among elites in the late nineteenth century. This development by no means led to a more egalitarian social and political system; it simply changed the shape of the elites. See Escott, *Many Excellent People*, pp. 217–19. David Carlton makes the same point for South Carolina in "'Builders of a New State,'" pp. 43–62.

28. Hannis Taylor, "Presidential Address," *Proceedings of the Alabama State Bar Association* 14 (1891): 59. On the distrust of southern reformers towards centralized power, see Link, *Paradox of Southern Progressivism*, pp. 3–30.

29. Ayers, *Promise of the New South*, pp. 409, 417–418; Wallenstein, *From Slave South to New South*, pp. 208, 212–13.

30. Ayers, *Vengeance and Justice*, pp. 245–46.

31. Bynum, "Reshaping the Bonds of Womanhood," pp. 321, 332–33.

32. Roark, *Masters without Slaves*, p. 203.

33. On the relationship between urbanization and legal patterns in the nineteenth-century South, see Bodenhamer, "Law and Disorder," pp. 109–19; Ayers, *Vengeance and Justice*, pp. 73–105, 172–73.

34. Bynum, "Reshaping the Bonds of Womanhood," pp. 326–27.

35. Not only will additional research in the local court records make it possible to explore the issue of rural/urban differences in greater detail, these records will provide us with the ability to depict a more textured portrait of how ordinary southerners interacted with the legal system and shaped it to their own needs. In particular, research at this level will provide a more rounded picture of women and African Americans in the South as historical actors in their own right, thus moving the scholarship on gender, race, and the law beyond the preoccupation with elite attitudes and values

that characterizes much of the present literature, including this study. For a fine foray into the local records of Piedmont North Carolina that demonstrates the promise of this new approach, see Bynum, *Unruly Women*.

36. O'Brien, *Legal Fraternity*, esp. pp. 79–92.

37. Armstead L. Robinson makes an important distinction between political Reconstruction and the "evolving social process" that continued after 1877 and "transformed all aspects of American life" in "Beyond the Realm of Social Consensus," p. 276.

38. Hahn, "Class and State in Postemancipation Societies," p. 86. On the relationship between Reconstruction and central state formation, see Bensel, *Yankee Leviathan*, pp. 366–415.

39. For an analysis heavily weighted toward northern and western developments, see Keller, *Affairs of State*, pp. 285–87, 461–72.

40. Link, *Paradox of Southern Progressivism*, 164–82, 304–11; Grantham, *Southern Progressivism*, pp. 178–99; Ayers, *Promise of the New South*, pp. 415–17; Hall et al., *Like a Family*, pp. 56–60. A similar dynamic was at work among northern reformers. See Boris, "Reconstructing the 'Family.'"

41. Link, *Paradox of Southern Progressivism*. On the intrusiveness and coerciveness of progressive social reforms, see Rothman, "State as Parent." For an insightful reading of the progressive campaign that views it not only as a movement spearheaded by elites but also as shaped by pressure from less powerful groups such as working-class women, see Gordon, "Family Violence, Feminism, and Social Control."

42. A useful discussion of the national vision of governance in the United States after the Civil War can be found in Keller, *Affairs of State*, pp. 289–318.

43. For a discerning analysis of the ambiguous legacy of Reconstruction, see Foner, *Reconstruction*, pp. 602–12.

44. Assessments of family public policy at the national level since the late nineteenth century and contemporary issues regarding justice and equity in the household can be found in Boris and Bardaglio, "Gender, Race, and Class," pp. 141–47; and Eisenstein, "State, the Patriarchial Family, and Working Mothers," pp. 52–56. Frances Fox Piven provides a less critical evaluation of the impact of the welfare state on the lives of women in "Women and the State."

BIBLIOGRAPHY

MANUSCRIPTS

Southern Historical Collection, University of North Carolina, Chapel Hill
  George Washington Allen Papers
  David Alexander Barnes Papers
  Battle Family Papers
  John W. Brown Diary, microfilm copy
  Richard Dozier Papers
  Augustin Harris Hansell Memoirs, microfilm copy
  Samuel H. Hempstead Letters
  Francis Nash Papers
  Richmond Mumford Pearson Papers
  David Schenck Books, microfilm copy
  Thomas Settle Papers
  William D. Valentine Diary

STATUTES AND LEGISLATIVE RECORDS

Alabama

Aikin, John G., comp. *A Digest of the Laws of the State of Alabama.* Philadelphia, 1833.

Brickell, Robert C., Peter Hamilton, and John P. Tillman, comps. *The Code of Alabama.* 2 vols. Nashville, 1887.

Clay, C. C., comp. *A Digest of the Laws of the State of Alabama.* Tuscaloosa, 1843.

Keyes, Wade, Fern M. Wood, and John D. Roquemore, comps. *The Code of Alabama.* Montgomery, 1877.

Martin, William L., comp. *The Code of Alabama.* 2 vols. Atlanta, 1897.

Meek, Alexander B., comp. *A Supplement to Aikin's Digest of the Laws of the State of Alabama.* Tuscaloosa, 1841.

Ormond, John J., Arthur P. Bagby, and George Goldthwaite, comps. *Code of Alabama.* Montgomery, 1852.

Toulmon, Harry, comp. *A Digest of the Laws of the State of Alabama.* Cahawba, 1823.

Walker, A. J., comp. *The Revised Code of Alabama.* Montgomery, 1867.

Arkansas

Ball, William McK., and Sam C. Roane, comps. *Revised Statutes of the State of Arkansas.* Boston, 1838.

English, E. H., comp. *A Digest of the Statutes of Arkansas.* Little Rock, 1848.

Gantt, Edward W., comp. *Statutes of Arkansas.* Little Rock, 1874.

Gould, Josiah, comp. *A Digest of the Statutes of Arkansas.* Little Rock, 1858.

Mansfield, W. W., comp. *A Digest of the Statutes of Arkansas.* Little Rock, 1884.

Sandels, L. P., and Joseph M. Hill, comps. *A Digest of the Statutes of Arkansas.* Columbia, Mo., 1894.

Steele, J., and J. M'Campbell, comps. *Laws of the Arkansas Territory.* Little Rock, 1835.

Florida

Blount, W. A., C. M. Cooper, and L. C. Massey, comps. *The Revised Statutes of the State of Florida.* Jacksonville, 1892.

Bush, Allen H., comp. *A Digest of Statute Law of Florida.* Tallahasee, 1872.

Duval, John P., comp. *Compilation of the Public Acts of the Legislative Council of the Territory of Florida.* Tallahasee, 1839.

McClellan, James F., comp. *A Digest of the Laws of the State of Florida.* Tallahasee, 1881.

Thompson, Leslie A., comp. *A Manual or Digest of the Statute Law of the State of Florida.* Boston, 1847.

Georgia

Acts of the General Assembly of the State of Georgia, 1865–1866. Milledgeville, 1866.

Candler, Allen D., ed. *The Colonial Records of the State of Georgia.* 26 vols. Atlanta, 1904–16.

Clark, R. H., T. R. R. Cobb, and D. Irwin, comps. *The Code of the State of Georgia.* Atlanta, 1861.

———. *The Code of the State of Georgia.* Atlanta, 1867.

Clayton, Augustin Smith, comp. *A Compilation of the Laws of the State of Georgia.* Augusta, 1813.

Cobb, Thomas R. R., comp. *A Digest of the Statute Laws of the State of Georgia.* 2 vols. Athens, 1851.

Hopkins, John L., Clifford Anderson, and Joseph R. Lamen, comps. *The Code of the State of Georgia.* 3 vols. Atlanta, 1896.

Hotchkiss, William A., comp. *Codification of the Statute Law of Georgia.* Savannah, 1845.

Irwin, David, George N. Lester, and W. B. Hill, comps. *The Code of the State of Georgia.* 2d ed. Macon, 1873.

Journal of the House of Representatives of the State of Georgia. Columbia, 1846.

Journal of the Senate of the State of Georgia. Columbia, 1846.

Lester, George N., C. Rowell, and W. B. Hill, comps. *The Code of the State of Georgia.* 4th ed. Atlanta, 1882.

Marbury, Horatio, and William H. Crawford, comps. *Digest of the Laws of the State of Georgia.* Savannah, 1802.

Prince, Oliver H., comp. *A Digest of the Laws of the State of Georgia*. Milledgeville, 1822.

———. *A Digest of the Laws of the State of Georgia*. 2d ed. Athens, 1837.

Louisiana

Acts Passed by the General Assembly of the State of Louisiana, 1900. Baton Rouge, 1900.

A Digest of the Civil Laws Now in Force in the Territory of Orleans. New Orleans, 1808.

Marr, Robert H., comp. *An Annotated Revision of the Statutes of Louisiana*. 3 vols. New Orleans, 1915.

Merrick, Edwin T., comp. *The Revised Civil Code of the State of Louisiana*. New Orleans, 1900.

Morgan, Thomas Gibbes, comp. *Civil Code of the State of Louisiana*. New Orleans, 1853.

Peirce, Levi, Miles Taylor, and William W. King, comps. *The Consolidation and Revision of the Statutes of the State*. New Orleans, 1852.

The Revised Civil Code of the State of Louisiana. New Orleans, 1870.

The Revised Statute Laws of the State of Louisiana. New Orleans, 1870.

Robinson, M. M., comp. *A Digest of the Penal Law of the State of Louisiana*. New Orleans, 1841.

Saunders, E. D., comp. *Revised Civil Code of Louisiana*. New Orleans, 1888.

Upton, Wheelock S., and Needler R. Jennings, comps. *Civil Code of the State of Louisiana*. New Orleans, 1838.

Voorhies, Albert, comp. *Revised Laws of Louisiana*. 2d ed. New Orleans, 1884.

Wolff, Solomon, comp. *Revised Laws of Louisiana*. New Orleans, 1897.

Mississippi

Campbell, J. A. P., comp. *The Revised Code of the Statute Laws of the State of Mississippi*. Jackson, 1880.

Campbell, J. A. P., Amos R. Johnston, and Amos Lovering, comps. *The Revised Code of the Statute Laws of the State of Mississippi*. Jackson, 1871.

Howard, V. E., and A. Hutchinson, comps. *Statutes of the State of Mississippi*. New Orleans, 1840.

Hutchinson, A., comp. *Code of Mississippi*. Jackson, 1848.

Laws of the State of Mississippi Passed at a Regular Session of the Mississippi Legislature, 1865. Jackson, 1866.

Poindexter, George, comp. *The Revised Code of the Law of Mississippi*. Natchez, 1824.

Sharkey, William L., William L. Harris, and Henry T. Ellett, comps. *The Revised Code of the Statute Laws of the State of Mississippi*. Jackson, 1857.

Thompson, R. H., George G. Dillard, and R. B. Campbell, comps. *The Annotated Code of the General Statute Laws of the State of Mississippi*. Nashville, 1892.

Toulmin, Harry, comp. *The Statutes of the Mississippi Territory*. Natchez, 1807.

Turner, Edward, comp. *Statutes of the Mississippi Territory*. Natchez, 1816.

Whitfield, A. H., T. C. Catchings, and W. H. Hardy, comps. *The Mississippi Code of 1906*. Nashville, 1906.

North Carolina

Battle, William H., comp. *Revisal of the Public Statutes of North Carolina.* Raleigh, 1873.

Clark, Walter, ed. *The State Records of North Carolina.* 16 vols. (numbered consecutively after a preceding series). Raleigh, 1886–1907.

Dortch, William T., John Manning, and John S. Henderson, comps. *The Code of North Carolina.* 2 vols. New York, 1883.

Haywood, John, comp. *A Manual of the Laws of North Carolina.* 2d ed. 2 vols. Raleigh, 1808.

———. *A Manual of the Laws of North Carolina.* 4th ed. Raleigh, 1819.

Moore, Bartholomew, and Asa Biggs, comps. *Revised Code of North Carolina.* Boston, 1855.

Nash, Fredrick, James Iredell, and William H. Battle, comps. *The Revised Statutes of the State of North Carolina.* 2 vols. Raleigh, 1837.

Parker, Mattie Erma Edwards, ed. *North Carolina Higher-Court Records, 1697–1701.* Raleigh, 1971.

Saunders, William L., ed. *Colonial Records of North Carolina.* 10 vols. Raleigh, 1886–90.

South Carolina

Bethea, Andrew J., comp. *Code of Laws of South Carolina.* 2 vols. Charlottesville, Va., 1912.

Breazeale, J. E., comp. *The Revised Statutes of South Carolina.* 2 vols. Columbia, 1894.

Brevard, Joseph, ed. *An Alphabetical Digest of the Public Statute Law of South Carolina.* 3 vols. Charleston, 1814.

Cooper, Thomas, and David J. McCord, eds. *The Statutes at Large of South Carolina.* 10 vols. Columbia, 1836–41.

Corbin, D. T., comp. *The Revised Statutes of the State of South Carolina.* Columbia, 1873.

James, Benjamin, comp. *A Digest of the Laws of South Carolina.* Columbia, 1822.

The Statutes at Large of South Carolina. 4 vols. (numbered consecutively after a preceding series). Columbia, 1873–75.

Tennessee

Caruthers, R. L., and A. O. P. Nicholson, comps. *A Compilation of the Statutes of Tennessee.* Nashville, 1836.

Meigs, Return J., and William F. Cooper, comps. *The Code of Tennessee.* Nashville, 1858.

Milliken, W. A., and John J. Vertrees, comps. *The Code of Tennessee.* Nashville, 1884.

Scott, Edward, comp. *Laws of the State of Tennessee.* 2 vols. Knoxville, 1821.

Shannon, R. T., ed. *Public and Permanent Statutes of a General Nature, Being an Annotated Code of Tennessee.* Nashville, 1896.

Thompson, Seymour D., and Thomas M. Steger, comps. *A Compilation of the Statute Laws of the State of Tennessee.* 2 vols. St. Louis, 1873.

Texas

Dallam, James Wilmer, comp. *A Digest of the Laws of Texas.* Baltimore, 1845.

Hartley, Oliver C., comp. *A Digest of the Laws of Texas.* Philadelphia, 1850.

Oldham, Williamson S., and George W. White, comps. *A Digest of the General Statute Laws of the State of Texas.* Austin, 1859.

Paschal, George W., comp. *A Digest of the Laws of Texas.* Galveston, 1866.

Revised Civil Statutes of the State of Texas. Austin, 1895.

Revised Civil Statutes of the State of Texas. Austin, 1912.

Revised Penal Code . . . of the State of Texas. 2d ed. St. Louis, 1889.

Revised Statutes of Texas. Galveston, 1879.

Revised Statutes of Texas. Austin, 1887.

Virginia

Burks, E. C., Waller R. Staples, and John W. Riely, comps. *The Code of Virginia.* Richmond, 1887.

A Collection of All Such Acts of the General Assembly of Virginia, of a Public and Permanent Nature, as Are Now in Force. Richmond, 1803.

Hening, William W., ed. *The Statutes at Large; Being a Collection of All the Laws of Virginia.* 13 vols. Richmond, 1809–23.

Leigh, B. W., comp. *The Revised Code of the Laws of Virginia.* 2 vols. Richmond, 1819.

Munford, George W., comp. *The Code of Virginia.* 2d ed. Richmond, 1860.

————. *Third Edition of the Code of Virginia.* Richmond, 1873.

Patton, John M., and Conway Robinson, comps. *Code of Virginia.* Richmond, 1849.

Pollard, John Garland, comp. *Supplement to the Code of Virginia.* Richmond, 1898.

Shepherd, Samuel, ed. *The Statutes at Large of Virginia, 1792–1806.* 3 vols. Richmond, 1835–36.

Tate, Joseph, comp. *Digest of the Laws of Virginia.* Richmond, 1823.

————. *Digest of the Laws of Virginia.* 2d ed. Richmond, 1841.

CASE REPORTS

Alabama
Alabama Reports, 1840–1900
Porter's Reports, 1834–39

Arkansas
Arkansas Reports, 1837–1900

Florida
Florida Reports, 1846–1900

Georgia
Dudley's Reports, 1830–33
Georgia Decisions, 1842–43
Georgia Reports, 1846–1900
R. M. Charlton's Reports, 1811–37

Louisiana
Louisiana Annual Reports, 1846–1900
Louisiana Reports, 1830–41
Martin's Reports, New Series, 1823–30
Martin's Reports, Old Series, 1809–23
Robinson's Reports, 1841–46

Mississippi
Mississippi Reports, 1818–1900

North Carolina
North Carolina Reports, 1778–1900

South Carolina
Bailey's Law Reports, 1828–32
Desaussure's Equity Reports, 1784–1816
Hill's Law Reports, 1833–37
McMullan's Law Reports, 1840–42
Nott and McCord's Law Reports, 1817–20
Richardson's Equity Reports, 1844–46, 1850–68
Richardson's Law Reports, 1844–46, 1850–68
South Carolina Reports, 1868–1900
Speer's Law Reports, 1842–44

Tennessee
Tennessee Chancery Reports, 1872–78
Tennessee Reports, 1791–1900

Texas
Texas Civil Appeal Reports, 1892–1900
Texas Criminal Appeals Reports, 1876–92
Texas Criminal Reports, 1892–1900
Texas Reports, 1846–1900

Virginia
Jefferson's Virginia Reports, 1730–40, 1768–72
Virginia Colonial Decisions, 1728–53
Virginia Decisions, 1870–1900
Virginia Reports, 1790–1900

Regional
Southeastern Reporter (Ga., S.C., N.C., Va.), 1887–1900
Southern Reporter (Ala., Fla., La., Miss.), 1887–1900
Southwestern Reporter (Ark., Tenn., Tex.), 1887–1900

LEGAL PERIODICALS

Alabama Bar Association Proceedings, 1879–99
Arkansas Bar Association Proceedings, 1882–89
Carolina Law Journal, 1830–31
Carolina Law Repository, 1813–16
Georgia Bar Association Proceedings, 1884–99
Louisiana Bar Association Proceedings, 1898–99
Memphis Law Journal, 1878–79
South Carolina Bar Association Transactions, 1885–91
Southern Law Journal and Reporter, 1879–80
Southern Law Review, 1872–74
Southern Law Review, n.s., 1875–83
Southern Law Times, 1885–86
Tennessee Bar Association Proceedings, 1885, 1888–99
Texas Bar Association Proceedings, 1882–99
Virginia Bar Association Reports, 1877–99
Virginia Law Journal, 1877–93
Virginia Law Register, 1895–99

NEWSPAPERS AND GENERAL PERIODICALS

De Bow's Review, 1846–64, 1866–70
Milledgeville (Ga.) Federal Union, 1845
Southern Literary Journal, 1835–38
Southern Literary Messenger, 1834–64
Southern Magazine (Baltimore), 1871–75
Southern Magazine (Louisville), 1892–95
Southern Quarterly Review, 1842–56
Southern Review (Charleston), 1828–32
Southern Review (Baltimore), 1867–78

BOOKS

Alexander, Adele Logan. *Ambiguous Lives: Free Women of Color in Rural Georgia, 1789–1879.* Fayetteville, Ark., 1991.
Amussen, Susan Dwyer. *An Ordered Society: Gender and Class in Early Modern England.* Oxford, 1988.
Andrews, Garnett. *Reminiscences of an Old Georgia Lawyer.* Atlanta, 1870.
Ash, Stephen V. *Middle Tennessee Society Transformed, 1860–1870: War and Peace in the Upper South.* Baton Rouge, La., 1988.
Axinn, Jane, and Herman Levin. *Social Welfare: A History of the American Response to Need.* New York, 1975.
Ayers, Edward L. *The Promise of the New South: Life After Reconstruction.* New York, 1992.

————. *Vengeance and Justice: Crime and Punishment in the Nineteenth-Century American South.* New York, 1984.

Baker, Jean H. *Affairs of Party: The Political Culture of Northern Democrats in the Mid-Nineteenth Century.* Ithaca, N.Y., 1983.

Baldwin, Joseph G. *The Flush Times of Alabama and Mississippi; A Series of Sketches.* 1853. New York, 1957.

Barker-Benfield, G. J. *The Horrors of the Half-Known Life: Male Attitudes Toward Women and Sexuality in Nineteenth-Century America.* New York, 1976.

Basch, Norma. *In the Eyes of the Law: Women, Marriage, and Property in Nineteenth Century New York.* Ithaca, N.Y., 1982.

Beard, Mary. *Woman as Force in History.* New York, 1946.

Benet, Mary Kathleen. *The Politics of Adoption.* New York, 1976.

Bensel, Richard Franklin. *Yankee Leviathan: The Origins of Central State Authority in America, 1859–1877.* Cambridge, England, 1990.

Benson, Mary Summer. *Women in Eighteenth-Century America: A Study of Opinion and Social Usuage.* New York, 1935.

Berlin, Ira. *Slaves without Masters: The Free Negro in the Antebellum South.* New York, 1974.

Berlin, Ira, Barbara J. Fields, Thavolia Glymph, Joseph P. Reidy, and Leslie S. Rowland, eds. *The Destruction of Slavery.* Ser. 1, vol. 1 of *Freedom: A Documentary History of Emancipation, 1862–1867.* New York, 1985.

Berlin, Ira, Joseph P. Reidy, and Leslie S. Rowland, eds. *The Black Military Experience.* Ser. 2 of *Freedom: A Documentary History of Emancipation, 1862–1867.* New York, 1982.

Berry, Mary Frances, and John W. Blassingame. *The Long Memory: The Black Experience in America.* New York, 1982.

Berthoff, Rowland. *An Unsettled People: Social Order and Disorder in American History.* New York, 1971.

Billings, Dwight B., Jr. *Planters and the Making of a "New South": Class, Politics, and Development in North Carolina, 1865–1900.* Chapel Hill, N.C., 1980.

Bishop, Joel Prentiss. *Commentaries on the Law of Marriage and Divorce.* Boston, 1852.

————. *Commentaries on the Law of Marriage and Divorce.* 2d ed. Boston, 1856.

Blackstone, William. *Blackstone's Commentaries on the Law of England.* Edited by George Sharswood. 2 vols. Philadelphia, 1875.

Blassingame, John W. *Black New Orleans, 1860–1880.* Chicago, 1973.

————. *The Slave Community: Plantation Life in the Antebellum South.* New York, 1972.

Bleser, Carol, ed. *The Hammonds of Redcliffe.* New York, 1981.

————. *Secret and Sacred: The Diaries of James Henry Hammond, a Southern Slaveholder.* New York, 1988.

Bloomfield, Maxwell H. *American Lawyers in a Changing Society, 1776–1876.* Cambridge, Mass., 1976.

Bodenhamer, David J., and James W. Ely Jr., eds. *Ambivalent Legacy: A Legal History of the South.* Jackson, Miss., 1984.

Boles, John B. *Black Southerners, 1619–1869.* Lexington, Ky., 1983.

Boydston, Jeanne, Mary Kelley, and Anne Margolis, eds. *The Limits of Sisterhood:*

The Beecher Sisters on Women's Rights and Women's Sphere. Chapel Hill, N.C., 1988.

Breen, T. H. *Tobacco Culture: The Mentality of the Great Tidewater Planters on the Eve of Revolution*. Princeton, N.J., 1985.

Breen, T. H., and Stephen Innes. *"Myne Owne Ground": Race and Freedom on Virginia's Eastern Shore, 1640–1676*. New York, 1980.

Brown, Richard D. *Modernization: The Transformation of American Life, 1600–1865*. New York, 1976.

Brownmiller, Susan. *Against Our Will: Men, Women and Rape*. New York, 1975.

Bruce, Dickson D., Jr. *Violence and Culture in the Antebellum South*. Austin, Tex., 1979.

Brundage, W. Fitzhugh. *Lynching in the New South: Georgia and Virginia, 1880–1930*. Urbana, Ill., 1993.

Burton, Orville Vernon. *In My Father's House Are Many Mansions: Family and Community in Edgefield, South Carolina*. Chapel Hill, N.C., 1985.

Bynum, Victoria E. *Unruly Women: The Politics of Social and Sexual Control in the Old South*. Chapel Hill, N.C., 1992.

Calhoun. Arthur W. *A Social History of the American Family*. 3 vols. Cleveland, 1917–19.

Carter, Dan T. *When the War Was Over: The Failure of Self-Reconstruction in the South, 1865–1867*. Baton Rouge, La., 1985.

Cash, W. J. *The Mind of The South*. New York, 1941.

Cashin, Joan E. *A Family Venture: Men and Women on the Southern Frontier*. New York, 1991.

Censer, Jane Turner. *North Carolina Planters and Their Children, 1800–1860*. Baton Rouge, La., 1984.

Chesnutt, Charles W. *The Wife of His Youth and Other Stories of the Color Line*. Ann Arbor, Mich., 1968.

Chopin, Kate. *The Awakening*. Edited by Margaret Culley. New York, 1976.

Clarke, Helen I. *Social Legislation: American Laws Dealing with Family, Child, and Dependent*. New York, 1940.

Clinton, Catherine. *The Other Civil War: American Women in the Nineteenth Century*. New York, 1984.

———. *The Plantation Mistress: Women's World in the Old South*. New York, 1982.

Cobb, James C. *Industrialization and Southern Society, 1977–1984*. Lexington, Ky., 1984.

Cobb, Thomas R. R. *An Inquiry into the Law of Negro Slavery in the United States of America*. 2 vols. Philadelphia, 1858.

Cohen, Maxwell T. *Race, Creed, and Color in Adoption Proceedings*. New York, 1964.

Collins, Bruce. *White Society in the Antebellum South*. London, 1985.

Cooper, William J., Jr. *Liberty and Slavery: Southern Politics to 1860*. New York, 1983.

Cott, Nancy F. *The Bonds of Womanhood: "Woman's Sphere" in New England, 1780–1835*. New Haven, Conn., 1977.

Daggett, Harriet Spiller. *Legal Essays on Family Law*. Baton Rouge, La., 1935.

Davis, Angela Y. *Women, Race, and Class*. New York, 1981.

Davis, Richard Beale. *Intellectual Life in the Colonial South, 1585–1763*. 3 vols. Knoxville, Tenn., 1978.

De Forest, John William. *Miss Ravenel's Conversion from Secession to Loyalty*. Edited by Gordon S. Haight. New York, 1955.

Degler, Carl N. *At Odds: Women and the Family in America from the Revolution to the Present*. New York, 1980.

——. *Neither Black nor White: Slavery and Race Relations in Brazil and the United States*. New York, 1971.

——. *Place Over Time: The Continuity of Southern Distinctiveness*. Baton Rouge, La., 1977.

D'Emilio, John, and Estelle B. Freedman. *Intimate Matters: A History of Sexuality in America*. New York, 1988.

Domínguez, Virginia R. *White by Definition: Social Classification in Creole Louisiana*. New Brunswick, N.J., 1986.

East, Charles, ed. *The Civil War Diary of Sarah Morgan*. Athens, Ga., 1991.

Eaton, Clement. *The Growth of Southern Civilization, 1790–1860*. New York, 1961.

Elkins, Stanley M. *Slavery: A Problem in American Institutional and Intellectual Life*. 2d ed. Chicago, 1969.

Eller, Ronald D. *Miners, Millhands, and Mountaineers: Industrialization of the Appalachian South, 1880–1930*. Knoxville, Tenn., 1982.

Escott, Paul D. *After Secession: Jefferson Davis and the Failure of Confederate Nationalism*. Baton Rouge, La., 1978.

——. *Many Excellent People: Power and Privilege in North Carolina, 1850–1900*. Chapel Hill, N.C., 1985.

Farber, Bernard. *Kinship and Class: A Midwestern Study*. New York, 1971.

Faulkner, William. *Absalom, Absalom!* New York, 1972.

Faust, Drew Gilpin. *James Henry Hammond and the Old South: A Design for Mastery*. Baton Rouge, La., 1982.

——. *A Sacred Circle: The Dilemma of the Intellectual in the Old South, 1840–1860*. Baltimore, 1977.

Fields, Barbara Jeanne. *Slavery and Freedom on the Middle Ground: Maryland during the Nineteenth Century*. New Haven, Conn., 1985.

Fitzhugh, George. *Sociology for the South*. Richmond, 1854.

Fliegelman, Jay. *Prodigals and Pilgrims: The American Revolution against Patriarchial Authority, 1750–1800*. New York, 1982.

Flynn, Charles L. *White Land, Black Labor: Caste and Class in Late Nineteenth-Century Georgia*. Baton Rouge, La., 1983.

Foner, Eric. *Nothing But Freedom: Emancipation and Its Legacy*. Baton Rouge, La., 1984.

——. *Reconstruction: America's Unfinished Revolution, 1863–1877*. New York, 1988.

Forsyth, William. *A Treatise on the Law Relating to the Custody of Infants*. London, 1850.

Fox, Robin. *The Red Lamp of Incest*. New York, 1980.

Fox-Genovese, Elizabeth. *Within the Plantation Household: Black and White Women of the Old South*. Chapel Hill, N.C., 1988.

Fox-Genovese, Elizabeth, and Eugene D. Genovese. *Fruits of Merchant Capital:*

Slavery and Bourgeois Property in the Rise and Expansion of Capitalism. New York, 1983.

Franklin, John Hope. *The Free Negro in North Carolina, 1790–1860.* New York, 1971.

———. *The Militant South, 1800–1861.* Cambridge, Mass., 1956.

Fredrickson, George M. *The Black Image in the White Mind: The Debate on Afro-American Character and Destiny, 1817–1914.* New York, 1971.

———. *White Supremacy: A Comparative Study in American and South African History.* New York, 1981.

Friedman, Jean E. *The Enclosed Garden: Women and Community in the Evangelical South, 1830–1900.* Chapel Hill, N.C., 1985.

Friedman, Lawrence M. *A History of American Law.* 2d ed. New York, 1985.

Gay, Peter. *The Bourgeois Experience: Victoria to Freud.* Vol. 1, *Education of the Senses.* New York, 1984.

Genovese, Eugene D. *Roll, Jordan, Roll: The World the Slaves Made.* New York, 1974.

———. *The World the Slaveholders Made: Two Essays in Interpretation.* New York, 1968.

Gerteis, Louis. *From Contraband to Freedman: Federal Policy toward Southern Blacks, 1861–1865.* Westport, Conn., 1973.

Ginzberg, Lori D. *Women and the Work of Benevolence: Morality, Politics, and Class in the Nineteenth-Century United States.* New Haven, Conn., 1990.

Goldstein, Joseph, Anna Freud, and Albert J. Solnit. *Beyond the Best Interests of the Child.* New York, 1973.

Goodell, William. *The American Slave Code in Theory and Practice.* 4th ed. New York, 1853.

Gordon, Linda. *Heroes of Their Own Lives: The Politics and History of Family Violence.* New York, 1988.

Grantham, Dewey W. *Southern Progressivism: The Reconciliation of Progress and Tradition.* Knoxville, Tenn., 1983.

Greenberg, Jack. *Race Relations and American Law.* New York, 1959.

Greenberg, Kenneth S. *Masters and Statesmen: The Political Culture of Slavery.* Baltimore, 1985.

Greene, Jack P. *Pursuits of Happiness: The Social Development of Early Modern British Colonies and the Formation of American Culture.* Chapel Hill, N.C., 1988.

Greven, Philip J., Jr. *The Protestant Temperament: Patterns of Child Rearing, Religious Experience, and the Self in Early America.* New York, 1977.

Grimké, Sarah. *Letters on the Equality of the Sexes and Other Essays.* Edited by Elizabeth Ann Bartlett. New Haven, Conn., 1988.

Griswold, Robert L. *Family and Divorce in California, 1850–1890: Victorian Illusions and Everyday Realities.* Albany, N.Y., 1982.

Grossberg, Michael. *Governing the Hearth: Law and the Family in Nineteenth Century America.* Chapel Hill, N.C., 1985.

Gutman, Herbert G. *The Black Family in Slavery and Freedom, 1750–1925.* New York, 1976.

Hahn, Steven. *The Roots of Southern Populism: Yeomen Farmers and the Transformation of the Georgia Upcountry, 1850–1890.* New York, 1983.

Hall, Jacquelyn Dowd, James Leloudis, Robert Korstad, Mary Murphy, LuAnn

Jones, and Christopher B. Daly. *Like a Family: The Making of a Southern Cotton Mill World*. New York, 1989.

Hall, Kermit L. *The Magic Mirror: Law in American History*. New York, 1989.

Hall, Kermit L., and James W. Ely Jr., eds. *An Uncertain Tradition: Constitutionalism and the History of the South*. Athens, Ga., 1989.

Hamilton, J. G. DeRoulhac, ed. *The Papers of Thomas Ruffin*. 4 vols. Raleigh, N.C., 1918–20.

Hawes, Joseph. *Children in Urban Society: Juvenile Delinquency in Nineteenth-Century America*. New York, 1971.

Henretta, James A., and Gregory H. Nobles. *Evolution and Revolution: American Society, 1600–1820*. Lexington, Mass., 1987.

Herman, Judith Lewis. *Father-Daughter Incest*. Cambridge, Mass., 1981.

Higginbothom, A. Leon, Jr. *In the Matter of Color: Race and the American Legal Process; The Colonial Period*. New York, 1978.

Hindus, Michael Stephen. *Prison and Plantation: Crime, Justice, and Authority in Massachusetts and South Carolina, 1767–1878*. Chapel Hill, N.C., 1980.

Hochheimer, Lewis. *A Treatise of the Law Relating to the Custody of Infants*. Baltimore, 1887.

Hoff, Joan. *Law, Gender, and Injustice: A Legal History of U.S. Women*. New York, 1991.

Horwitz, Morton J. *The Transformation of American Law, 1780–1960*. Cambridge, Mass., 1977.

Howard, George E. *A History of Matrimonial Institutions*. 3 vols. Chicago, 1901.

Hundley, Daniel R. *Social Relations in Our Southern States*. New York, 1860.

Hurd, Rollin C. *A Treatise on the Right of Personal Liberty, and on the Writ of Habeas Corpus*. Albany, N.Y., 1858.

Hurst, James Willard. *Law and the Conditions of Freedom in the Nineteenth-Century United States*. Madison, Wis., 1956.

Ireland, Robert. *County Courts in Antebellum Kentucky*. Lexington, Ky., 1972.

Isaac, Rhys. *The Transformation of Virginia, 1740–1790*. Chapel Hill, N.C., 1982.

Jacobs, Harriet A. *Incidents in the Life of a Slave Girl, Written by Herself*. Edited by Jean Fagan Yellin. Cambridge, Mass., 1987.

Jimerson, Randall C. *The Private Civil War: Popular Thought during the Sectional Conflict*. Baton Rouge, La., 1988.

Johnson, Guion Griffis. *Ante-Bellum North Carolina: A Social History*. Chapel Hill, N.C., 1937.

Johnson, Michael P. *Toward a Patriarchal Republic: The Secession of Georgia*. Baton Rouge, La., 1977.

Johnson, Michael P., and James L. Roark. *Black Masters: A Free Family of Color in the Old South*. New York, 1984.

———, eds. *No Chariot Let Down: Charleston's Free People of Color on the Eve of the Civil War*. New York, 1986.

Johnston, James Hugo. *Race Relations in Virginia and Miscegenation in the South, 1776–1860*. Amherst, Mass., 1970.

Jones, Jacqueline. *Labor of Love, Labor of Sorrow: Black Women, Work, and the Family from Slavery to the Present*. New York, 1985.

Jordan, Winthrop D. *White Over Black: American Attitudes toward the Negro, 1550–1812*. Baltimore, 1969.

Kadushin, Alfred. *Child Welfare Services.* 3d ed. New York, 1980.

Kairys, David, ed. *The Politics of Law: A Progressive Critique.* New York, 1982.

Keller, Morton. *Affairs of State: Public Life in Late Nineteenth Century America.* Cambridge, Mass., 1977.

Kemble, Frances Anne. *Journal of a Residence on a Georgian Plantation in 1838–1839.* Edited by John A. Scott. Athens, Ga., 1984.

Kennedy, John Pendleton. *Swallow Barn; or, A Sojourn in the Old Dominion.* New York, 1962.

Kenzer, Robert C. *Kinship and Neighborhood in a Southern Community: Orange County, North Carolina.* Knoxville, Tenn., 1987.

Kerber, Linda K. *Women of the Republic: Intellect and Ideology in Revolutionary America.* Chapel Hill, N.C., 1980.

Kolchin, Peter. *First Freedom: The Responses of Alabama's Blacks to Emancipation and Reconstruction.* Westport, Conn., 1972.

Kulikoff, Allan. *Tobacco and Slaves: The Development of Southern Cultures in the Chesapeake, 1680–1800.* Chapel Hill, N.C., 1986.

Lebsock, Suzanne. *The Free Women of Petersburg: Status and Culture in a Southern Town, 1784–1860.* New York, 1984.

Lerner, Gerda. *The Creation of Patriarchy.* New York, 1986.

Lévi-Strauss, Claude. *The Elementary Structures of Kinship.* Boston, 1969.

Lewis, Jan. *The Pursuit of Happiness: Family and Values in Jefferson's Virginia.* New York, 1983.

Link, William A. *The Paradox of Southern Progressivism, 1880–1930.* Chapel Hill, N.C., 1992.

Litwack, Leon F. *Been in the Storm So Long: The Aftermath of Slavery.* New York, 1979.

Lurie, Jonathan. *Law and the Nation, 1865–1912.* New York, 1983.

Lystra, Karen. *Searching the Heart: Women, Men, and Romantic Love in Nineteenth-Century America.* New York, 1989.

MacKinnon, Catharine A. *Toward a Feminist Theory of the State.* Cambridge, Mass., 1989.

McLaurin, Melton A. *Celia, A Slave.* Athens, Ga., 1991.

McMillen, Sally G. *Motherhood in the Old South: Pregnancy, Childbirth, and Infant Rearing.* Baton Rouge, La., 1990.

———. *Southern Women: Black and White in the Old South.* Arlington Heights, Ill., 1992.

Martineau, Harriet. *Society in America.* Edited by Seymour Martin Lipset. Garden City, N.Y., 1962.

Massey, Mary Elizabeth. *Bonnet Brigades.* New York, 1966.

Mencke, John G. *Mulattoes and Race Mixture: American Attitudes and Images, 1865–1918.* Ann Arbor, Mich., 1979.

Mintz, Steven. *A Prison of Expectations: The Family in Victorian Culture.* New York, 1983.

Mintz, Steven, and Susan Kellogg. *Domestic Relations: A Social History of American Family Life.* New York, 1988.

Mohr, Clarence L. *On the Threshold of Freedom: Masters and Slaves in Civil War Georgia.* Athens, Ga., 1986.

Morgan, Edmund S. *American Freedom, American Slavery: The Ordeal of Colonial Virginia*. New York, 1975.
——— . *Virginians at Home: Family Life in the Eighteenth Century*. Williamsburg, Va., 1952.
Morris, Richard B. *Studies in the History of American Law*. New York, 1930.
Murray, Janet Horowitz, ed. *Strong-Minded Women and Other Lost Voices from Nineteenth-Century England*. New York, 1982.
Myers, Robert M., ed. *The Children of Pride: A True Story of Georgia and the Civil War*. New Haven, Conn., 1972.
Nash, Gary B. *Red, White, and Black: The Peoples of Early America*. 2d ed. Englewood Cliffs, N.J., 1982.
Nieman, Donald G. *To Set the Law in Motion: The Freedmen's Bureau and the Legal Rights of Blacks, 1865–1868*. Westport, Conn., 1976.
Norton, Mary Beth. *Liberty's Daughters: The Revolutionary Experience of American Women, 1750–1850*. Boston, 1980.
Oakes, James. *The Ruling Race: A History of American Slaveholders*. New York, 1982.
——— . *Slavery and Freedom: An Interpretation of the Old South*. New York, 1990.
O'Brien, Gail Williams. *The Legal Fraternity and the Making of a New South Community, 1848–1882*. Athens, Ga., 1986.
Ownby, Ted. *Subduing Satan: Religion, Recreation, and Manhood in the Rural South, 1865–1920*. Chapel Hill, N.C., 1990.
Owsley, Frank. *Plain Folk of the Old South*. Baton Rouge, La., 1949.
Paludan, Phillip Shaw. *Victims: A True Story of the Civil War*. Knoxville, Tenn., 1981.
Paul, Arnold M. *Conservative Crisis and the Rule of Law: Attitudes of Bar and Bench, 1887–1895*. New York, 1969.
Peck, Evelyn Foster. *Adoption Laws in the United States*. Washington, D.C., 1925.
Perkin, Joan. *Women and Marriage in Nineteenth-Century England*. Chicago, 1989.
Peterson, Thomas Virgil. *Ham and Japeth: The Mythic World of Whites in the Antebellum South*. Metuchen, N.J., 1978.
Platt, Anthony M. *The Child Savers: The Invention of Delinquency*. Chicago, 1969.
Pleck, Elizabeth. *Domestic Tyranny: The Making of Social Policy Against Family Violence from Colonial Times to the Present*. New York, 1987.
Poster, Mark. *Critical Theory of the Family*. New York, 1978.
Rabinowitz, Howard N. *Race Relations in the Urban South, 1865–1890*. New York, 1978.
Rabkin, Peggy A. *Father to Daughters: The Legal Foundation of Female Emancipation*. Westport, Conn., 1980.
Rable, George C. *Civil Wars: Women and the Crisis of Southern Nationalism*. Urbana, Ill., 1989.
Reidy, Joseph P. *From Slavery to Agrarian Capitalism in the Cotton Plantation South: Central Georgia, 1800–1880*. Chapel Hill, N.C., 1992.
Ripley, C. Peter. *Slaves and Freedmen in Civil War Louisiana*. Baton Rouge, La., 1976.
Roark, James L. *Masters without Slaves: Southern Planters in the Civil War and Reconstruction*. New York, 1977.

Roberts, David. *Paternalism in Early Victorian England.* New Brunswick, N.J., 1979.

Robinson, William M. *Justice in Grey: A History of the Judicial System of the Confederate States of America.* Cambridge, Mass., 1941.

Roeber, A. G. *Faithful Magistrates and Republican Lawyers: Creators of Virginia Legal Culture, 1680–1810.* Chapel Hill, N.C., 1981.

Rose, Willie Lee. *Rehearsal for Reconstruction: The Port Royal Experiment.* New York, 1964.

———. *Slavery and Freedom.* Edited by William W. Freehling. New York, 1982.

Rosengarten, Theodore. *Tombe: Portrait of a Cotton Planter.* New York, 1987.

Rothman, David J. *The Discovery of the Asylum: Social Order and Disorder in the New Republic.* Boston, 1971.

Ruggiero, Guido. *The Boundaries of Eros: Sex Crime and Sexuality in Renaissance Venice.* New York, 1985.

Rutman, Darrett B., and Anita H. Rutman. *A Place in Time: Middlesex County, Virginia, 1650–1750.* New York, 1984.

Ryan, Mary P. *Cradle of the Middle Class: The Family in Oneida County, New York, 1790–1865.* New York, 1981.

Salmon, Marylynn. *Women and the Law of Property in Early America.* Chapel Hill, N.C., 1986.

Schochet, Gordon J. *Patriarchalism in Political Thought: The Authoritarian Family and Political Speculation and Attitudes, Especially in Seventeenth-Century England.* New York, 1975.

Schouler, James. *A Treatise on the Law of Domestic Relations.* 2d ed. Boston, 1874.

Schwarz, Philip J. *Twice Condemned: Slaves and the Criminal Laws of Virginia, 1705–1865.* Baton Rouge, La., 1988.

Scott, Ann Firor. *The Southern Lady: From Pedestal to Politics, 1830–1930.* Chicago, 1970.

Sennett, Richard. *Authority.* New York, 1980.

Shepher, Joseph. *Incest: A Biosocial View.* New York, 1983.

Simkins, Francis Butler, and James Welch Patton. *The Women of the Confederacy.* New York, 1936.

Sklar, Kathryn Kish. *Catharine Beecher: A Study in American Domesticity.* New York, 1976.

Smith, Carl S., John P. McWilliams Jr., and Maxwell Bloomfield. *Law and American Literature: A Collection of Essays.* New York, 1983.

Smith, Daniel Blake. *Inside the Great House: Planter Family Life in Eighteenth-Century Chesapeake Society.* Ithaca, N.Y., 1980.

Smith-Rosenberg, Carroll. *Disorderly Conduct: Visions of Gender in Victorian America.* New York, 1985.

Southworth, E. D. E. N. *Ishmael; or, In the Depths.* 1863. Philadelphia, 1876.

Spindel, Donna J. *Crime and Society in North Carolina, 1663–1776.* Baton Rouge, La., 1989.

Spruill, Julia Cherry. *Women's Life and Work in the Southern Colonies.* New York, 1972.

Stampp, Kenneth. *The Peculiar Institution: Slavery in the Ante-Bellum South.* New York, 1956.

Stansell, Christine. *City of Women: Sex and Class in New York, 1789–1860.* New York, 1986.

Stephenson, Gilbert T. *Race Distinctions in American Law.* New York, 1910.

Sterkx, H. E. *Partners in Rebellion: Alabama Women in the Civil War.* Rutherford, N.J., 1970.

Stone, Lawrence. *The Family, Sex, and Marriage in England, 1500–1800.* New York, 1977.

———. *Road to Divorce: England, 1530–1987.* Oxford, 1990.

Stowe, Steven M. *Intimacy and Power in the Old South: Ritual in the Lives of the Planters.* Baltimore, 1987.

Sydnor, Charles S. *The Development of Southern Sectionalism, 1819–1848.* Baton Rouge, La., 1948.

Takaki, Ronald T. *Iron Cages: Race and Culture in Nineteenth-Century America.* New York, 1979.

Taylor, Rosser H. *Ante-Bellum South Carolina: A Social and Cultural History.* Chapel Hill, N.C., 1942.

Taylor, William R. *Cavalier and Yankee: The Old South and American National Character.* New York, 1961.

Thomas, Emory M. *The Confederacy as a Revolutionary Experience.* Englewood Cliffs, N.J., 1971.

———. *The Confederate Nation, 1861–1865.* New York, 1979.

Thompson, E. P. *Whigs and Hunters: The Origin of the Black Act.* New York, 1975.

Thornton, J. Mills, III. *Politics and Power in a Slave Society: Alabama, 1800–1860.* Baton Rouge, La., 1978.

Thorpe, Thomas B. *The Master's House; or, Scenes Descriptive of Southern Life.* New York, 1854.

Thurston, Henry W. *The Dependent Child: A Story of Changing Aims and Methods in the Care of Dependent Children.* New York, 1930.

Tigar, Michael E., and Madeleine R. Levy. *Law and the Rise of Capitalism.* New York, 1977.

Tindall, George B. *South Carolina Negroes, 1877–1900.* Columbia, S.C., 1952.

Tong, Rosemarie. *Women, Sex, and the Law.* Totowa, N.J., 1984.

Tourgée, Albion W. *A Fool's Errand: A Novel of the South during Reconstruction.* Edited by George M. Fredrickson. New York, 1966.

Trattner, Walter I. *From Poor Law to Welfare State: A History of Social Welfare in America.* 2d ed. New York, 1979.

Trumbach, Randolph. *The Rise of the Egalitarian Family: Aristocratic Kinship and Domestic Relations in Eighteenth-Century England.* New York, 1978.

Tucker, George. *The Valley of the Shenandoah; or, Memoirs of the Graysons.* New York, 1824.

Tushnet, Mark. *The American Law of Slavery, 1810–1860: Considerations of Humanity and Interest.* Princeton, N.J., 1981.

Twain, Mark. *The Tragedy of Pudd'nhead Wilson.* New York, 1964.

Tyler, Ransom H. *Commentaries on the Law of Infancy.* 2nd ed. Albany, N.Y., 1882.

Vernier, Chester G. *American Family Laws.* 6 vols. Stanford, Calif., 1931–38.

Wallenstein, Peter. *From Slave South to New South: Public Policy in Nineteenth-Century Georgia.* Chapel Hill, N.C., 1987.

Warbasse, Elizabeth Bowles. *The Changing Legal Rights of Married Women, 1800–1861.* New York, 1987.

Wayne, Michael. *The Reshaping of Plantation Society: The Natchez District, 1860–1880.* Baton Rouge, La., 1984.

Weeks, Jeffrey. *Sex, Politics and Society: The Regulation of Sexuality since 1800.* London, 1981.

Wharton, Vernon L. *The Negro in Mississippi, 1865–1890.* Chapel Hill, N.C., 1947.

White, Deborah Gray. *Ar'n't I a Woman? Female Slaves in the Plantation South.* New York, 1985.

Whitmore, William H. *The Law of Adoption in the United States.* Albany, N.Y., 1876.

Wiener, Jonathan M. *Social Origins of the New South: Alabama, 1860–1885.* Baton Rouge, La., 1978.

Wikramanayake, Marina. *A World in Shadow: The Free Blacks in Ante-bellum South Carolina.* Columbia, S.C., 1973.

Williams, Jack K. *Vogues in Villainy: Crime and Retribution in Ante-Bellum South Carolina.* Columbia, S.C., 1959.

Williamson, Joel. *After Slavery: The Negro in South Carolina during Reconstruction, 1861–1877.* New York, 1975.

——— . *The Crucible of Race: Black-White Relations in the American South since Emancipation.* New York, 1984.

——— . *New People: Miscegenation and Mulattoes in the United States.* New York, 1980.

Wilson, Charles Reagan, and William Ferris, eds. *Encyclopedia of Southern Culture.* 4 vols. New York, 1991.

Wilson, Theodore B. *The Black Codes of the South.* University, Ala., 1965.

Wishy, Bernard. *The Child and the Republic: The Dawn of Modern American Child Nurture.* Philadelphia, 1968.

Wisner, Elizabeth. *Social Welfare in the South: From Colonial Times to World War I.* Baton Rouge, La., 1970.

Witmer, Helen L., Elizabeth Herzog, Eugene A. Weinstein, and Mary E. Sullivan. *Independent Adoptions: A Follow-Up Study.* New York, 1963.

Wolfram, Sybil. *In-Laws and Outlaws: Kinship and Marriage in England.* London, 1987.

Wood, Forrest G. *Black Scare: The Racist Response to Emancipation and Reconstruction.* Berkeley, Calif., 1968.

Wood, Peter H. *Black Majority: Negroes in Colonial South Carolina from 1670 through the Stono Rebellion.* New York, 1974.

Woodward, C. Vann. *Origins of the New South, 1877–1913.* Baton Rouge, La., 1951.

Woodward, C. Vann, ed. *Mary Chesnut's Civil War.* New Haven, Conn., 1981.

Wooster, Ralph A. *The People in Power: Courthouse and Statehouse in the Lower South, 1850–1860.* Knoxville, Tenn., 1969.

——— . *Politicians, Planters, and Plain Folk: Courthouse and Statehouse in the Upper South, 1850–1860.* Knoxville, Tenn., 1975.

Wright, Gavin. *Old South, New South: Revolutions in the Southern Economy since the Civil War.* New York, 1986.

———. *The Political Economy of the Cotton South: Households, Markets, and Wealth in the Nineteenth Century.* New York, 1978.

Wyatt-Brown, Bertram. *Southern Honor: Ethics and Behavior in the Old South.* New York, 1982.

Zainaldin, Jamil. *Law in Antebellum Society: Legal Change and Economic Expansion.* New York, 1983.

Zelizer, Viviana A. *Pricing the Priceless Child: The Changing Social Value of Children.* New York, 1985.

ARTICLES, DISSERTATIONS, AND UNPUBLISHED PAPERS

Alpert, Jonathan L. "The Origins of Slavery in the United States—The Maryland Precedent." *American Journal of Legal History* 14 (July 1970): 189–221.

Anderson, Nancy Fix. "Cousin Marriage in Victorian England." *Journal of Family History* 11 (1986): 285–301.

———. "The 'Marriage with a Deceased Wife's Sister Bill' Controversy: Incest Anxiety and the Defense of Family Purity in Victorian England." *Journal of British Studies* 21 (Spring 1982): 67–82.

"An Exchange on Critical Legal Studies Between Robert W. Gordon and William Nelson." *Law and History Review* 6 (Spring 1988): 139–86.

Applebaum, Harvey M. "Miscegenation Statutes: A Constitutional and Social Problem." *Georgetown Law Journal* 53 (Fall 1964): 49–91.

Areen, Judith. "Intervention between Parent and Child: A Reappraisal of the State's Role in Child Neglect and Abuse Cases." *Georgetown Law Journal* 63 (March 1975): 887–937.

Armao, Agnes Orsatti. "In Search of a New God: Law in Nineteenth-Century America." *Journal of Legal History* 4 (September 1983): 38–55.

Arnold, Marybeth Hamilton. "'The Life of a Citizen in the Hands of a Woman': Sexual Assault in New York City, 1790 to 1920." In *Passion and Power: Sexuality in History*, edited by Kathy Peiss and Christina Simmons, pp. 35–56. Philadelphia, 1989.

Ash, Stephen V. "Poor Whites in the Occupied South, 1861–1865." *Journal of Southern History* 57 (February 1991): 39–62.

Avins, Alfred. "Anti-Miscegenation Laws and the Fourteenth Amendment: The Original Intent." *Virginia Law Review* 52 (November 1966): 1224–55.

Babier, Carl J. "A Historical Comment on the Substantive Adoption Law of Louisiana." *Loyola Law Review* 15 (1968–69): 297–306.

Bardaglio, Peter. "The Children of Jubilee: African-American Childhood in Wartime." In *Divided Houses: Gender and the Civil War*, edited by Catherine Clinton and Nina Silber, pp. 213–19. New York, 1992.

———. "'An Outrage upon Nature': Incest and the Law in the Nineteenth-Century South." In *In Joy and in Sorrow: Women, Family, and Marriage in the Victorian South, 1830–1900*, edited by Carol Bleser, pp. 32–51. New York, 1991.

Bartlett, Helen R. "Eighteenth Century Georgia Women." Ph.D. diss., University of Maryland, 1939.

Basch, Norma. "The Emerging Legal History of Women in the United States: Property, Divorce, and the Constitution." *Signs* 12 (Autumn 1986): 97–117.

———. "Equity vs. Equality: Emerging Concepts of Women's Political Status in the Age of Jackson." *Journal of the Early Republic* 3 (Fall 1983): 297–318.

———. "Invisible Women: The Legal Fiction of Marital Unity in Nineteenth-Century America." *Feminist Studies* 5 (Summer 1979): 346–66.

Begus, Sarah, and Pamela Armstrong. "Daddy's Right: Incestuous Assault." In *Families, Politics, and Public Policy: A Feminist Dialogue on Women and the State*, edited by Irene Diamond, pp. 236–49. New York, 1983.

Benedict, Michael Les. "The Problem of Constitutionalism and Constitutional Liberty in the Reconstruction South." In *An Uncertain Tradition: Constitutionalism and the History of the South*, edited by Kermit L. Hall and James W. Ely Jr., pp. 225–49. Athens, Ga., 1989.

Ben-Or, Joseph. "The Law of Adoption in the United States: Its Massachusetts Origins and the Statute of 1851." *New England Historical and Genological Register* 130 (1976): 259–69.

Berlin, Ira, Francine C. Cary, Steven F. Miller, and Leslie S. Rowland. "Family and Freedom: Black Families in the American Civil War." *History Today* 37 (January 1987): 8–15.

Berlin, Ira, Steven F. Miller, and Leslie S. Rowland. "Afro-American Families in the Transition from Slavery to Freedom." *Radical History Review* 42 (Fall 1988): 89–121.

Berry, Mary Frances. "Judging Morality: Sexual Behavior and Legal Consequences in the Late Nineteenth-Century South." *Journal of American History* 78 (December 1991): 835–56.

Billings, Warren M. "The Cases of Fernando and Elizabeth Key: A Note on the Status of Blacks in Seventeenth-Century Virginia." *William and Mary Quarterly* 30 (July 1973): 467–74.

Blackburn, D. R. N. "Incest." *Criminal Law Magazine and Reporter* 17 (July 1895): 389–99.

Blake, Russell Lindley. "Ties of Intimacy: Social Values and Personal Relationships of Antebellum Slaveholders." Ph.D. diss., University of Michigan, 1978.

Bleser, Carol. "The Perrys of Greenville: A Nineteenth-Century Marriage." In *The Web of Southern Social Relations: Women, Family, and Education*, edited by Walter J. Fraser, R. Frank Saunders Jr., and Jon L. Wakelyn, pp. 72–89. Athens, Ga., 1985.

Bleser, Carol, and Frederick M. Heath. "The Clays of Alabama: The Impact of the Civil War on a Southern Marriage." In *In Joy and in Sorrow: Women, Family, and Marriage in the Victorian South*, edited by Carol Bleser, pp. 135–53. New York, 1991.

Bloomfield, Maxwell H. "Image of Lawyer." In *Encyclopedia of Southern Culture*, edited by Charles Reagan Wilson and William Ferris, 2:698–700. New York, 1991.

———. "Law and Southern Society." In *Encyclopedia of Southern Culture*, edited by Charles Reagan Wilson and William Ferris, 2:669–77. New York, 1991.

———. "The Texas Bar in the Nineteenth Century." *Vanderbilt Law Review* 32 (January 1979): 261–76.

Boatwright, Eleanor M. "The Political and Civil Status of Women in Georgia, 1783–1860." *Georgia Historical Quarterly* 25 (December 1941): 301–24.

Bodenhamer, David J. "Criminal Justice." In *Encyclopedia of Southern Culture*, edited by Charles Reagan Wilson and William Ferris, 2:682–84. New York, 1991.

———. "The Efficiency of Criminal Justice in the Antebellum South." *Criminal Justice History* 3 (1982): 81–95.

———. "Law and Disorder in the Old South: The Situation in Georgia, 1830–1860." In *From the Old South to the New: Essays on the Transitional South*, edited by Walter J. Fraser Jr. and Winfred B. Moore Jr., pp. 109–19. Westport, Conn., 1981.

Boris, Eileen. "Reconstructing the 'Family': Women, Progressive Reform, and the Problem of Social Control." In *Gender, Class, Race, and Reform in the Progressive Era*, edited by Noralee Frankel and Nancy S. Dye, pp. 73–86. Lexington, Ky., 1991.

Boris, Eileen, and Peter Bardaglio. "Gender, Race, and Class: The Impact of the State on the Family and Economy, 1790–1945." In *Families and Work*, edited by Naomi Gerstel and Harriet Engle Gross, pp. 132–51. Philadelphia, 1987.

———. "The Transformation of Patriarchy: The Historic Role of the State." In *Families, Politics, and Public Policy: A Feminist Dialogue on Women and the State*, edited by Irene Diamond, pp. 70–93. New York, 1983.

Breen, T. H. "A Changing Labor Force and Race Relations in Virginia, 1660–1710." *Journal of Social History* 7 (Fall 1973): 3–25.

Brosnan, John Francis. "The Law of Adoption." *Columbia Law Review* 22 (April 1922): 332–42.

Brown, Carol. "Mothers, Fathers, and Children: From Private to Public Patriarchy." In *Women and Revolution: A Discussion of the Unhappy Marriage of Marxism and Feminism*, edited by Lydia Sargent, pp. 239–67. Boston, 1981.

Brown, Elizabeth G. "Husband and Wife—Memorandum on the Mississippi Woman's Law of 1839." *Michigan Law Review* 42 (April 1944): 1110–21.

Brown, Theodore, Jr. "The Tennessee County Courts under the North Carolina and Territorial Governments: The Davidson County Court of Pleas and Quarter Sessions, 1783–1796, as a Case Study." *Vanderbilt Law Review* 32 (January 1979): 349–412.

Bryant, Jonathan M. "Market Revolution in Black and White: Law and the Freedpeople in Reconstruction Georgia, 1865–1880." Paper delivered at the Baltimore-Washington Legal History Symposium, March 1994, University of Baltimore Law School.

Bugea, James A. "Adoption in Louisiana: Its Past, Present, Future." *Loyola Law Review* 3 (June 1945): 1–31.

———. "Comment: Adoption." *Louisiana Law Review* 1 (November 1938): 196–203.

Burnham, Margaret A. "An Impossible Marriage: Slave Law and Family Law." *Law and Inequality* 5 (July 1987): 187–225.

Butler, Reginald D. "Exploitation and Opportunity: The Institutions of Juvenile Apprenticeship." Paper delivered at the New Directions in North American Slavery Studies Workshop, October 1993, Johns Hopkins University.

Bynum, Victoria. "On the Lowest Rung: Court Control Over Poor White and Free Black Women." *Southern Exposure* 12 (November–December 1984): 40–44.

————. "Reshaping the Bonds of Womanhood: Divorce in Reconstruction North Carolina." In *Divided Houses: Gender and the Civil War*, edited by Catherine Clinton and Nina Silber, pp. 320–33. New York, 1992.

Carlton, David. " 'Builders of a New State'—The Town Classes and Early Industrialization of South Carolina, 1880–1907." In *From the Old South to the New: Essays on the Transitional South*, edited by Walter J. Fraser Jr. and Winfred B. Moore Jr., pp. 43–52. Westport, Conn., 1981.

Carr, Lois Green. "The Development of the Maryland Orphans' Court, 1654–1715." In *Law, Society, and Politics in Early Maryland*, edited by Aubrey C. Land, Lois Green Carr, and Edward C. Papenfuse, pp. 41–62. Baltimore, 1977.

Carr, Lois Green, and Lorena S. Walsh. "The Planter's Wife: The Experience of White Women in Seventeenth Century Maryland." In *A Heritage of Her Own: Toward a New Social History of American Women*, edited by Nancy F. Cott and Elizabeth H. Pleck, pp. 25–57. New York, 1979.

Cashin, Joan. " 'Since the War Broke Out': The Marriage of Kate and William McLure." In *Divided Houses: Gender and the Civil War*, edited by Catherine Clinton and Nina Silber, pp. 200–212. New York, 1992.

————. "The Structure of Antebellum Families: 'The Ties that Bound us Was Strong.' " *Journal of Southern History* 56 (February 1990): 55–70.

Censer, Jane Turner. " 'Smiling through Her Tears': Ante-Bellum Southern Women and Divorce." *American Journal of Legal History* 25 (January 1981): 24–47.

Chused, Richard H. "Married Women's Property Law: 1800–1850." *Georgetown Law Journal* 71 (June 1983): 1359–1425.

Clinton, Catherine. "Bloody Terrain: Freedwomen, Sexuality and Violence During Reconstruction." *Georgia Historical Quarterly* 76 (Summer 1992): 313–32.

————. "Caught in the Web of the Big House: Women and Slavery." In *The Web of Southern Social Relations: Women, Family, and Education*, edited by Walter J. Fraser, R. Frank Saunders Jr., and Jon L. Wakelyn, pp. 19–34. Athens, Ga., 1985.

————. " 'Southern Dishonor': Flesh, Blood, Race, and Bondage." In *In Joy and in Sorrow: Women, Family, and Marriage in the Victorian South, 1830–1900*, edited by Carol Bleser, pp. 52–68. New York, 1991.

Cogan, Neil Howard. "Juvenile Law, Before and After the Entrance of 'Parens Patriae.' " *South Carolina Law Review* 22 (Spring 1970): 147–81.

Cott, Nancy F. "Notes Toward an Interpretation of Antebellum Childrearing." *Psychohistory Review* 6 (Spring 1978): 4–20.

————. "Passionlessness: An Interpretation of Victorian Sexual Ideology, 1790–1850." *Signs* 4 (Winter 1978): 219–36.

Custer, Lawrence B. "The Origins of the Doctrine of 'Parens Patriae.' " *Emory Law Journal* 27 (Spring 1978): 195–208.

Degler, Carl N. "Slavery and the Genesis of American Race Prejudice." *Comparative Studies in Society and History* 2 (October 1959): 49–66.

————. "Thesis, Antithesis, Synthesis: The South, the North, and the Nation." *Journal of Southern History* 53 (February 1987): 3–18.

DePauw, Linda Grant. "Women and the Law: The Colonial Period." *Human Rights* 6 (Winter 1977): 107–14.

Derdeyn, André P. "Child Custody Contests in Historical Perspective." *American Journal of Psychiatry* 133 (December 1976): 1369–76.

Dorsey, James R. "Race as a Consideration in Adoption and Custody Proceedings." *University of Illinois Law Forum* 2 (1969): 256–66.

Duvall, Severn. "*Uncle Tom's Cabin*: The Sinister Side of the Patriarchy." *New England Quarterly* 36 (March 1963): 3–22.

Easterly, Ernest S., III. "Common Law." In *Encyclopedia of Southern Culture*, edited by Charles Reagan Wilson and William Ferris, 2:680–81. New York, 1991.

Edwards, Laura F. "Sexual Violence and the Politics of Reconstruction." Paper delivered at the annual meeting of the American Historical Association, January 1994, San Francisco.

——— . "Sexual Violence, Gender, Reconstruction, and the Extension of Patriarchy in Granville County, North Carolina." *North Carolina Historical Review* 68 (July 1991): 237–60.

Einbinder, Michael P. "The Legal Family—A Definitional Analysis." *Journal of Family Law* 13 (1973): 781–802.

Eisenstein, Zillah. "The State, the Patriarchial Family, and Working Mothers." In *Families, Politics, and Public Policy: A Feminist Dialogue on Women and the State*, edited by Irene Diamond, pp. 41–58. New York, 1983.

Ely, James W., Jr. "Law in a Republican Society: Continuity and Change in the Legal System of Postrevolutionary America." In *Perspectives on Revolution and Evolution*, edited by Richard A. Preston, pp. 46–65. Durham, N.C., 1979.

——— . "Poor Laws of the Post-Revolutionary South, 1776–1800." *Tulsa Law Journal* 21 (Fall 1985): 1–22.

——— . " 'That no office whatever be held during life or good behavior': Judicial Impeachments and the Struggle for Democracy in South Carolina." *Vanderbilt Law Review* 30 (March 1977): 167–208.

——— . " 'There are few subjects in political economy of greater difficulty': The Poor Laws of the Antebellum South." *American Bar Foundation Research Journal* 4 (Fall 1985): 849–79.

Ely, James W., Jr., and David J. Bodenhamer. "Regionalism and American Legal History: The Southern Experience." *Vanderbilt Law Review* 39 (April 1986): 539–67.

Escott, Paul D. "Poverty and Government Aid for the Poor in Confederate North Carolina." *North Carolina Historical Review* 61 (October 1984): 462–80.

Farmer, Fannie Memory. "Legal Practice and Ethics in North Carolina, 1820–1860." *North Carolina Historical Review* 30 (July 1953): 329–53.

Faust, Drew Gilpin. "Altars of Sacrifice: Confederate Women and the Narratives of War." *Journal of American History* 76 (March 1990): 1200–1228.

——— . "Culture, Conflict, and Community: The Meaning of Power on an Antebellum Plantation." *Journal of Social History* 14 (Fall 1980): 83–97.

——— . "A Southern Stewardship: The Intellectual and the Proslavery Argument." *American Quarterly* 31 (Spring 1979): 63–80.

——— . " 'Trying to Do a Man's Business': Slavery, Violence and Gender in the American Civil War." *Gender & History* 4 (Summer 1992): 197–214.

Fields, Barbara J. "Ideology and Race in American History." In *Region, Race, and Reconstruction: Essays in Honor of C. Vann Woodward*, edited by J. Morgan Kousser and James M. McPherson, pp. 143–77. New York, 1982.

——— . "The Nineteenth-Century American South: History and Theory." *Plantation Society in the Americas* 2 (April 1983): 7–27.

Flanigan, Daniel J. "The Criminal Law of Slavery and Freedom, 1800–1868." Ph.D. diss., Rice University, 1973.

———. "Criminal Procedure in Slave Trials in the Antebellum South." *Journal of Southern History* 40 (November 1974): 537–64.

Foster, Henry H., and Doris Jonas Freed. "Child Custody." *New York University Law Review* 39 (May 1964): 423–43.

Fox-Genovese, Elizabeth. "Family and Female Identity in the Antebellum South: Sarah Gayle and Her Family." In *In Joy and in Sorrow: Women, Family, and Marriage in the Victorian South, 1830–1900*, edited by Carol Bleser, pp. 15–31. New York, 1991.

Frankel, Noralee. "Federal and State Policy in Mississippi, 1862–70: Legal Patriarchy and Rural Black Women." Paper delivered at the annual meeting of the American Historical Association, December 1980, Washington, D.C.

Freedman, Estelle B. "Sexuality in Nineteenth-Century America: Behavior, Ideology, and Politics." *Reviews in American History* 10 (December 1982): 196–215.

Freyer, Tony A. "Law and the Antebellum Southern Economy: An Interpretation." In *Ambivalent Legacy: A Legal History of the South*, edited by David J. Bodenhamer and James W. Ely Jr., pp. 49–68. Jackson, Miss., 1984.

Friedman, Lawrence M. "The Law between the States: Some Thoughts on Southern Legal History." In *Ambivalent Legacy: A Legal History of the South*, edited by David J. Bodenhamer and James W. Ely Jr., pp. 30–46. Jackson, Miss., 1984.

———. "Legal Culture and Social Development." *Law and Society Review* 4 (August 1969): 29–44.

Fuke, Richard Paul. "Planters, Apprenticeship, and Forced Labor: The Black Family Under Pressure in Post-Emancipation Maryland." *Agricultural History* 62 (Fall 1988): 57–74.

Gehman, Mary. "Toward an Understanding of the Quadroon Society of New Orleans." In *Southern Women*, edited by Caroline Matheny Dillman, pp. 47–54. New York, 1988.

Genovese, Eugene. " 'Our Family, White and Black': Family and Household in the Southern Slaveholders' World View." In *In Joy and in Sorrow: Women, Family, and Marriage in the Victorian South, 1830–1900*, edited by Carol Bleser, pp. 69–87. New York, 1991.

———. "Slavery in the Legal History of the South and the Nation." *Texas Law Review* 59 (May 1981): 969–98.

Genovese, Eugene D., and Elizabeth Fox-Genovese. "Slavery, Economic Development, and the Law: The Dilemma of the Southern Political Economists, 1800–1860." *Washington and Lee Law Review* 41 (Winter 1984): 1–29.

Getman, Karen A. "Sexual Control in the Slaveholding South: The Implementation and Maintenance of a Racial Caste System." *Harvard Women's Law Journal* 7 (Spring 1984): 115–52.

Gillman, Susan. " 'Sure Identifiers': Race, Science, and the Law in Twain's *Pudd'nhead Wilson*." *South Atlantic Quarterly* 87 (Spring 1988): 195–218.

Goda, Paul S. "The Historical Evolution of the Concept of Void and Voidable Marriages." *Journal of Family Law* 7 (Summer 1967): 297–308.

Gordon, Linda. "Family Violence, Feminism, and Social Control." *Feminist Studies* 12, no. 3 (Fall 1986): 458–73.

Gorn, Elliott J. " 'Gouge and Bite, Pull Hair and Scratch': The Social Significance of

Fighting in the Southern Backcountry." *American Historical Review* 90 (February 1985): 18–43.

Greenberg, Kenneth S. "The Nose, the Lie, and the Duel in the Antebellum South." *American Historical Review* 95 (February 1990): 57–74.

Griswold, Robert L. "Adultery and Divorce in Victorian America, 1800–1900." *Legal History Program Working Papers*, ser. 1 (March 1986): 1–50.

———. "Divorce and the Legal Redefinition of Victorian Manhood." In *Meanings for Manhood: Constructions of Masculinity in Victorian America*, edited by Mark C. Carnes and Clyde Griffen, pp. 96–110. Chicago, 1990.

———. "The Evolution of the Doctrine of Mental Cruelty in Victorian American Divorce, 1790–1900." *Journal of Social History* 20 (Autumn 1986): 127–48.

———. "Sexual Cruelty and the Case for Divorce in Victorian America." *Signs* 11 (1986): 529–41.

Grossberg, Michael. "Crossing Boundaries: Nineteenth-Century Domestic Relations Law and the Merger of Family and Legal History." *American Bar Foundation Research Journal* 4 (Fall 1985): 799–847.

———. "Guarding the Altar: Physiological Restrictions and the Rise of State Intervention in Matrimony." *American Journal of Legal History* 26 (July 1982): 197–226.

———. "Institutionalizing Masculinity: The Law as a Masculine Profession." In *Meanings for Manhood: Constructions of Masculinity in Victorian America*, edited by Mark C. Carnes and Clyde Griffen, pp. 133–51. Chicago, 1990.

———. "Law and the Family in Nineteenth Century America." Ph.D. diss., Brandeis University, 1979.

———. "Who Gets the Child? Custody, Guardianship, and the Rise of a Judicial Patriarchy in Nineteenth-Century America." *Feminist Studies* 9 (Summer 1983): 235–60.

Grossman, Susan J. "A Child of A Different Color: Race as a Factor in Adoption and Custody Proceedings." *Buffalo Law Review* 17 (Winter 1968): 303–47.

Gundersen, Joan R., and Gwen Victor Gampel. "Married Women's Legal Status in Eighteenth-Century New York and Virginia." *William and Mary Quarterly* 39 (January 1982): 114–34.

Hagler, D. Harland. "The Ideal Woman in the Antebellum South: Lady or Farmwife?" *Journal of Southern History* 46 (August 1980): 405–18.

Hahn, Steven. "Class and State in Postemancipation Societies: Southern Planters in Comparative Perspective." *American Historical Review* 95 (February 1990): 75–98.

———. "Hunting, Fishing, and Foraging: Common Rights and Class Relations in the Postbellum South." *Radical History Review* 26 (1982): 37–64.

Hall, Jacquelyn Dowd. " 'The Mind That Burns in Each Body': Women, Rape, and Racial Violence." In *The Powers of Desire: The Politics of Sexuality*, edited by Ann Snitow, Christine Stansell, and Sharon Thompson, pp. 328–49. New York, 1983.

Hall, Jacquelyn Dowd, and Anne Firor Scott. "Women in the South." In *Interpreting Southern History: Historiographical Essays in Honor of Sanford W. Higginbotham*, edited by John B. Boles and Evelyn Thomas Nolen, pp. 454–509. Baton Rouge, La., 1987.

Hall, Kermit L. "The Judiciary on Trial: State Constitutional Reform and the Rise of an Elected Judiciary, 1846–1860." *Historian* 45 (May 1983): 337–54.

———. "The 'Route to Hell' Retraced: The Impact of Popular Election on the Southern Appellate Judiciary, 1832–1920." In *Ambivalent Legacy: A Legal History of the South*, edited by David J. Bodenhamer and James W. Ely Jr., pp. 229–55. Jackson, Miss., 1984.

Hall, Peter Dobkin. "Marital Selection and Business in Massachusetts Merchant Families, 1700–1900." In *The American Family in Social-Historical Perspective*, edited by Michael Gordon, pp. 101–14. 2d ed. New York, 1978.

Hamilton, Adelbert. "Miscegenetic Marriages." *Central Law Journal* 13 (August 1881): 121–24.

Hay, Douglas. "Property, Authority and the Criminal Law." In *Albion's Fatal Tree: Crime and Society in Eighteenth-Century England*, by Douglas Hay, Peter Linebaugh, John G. Rule, E. P. Thompson, and Cal Winslow. pp. 17–63. New York, 1975.

Helis, Thomas W. "Of Generals and Jurists: The Judicial System of New Orleans Under Union Occupation, May 1862–April 1865." *Louisiana History* 29 (Spring 1988): 143–62.

Hindus, Michael S. "Black Justice Under White Law: Criminal Prosecutions of Blacks in Antebellum South Carolina." *Journal of American History* 63 (December 1976): 575–99.

Hine, Darlene Clark. "Rape and the Inner Lives of Black Women in the Middle West: Preliminary Thoughts on the Culture of Dissemblance." *Signs* 14 (Spring 1989): 912–20.

Hodes, Martha. "The Sexualization of Reconstruction Politics: White Women and Black Men in the South after the Civil War." *Journal of the History of Sexuality* 3 (January 1993): 402–17.

———. "Wartime Dialogues on Illicit Sex: White Women and Black Men." In *Divided Houses: Gender and the Civil War*, edited by Catherine Clinton and Nina Silber, pp. 230–42. New York, 1992.

Hoffer, Peter C. "Disorder and Deference: The Paradoxes of Criminal Justice in the Colonial Tidewater." In *Ambivalent Legacy: A Legal History of the South*, edited by David J. Bodenhamer and James W. Ely Jr., pp. 187–201. Jackson, Miss., 1984.

Howington, Arthur F. " 'Not in the Condition of a Horse or an Ox': *Ford v. Ford*, the Law of Testamentary Maumission and the Tennessee Court's Recognition of Slave Humanity." *Tennesee Historical Quarterly* 34 (Fall 1975): 249–63.

Huard, Leo Albert. "The Law of Adoption: Ancient and Modern." *Vanderbilt Law Review* 9 (June 1956): 743–63.

Hubert, Léon D., Jr. "Comment: The Rights of Descendants of Adopted Children in Louisiana in the Estate of the Adoptive Parent." *Tulane Law Review* 8 (April 1934): 431–36.

Hughes, Graham. "The Crime of Incest." *Journal of Criminal Law, Criminology and Police Science* 55 (September 1964): 322–31.

Inker, Monroe L., and Charlotte Anne Perretta. "A Child's Right to Counsel in Custody Cases." *Family Law Quarterly* 5 (March 1971): 108–20.

Ireland, Robert M. "Frenzied and Fallen Females: Women and Sexual Dishonor in the Nineteenth-Century United States." *Journal of Women's History* 3 (Winter 1992): 95–117.

———. "Law and Disorder in Nineteenth Century Kentucky." *Vanderbilt Law Review* 32 (January 1979): 281–99.

———. "The Libertine Must Die: Sexual Dishonor and the Unwritten Law in the Nineteenth-Century United States." *Journal of Social History* 23 (Fall 1989): 27–44.

Johnson, Guion Griffis. "Courtship and Marriage Customs in Ante-Bellum North Carolina." *North Carolina Historical Review* 8 (October 1931): 384–402.

Johnson, Michael P. "Planters and Patriarchy: Charleston, 1800–1860." *Journal of Southern History* 46 (February 1980): 45–72.

Jones, Jacqueline. " 'My Mother Was Much of a Woman': Black Women, Work, and the Family under Slavery." *Feminist Studies* 8 (Summer 1982): 235–69.

Jordan, Winthrop D. "Modern Tensions and the Origins of American Slavery." *Journal of Southern History* 28 (February 1962): 18–30.

Kagan, Robert A., Bliss Cartwright, Lawrence M. Friedman, and Stanton M. Wheeler. "The Business of State Supreme Courts, 1870–1970." *Stanford Law Review* 30 (November 1977): 121–56.

Kantor, Shawn Everett, and J. Morgan Kousser. "Common Sense or Commonwealth? The Fence Law and Institutional Change in the Postbellum South." *Journal of Southern History* 59 (May 1993): 201–42.

Kawashima, Yasuhide. "Adoption in Early America." *Journal of Family Law* 20 (1982): 677–96.

Kelly, Henry A. "Kinship, Incest, and the Dictates of Law." *American Journal of Jurisprudence* 14 (1969): 69–78.

Kern, Stephen. "Explosive Intimacy: Psychodynamics of the Victorian Family." In *The New Psychohistory*, edited by Lloyd de Mause, pp. 29–53. New York, 1975.

Konig, David Thomas. "Country Justice: The Rural Roots of Constitutionalism in Colonial Virginia." In *An Uncertain Tradition: Constitutionalism and the History of the South*, edited by Kermit L. Hall and James W. Ely Jr., pp. 63–82. Athens, Ga., 1989.

Kulikoff, Allan. " 'Throwing the Stocking,' A Gentry Marriage in Provincial Maryland." *Maryland Historical Magazine* 71 (Winter 1976): 516–21.

Lasok, Dominik. "Virginia's Bastardy Laws: A Burdensome Heritage." *William and Mary Law Review* 9 (Winter 1967): 402–29.

Lebsock, Suzanne. "Free Black Women and the Question of Matriarchy: Petersburg, Virginia, 1784–1820." *Feminist Studies* 8 (Summer 1982): 271–92.

———. "Radical Reconstruction and the Property Rights of Southern Women." *Journal of Southern History* 43 (May 1977): 195–216.

Leslie, Virginia Kent Anderson. "A Myth of the Southern Lady: Antebellum Proslavery Rhetoric and the Proper Place Of Woman." In *Southern Women*, edited by Caroline Matheny Dillman, pp. 19–33. New York, 1988.

Levine, Richard Steven. "Caveat Parens: A Demystification of the Child Protection System." *University of Pittsburgh Law Review* 35 (Fall 1973): 1–52.

Lévi-Strauss, Claude. "The Family." In *Man, Culture, and Society*, edited by Harry L. Shapiro, pp. 261–85. New York, 1956.

Lloyd, Jane. "The Management of Incest: An Overview of Three Inter-Related Systems—The Family, The Legal, and the Therapeutic." *Journal of Social Welfare Law* (January 1982): 16–28.

Long, William Ellison. "Adoption in South Carolina." *South Carolina Law Quarterly* 9 (Winter 1957): 210–31.

Manchester, Anthony H. "Incest and the Law." In *Family Violence: An International and Interdisciplinary Study*, edited by John M. Eekelaar and Sanford N. Katz, pp. 487–517. Toronto, 1978.

Mann, Susan A. "Slavery, Sharecropping, and Sexual Inequality." *Signs* 14 (Spring 1989): 774–98.

Marcus, Stephen H. "Equal Protection: The Custody of the Illegitimate Child." *Journal of Family Law* 11 (1971): 1–48.

McCurry, Stephanie. "The Politics of Yeoman Households in South Carolina." In *Divided Houses: Gender and the Civil War*, edited by Catherine Clinton and Nina Silber, pp. 22–38. New York, 1992.

———. "The Two Faces of Republicanism: Gender and Proslavery Politics in Antebellum South Carolina." *Journal of American History* 78 (March 1992): 1245–64.

McFarlane, Catherine N. "The Mississippi Law on Adoptions." *Mississippi Law Journal* 10 (April 1938): 239–54.

McGough, Lucy S., and Lawrence M. Shindell. "Coming of Age: The Best Interests of the Child Standard in Parent–Third Party Custody Disputes." *Emory Law Journal* 27 (Spring 1978): 209–45.

McKinney, Gordon B. "Women's Role in Civil War Western North Carolina." *North Carolina Historical Review* 69 (January 1992): 37–56.

McKnight, Joseph W. "Family Law." In *Encyclopedia of Southern Culture*, edited by Charles Reagan Wilson and William Ferris, 2:686–91. New York, 1991.

———. "Texas Community Property Law—Its Cause of Development and Reform." In *Essays in the Law of Property*, by Harvey L. Davis, John L. Fitzgerald, Joseph W. McKnight, and Howard J. Taubenfeld. pp. 30–57. Dallas, 1975.

McLoughlin, William G. "Evangelical Childrearing in the Age of Jackson: Francis Wayland's Views on When and How to Subdue the Willfulness of Children." *Journal of Social History* 9 (Fall 1975): 20–43.

McPherson, James M. "Antebellum Southern Exceptionalism: A New Look at an Old Question." *Civil War History* 29 (September 1983): 230–44.

Merlin, William. "The Tennessee Law of Adoption." *Vanderbilt Law Review* 3 (April 1950): 627–43.

Mills, Gary B. "Miscegenation and the Free Negro in Antebellum 'Anglo' Alabama: A Reexamination of Southern Race Relations." *Journal of American History* 68 (June 1981): 16–34.

Mintz, Steven. "Regulating the American Family." *Journal of Family History* 14 (1989): 387–408.

Mnookin, Robert H. "Child-Custody Adjudication: Judicial Functions in the Face of Indeterminacy." *Law and Contemporary Problems* 39 (Summer 1975): 226–93.

Moncrief, Sandra. "The Mississippi Married Women's Property Act of 1839." *Journal of Mississippi History* 47 (May 1985): 110–25.

Morgan, Gwenda. "Law and Social Change in Colonial Virginia: The Role of the Grand Jury in Richmond County, 1692–1776." *Virginia Magazine of History and Biography* 95 (October 1987): 453–80.

Myers, John B. "The Freedman and the Law in Post-Bellum Alabama, 1865–1867." *Alabama Review* 23 (January 1970): 56–69.

Nash, A. E. Keir. "Fairness and Formalism in the Trials of Blacks in the State Supreme Courts of the Old South." *Virginia Law Review* 56 (February 1970): 64–100.

———. "A More Equitable Past? Southern Supreme Courts and the Protection of the Antebellum Negro." *North Carolina Law Review* 78 (February 1970): 197–242.

———. "Negro Rights and Judicial Behavior in the Old South." Ph.D. diss., Harvard University, 1967.

———. "Negro Rights, Unionism, and Greatness on the South Carolina Court of Appeals: The Extraordinary Chief Justice John Belton O'Neall." *South Carolina Law Review* 21 (Spring 1969): 141–90.

———. "Reason of Slavery: Understanding the Judicial Role in the Peculiar Institution." *Vanderbilt Law Review* 32 (January 1979): 7–218.

———. "The Texas Supreme Court and Trial Rights of Blacks, 1845–1860." *Journal of American History* 58 (December 1971): 622–42.

Nieman, Donald G. "Black Political Power and Criminal Justice: Washington County, Texas, 1868–1884." *Journal of Southern History* 55 (August 1989): 391–420.

Norton, Mary Beth. "The Evolution of White Women's Experience in Early America." *American Historical Review* 89 (June 1984): 593–619.

Norvell, James R. "The Reconstruction Courts of Texas, 1867–1873." *Southwestern Historical Quarterly* 62 (October 1958): 141–63.

Note. "Alternatives to 'Parental Right' in Child Custody Disputes Involving Third Parties." *Yale Law Journal* 73 (November 1963): 151–70.

———. "Adoption in Virginia." *Virginia Law Review* 38 (May 1952): 544–53.

———. "Intermarriage with Negroes—A Survey of State Statutes." *Virginia Law Register*, n.s., 13 (September 1927): 311–18.

———. "The Law of Adoption." *American Law Review* 9 (October 1874): 74–84.

Ortner, Sherry B. "The Virgin and the State." *Feminist Studies* 4 (October 1978): 19–35.

Oster, Alan M. "Custody Proceeding: A Study of Vague and Indefinite Standards." *Journal of Family Law* 5 (Spring 1965): 21–38.

Padgett, J. A. "The Status of Slaves in Colonial North Carolina." *Journal of Negro History* 14 (July 1929): 300–327.

Padgug, Robert A. "Sexual Matters: On Conceptualizing Sexuality in History." In *Passion and Power: Sexuality in History*, edited by Kathy Peiss and Christina Simmons, pp. 35–56. Philadelphia, 1989.

Painter, Nell Irvin. "Of *Lily*, Linda Brent, and Freud: A Non-Exceptionalist Approach to Race, Class, and Gender in the Slaveholding South." *Georgia Historical Quarterly* 76 (Summer 1992): 241–59.

———. "'Social Equality,' Miscegenation, Labor, and Power." In *The Evolution of Southern Culture*, edited by Numan V. Bartley, pp. 47–67. Athens, Ga., 1988.

Palmer, Paul C. "Miscegenation as an Issue in the Arkansas Constitutional Convention of 1868." *Arkansas Historical Quarterly* 24 (Summer 1965): 99–119.

———. "Servant into Slave: The Evolution of the Legal Status of the Negro Laborer in Colonial Virginia." *South Atlantic Quarterly* 65 (Summer 1966): 355–70.

Parsons, Talcott. "The Incest Taboo in Relation to Social Structure." In *The Family: Its Structures & Functions*, edited by Rose Laub Coser, pp. 13–30. 2d ed. New York, 1974.

Phifer, Edward W. "Slavery in Microcosm: Burke County, North Carolina." *Journal of Southern History* 28 (May 1962): 137–65.

Phillips, Cyrus E., IV. "Miscegenation: The Courts and the Constitution." *William and Mary Law Review* 8 (Fall 1966): 133–42.

Pittman, R. Carter. "The Fourteenth Amendment: Its Intended Effect on Anti-Miscegenation Laws." *North Carolina Law Review* 43 (December 1964): 92–109.

Piven, Frances Fox. "Women and the State: Ideology, Power, and the Welfare State." *Socialist Review* 14 (March/April 1984): 11–19.

Polan, Diane. "Toward a Theory of Law and Patriarchy." In *The Politics of Law: A Progressive Critique*, edited by David Kairys, pp. 294–303. New York, 1982.

Presser, Stephen B. "The Historical Background of the American Law of Adoption." *Journal of Family Law* 11 (1971): 443–516.

Preyer, Kathryn. "Crime, the Criminal Law and Reform in Post-Revolutionary Virginia." *Law and History Review* 1 (Spring 1983): 53–85.

Rabinowitz, Howard N. "The Origins of a Poststructural New South: A Review of Edward L. Ayers's *The Promise of the New South: Life After Reconstruction*." *Journal of Southern History* 59 (August 1993): 505–15.

Reidy, Joseph P. "The Unfinished Revolution: White Planters and Black Laborers in the Georgia Black Belt, 1865–1910." Paper delivered at the annual meeting of the Organization of American Historians, April 1980, Washington, D.C.

Richards, Mary Stovall. "All Our Connections: Kinship, Family Structure, and Dynamics Among White Families in the Mid-Nineteenth Century Central South." *Tennessee Historical Quarterly* 50 (Fall 1991): 142–51.

Rifkin, Janet. "Toward a Theory of Law and Patriarchy." *Harvard Women's Law Journal* 3 (Spring 1980): 83–95.

Ripley, C. Peter. "The Black Family in Transition: Louisiana, 1860–1865." *Journal of Southern History* 41 (August 1975): 369–80.

Robinson, Armstead L. "Beyond the Realm of Consensus: New Meanings of Reconstruction for American History." *Journal of American History* 68 (September 1981): 276–97.

Roeber, A. G. "Authority, Law, and Custom: The Rituals of Court Day in Tidewater Virginia, 1720–1750." *William and Mary Quarterly* 37 (January 1980): 29–52.

Rosenberg, Charles E. "Sexuality, Class, and Role in Nineteenth-Century America." *American Quarterly* 25 (May 1973): 131–53.

Ross, Ellen, and Rayna Rapp. "Sex and Society: A Research Note from Social History and Anthropology." In *The Powers of Desire: The Politics of Sexuality*, edited by Ann Snitow, Christine Stansell, and Sharon Thompson, pp. 51–73. New York, 1983.

Rothman, David J. "The State as Parent: Social Policy in the Progressive Era." In *Doing Good: The Limits of Benevolence*, by Willard Gaylin, Ira Glasser, Steven Marcus, and David J. Rothman, pp. 69–95. New York, 1978.

Royce, David, and Anthony A. Waits. "The Crime of Incest." *Northern Kentucky Law Review* 5 (1978): 191–206.

Rutman, Darrett B., and Anita H. Rutman. " 'Now-Wives and Sons-in-Law':

Parental Death in a Seventeenth-Century Virginia County." In *The Chesapeake in the Seventeenth Century: Essays on Anglo-American Society*, edited by Thad W. Tate and David L. Ammerman, pp. 153–82. New York, 1979.

Sachse, Harry R. "The Evolution of the Regime of Tutorship in Louisiana." *Louisiana Law Review* 16 (February 1956): 412–30.

St. Clair, Kenneth E. "Judicial Machinery in North Carolina in 1865." *North Carolina Historical Review* 30 (July 1953): 415–39.

Salmon, Marylynn. "The Legal Status of Women in Early America: A Reappraisal." *Law and History Review* 1 (Spring 1983): 129–51.

———. " 'Life, Liberty, and Dower': The Legal Status of Women After the American Revolution." In *Women, War, and Revolution*, edited by Carol R. Berkin and Clara M. Lovett, pp. 85–106. New York, 1980.

———. "Republican Sentiment, Economic Change, and the Property Rights of Women in American Law." In *Women in the Age of the American Revolution*, edited by Ronald Hoffman and Peter J. Albert, pp. 447–75. Charlottesville, Va., 1989.

———. "Women and Property in South Carolina: The Evidence from Marriage Settlements, 1730–1830." *William and Mary Quarterly* 39 (October 1982): 655–85.

Schafer, Judith K. " 'Open and Notorious Concubinage': The Emancipation of Slave Mistresses by Will and the Supreme Court in Antebellum Louisiana." *Louisiana History* 28 (Spring 1987): 115–82.

Schauinger, Joseph H. "William Gaston and the Supreme Court of North Carolina." *North Carolina Historical Review* 21 (April 1944): 97–117.

Schuhmann, George. "Miscegenation: An Example of Judicial Recidivism." *Journal of Family Law* 8 (1968): 69–78.

Schwarz, Philip J. "Forging the Shackles: The Development of Virginia's Criminal Code for Slaves." In *Ambivalent Legacy: A Legal History of the South*, edited by David J. Bodenhamer and James W. Ely Jr., pp. 125–46. Jackson, Miss., 1984.

Scott, Joan W. "Gender: A Useful Category of Historical Analysis." *American Historical Review* 91 (December 1986): 1053–75.

Scott, Rebecca J. "The Battle over the Child: Child Apprenticeship and the Freedmen's Bureau in North Carolina." In *Growing Up in America: Children in Historical Perspective*, edited by N. Ray Hiner and Joseph M. Hawes, pp. 193–207. Urbana, Ill., 1985.

Seligman, Brenda Z. "The Incest Barrier: Its Role in Social Organization." *British Journal of Psychology* 22 (January 1932): 250–76.

Semonche, John E. "Common-Law Marriage in North Carolina: A Study in Legal History." *American Journal of Legal History* 9 (October 1965): 320–49.

Senese, Donald. "Building the Pyramid: The Growth and Development of the State Court System in Antebellum South Carolina, 1800–1860." *South Carolina Law Review* 24 (1972): 357–79.

Shalhope, Robert E. "Thomas Jefferson's Republicanism and Antebellum Southern Thought." *Journal of Southern History* 42 (November 1976): 529–56.

Shepard, E. Lee. "Breaking into the Profession: Establishing a Law Practice in Antebellum Virginia." *Journal of Southern History* 48 (August 1982): 393–410.

———. "The First Law Journals in Virginia." *Law Library Journal* 79 (Winter 1987): 33–52.

————. "Lawyers Look at Themselves: Professional Consciousness and the Virginia Bar, 1770–1850." *American Journal of Legal History* 25 (January 1981): 1–23.

Sims, George C. "Adoption by Estoppel: History and Effect." *Baylor Law Review* 15 (Spring 1963): 162–78.

Smith, Daniel Blake. "Mortality and Family in the Colonial Chesapeake." *Journal of Interdisciplinary History* 8 (Winter 1978): 403–27.

Smits, David D. " 'Abominable Mixture': Toward the Repudiation of Anglo-Indian Intermarriage in Seventeenth-Century Virginia." *Virginia Magazine of History and Biography* 95 (April 1987): 157–92.

Snellings, Breard. "Comment: Civil Effects of Adoption on the Descent of Property by Inheritance in Louisiana." *Tulane Law Review* 13 (February 1939): 287–96.

Spindel, Donna J., and Stuart W. Thomas Jr. "Crime and Society in North Carolina, 1663–1740." *Journal of Southern History* 49 (May 1983): 223–44.

Stanley, Amy Dru. "Beggars Can't Be Choosers: Compulsion and Contract in Postbellum America." *Journal of American History* 78 (March 1992): 1265–93.

————. "Conjugal Bonds and Wage Labor: Rights of Contract in the Age of Emancipation." *Journal of American History* 75 (September 1988): 471–500.

Stephenson, Mason W., and D. Grier Stephenson Jr. " 'To Protect and Defend': Joseph Henry Lumpkin, the Supreme Court of Georgia, and Slavery." *Emory Law Journal* 25 (Summer 1976): 579–608. Reprinted in *The Law of American Slavery: Major Historical Interpretations*, edited by Kermit L. Hall, pp. 522–51. New York, 1987.

Storke, Fredric P. "The Incestuous Marriage—Relic of the Past." *University of Colorado Law Review* 36 (Summer 1964): 473–99.

Stowe, Steven M. "The Rhetoric of Authority: The Making of Social Values in Planter Family Correspondence." *Journal of American History* 73 (March 1987): 916–33.

————. "The 'Touchiness' of the Gentleman Planter: The Sense of Esteem and Continuity in the Antebellum South." *Psychohistory Review* 8 (Winter 1979): 6–15.

Strong, Bryan. "Toward a History of the Experiential Family: Sex and Incest in the Nineteenth-Century Family." *Journal of Marriage and the Family* 35 (August 1973): 457–66.

Sunley, Robert. "Early Nineteenth-Century American Literature on Child Rearing." In *Childhood in Contemporary Cultures*, edited by Margaret Mead and Martha Wolfenstein, pp. 150–67. Chicago, 1955.

Sydnor, Charles S. "The Southerner and the Laws." *Journal of Southern History* 6 (February 1940): 3–23.

"Symposium: The Legal History of the South." *Vanderbilt Law Review* 32 (January 1979).

Taub, Nadine, and Elizabeth M. Schneider. "Perspectives on Women's Subordination and the Role of Law." In *The Politics of Law: A Progressive Critique*, edited by David Kairys, pp. 1176–39. New York, 1982.

Tillett, Wilbur Fisk. "Southern Womanhood as Affected by the War." *Century* 43 (November 1891): 9–16.

Toplin, Robert Brent. "Between Black and White: Attitudes toward Southern Mulattoes, 1830–1861." *Journal of Southern History* 45 (May 1979): 185–200.

Treckel, Paula A. " 'To Comfort the Heart': English Women and Families in the Settlement of Colonial Virginia." In *Looking South: Chapters in the Story of an American Region*, edited by Winfred B. Moore Jr. and Joseph F. Tripp, pp. 133–52. Westport, Conn., 1989.

Tushnet, Mark. "The American Law of Slavery, 1810–1860: A Study in the Persistence of Legal Autonomy." *Law and Society Review* 10 (Fall 1975): 119–86.

———. "Approaches to the Study of the Law of Slavery." *Civil War History* 25 (December 1979): 329–38.

———. "A Marxist Analysis of American Law." *Marxist Perspectives* 1 (Spring 1978): 96–116.

Wadlington, Walter J., III. "Adoption of Persons Under Seventeen in Louisiana." *Tulane Law Review* 36 (February 1962): 201–27.

———. "The *Loving* Case: Virginia's Miscegenation Statute in Historical Perspective." *Virginia Law Review* 52 (November 1966): 1189–1223.

Wald, Michael S. "State Intervention on Behalf of 'Neglected' Children: A Search for Realistic Standards." *Stanford Law Review* 27 (April 1975): 985–1040.

Walsh, Lorena S. "Child Custody in the Early Colonial Chesapeake: A Case Study." Paper delivered at the Fifth Berkshire Conference on the History of Women, June 1981, Vasser College.

———. "The Experience and Status of Women in the Chesapeake, 1750–1775." In *The Web of Southern Social Relations: Women, Family, and Education*, edited by Walter J. Fraser, R. Frank Saunders Jr., and Jon L. Wakelyn, pp. 1–18. Athens, Ga., 1985.

———. " 'Till Death Us Do Part': Marriage and Family in Seventeenth-Century Maryland." In *The Chesapeake in the Seventeenth Century: Essays on Anglo-American Society and Politics*, edited by Thad W. Tate and David L. Ammerman, pp. 126–52. New York, 1979.

Walters, Ronald G. "The Erotic South: Civilization and Sexuality in American Abolitionism." *American Quarterly* 25 (May 1973): 176–201.

———. "The Family and Ante-bellum Reform." *Societas* 3 (Summer 1973): 223–34.

———. "Sexual Matters as Historical Problems: A Framework of Analysis." *Societas* 6 (Summer 1976): 157–75.

Welter, Barbara. "The Cult of True Womanhood: 1820–1860." *American Quarterly* 18 (Summer 1966): 151–74.

White, G. Edward. "The Appellate Opinion as Historical Source Material." *Journal of Interdisciplinary History* 1 (Spring 1971): 491–507.

Whites, LeeAnn. "The Civil War as a Crisis in Gender." In *Divided Houses: Gender and the Civil War*, edited by Catherine Clinton and Nina Silber, pp. 3–21. New York, 1992.

Wiecek, William M. " 'Old Times There Are Not Forgotten': The Distinctiveness of the Southern Constitutional Experience." In *An Uncertain Tradition: Constitutionalism and the History of the South*, edited by Kermit L. Hall and James W. Ely Jr., pp. 159–97. Athens, Ga., 1989.

———. "The Statutory Law of Slavery and Race in the Thirteen Mainland Colonies of British America." *William and Mary Quarterly* 34 (April 1977): 258–80.

Wiener, Jonathan M. "Female Planters and Planters' Wives in Civil War and Reconstruction: Alabama, 1850–1870." *Alabama Review* 30 (April 1977): 135–49.

Wohl, Anthony S. "Sex and the Single Room: Incest among the Victorian Working

Classes." In *The Victorian Family: Structure and Stresses*, edited by Anthony S. Wohl, pp. 197–216. New York, 1978.

Wood, Donald E. "Characterization of the Daughter as an Accomplice in Incest Prosecutions: Does Texas Immunize the Father?" *Houston Law Review* 20 (1983): 1129–56.

Woodman, Harold D. "Post–Civil War Southern Agriculture and the Law." *Agricultural History* 53 (January 1979): 319–37.

———. "Sequel to Slavery: The New History Views the Postbellum South." *Journal of Southern History* 43 (November 1977): 523–54.

Wriggins, Jennifer. "Rape, Racism, and the Law." *Harvard Women's Law Journal* 6 (Fall 1983): 103–41.

Wyatt-Brown, Bertram. "Community, Class, and Snopesian Crime: Local Justice in the Old South." In *Class, Conflict, and Consensus: Antebellum Southern Community Studies*, edited by Orville Vernon Burton and Robert C. McMath Jr., pp. 173–206. Westport, Conn., 1976.

———. "The Ideal Typology and Ante-Bellum Southern History: A Testing of a New Approach." *Societas* 5 (Winter 1975): 1–29.

Yanuck, Julius. "Thomas Ruffin and North Carolina Slave Law." *Journal of Southern History* 21 (November 1955): 456–75.

Younger, Richard D. "Southern Grand Juries and Slavery." *Journal of Negro History* 40 (April 1955): 166–78.

Zainaldin, Jamil S. "The Emergence of a Modern American Family Law: Child Custody, Adoption, and the Courts, 1796–1851." *Northwestern University Law Review* 73 (February 1979): 1038–89.

Zuckerman, Michael. "Children's Rights: The Failure of 'Reform.'" *Policy Analysis* 2 (Summer 1976): 371–85.

———. "William Byrd's Family." *Perspectives in American History* 12 (1979): 255–311.

INDEX

woman and rape, 195, 198; on consent and incest, 203

Alcorn, Gov. James L.: on slavery and state authority, 126

Alexander, Adele Logan, 57

Allen, Alexander A.: on election to circuit court, 19

Alston, James, 94

Anderson, Justice Francis T.: on maternal preference, 144

Antimiscegenation laws: goal of, 49–50; in colonial South, 51–54; in colonial North, 54, 255 (n. 68); in antebellum South, 59, 256–58 (n. 94), 258 (n. 96), 259 (n. 100); after Reconstruction, 179, 180–81; constitutionality of, 182–86; and tests of marital fitness, 184, 292 (n. 38); on status of children, 186–87; on marrying out of state, 187–88, 293 (n. 51); and expansion of state intervention, 188–89. See also Adultery; Fornication; Interracial marriage; Miscegenation

Appellate opinions: as historical evidence, xvii–xviii, 38–39

Apprenticeship, 107, 111; of African American children, xv, 99, 104, 161–63; and legal education, 14; and poverty, 98, 103–4, 157; in colonial South, 102; postrevolutionary developments in, 102–3; and best interests of the child, 103; and involuntary indentures, 103–4

Arkansas Constitutional Convention, 177

Arkansas legislation: on married women's property rights, 32; on forbidden degrees of marriage, 42, 202

Arkansas Supreme Court: on mental cruelty, 33; on affinal marriages, 42; on execution of blacks for attempted rape, 66; on reputation of woman and rape, 73, 74, 194; on regulation of apprenticeship, 103; on gender roles and child custody, 140; on child support, 146; on paternal custody rights, 147–48; on tender years doctrine, 151–52; on voluntary transfer agreements, 156; on parental child abuse, 158; on adoption and inheritance, 170; on attempted rape of black female, 197; on force in rape, 199; on cousin marriages, 203; on proceduralism in incest trials, 205

Ayers, Edward L., 77

Baldwin, Joseph G.: Flush Times of Alabama and Mississippi, The, 13; on mercenary lawyer, 13

Banks, Gen. Nathan P., 123

Barbour, Charlie: on end of slavery, 116

Barden, Jesse, 63

Barden v. Barden (divorce), 63–64

Barefoot, Scion, 45–46

Barnes, Judge David Alexander: letter to, 125

Barnett v. State (rape), 195

Barrow, Bennett H.: on lynching of slaves, 77

Baskette, Victoria, 169

Battle, Jeremiah, 16

Battle, William, 16

Bell, Justice James H.: on maternal transfer of custody, 101

Berry, Mary Frances, 187

Best interests of the child, doctrine of: and judicial discretion, 82, 93, 95; antebellum development of, 90–97; and disputes with surrogate parents, 97, 99, 105; and apprenticeship, 103; and adoption, 168, 169. See also Child custody, law of

Bigamy: and incest, 45–46; and slave unions, 133–34

Bishop, Joel, 183

Black, Daniel, 155

Black belt: opening up of, xv; and crisis of, 1850s, 118

Black Codes, 126, 212; and labor discipline, 125–26; and apprenticeship, 162–63; and interracial marriage, 179

Blackstone, William: on paternal custody rights, 80

Blassingame, John, 179

Bleckley, Chief Justice L. E.: on mob violence, 216

Bloomfield, Maxwell, xii

Border states, xvii

Breckinridge, W. C. P.: on importance of law, 218–19; involvement in domestic scandal, 302 (n. 13)

Brown, Genie, 191

Brown, John W.: on setting up legal practice, 15; on Union occupation in Arkansas, 124

Bullard, Justice Henry, 88

Bunn, Chief Justice Henry G.: on gender roles and child custody, 140

Burns v. State (miscegenation), 183

Burwell, James, 210

Butler, Gen. Benjamin F., 123

Byrd, William, II: on the patriarchal ideal, 25

Calhoun, John, 121

Carolina Law Journal: on need to upgrade bar, 16

Carolina Law Repository: on role of judge, 21

Carr, Ascenith Ann, 143

Carr, Justice Dabney: on rights of parents to apprentice child, 103

Carroll, C. R.: on southern lady, 83

Cash, W. J.: on southern frontier and growth of state, 10; on southern distrust of authority, 20

Catawba Superior Court, 128

Cato v. State (rape), 75

Charleston Mercury: on interracial marriage, 61

Charles v. State (rape), 66

Charlton, Justice Robert: on judicial discretion in custody disputes, 86; on best interests of child, 105

Chatham Superior Court, 86

Chesapeake, colonial, 24–25, 51–54, 250 (n. 30)

Chesnut, Mary: on sexual relations between masters and slaves, 56–57; on wartime sacrifice, 130

Chesnutt, Charles W.: *Wife of His*

Youth, The, 214; on lynching in New South, 214–15

Child-care institutions: and racial segregation, 159; and environmentalism, 159–60; custodial authority of, 160–61; and state paternalism, 161

Child custody, law of, xiv, xvii, xviii, 117; and parental fitness, 80, 81–82, 96, 98, 137, 145, 149, 151, 161, 165; and English common law, 80–81, 97, 140; maternal versus paternal rights in, 80–97 passim, 137–48 passim; and guardianship, 81, 85–86, 100–101, 148, 164; in colonial South, 81, 97–98; role of judicial discretion in, 81–82, 84–87, 93–95, 98–99, 137, 148, 149–50, 157, 159, 164–65; postrevolutionary developments in, 81–84, 98–99; and best interests of the child, 82, 93–95, 96, 137, 140, 148, 149–50, 154–56, 164, 165; and gender roles, 82–83, 139–40, 142–43, 145, 148, 151; and abuse of patriarchal authority, 86–87, 89, 92, 142; and adultery, 88, 90, 92, 143, 145; and illegitimate children, 91–92; and marital dissolution, 92, 95, 100, 142–43, 148; codification of, 95; and surrogate parents, 97–100, 149–57; tender years doctrine in, 101, 138–40, 151–52; and voluntary transfer agreements, 101–2, 155–57, 164; role of class in, 103–5, 151, 152–53, 157–58, 161; and infant discretion rule, 140–41, 153–54; and desertion, 143–45; and new ties rule, 149, 154–55; and child-care institutions, 159–61; and domestic Reconstruction, 227. *See also* Maternal preference; Maternal rights; Paternal rights

Childhood: and ideology of domesticity, 82–83, 93–94; and antebellum reformers, 83; role of maternal care in, 83; and individualism, 83, 89, 107, 111, 165. *See also* Motherhood; Parenthood

Child-labor reform, 159, 226

Dabney, R. L.: attacks reforms in domestic relations, 135
Daniel, Mary, 37, 64
De Bow, J. D. B.: on organic notion of law, 6; on role of law in slavery, 28
De Bow's Review: on the southern household, xiv; on county courts, 10; on divorce and property rights, 120; on interracial marriage, 180
De Forest, John William: on labor discipline and former slaves, 124; *Miss Ravenal's Conversion*, 125
Degler, Carl N., 93
Denman, Justice Leroy: on parental authority and state paternalism, 150–51
Desaussure, Chancellor Henry: on paternal custody rights, 90
Desertion: as grounds for divorce, 33; and child custody rights, 143
Dew, Thomas R.: on sexual double standard, 4; on sexual nature of women, 73; on southern lady, 82
Dickson, Amanda America, 186
Dickson, David, 186
Diggs, Kitty, 115
Disfranchisement, 223
Divorce, xiv, 80, 81, 107, 117, 119; reforms before Civil War, xvi, 32; in colonial South, 32; and desertion, 33; and mental cruelty, 33; and concept of fault, 34; and gender roles, 34; and miscegenation, 63; and child custody, 92, 95, 100, 142, 148; and southern conservatives, 120; and adultery, 134; reforms during Reconstruction, 134; in Reconstruction North Carolina, 225, 281 (n. 56); reform and domestic Reconstruction, 227
Dodd, Evelyn Baker: on Confederate women, 213
Domesticity, ideology of: in antebellum North, 24; and child rearing, 82–83; in antebellum South, 84; and child custody, 91, 93–94, 148; and antislavery debate, 119–20. *See also* Separate spheres, doctrine of

Domestic Reconstruction, 129–36, 226–28
Dozier, A. W.: on blacks serving on juries, 128–29
Duffel, Justice A.: on rights of adoptive parents, 109
DuPont, Chief Justice Charles H.: on proceduralism in slave trials, 70–71

Eakin, Justice John Eakin: on tender years doctrine, 151–52
Edgefield, S.C., 130, 162
Eliot, Elton: on southern lady, 142
Ely, James, Jr., 104
Emancipation: and southern household, xvi; and parental rights of former slaves, 115–16; and labor system, 124–25; impact on southern social relations, 131, 137, 174, 176; and African American families, 132–33; and apprenticeship of black children, 161–63; and miscegenation, 177–89 passim; and politics of rape, 189–90, 195; and postwar legal change, 225–26
English, Chief Justice E. H. English: on parental child abuse, 158
English common law: in colonial South, 7; and dower rights, 31; and incest, 40, 44, 46, 204; and antimiscegenation statutes, 51, 61; and status-of-the-father rule, 53; and paternal custody rights, 80–81, 147; and bastardy, 91; and emphasis on blood ties, 97, 170; and guardianship, 100; and opposition to adoption, 107, 169, 172; and age of discretion, 140
Equity courts: and protection of married women's property, 31–32
Evangelicals, southern: and male immorality, 139; and moral reform, 142–43, 223
Evans, Laura, 143
Ewell, Dabney, 47
Ewell v. State (incest), 47
Ex parte Boaz (custody), 87
Ex parte Ralston (custody), 85

Farber, Bernard, 43

Felton, Rebecca Latimer: on slavery, xiii

Finley, Justice W.: on adoption and new ties, 168–69

Fitzhugh, George: on dynamic nature of law, 22; on household patriarchy, 27, 244 (n. 86); on moral superiority of women, 138

Flanigan, Daniel, 206

Florida legislation: on married women's property rights, 32; on forbidden degrees of marriage, 42; on accomplice testimony, 207

Florida Supreme Court: on due process for slaves, 70–71; on force in rape, 75; on infant discretion rule, 140–41; on desertion and maternal custody rights, 144–45

Folkes, Justice William C.: on rights of adoptive parents, 167

Foner, Eric, xvi

Food shortages: during Civil War, 122

Ford v. Ford (slavery), 29

Fornication: between whites and blacks, 49, 51, 53, 179, 181, 185, 260 (n. 112), 263 (n. 131); interracial marriage as, 62, 180; and incest prosecutions, 203–4, 205, 209

Forstall, Oscar, 166

Foster v. Alston (custody), 94–95

Fourteenth Amendment, 182, 184, 187

Fox-Genovese, Elizabeth, 66, 84

Frasher, Charles, 184

Fredrickson, George, 54

Free blacks, 29; and divorce, 34; and interracial marriage, 52; in post-revolutionary South, 55, 58–60; and rape, 72, 76, 77; and state intervention in families, 79, 98; and apprenticeship, 99, 104, 161

Freedmen's Bureau: and apprenticeship of black children, 79, 98, 104, 161; and enforcement of labor discipline, 124–25; and rule of law, 127; and

marriage of former slaves, 132; and child custody, 145–46

Fullilove v. Banks (custody), 153

Galloway, Abraham H., 178

Gardenhire v. Hinds (custody): on rights of surrogate parents, 149

Garland, Justice Rice: on paternal custody rights, 100

Gaston, William Justice: on judges and legal formalism, 22

Gender: and southern legal culture, xv, 17–18, 220; roles in antebellum households, 24, 82–84, 93–94; and organic model of southern society, 27; and divorce, 34, 134; and sexual dynamics of slave South, 38–39; and child custody, 96–97, 139–40, 142–43, 145, 148, 284 (n. 43); roles during Civil War, 129–30; as category in law, 227

George v. State (rape), 67–68

Georgia Bar Association, 135, 219; and forum on lynching, 217–18

Georgia legislation: on forbidden degrees of marriage, 41, 202; on ban against castration of slaves, 64; on rape of slave woman, 68–69; on guardianship, 85–86; on judicial discretion in custody disputes, 95, 272 (n. 60); on adoption, 110; on parental fault, 142; on husband as head of family, 148; on child neglect and abuse, 159

Georgia Supreme Court, 17, 216; on attempted rape of white woman by slave, 37; on judicial discretion in incest cases, 47; on chastity and rape, 73; on maternal unfitness due to adultery, 88; on paternal custody rights, 100, 163–64; on married women's property rights, 135; on tender years doctrine, 138; on rights of legal guardian, 152; on new ties rule, 154; on voluntary transfer agreements, 156, 164; on custodial authority of child-care institutions, 160; on apprenticeship of black chil-

181, 193, 205–9; and faith in blood ties, 97, 99, 105, 109; and Reconstruction politics, 127–28; and psychological notion of parenthood, 150

Keith, James Justice: on parental fault, 143
Keller, Morton, 175
Kemble, Fanny: and sexual exploitation of slave women, 67
Kennedy, John Pendleton: on county courthouse scene, 11; on gentleman lawyer, 13; on justices of the peace, 16; *Swallow Barn*, 11, 13, 16–17
Kentucky Supreme Court: on humanity of slave, 30
Ker, Anatole, 168
Kershaw, Thomas, 99
King, Anna, 93
Kinship, 106; networks, 14, 23–24, 84; systems and marriage, 43–44; role of in apprenticeship, 102; during Civil War, 130; and child custody, 150
Ku Klux Klan, 127, 198

Labor relations: in postwar South, 124–25, 161–62
Lacy, Justice Benjamin: on new family ties, 154–55; on voluntary transfer agreements, 155–56
Lagrone, Julia, 197
Latham, C. Fannie, 144
Latham, Robert E., 144
Lawson v. Scott (custody), 91
Lawyers, southern: in colonial South, 8–9; images of, 9, 13, 221; and legal education, 14, 221–22; and mobility, 14–15; and professional standards, 16, 220–22; and judicial delay, 216–17; racial attitudes of, 217–18; role of in New South, 218–20; postwar masculine ideals of, 220; and progressivism, 222–24; in rural areas, 225
Legal conservatism: in New South, 218–20

Legal culture, southern, xvii; distinctiveness of, xii, xv, 36, 227; transformation of, xv, 129; during antebellum period, 5–23 passim; during Civil War, 121–23; during Reconstruction, 123–36 passim; and New South, 214–26 passim. *See also* Judiciary, southern; Lawyers, southern; Legal formalism
Legal formalism: and southern judiciary, xvi, 22, 72, 205–6
Lewis, H. T.: on lynching and black rapists, 217
Lewis, Julia Francis, 186
Lilienthal, Mrs. Theodore, 172
Limestone County, Tex., 195
Lincoln, Abraham, 121
Lindsey v. Lindsey (custody), 88
Little Rock, Ark., 5, 15
Localism, 12, 19, 23
Lord Hale: on false accusations of rape, 201
Lost Cause, 130, 213
Louisiana legislation: on status of slave, 28; on forbidden degrees of marriage, 42, 202; on adoption, 107–8; on parental fault, 142; on guardianship, 273–74 (n. 77)
Louisiana Supreme Court: on interracial marriage, 62; on paternal custody rights, 84–85, 99–100; on maternal unfitness due to adultery, 88; on apprenticeship transfers, 103; on adoption and inheritance, 108, 172, 173; on rights of adoptive parents, 108–9, 166, 167–68; on matrimonial consent and rape, 200
Louisville, Ky., 15
Lower South: and West Indies racial pattern, 60
Loyal Georgian, 195
Lumpkin, Justice Joseph Henry: on attempted rape of white woman by slave, 37–38, 64–65
Lynching: in slave South, 77; and racial crisis in New South, 212–13, 214–18; and class fears, 216

Mabry, Chief Justice Milton H.: on desertion and maternal custody rights, 144–45

McAlister, Justice William K.: on adoption and best interests of the child, 169

McCurry, Stephanie, 120

McDonald, Justice Charles J.: on rights of adoptive parents, 111–12

McGrew, William, 206

McGrew v. State (incest), 206

McGuire, Maggie, 209

McKie, Thomas, 162

MacKinnon, Catharine A., 77

McShan v. McShan (custody), 146

Major (slave), 70

Mansfield, Lord, 82

Manumission laws, 57

Marr, Justice D. P.: on rights of adoptive parents, 167

Marriage: and forbidden degrees, 41–42, 202–3; traditional view of, 42; and romantic love, 43; and contractualism, 79; rates after Civil War, 130–31; among former slaves, 132–34; and limits of contractualism, 177, 183–84; and rape law, 200. *See also* Incest; Interracial marriage; Married women's property rights

Married women's property rights, xiv, 117, 119; and equity courts, 31–32; antebellum statutory developments in, 32; during Reconstruction, 134–35; and domestic Reconstruction, 227

Martineau, Harriet: on sexual exploitation of slave women, 57

Maryland, legislation: on miscegenation, 51–52, 253–54 (n. 62, 63); on status of mulatto offspring, 52, 53

Massachusetts legislation: on miscegenation, 54; on adoption, 110

Massey, John Needham, 111

Maternal preference: and illegitimate children, 91; and child custody, 138–39, 144, 148, 151–52, 164. *See also* Child custody, law of; Maternal rights

Maternal rights: and child custody, 80, 83–84, 137–39, 164, 272 (n. 60); and guardianship, 85–86, 100–101, 164, 273–74 (n. 77); and illegitimate children, 91–92. *See also* Child custody, law of

Matthews, Judge H. A.: on married women's property rights, 135

Maxwell, Chief Justice Augustus E.: on infant discretion rule, 141

Meek, Samuel: on importance of lawyers, 220

Mercer, James, 203

Mercer v. State (incest), 204, 207–8

Merrick, Chief Justice E. T.: on private adoption acts, 108

Merritt, Hugh, 154

Merritt v. Swimley (custody), 154–55

Michigan Supreme Court: on psychological coercion in incest, 210–11

Middleton, Maria, 178

Miller, Lillian Belle, 144

Miller, Nunn, 37

Minor, Lucian: on model lawyer, 16

Miscegenation, xvii, xviii, 38, 48–64 passim, 176–89 passim, 227; between white men and black women, 49, 54–55, 56–57, 179–80; and demographic conditions in New World, 50–51; between white women and black men, 51–55, 63, 178–79, 259 (n. 104); as grounds for divorce, 63–64; and white anxiety in postwar South, 177; rates in postwar South, 178; convictions and postwar rates of reversal, 181; and late-nineteenth-century views of heredity, 185, 292 (n. 38). *See also* Antimiscegenation laws; Interracial marriage

Mississippi legislation: on married women's property rights, 32; on rape of female slave under twelve, 68; on paternal custody rights, 91; on adoption, 110, 111; on forbidden degrees of marriage, 202

Mississippi Supreme Court: on incest and social order, 39–40; on slave women and rape law, 67–68; on female credibility in rape cases, 74; on paternal unfitness, 92; on judicial discretion in custody awards, 94–95; on tender years doctrine, 101; on role of class in custody awards, 146, 152–53; on maternal custody rights, 164; on adoption and inheritance, 171; on supervision of juries in rape cases, 193; on proceduralism in incest trials, 205

Mitchell, Dr. John J., 86

Mooney v. State (rape), 200

Moore v. State (miscegenation), 181

Morgan, Edmund, 23

Morgan, Sarah: on death of brothers in Civil War, 130

Motherhood, 79–80, 83–84, 119, 138–139, 144

Mulattoes: and miscegenation in slave South, 48–49, 51–61 passim, 63; and apprenticeship, 104; and miscegenation in postwar South, 177–78, 214–15

Munro, G. P.: on lawyers and mob violence, 218

Nash, Frederick: on circuit riding, 18

New Orleans, La., 123, 178, 179

New Orleans Times: on postwar interracial socializing, 178

New South: continuity and change in, 176; role of lawyers in, 218–20; bar associations in, 220–22; and progressivism, 222–24; child labor movement in, 226. *See also* Lynching

New ties rule, 154–55, 168–69

New York Supreme Court: on rights of surrogate parents, 99; on informal transfers of custody, 102

Nicholls, Chief Justice Francis T.: on rights of adoptive parents, 168

Nisbet, Judge Eugenius A.: on judicial discretion in incest cases, 47

Noe, Catherine, 173

North: domestic relations in, xii–xiii, 117–19; and postrevolutionary attitude toward bench and bar, 9; and inefficiency of legal system, 11–12;

and penitentiary, 12; reformers in, 14, 83, 117–20, 159; republicanism in, 20, 30; household in, 24, 117; and restrictions on marriage, 42, 54, 59, 181; and ideology of passionlessness, 73; decline of paternal rights in, 79, 81–82; divorce in, 81; ideology of domesticity in, 82, 84, 93, 119; women's networks in, 84; child rearing in, 89; adoption in, 107, 110, 111; and rule of law, 127; domestic Reconstruction in, 226–27. *See also* Judiciary, northern

North Carolina legislation: on forbidden degrees of marriage, 42, 202; on racial identification, 58; on ban against castration of slaves for rape, 64; on adultery, 134; on children of interracial marriage, 186; on incestuous sexual intercourse, 203

North Carolina Supreme Court, 14, 17, 20, 22, 121, 127; on judicial discretion in divorce suits, 33; on divorce and wife abuse, 33–34; on interracial marriage, 62, 182, 187, 188; on miscegenation as grounds for divorce, 63; on proceduralism in rape trials, 71; on apprenticeship of free black children, 104; on child abuse, 105; on adultery as grounds for divorce, 134; on infant discretion rule, 140, 153–54; on role of class in custody awards, 153; on voluntary transfer agreements, 164; on children of interracial marriage, 186; on rape by black man, 190; on intent in attempted rape, 194; on proceduralism in rape trials, 196–97; on rape and matrimonial consent, 200; on incest, 201–2

Nott, Justice Abraham: on rape of child by white man, 65

Obermeyer, Simon: on status of adopted child, 174

O'Brien, Gail William, 218

Odum, Elizabeth, 45

Old Southwest, 23

O'Neall, John Belton: *Negro Law of South Carolina, The*, 60; on racial identification by juries, 60
Orange County, N.C., 130
Orphanages, 159–60
Owens v. Owens (custody), 143

Pace and Cox v. State (miscegenation), 185
Pace v. Klink (adoption), 172
Page, Thomas Nelson: on southern lawyers, 221
Painter, Nell Irvin, 212
Pape, Emelia, 147
Parens patriae, doctrine of: English origins, 80–81, 268 (n. 7); and child custody, 82; and parental custody rights, 97, 149
Parental fault, 92–93, 142–45
Parenthood: and contractualism, 79, 137, 149, 158; as personal trust, 97, 105, 165; and blood ties, 97–99, 102, 105–6, 137; psychological notion of, 149–50, 154–57, 165. *See also* Childhood; Motherhood
Parkerson, W. S.: on restricting admission to bar, 221
Paternalism: and antebellum planters, 25–26; and slave law, 29–31; and sexual exploitation of slave women, 57, 66; of English ruling classes, 81; of southern judges, 92, 103, 133–34, 142, 148, 191, 197; and postwar planters, 124, 162; and married women's property rights, 134–35; protection versus control in, 201; and patriarchy, 242 (n. 70). *See also* State paternalism
Paternal rights: traditional nature of in custody law, 80–81; decline of in custody law, 82, 95–97, 138, 147–48, 151–52; in antebellum South, 84–89, 99–100, 109; and responsibility to provide support, 89, 145, 147. *See also* Child custody, law of
Patriarchy: in slave South, xi, xiii–xiv, 24–28, 35–36, 89, 117; and incest,

40, 210–12; and rape, 65, 189; and child custody, 80–81, 88, 94–95, 96–97; decline of in antebellum North, 117; and rape, 189; and law in postwar South, 215, 224, 227; definition of, 241–43 (n. 70). *See also* Household patriarchy
Pearson, Chief Justice Richmond M., 14, 17; on wife abuse and divorce, 34; on Reconstruction politics, 127–28; on adultery committed by wife, 134; on infant discretion rule, 153–54; on intent in attempted rape, 194
Pell, Edward Leigh: on lynching, 215
Penitentiary, 12
Pennsylvania, legislation: on miscegenation, 54
Pierce v. Massenburg (apprenticeship), 103
Planters: and republicanism, xi–xii, 20, 118; and southern law, xvi; and honor, 6–7; and kinship networks, 23–24; as patriarchs, 25–28, 57, 66, 89, 117; and crisis of 1850s, 35, 118; and cousin marriage, 44; and paternalism after emancipation, 124, 162; and postwar labor system, 126–27, 131; and apprenticeship of African Americans, 161–62
Pleasant v. State (rape), 73
Poor laws, 103–4
Poor whites: and divorce, 34; and state intervention in families, 79–80, 98, 103–4, 161; during Civil War, 123–24; and disfranchisement, 223
Porath, Ernest, 210
Porter, B. F.: on self-image of lawyer, 16
Porter, Nimrod: on guerrilla forces in Tennessee, 123
Power, Félicité Blanche, 108
Prather, Jennet, 90
Prather, William, 90
Prather v. Prather (custody), 90
Prescott, Jeannette, 168
Presidential Reconstruction, 125, 126

Progressivism, southern: origins of, xvi, 222–24; limits on, 227
Property crimes, 122, 124
Punishment of Incest Act (1908), 44

Quadroon balls, 56

Race: relations and patriarchy, xi; and southern legal culture, xv; and organic model of southern society, 27; and sexuality, 38, 50; and state intervention in household, 50, 188–89; statutory definitions of, 58–59; relations in Lower South, 60–62; relations after emancipation, 124–26; relations under Radical Reconstruction, 126–28; relations and community control, 179–80, 212–13; and lynching, 214–16; and New South lawyers, 217–18. *See also* African Americans; Miscegenation; Rape; Slavery; White supremacy
Radical Reconstruction: and expansion of state authority, 126; local and state courts under, 126; policies of, 126, 129; and state constitutions, 126, 134–35; and race relations, 127; and debate over miscegenation, 177–78, 180, 182–83. *See also* Freedmen's Bureau; Reconstruction
Rape, xvi, xvii, xviii, 64–78 passim, 189–201 passim, 227; of white woman by slave, 37–38, 64–65, 74–75; and incestuous assault, 45, 74, 203–4; and colonial legislation, 64; and poor white women, 64, 74–75, 197–98, 201; as theft of honor, 65, 72; and antebellum legislation, 65–66, 76, 77; and slave women, 66–69; and reputation of woman, 72, 75, 198–99; and consent, 72–73, 77, 194; and credibility of female testimony, 73–74, 194; and force, 75–77, 199; and postwar legislation, 190; and race after the Civil War, 191–97; and age of consent, 199; and use of fraud, 199–200; and matrimonial consent, 200; as cause

for lynching, 213, 215. *See also* Rape, attempted
Rape, attempted: racial disparities in punishments for, 66, 77, 289; and issue of coercion, 76; and evidence of intent, 193–94. *See also* Rape
Reconstruction: as social process, xvi, 174, 226; and married women's property rights, 32, 134; and divorce reform, 33, 134; political polarization during, 128–29; and southern legal change, 131–36; and miscegenation, 177–80, 182–84; and racial violence, 195, 212. *See also* Presidential Reconstruction; Radical Reconstruction
Redeemers, 129, 136, 183
Reformers, southern: and child-saving movement, 159; attitude toward law of, 223; and state government, 224; and child labor, 226; and state paternalism, 226. *See also* Progressivism, southern
Regionalism: and southern legal history, xii; and domestic-relations law, xiii; and republicanism, 20; and domestic governance, 227; and attitudes toward law, 239 (n. 34)
Reproduction: social construction of, 52–53
Republican family, ideal of, xiii
Republicanism, southern, xi–xiii, 20, 22–23, 30, 120
Republican mother, ideal of, 83
Rex v. Delaval (custody), 82
Rice, Pvt. Spotswood, 115
Richardson, Judge J. S.: on incestuous marriages, 46
Richmond, Va., 122
Richmond Superior Court, 85
Riots: during Civil War, 122
Rives, Robert, 111
Rives v. Sneed (adoption), 111
Roark, James, 225
Rowan, John, 15
Ruffin, Chief Justice Thomas, 17; on popular election of judiciary, 19–20; on domestic paternalism, 26; on

divorce reform, 33; on miscegenation as grounds for divorce, 63; on proceduralism in rape trials, 71

Russell v. Russell (adoption), 171

St. Louis, Mo., 115

Salisbury, N.C., 122

Sanders, John K., 172

Sayre, Nathan, 57

Schenck, David: on breaking into legal profession, 14; on blacks serving on juries, 128

Scott, Justice Christopher: on mental cruelty, 33

Scroggins, Marville, 63

Secession, 121; and southern republicanism, xii; household theory of, xiv, 117–19, 121

Separate spheres, doctrine of: in North, 24; and child-custody law, 120, 144, 148. *See also* Domesticity, ideology of

Settle, Justice Thomas: on consequences of secession, 121; on election fraud and violence, 128; letter to, 129

Sexuality: and patriarchy, xi, 38, 227, 253 (n. 53); social construction of, 39; and Victorian family life, 39; and race, 48, 50, 117; of female as male property, 65; and politics in postemancipation South, 189. *See also* Incest; Miscegenation; Rape

Sharkey, Chief Justice William Lewis: on female credibility in rape cases, 74; on paternal custody rights, 94

Shell, Dick, 199

Shly, Justice John: on best interests of child, 93

Shumate, I. E.: attacks growth of state, 219

Silver Bluff, S.C., 4

Simrall, Chief Justice Horatio F.: on mother's ability to support children, 146

Slater, Anne, 145

Slave codes, 29

Slavery: and domestic-relations law, xi; and southern households, xiii, 118;

and southern social relations, xv, 35, 131; and southern legal culture, 23; and southern republicanism, 30; and lack of legal protection for slave families, 31; and interracial sex, 48, 54, 56; and southern family life, 105, 112. *See also* Slavery, law of; Slave women

Slavery, law of, xiv, 22, 28, 68, 117; and procedural rights of slaves, xvi; and slave-trial courts, 8, 69, 263–64 (n. 144); and grand juries in, 30; and slave patrols, 30; and slave families, 31, 98; and rape, 64–71

Slave women, 24; sexual exploitation of, 56, 66; and rape law, 66–68

Sliwinski, Clara, 199

Smith, Gov. William: and wartime food shortages, 122

Sneed, Dudley, 111–12

Somerville, Justice Henderson M.: on inheritance rights of adopted child, 172

South: definition of, xvii

South Carolina Bar Association: on professional self-policing, 222

South Carolina legislation: on forbidden degrees of marriage, 41; on racial identification, 59; on apprenticeship of black children, 162; on interracial marriage, 179; on incestuous sexual intercourse, 203

South Carolina Supreme Court: on strict construction of incest statutes, 45–46; on racial identification, 59–60; on interracial marriage, 61–62; on proceduralism in rape trials, 65; on judicial discretion in custody disputes, 86; on spousal testimony in incest trials, 207

Southern lady, ideal of, 82–83, 142, 213

Southern Law Review: on status of adopted child, 174; on the legal profession, 221–22

Southern Literary Journal: on southern lady, 83

Southern Literary Messenger: on adversity in southern bar, 15; on the model lawyer, 16; on role of government, 21; on importance of motherhood, 94; attacks Harriet Beecher Stowe, 119–20

Southern Quarterly Review: on judicial accountability, 20; on woman's place in home, 26–27; on child custody, 96; on divorce reform, 120

Southern Review: on legal reform, 222

Southworth, E. D. E. N.: on child custody, 138; *Ishmael*, 138

Spoonts, M. A.: on postwar legal profession, 220

Staples, Justice Waller R.: on desertion and maternal custody rights, 144

State, southern attitude toward, 20–21, 78, 117, 121, 223–24. *See also* Republicanism, southern; State paternalism

State bar associations: in New South, 220; and professional standards, 221

State governments: antebellum policies of, 21; and wartime expansion, 121–22; under Radical Reconstruction, 129; and late-nineteenth-century reform, 224

State paternalism: definition of, xv–xvi; in slave South, 35–36; and child custody, 148, 150; in postwar South, 157, 161, 174, 219–20, 224, 226–27; role of legislature and bar in, 236 (n. 15)

State statutes: as historical evidence, xvii

State v. Barefoot (incest), 45–46

State v. Bell (miscegenation), 187–88

State v. Grisby (child abuse) 158

State v. Kilvington (custody), 160–61

State v. Mann (slavery), 17

State v. Martin (rape), 71

State v. Powell (rape), 196–97

State v. Ross (miscegenation), 188

Stephen (slave), 37; and *Stephen v. State* (rape), 37–38, 64–65

Stone, Chief Justice George W.: on rape as fraud, 76; on inheritance rights of adopted child, 171

Stowe, Harriet Beecher, xiv; *Uncle Tom's Cabin*, xiv, 119; attacks slavery, 119–20

Streight, James P., 169

Strickland, John J.: on judicial inefficiency, 216

Succession of Forstall (adoption), 166

Succession of Haley (adoption), 168

Sydnor, Charles, 23

Taliaferro, Justice J. G.: on rights of adoptive parents, 166

Taylor, Hannis: on state paternalism, 224

Taylor v. Deseve (adoption), 166–67

Taylor v. State (incest), 209

Tender years doctrine: 101, 138–40, 151–52. *See also* Child custody, law of

Tennessee Bar Association, 219

Tennessee Industrial School, 160

Tennessee legislation: on custodial authority of child-care institution, 159; on rape and capital punishment, 190

Tennessee Supreme Court: on humanity of slave, 29; and prosecution of incestuous assault, 47; on insufficiency of evidence in rape prosecution, 69–70; on evidence of woman's race in rape prosecutions, 71; on patriarchal nature of English common law, 81; on maternal rights to illegitimate children, 91; on transfer of apprenticeship, 103; on parental right to punish children, 105; on maternal unfitness due to adultery, 143; on rights of surrogate parents, 149; on custodial authority of child-care institutions, 160–61; on rights of adoptive parents, 167, 169; on adoption and inheritance, 173–74; on miscegenation, 182, 187–88; on proceduralism in rape trials, 193; on reputation of woman in rape prosecutions, 198; on strict construction of incest statutes, 204–5; on due process in incest trials, 205

maternal custody rights, 143; on parental fault, 143–44; on paternal capacity to provide support, 145; on new ties rule, 154–55; on voluntary transfer agreements, 155–56; on proceduralism in miscegenation trials, 181; on children of interracial marriage, 186

Warton, Joe, 193
Washaw v. Gimble (custody), 156
Washington County, Tex., 126
Watson, Thomas: on wartime class tensions, 123
Wear, W. C.: on decline of legal profession, 221
Weatherly, James: on need for legal reform, 216–17
White, LeeAnn, 118
White supremacy, 189, 212; and sexuality, 38; and hostility toward miscegenation, 48–49; and criminal justice in postwar South, 126; and southern lawyers, 217; and interracial sex and marriage, 227. *See also* Race
White women: and sexual double standard, 4–5; role of on plantation, 24; antebellum legal status of, 31–34, 117; as symbol of racial purity, 57–58, 65, 191, 213; and class in rape cases, 64, 72, 74, 197–98, 201; and race in rape cases, 64–65, 193–95; and prior sexual history in rape cases, 72–74; and sexuality in antebellum South, 73; and ideology of domesticity, 82–84; during Civil War, 122, 129–30; and lynching hysteria, 212–13, 217–18. *See also* Gender; Miscegenation; Rape; Southern lady, ideal of
Whitfield, Ga., 122
Whitner, Justice Joseph N.: on judicial discretion in custody disputes, 95
Wiecek, William, xvii
William and Mary College, 18
Williams, Fern, 197
Williamsburg, Va., 8
Williams v. Williams (custody), 90–91
Wisconsin Supreme Court: on psychological coercion in incest, 210
Women. *See* African American women; Gender; Slave women; White women
Worth, Gov. Jonathan: on ensuring impartial justice, 125
Wright, W. W.: on miscegenation, 48, 49; on mulattoes, 58
Wyatt-Brown, Bertram, 12, 106

Yeomen: and support for secession, xii, 118; as patriarchs, 27–28, 117